The Many Gospels *of* Jesus

Sorting Out the Story of the Life of Jesus

Philip W. Comfort | Jason Driesbach

TYNDALE HOUSE PUBLISHERS, INC.
CAROL STREAM, ILLINOIS

Visit Tyndale's exciting Web site at www.tyndale.com

TYNDALE and Tyndale's quill logo are registered trademarks of Tyndale House Publishers, Inc.

The Many Gospels of Jesus: Sorting Out the Story of the Life of Jesus

Copyright © 2008 by Philip W. Comfort and Jason Driesbach. All rights reserved.

Cover photo copyright © by stock.xchng. All rights reserved.

Designed by Erik M. Peterson

Edited by Cara Lacey

Library of Congress Cataloging-in-Publication Data

Comfort, Philip Wesley.
    The many Gospels of Jesus : sorting out the story of the life of Jesus / Philip W. Comfort and Jason Driesbach.
    p. cm.
    Includes bibliographical references.
    ISBN-13: 978-1-4143-1604-8 (hc)
    ISBN-10: 1-4143-1604-6 (hc)
    1. Jesus Christ—Biography. I. Driesbach, Jason. II. Title.
    BT301.3.C66 2007
    226'.06—dc22   2007046766

Printed in the United States of America

14   13   12   11   10   09   08
7   6   5   4   3   2   1

TABLE of CONTENTS

PREFACE

I t might be said that all scholars make judgment calls about what is orthodox or heretical based on their own prejudices or schools of thought. We
each have our own horizon of expectations that we bring to the reading
of any text. But what Jason and I hope to accomplish in this volume is simply to explain why some books were included in the Bible and some were not
and to allow others the opportunity we have had to examine the evidence.
To that end, we have included the text of many significant Gnostic Gospels,
as well as other writings that some have put forward as equal in validity and
veracity to the four Gospels found in the Bible. Further, we have tried to
explain in an even-handed manner the history of these books and why only
four Gospels were chosen as Scripture.

To help you understand how I personally approached this study, I think it
would be helpful to tell how I came to be interested in the enigmatic subject
of ancient writings, the biblical text, and textual criticism. In many ways,
this book is the result of a long spiritual search. But it is also the product of
extensive academic research.

SPIRITUAL JOURNEY

In my early days, I rejected Christianity. My faith in Christ came at the end
of a long and broad search for spiritual truth.

In many ways, I was a child of the sixties—of that spiritual revolution in
America propelled by a rejection of materialism, a longing for world peace
and unity, and a quest for spiritual reality. Anyone alive at the time knows it
was a time of extreme idealism, experimentation, and exploration.

I shared the aspirations of my peers for a new community. I rejected my
heritage, which was rooted in materialism, traditional Christian religion,
and good old American conservatism. I wanted to return to nature and make
an Eden for myself and others. In that idealistic mind-set, without knowing
it, I was seeking God—or rather, God was seeking me.

Perhaps the best place to pick up the story is in the summer of 1967,
when I was sixteen. The Beatles had already broken onto the scene, the Roll-
ing Stones were just emerging, and I was home for the summer from my first
year at Choate (now the coeducational Choate Rosemary Hall), a prepara-
tory school that John F. Kennedy and other notables had attended.

I didn't fit in at Choate. I wasn't smart, and I wasn't preppy. Fortunately,
my roommate, Ray Hitchcock, was of the same ilk, so we got along well with
each other. We both struggled with our studies, and we both hated being

away from girls and rock 'n' roll. But we made it through the year and parted ways to enjoy the summer.

In late July, I received a phone call from Ray's mother, who sobbed hysterically as she told me again and again, "Ray was killed—he was killed—in a car accident."

That night as I lay in bed, I told God (whoever he was), "I'm afraid of you. How can someone be alive one moment and then dead the next? What *is* life?" It was the first time I talked to God in a real way and the first time I thought about the meaning of life. I had attended an Episcopal church as a child and was even an acolyte, but I had never really encountered God.

Something strange happened next. When I told my father about Ray and my feelings about God, he talked to me about Jesus. Though at the time I couldn't understand what he was saying, it comforted me. When I woke up the next morning, something was different. I felt that someone or something was with me—a kind of presence. To this day, I believe that it was real. I was different.

I gradually began to lose my taste for the kind of life my friends and I had lived. I became more and more of a loner and a thinker. I began to read poetry and philosophy and to write poetry. I was searching for the meaning of life and of my own existence. Reading let me know what others believed; writing was a way of searching myself to discover what I believed. In a poem in memory of Ray, I wrote that "his death gave life to me." If Ray had not died, I don't know that I would have sought the meaning of life when I did.

Nature became to me the expression of God. He could be seen in every living thing. I used to love taking walks in the woods near our home, contemplating the natural beauty and writing poetry. Sometimes, for a brief moment, I would sense God's presence. I had flashes of realization that there was a God and that he was out there somewhere. I tried not to think about it but would find myself doing just that. *I know that there is a God—but who is he?*

Of the many books I read in those days, I especially enjoyed the poetry of Kahlil Gibran, William Blake, and Dylan Thomas—men who loved nature and seemed to have a mystical relationship with God. And whenever I read the word *Jesus*, my heart felt warm. I really liked Jesus. I liked what I read about him, and I thought it would be wonderful if I could be like him. *But what does Jesus have to do with God?* I wondered. *Is he really God's Son?*

The summer after I graduated from Choate, some of my friends took a trip to the West Coast, and they told me about a Christian commune in Oregon called Living Springs, where they'd had some kind of experience with Jesus. A man named Gar, who had come back from Oregon with my friends, told me something I will never forget.

He pointed to one of those pictures that are meant to look like Jesus said, "That's not Jesus." When I asked how he knew, he said, "Jesus is in me." Startled, I asked, "How could that be?"

Then he told me of his experience, of how he had accepted Christ into his heart—the same thing that had happened to my friends.

This was something new. Up until that point, I had believed that there was a God, I had somehow felt that Jesus had something to do with him, and I had somewhat tried to model my life after his, in spite of all my failures. But I had never heard that Jesus could come and live in me.

Gar told me that it was a matter of faith and that I could never figure it out with my mind. My thinking could take me only so far, and then I would have to take a leap of faith.

I had heard about the "leap of faith" before, from the writings of Søren Kierkegaard. But I never imagined it meant receiving Jesus into my heart. How could I receive someone into myself whom I didn't see or know? And how did I know he was out there? And if he was out there, then that must mean he was alive. I continued to think about this over the summer, even as I hitchhiked to upstate New York to attend what was to become an amazing musical and historical event: the Woodstock Festival.

For me, the Woodstock experience was so powerful that I was reinfused with hope for an alternative society to rise up in this country. I forgot about Jesus for a while and instead tuned in to whatever natural or alternative spiritual ideas were moving around me at the time.

The following autumn, I began attending Kent State University, where I had the opportunity to spend time with a well-known poet from the Beat generation who was also a Buddhist monk. I had been attracted to eastern religions; Buddhism, in particular. But although my mind was obviously open to alternate spiritual routes, the end I sought was still God. And the more I observed and listened to this poet during those few days, the more it became clear that he did not depend on God. It also became clear to me that, contrary to Buddhist teaching, there was no great light within me awaiting discovery. According to my experience, there was nothing within me but darkness. God was outside me, not within me. I needed God to come into me.

My frustration escalated in early May 1970, when our campus became the scene of student riots and the infamous National Guard shootings. Eleven students were shot and four killed. As I saw it, the government was killing the youth movement, which held such promise in the sixties. As the movement was dying, I found myself dying inside as well.

I made a radical decision: I was going to hitchhike to the Christian commune in Oregon and find out for myself if Jesus was real. I took a Bible with me and read it; and I kept a journal every day of my travels. I remember thinking that I was on my way to meet Jesus. I had a sense that I was leaving my old life behind and was about to begin a new one.

After many days and many rides, I reached my destination: Quines Creek, Oregon. It wasn't much more than a gas station, a general store, and a long road leading up to the Living Springs commune. As I walked up that dusty road, my heart beat faster. I was nervous. Then a pickup truck pulled up and the two men inside asked me where I was going. They turned out to be leaders at Living Springs. When they asked why I had come, I told them, "I want to go on with Jesus."

The farm was lovely, but I was not restful enough to enjoy the idyllic scene. I had come for a purpose. Gar happened to be there, and after we greeted each other, I told him, too, of my desire to go on with Jesus. His reply was strange: "Are you sure?" He warned me that if I received Jesus, I could never go back to my old world. "It's like a fish out of water that can't go back."

That night, I thought about his words; and the whole next morning, while I was weeding in the garden, as all members of the commune did, I debated with myself. *Should I receive Jesus? Can I still do the things I enjoyed doing before? What will happen?* All the questions and doubts ran through me. *What am I doing? Why did I come all the way from Ohio to Oregon?*

At the same time, something else was moving in me, urging me, persuading me, coaxing me to do something. Finally, I put down my hoe and went up to the lodge. I told the few people sitting there that I had to pray, that I wanted to receive Jesus right then. I was nervous and trembling inside, unsure what I should even say or pray. But as soon as I said, "Jesus, I need you," I was flooded with his Spirit, and I felt an electric flow, like a surge of rushing water, cleansing my being. It was warm and loving and personal. It was Jesus. I knew it.

The person whose presence I had sensed before had now, at long last, come into me. I felt as light as a feather. No burden—I was liberated! Suddenly full of joy, I leaped up and ran past the stream and up the side of the mountain. My smile seemed too big, and the ecstasy too great. It seemed that the whole of the Oregon sky couldn't contain it. And, oh, was that sky blue, and those pine trees green! Oregon smelled to me then like heaven itself. Christ was alive!

ACADEMIC JOURNEY

After this experience, I hitchhiked home and began a new life as a disciple of Jesus Christ. This meant finding other Christians and meeting with them, communicating with Jesus through spiritual exercises—such as prayer, Bible reading, and listening to others explain the Bible—and persisting in these. Within a few years, I had heard so many different notions and was being urged to adopt so many different kinds of spiritual practices that my head was spinning. At the same time, my idealism and longing for unity led me to promote Christian oneness. This, too, was bewildering, because so many Christians were entrenched in teachings and practices that kept them divided from others.

During these early years, I fulfilled my two-year alternative military service (I was a conscientious objector) and then completed a B.A. in English at Cleveland State University, followed by an M.A. in English from Ohio State. My beloved wife, Georgia, and I were married and eventually had our three sons, Jeremy, John, and Peter. I became a schoolteacher, and I also spent several years in full-time Christian ministry, teaching the Bible to college students. As time went on, it became increasingly clear to me that I needed to study Greek so that I could read the New Testament in its original language. I needed it for myself because I was weary and wary of so many teachings that just didn't seem right. And I needed it for those who listened to me teach because I wanted to give them the very words of Jesus.

I completed first-year Greek at Trinity Lutheran Seminary and began graduate studies in the classics department at Ohio State. After taking a few classes in classical Greek, I signed up for a class in the New Testament Gospels. I was so excited to read the Gospels. On the first day of class, the professor told us to purchase a copy of the Greek New Testament[1] and then read the first chapter of Mark's Gospel. I did the reading with great satisfaction: I immediately understood nearly all of it, having already become somewhat fluent in Greek.

What I didn't understand were all the notes at the bottom of the pages, which seemed to list different readings from what was in the text. For example, the very first verse of Mark says, "the Gospel of Jesus Christ, Son of God," with a marginal note—in Greek, of course—indicating that some manuscripts read, "the Gospel of Jesus Christ." I was baffled. I had thought there was only one Greek New Testament. How could there be different readings of the same verse? I had studied Greek so as to read the text in its original language, but now I was discovering that the original reading could be in any one of several ancient manuscripts.

I discussed my dilemma with the professor, who then briefly explained to me that various editors had decided which readings went into the text and which readings were relegated to the margin. The art and science behind this decision-making process is what is called *textual criticism.*

After that day, I determined not only to read the New Testament in the original language but also to ascertain the original wording through studying the actual Greek manuscripts of the New Testament. I continued graduate studies in Greek texts and textual criticism at Ohio State, as well as at Case Western Reserve University and John Carroll University. After this, I completed a doctoral degree at the University of South Africa, writing a thesis titled "Scribes as Readers: A New Look at New Testament Textual Criticism according to Reader Reception Theory."

During these years and the decade thereafter, I studied all the early manuscripts of the New Testament. I traveled to several places around the world to examine actual manuscripts, places such as the University of Michigan; the Smithsonian; Harvard University; the Ashmolean Museum and Magdalene College in Oxford, England; the Bibliotheque Nationale in Paris, France; and the Bodmer Library in Cologny-Geneva, Switzerland (Bibliotheca Bodmeriana).

I collected the best photographs of all the New Testament manuscripts dated prior to the fourth century. I examined all the manuscripts word for word and published a volume (with David Barrett) of the complete, up-to-date transcription of these manuscripts: *The Text of the Earliest New Testament Greek Manuscripts.* I also wrote several books in the area of textual criticism: *Early Manuscripts and Modern Translations of the New Testament, The Quest for the Original Text of the New Testament,* and *Encountering the Manuscripts: An Introduction to New Testament Paleography and Textual Criticism.* I have also had the privilege of being a member of a group of translators who produced the New Living Translation (NLT); I served as a textual critic and as New Testament Coordinating Editor.

THE TRUSTWORTHINESS OF THE GOSPELS

Having studied every word of the Gospels in the earliest manuscripts, as well as having studied and applied the principles of textual criticism, I can say with confidence that the original wording of the four Gospels—Matthew, Mark, Luke, and John—can be reconstructed with a higher degree of certainty than any other book in antiquity because we have so many ancient source manuscripts and because so many competent scholars have given themselves to this task. For example, scholars know that John did not write the story of the woman caught in adultery (traditionally placed at John 7:53–8:11) because it does not appear in any of the earliest manuscripts. And we know that the Lord's Prayer (Matthew 6:9-13) ends with "deliver us from evil" because it finishes that way in the earliest manuscripts and because there are at least five different appended endings, including the well-known verbiage: "for yours is the kingdom and the power and the glory forever and ever, amen." And the list goes on.

It might be tempting to think that Christians are wrong about much of what Jesus actually said because there are so many differences among the manuscripts. But this simply isn't true. Many scholars know quite accurately nearly everything Jesus said, as recorded in the Gospels.

Where there are significant differences among Jesus' words within the reliable manuscripts, most responsible English translators will note these. This is the case in such versions as the New International Version, New Revised Standard Version, English Standard Version, and New Living Translation, to name a few. As I worked on the NLT New Testament, I kept very close watch on what significant textual variants should be listed in the margin. These notes often inform readers about certain variant readings that have not been accepted into the text of their translation—as, for example, the ending to the Lord's Prayer in Matthew 6:13, noted previously. In other words, translators give readers the courtesy of telling them about certain words that no longer appear in their translation but still do appear in older translations, such as the King James Version. The translators know full well that these readings are not original.

More importantly, there are notes in the margin of most translations, or "textual notes," that indicate variant readings (different wordings) that have equal or nearly equal evidence among the manuscripts. For example, in John 1:34, some very early manuscripts read, "he is the Son of God," whereas other early manuscripts read, "he is the Chosen One of God"—the reading selected for the NLT, in fact. But relative to the volume of material in the Gospels, there are actually very few textual variants that fall into this category. According to current scholarship, there would be some substantial debate on wording in the following verses (see NLT text and marginal notes): Matthew 3:16; 6:33*; 12:47; 13:35*; 16:2-3*; 16:21; 18:15*; 19:9*; 21:44*; 23:38*; 27:16; 27:49.

Mark 1:1; 1:41; 3:14; 6:3; 6:14; 7:4; 10:7*; 14:68; various endings after 16:8*.

Luke 3:22; 4:44; 10:1; 14:5*; 18:11*; 22:19b-20*; 22:43-44*.

John 1:34; 3:13*; 5:44*; 8:57; 9:38-39; 10:8*; 10:29*; 11:25*; 14:7*; 14:17*; 21:18*.

This totals about forty verses in the Gospels—out of about 3,778 (give or take those few passages whose authenticity are in question), which is about one hundredth of a percent. And more often than not, the textual difference in the verse has to do with only one or two words. Of the verses recording Jesus' speech, only twenty-one (marked above with asterisks) are in some question; and again, most of these pertain to only one- or two-word differences per verse. As in most fields of study, those on either extreme of textual criticism can find much to dispute. But there is very little that Jesus said, as recorded in the canonical Gospel writings, that is debated among centrist, modern textual critics.

The bottom line is that we have an accurate record in the Gospels of all Jesus' words. Responsible translators do their best to put those words in the text of their translations and then footnote any alternative readings in the margins. Either way, whether in the text or the margin, we have the words of Jesus.

Thus far, I have addressed only the issue of textual criticism of the wording in actual manuscripts. There is also what is called *source criticism,* which has encouraged a kind of distrust of the authenticity of the four Gospels. Source critics have set out to determine what Jesus actually said, as distinct from what the four Gospel writers purportedly put in his mouth as they wrote.

But the entire exercise of source criticism is largely theoretical. Because no one knows what Jesus said prior to what is stated in the Gospel writings, what various source critics, such as those in the Jesus Seminar, have done amounts to setting themselves as judges over what statements came from Jesus authentically and what statements were creations of the Gospel writers. Unless there are other documents with Jesus' words that predate or were concurrent with the Gospels, no scholar *can* establish criteria for judgment.

For example, some source critics have tried to date the four canonical Gospels and some noncanonical Gospels—the *Gospel of Thomas* and the *Gospel of Mary*—all to the second century—thereby gaining two other documents whereby they can pass judgment on Matthew, Mark, Luke, and John. However, it is almost universally recognized that the four Gospels were penned in the first century and that all others came in the second century or thereafter (see chapter three). Thus, the authenticity of Jesus' statements in the noncanonical Gospels should be judged by what we see in the canonical Gospels, not vice versa.

My background is not conservative. Even in my biblical studies, I was in an educational context that more than leaned toward a liberal interpretation of the texts. Yet through my studies I have come to believe without question that the four Gospels are authentic, God-inspired, trustworthy records of the life, words, and ministry of Jesus Christ of Nazareth. Of the many other Gospels which appear in this volume (see chapter six), I can say that some do seem genuine; namely, the *Egerton Gospel,* the *Gospel of the Nazareans,* the *Gospel of Peter,* and two Gospels of unknown origin (known to Bible scholars as P. Oxyrhynchus 840 and P. Oxyrhynchus 1224). I can also say that some of the words of Jesus recorded in still other Gospels also appear to be authentic—as in the *Gospel of Thomas,* which contains genuine Jesus sayings (as affirmed by the four Gospels) and other statements that have the ring of truth about them. Concerning statements in other Gospels, scholars are divided on which are genuine and which are fabrications. But all who care to take a respectful, responsible look are invited to do so here. On some of the finer points, we must all decide by careful study and—may we not forget—by prayer.

One final note on the writing of this manuscript: My colleague, Jason Driesbach, has contributed equally to this book in his hours of research and fine writing. Wherever we have used the first person voice, however, we have done so simply to reflect a discovery or conclusion I came to as a result of my personal research.

Philip Comfort

Getting At the Facts:
You Decide

Throughout the ages, the identity of Jesus of Nazareth has been scrutinized. Was he a real historical figure, or just the creation of some deluded disciples? Was he just a prophet, or the Son of God? Was he really a miracle worker who raised the dead, walked on water, and rose again after being crucified?

The four Gospels in the Bible—Matthew, Mark, Luke, and John—have been the main source of our knowledge about Jesus for hundreds of years. Other writings about Jesus were generally considered suspect. But recently, more and more readers, not just scholars, have been delving into other written Gospels about Jesus in an effort to get a different view of him. Most of these other Gospels are known as "Gnostic" Gospels, because they depict Jesus as presenting various secrets to select disciples about knowing deeper spiritual truths (gnostic is Greek for "knowledge"). And, for reasons we will see, these Gnostic Gospels were not accepted into the canon of Scripture—the list of books accepted for inclusion in the Bible.

What was once merely a point of debate among Bible scholars and historians has now come to the forefront in the regular media. When you see different people being interviewed on various talk shows and hear the discussions about some ancient Gospel manuscripts behind *The Da Vinci Code* or *The Jesus Family Tomb,* you will notice that people are now talking about more Gospels than the standard four.

The Da Vinci Code claims that "more than eighty gospels were considered for the New Testament, yet only four were accepted for inclusion" (p. 231)—which sounds like eighty books were submitted to a panel of critics, who decided that seventy-six of them should be rejected and four accepted! This is a gross exaggeration and a misrepresentation of historical facts. First, there were no more than fifty Gospels; in addition, the number is actually closer to thirty because the other twenty are known only by references in other writings. In other words, there are extant portions of about thirty Gospels. And it should be noted that only a minority of these Gospels were widespread. Many were not known to Christians in other locales.

Some scholars believe that certain church authorities kept these other Gospels from people, first by labeling them Gnostic Gospels (i.e., Gospels tainted by teachings that differ from orthodoxy), then by banning these Gospels from being read in church gatherings. These same scholars, of whom Elaine Pagels and Helmut Koester are primary advocates, tell us that these other Gospels simply present a different, viable view of Jesus and his teachings. They are glad that recent discoveries of the lost Gospels or apocryphal Gospels (*apocryphal* meaning "hidden") have now brought to light documents that need to be esteemed side by side with the four Gospels.

Without going into too much detail here, it should be said that there was no one ecclesiastical person in the second or the third century who had the power to control what Christians read. Pagels and others like to point to Irenaeus, bishop of Lyons (ca. 180), whom they say single-handedly censored all the Gospels other than the four. But, given the fact that apostles John and Paul were not successful in routing out Gnosticism, the idea that Irenaeus finished the job is unlikely at best. Paul attacked a certain early form of Gnosticism in his Epistle to the Colossians, and John attacked another form of it in his letters. Yet Gnosticism continued in various sectors of the church for centuries to come. The point is that churches were local entities exercising autonomy. At most, they answered to a regional bishop. Full-blown, universal church authority, as one sees in the Roman church today, did not exist until the late fourth century, at the earliest.

Contrary to the view of Pagels and others, the Gnostic or apocryphal Gospels were generally rejected by many Christians, not just a powerful figure such as Irenaeus, over a period of from one hundred to two hundred years because they found these Gospels not to be inspired by God, non-authoritative as to authorship, and questionable as to content (contradictory to the earliest apostolic literature). And so Christians stopped reading them. It was as simple as that. The acceptance and rejection happened through a process of what you could call general Christian consumption and discernment.

But we live in an age of pluralism, where giving all religions equal status as pathways to God is thought to be as fair and decent as giving all races equal status as human beings. The same is now happening with the Gospels, in that various scholars and popular writers are trying to promote the notion that all the Gospels provide equally valid presentations of Jesus Christ and so should be treated equally. On one hand, this kind of approach can inspire us beyond the confines of our narrow biases. On the other hand, that particular view could become a bias in itself, making equal every claimant to the term

Gospel and thus draining each true Gospel of its clarity and power. However, it is our belief that the power of the true Gospel prevails, so that readers with discernment would arrive at the same judgments as did our early brothers and sisters: The four Gospels have the flavor of life and truth, whereas the others simply do not.

What we've said above does not preclude Christians from another idea, which nevertheless might be radical to some. That is, the idea of accepting another Gospel—a fifth one, let's say—if one would present itself as being an eyewitness account of Jesus Christ. There are a few fragmentary Gospels which in our opinion appear to be true accounts of Jesus' teaching and actions. We are thinking of the *Egerton Gospel*, P. Oxyrhynchus 840, and P. Oxyrhynchus 1224, as well as the *Gospel of the Ebionites* and the *Gospel of Peter* (each of these is presented in chapter 6). The obstacle to accepting these writings on equal par with the canonical Gospels is that there is not enough extant text to make a complete judgment. The possibility of another Gospel is not blindly ruled out but carefully considered and, if necessary, just as carefully rejected.

What, then, is the difference between the four canonical Gospels and their fellows? In this book you will discover that the following five differences exist, to the general agreement of biblical scholars. The four Gospels (1) were written on the basis of eyewitness authority; (2) were written in the first century; (3) have substantial second-century manuscript support; (4) were written as memoirs of the apostles in the form of narratives; and (5) ring true and accord with what the apostles taught about Jesus.

On the other hand, the noncanonical Gospels were not eyewitnesses' accounts; in fact, most were *pseudepigrapha* ("falsely inscribed"), pseudonymous or anonymous writings. These Gospels were written in the second century or thereafter; they usually have no manuscript support earlier than the third century or no Greek manuscript support at all. They were written in the form of dialogues or sayings, thereby revealing the authors' lack of credibility as eyewitnesses; and they lacked that ring of truth, failing to accord with what the apostles taught about Jesus. Many of these kinds of Gospels are gnostic in character, as we will explain later in this book.

In recent years the public has been introduced to the *Gospel of Judas*, accompanied by the hype that it provides a brand new look at Jesus and his betrayer, Judas, who now becomes hero rather than villain. This Gospel is a perfect example of those writings the church rejected in that it is not an eyewitness account. It was written in the second century, the earliest manuscript is a Coptic translation of the early fourth century, it is mainly a dialogue between Jesus and Judas, and it does not accord with the truths about Jesus originally presented elsewhere by the apostles. The following pages will make it very clear that this Gospel—and many others—was rejected by early Christians because its content is false and its presentation is gnostic.

The fact is that the four Gospels were written in the first century, and all other subsequent Gospels were not accepted into the canon because they did not meet the standards of what constitutes "Scripture" for Christians. Some of the most renowned noncanonical Gospels are the *Gospel of Thomas,* the *Gospel of Judas,* the *Gospel of Philip,* and the *Gospel of Mary.* Although these Gospels have the name of famous people, there is no serious scholar who actually thinks Mary or the apostles Thomas, Judas, or Philip wrote these Gospels. That is why these Gospels are called pseudepigraphic—that is, having authors' names erroneously ascribed to them. Furthermore, there is not one serious textual scholar who thinks that any of these noncanonical Gospels was written during the first century—which is known as the apostolic age, the time during which the apostles of Jesus were alive.

However, in order to narrow the gap between the time the four Gospels were written and some of the Gnostic Gospels were written (and so further justify claims to those Gospels' equality), there are those who stretch forward the time of the writing of the four Gospels to late first or early second century and then stretch backward the time of the writing of the Gnostic Gospels to early second century. This is the fallacious view, for example, of Michael Baigent in his book *The Jesus Papers,* wherein he tells readers that the *Gospel of Mary of Magdala* "was dated to early in the second century A.D. So, like the *Gospel of Thomas,* it has as much claim to validity as the Gospels in the New Testament."[1] This dating is erroneous, as we will argue in coming pages.

We wrote this book out of our convictions as committed scholars and with these purposes: (1) to explain why the four Gospels were the only writings accepted as authoritative by the early Christians; (2) to give readers some background on what manuscripts have been discovered in the last one hundred years, since these discoveries have brought to light very early copies of the Gospels, as well as some interesting copies of noncanonical Gospels; (3) to explain what Gnosticism is, since many of the noncanonical Gospels were written by gnostic writers; and (4) to present the other important noncanonical Gospels with a description of their content and a brief assessment of their worth.

However, the ultimate critic is you, the reader. *You* need to read the four Gospels (Matthew, Mark, Luke, and John) and then compare the noncanonical Gospels to them. Which ones have the ring of truth? It is not enough for you to just hear from various broadcasts, books, and magazines a few tantalizing quotes from these other Gospels—and then to consent to the view of some who want you to believe that the other Gospels provide just as valid a testimony to life and deeds of Jesus Christ as do the canonical four Gospels. Our major objective will have been achieved if this book—by providing all the evidence—will assist you in your discernment of this important matter.

In this volume we have provided an English translation of all the books that can be called Gospels, where there are extant manuscripts. Several Gospels are lost, with no manuscript evidence whatsoever, although we have been able to provide excerpts of some of these lost Gospels through the citations of various church fathers. In each case where there are no extant excerpts, we provide a description of the Gospel. We have also given descriptions (but not translations) of the less-known Infancy Gospels and the Passion and Resurrection Gospels.

This volume contains my new translations of three unknown Gospels (P. Oxyrhynchus 406, 840, and 1224), the P. Köln 608 portion of the *Egerton Gospel*, as well as a rendering of two manuscripts of the *Gospel of Mary* (P. Oxyrhynchus 3525 and 4009).

A note on the translations: In all translations, we have used ellipses to indicate gaps in the manuscripts, and we have occasionally added words in brackets to make the English more intelligible.

There is a translation of all excerpts extant in the writings of the church fathers, as well as of extant manuscripts of the following Gospels:

> Gospel of Matthew
> Gospel of Mark
> Gospel of Luke
> Gospel of John
> *Egerton Gospel*
> *Gospel of the Nazareans*
> *Gospel of Peter*
> *Unknown Gospel* (P. Oxyrhynchus 840)
> *Unknown Gospel* (P. Oxyrhynchus 1224)
> *Gospel of the Ebionites*
> *Gospel of the Egyptians*
> *Gospel According to the Hebrews*
> *Gospel of Judas*
> *Gospel of Mary*
> *Gospel of Philip*
> *Gospel of Thomas*
> *Gospel of Truth*

PART I

Getting At *the* Facts

CHAPTER 1

What Is a Gospel?

When it comes to writings about Jesus, some professors of religion have promoted the idea that some of the noncanonical writings, such as the *Gospel of Thomas* and the *Gospel of Mary,* are just as valid as the four Gospels that were included in the canon. Thus, the purposes of this chapter are to examine just what a Gospel is, to explain why each of the four Gospels can legitimately be deemed a Gospel, and to see how the four Gospels were accepted into the New Testament canon.

WHAT IS A GOSPEL?

Since this book is about the many Gospels of Jesus, it is important for us to define just what a Gospel is. First of all, we need to understand that Gospels were considered to be "published" books. As recorded by Eusebius, Irenaeus tells us that Mark and Luke "published their Gospels." Irenaeus used the Greek term *ekdosis,* the standard term for the public dissemination of any writing. Similarly, Irenaeus wrote, "John, the disciple of the Lord, he who had leaned on his breast, also published (*exedōke*) the Gospel, while living at Ephesus in Asia."[1] This term was used for the official publication of a book, the master copy (*archetype*) from which other copies would be made. For Mark, Luke, or John to "publish" their Gospels meant that they each made an official publication of their book, a master copy from which further copies would be made for distribution.[2]

Interestingly, the term *gospel* (Greek *euaggelion*) was not used as a descriptor of these written accounts until the middle of the second century.[3] Before these books were called Gospels, they were called narratives and memoirs. A narrative tells a story; a memoir is a narrative composed from personal experience. A memoir could be autobiographical or biographical. The four Gospels are biographical memoirs.

Literary Genre

When Luke mentioned the written accounts about Jesus' life that were current in the first century, he called them narratives.[4] Papias of Hierapolis described the Gospel of Mark as containing "memoirs" (Greek *apomnemoneumata*) drawn from Peter's sayings.[5,6] Justin Martyr, a Christian philosopher by profession, also used the word *memoirs* to describe the Gospels. Significantly, *memoirs* were a recognized literary form. Such writings contained the sayings or actions of specific individuals and were set in narrative framework that was transmitted by memory. Because of the culture's highly developed memory currency, this means that they were reliable.

The description of the Gospels as memoirs would place them in the same literary category as Xenophon's *memorabilia*[7] of Plato's life. Memoirs are not necessarily full-fledged biographies, as modern readers might think. Luke comes closest to presenting the full life story of Jesus Christ, from birth to death; but even so, Luke was ultimately more concerned with presenting what Jesus did and said during his public ministry than in presenting a biography. In fact, when commenting on his own Gospel, Luke told Theophilus, "In my former book . . . I wrote about all that Jesus began to do and to teach until the day he was taken up to heaven."[8]

The fourth Gospel concludes with the same emphasis: "Jesus did many other miraculous signs in the presence of his disciples, which are not recorded in this book. But these are written that you may believe that Jesus is the Christ, the Son of God."[9]

Even though the four Gospels are not full-fledged biographies, first-century readers would have been familiar with biographies of great men and likely would have recognized that the four Gospels were in a limited way somewhat like other biographies of their day, such as Xenophon's *Memorabilia* or Plato's *Dialogues*. Other biographies appeared in the Greco-Roman world that were more popular in nature, such as the *Life of Aesop* and the *Life of Homer*. The four Gospels could be included in this category of biography on the basis of structure and style.[10]

The Gospels, as with the popular biographies of the day, have a fundamentally chronological framework that follows the subject's life and is amplified by anecdotes, maxims, speeches, and documents. Most of these biographies were didactic in that they presented the subject as a paradigm of virtue. For example, Plutarch's *Lives,* written at the end of the first century and very popular throughout the Greco-Roman world, is like the Gospels in that the general scheme was to tell of the birth, youth, character, achievements, and circumstances of death of each subject, interspersed with frequent ethical reflections and anecdotes.

So the primary importance of the Gospels is that they are written records of Jesus' speech and actions. Of course, each Gospel is not just a chronological display of what Jesus said and did, as if it were some kind of diary. Each Gospel is a story with a crafted narrative produced to be a work of literature. Gamble elaborates: "The Gospels were written in a literary context with literary skills and a literary view to readership. . . . Each of these authors [Matthew, Mark, Luke, and John] was self-consciously engaged in literary composition and therefore sensible not only of his own compositional techniques and theological aims, but also of the prospects for valuation, circulation, and use of his work."[11]

Literary Style

Each of the four Gospels, as we refer to the canonical Gospels, demonstrates its writer's use of different literary techniques in his individual portrayal of Jesus Christ. Matthew pointed to prophetic fulfillment to move his narrative along; Mark used fast-paced, dramatic action; Luke highlighted historical details to frame the narrative; and John specialized in eyewitness accounts and monologues. What made these Gospels different from any other memoirs or biographies was that they were about Jesus Christ, who was stupendously different from all other men because of his claim to be the Son of God come to earth from heaven. And Jesus' message was radically different from that of other men. For example, his Beatitudes, though similar in form to the Old Testament beatitudes found in Psalms and Proverbs, promise eschatological (ultimate, not temporal) benefits to those who are meek, pure, and poor. Furthermore, the story of Jesus' life is unique: He came from heaven to be born of a virgin; he proclaimed salvation and eternal life for all who believe in him as the Messiah and Son of God; he was crucified as a criminal; he was raised from the dead and appeared to his disciples; and then he ascended to heaven.

The Gospel writers were inspired by witnessing these events, and they were inspired by God himself when they wrote about them. The apostles had not forgotten or misremembered these events when they penned them. Jesus himself guarded against this; he specifically told his disciples that he would send them the Spirit to help them remember everything he had told them.[12] This Spirit, the Spirit of Jesus, guided the disciples when they composed their narratives and memoirs. And so the Gospels—that is, those accepted into the canon of Scripture—are inspired by God.

It is no wonder that the early Christians accepted the writings of the four Gospels and generally dismissed the other Gospels. None of these other Gospels were written by other eyewitnesses, nor were they written in the first century. If a fifth Gospel had been written by an apostle or eyewitness, the early Christians would have been reading it and treasuring it as a sacred text. But there is no such fifth Gospel, or sixth, or seventh, as we shall see in the following chapters.

One of the striking features of nearly all the noncanonical Gospels is that they are not narratives. Rather, they largely consist of so-called sayings of Jesus. The *Gospel of Thomas,* for example, is a composition of 114 sayings, without any narrative. There is no story line because the writers of these Gospels were not there when Jesus spoke and worked his miracles. They were not eyewitnesses, so their writings are not memoirs.

So then, the Gospels that have been accepted as Scripture are—and were from early on—published biographical memoirs of the life of Jesus of Nazareth, as written by his inspired apostles, those who had witnessed his life and ministry.

THE FOUR GOSPELS: EYEWITNESS ACCOUNTS

The four Gospels are the documents that record Jesus' words and deeds, written by eyewitnesses. Since Jesus himself did not leave any written records that we know of, we must rely on the accounts of those who were his companions for the true accounts of his life and words. By way of analogy, we could consider the writings of Plato and Xenophon about Socrates. As far as we know, Socrates wrote nothing. What we know about Socrates comes from two of his disciples, Plato and Xenophon. Likewise, what we know about Jesus comes from a few of his disciples.

What kept these disciples—whether of Plato or of Jesus—from composing fabrications? The answer is straightforward: the living presence of other disciples who could challenge fabricators on anything they said. One among "the Twelve," Jesus' hand-picked disciples, could have testified against any falsification. Even Matthias, who replaced the traitor Judas Iscariot, had been present for Jesus' earthly ministry.[13] There was also a group of seventy-two other disciples, and even more witnesses than these.[14] According to 1 Corinthians 15:6, Jesus had at least five hundred followers by the time he finished his ministry, all of whom witnessed the risen Christ. Most of these were still alive at the time of Paul's writing. Since 1 Corinthians is usually dated around A.D. 56–57, Paul made this statement just a few years prior to the time the synoptic Gospels—Matthew, Mark, and Luke—were composed. Any of the original witnesses could have exposed false writings concerning Jesus.[†] Of these five hundred disciples, 120 remained in Jerusalem to begin the church.[15] After the church began, the early believers relied on

---

[†]The synoptics were those that took a distinctly parallel view or "story line," whereas the Gospel of John diverged from the others in its perspective as well as its plot.

the apostles' words to teach them about Jesus' life and ministry.[16] This oral transmission of Jesus' life and teachings, together with the Old Testament, provided the spiritual sustenance for the early Christians.

During the days of the early church, various disciples and/or other Christians put together collections of Jesus' deeds and his sayings, or *logia*.[17] Scholars have called this collection "Q," from the German word *Quelle,* meaning "source," because it is thought that the synoptic Gospel writers, especially Matthew and Luke, used it as their source in writing the Gospels.

Papias of Hierapolis (A.D. 60–130) was a scholarly historian who collected oral and written traditions about Jesus. He knew Polycarp, a first-century bishop of Smyrna, and had heard the apostle John preach. In his writing known as *Explanation of the Sayings of the Lord,* Papias said that Matthew had collected the logia of Jesus in the Aramaic or Hebrew languages prior to composing his Gospel.[18] As one of the apostles who accompanied Jesus for three years, Matthew was an eyewitness of Jesus' ministry. As a customs collector, Matthew would have regularly used shorthand to keep track of people's taxes. He could have easily employed this practice in taking notes on Jesus' sermons and then later transferred the shorthand to a fuller, written form. This would not have been unusual in those days. Thus, Matthew's Gospel in limited form may have existed in writing—perhaps originally in Aramaic, a language Jesus spoke—as early as the A.D. 30s.

Later, Matthew composed an entire Gospel narrative built around Jesus' sayings. The importance of this is that, unlike the Gnostic Gospels, most of Matthew's Gospel is based on on-the-spot, eyewitness records. In essence, it was composed concurrently with the history being observed—much like a traveling journalist would do. Papias also described the Gospel of Mark as containing reminiscences or memoirs drawn from Peter's sayings about Jesus' life and ministry.[19] Peter remembered Jesus' words and passed them on to Mark, who then wrote them down as he heard them (see discussion on Mark in chapter 5).

The inspiration for writing the Gospels didn't begin when the authors set pen to papyrus; the inspiration began when the disciples Matthew, Peter (for whom Mark wrote), and John were enlightened by their encounters with Jesus Christ, the Son of God. The apostles' experiences with him altered their lives forever, imprinting on their souls' unforgettable images of the revealed God-man, Jesus Christ.

This is what John was speaking of in the prologue to his Gospel when he declared, "The Word became flesh and lived among us, and we have seen his glory."[20] The "we" refers to those eyewitnesses of Jesus' glory—the apostles, or disciples, who lived with Jesus for more than three years. This reminiscence is expanded upon in John's prologue to his first Epistle, where he says, "We have heard him, touched him, seen him, and looked upon him."[21] In both the Gospel and this Epistle, the verbs are in the perfect tense, denoting a past action with a present, abiding effect. Those past encounters with Jesus were never forgotten by John; they lived with him and stayed with him as an inspiration until the day—many years later—he wrote of them in his Gospel.

Specific examples of eyewitness remembrances are scattered throughout the Gospels. Take, for example, how both Peter (as recorded by Mark) and John recalled Jesus' emotional condition on certain occasions. Peter recalled how Jesus looked at certain religious leaders with anger, being grieved at their hard-heartedness.[22] Peter also recalled how Jesus sighed deeply in his spirit when the religious leaders asked him for a miraculous sign.[23] John vividly remembered Jesus' emotional condition before raising Lazarus from the dead. John said he groaned in his spirit, he wept, and he was deeply agitated.[24] John noted this same deep spiritual agitation when Jesus proclaimed his coming death and when he told his disciples that one of them would betray him.[25] These descriptions come from those who were with Jesus.

The Gospels of Mark and John also have some other striking examples of eyewitness writing. In Mark's Gospel we are given record of how Peter remembered the actual Aramaic words Jesus used at certain occasions. (Mark did not translate them into Greek.) When Jesus raised a little girl from death, he said, *Talitha, koum*—"Little girl, rise."[26] When Jesus healed a mute person, he sighed and said, *Ephphatha*—"Be opened."[27] Peter was with Jesus when these miracles happened. When Jesus was in the Garden of Gethsemane, he was praying to *Abba*, which means "Father."[28] And on the cross Jesus cried out *Eloi, Eloi, lema sabachthani*—"My God, my God, why have you abandoned me?"[29] Mark's Gospel is also full of detailed healing accounts.[30] John's Gospel also includes some colorful details only an eyewitness could provide. John recalled the exact day and hour he first followed Jesus.[31] At the wedding in Cana of Galilee, he remembered that there were six stone water jars, each of which could hold twenty to thirty gallons.[32] He spoke of a particular pool near the Sheep Gate in Jerusalem that had five porches[33]—a statement doubted by many scholars until it was recently affirmed by archaeology. John remembered that Jesus was cooking fish on a charcoal fire when seven of the disciples came to shore, hauling behind them the miraculous catch of fish.[34] John never forgot how many fish were in that net: 153. Such details are the telltale signs of eyewitness writing.

The written Gospels became the fixed form of what had been passed down through the teachings of the disciples for several decades. The early Christians first *heard* about Jesus' words and deeds; in due course, they could *read* about them, as well. Luke told his readers that he wrote his

Gospel narrative to affirm what Theophilus (evidently a new Christian) had already been taught. The Greek expression in Luke 1:4 is very revealing. In an expanded rendering, it could be translated "that you might know the certainty of the words you have been taught by word of mouth"(NIV). Theophilus, typical of most Christians in that era, had received the sayings, or logia, of Jesus by oral recitation. But Luke thought Theophilus would benefit from a written affirmation of what he had been taught orally. It is important to note that Luke didn't say his written account would redact or change the oral account in any way; rather, the written message would affirm or substantiate the oral ("that you might know the certainty/veracity of the things you have been taught"). As such, the written Gospel became an accurate extension and continuation of the oral teaching. Furthermore, Luke's Gospel was based on the testimony of those people who had been "eyewitnesses and servants of the word"[35]—that is, the message of Jesus. They had heard Jesus' teachings, seen his miraculous deeds, and then faithfully passed them on to others.

Before the apostles, who were eyewitnesses of Jesus, made their exodus from this life to the next, they wanted to leave the church a written testimony of Jesus' words and life. Two of the four Gospel writers, Matthew and John, were apostles. John, "the disciple Jesus loved," claims eyewitness authenticity for his Gospel.[36] Matthew makes no such claim for himself, but the testimony of early church history affirms it repeatedly. Mark wrote for the apostle Peter just a short time before Peter was martyred. Luke was not an eyewitness, but he based his Gospel on eyewitness accounts.

So three of the Gospels—Matthew, Mark, and John—were written by those who were eyewitnesses of Jesus. And Luke wrote his Gospel based on the testimony of those who were eyewitnesses.[37] All four of these Gospels affirmed what the apostles of Jesus had been teaching about Jesus for several decades. The early Christians trusted these writings because of this. Perhaps they had learned this principle from Jesus, who emphasized again and again that the disciples would testify of what they saw and heard.[38] Significantly, the person who would replace Judas as the twelfth apostle had to be someone who had been with Jesus throughout his ministry and had witnessed his resurrection.

The early Christians did not trust the teachings or writings of those who had not been eyewitnesses of Jesus as providing apostolic truth. This is not to say that they didn't appreciate the teachings and writings of others who were Christians but had not seen Jesus—they did. However, they drew the line when it came to eyewitness, apostolic authority behind a teaching or writing. And this, quite simply, is why the early Christians did not accept any other writings—no matter how good—about Jesus' life. Only four written Gospels met the requirement of apostolic authority.

COLLECTIONS OF THE FOUR GOSPELS

Because the Gospels were individual publications from their inception, it took a while for a collection of these four books to be made. During the first and early second centuries, each Gospel primarily had its own independent life. But by the middle of the second century, it appears that churches or individuals began to make codex collections of the Gospels. Various church fathers, such as Justin Martyr and Irenaeus, were speaking of a fourfold Gospel collection in the second century. And various Christians started putting together the four Gospels into one book. This would have been physically impossible with the form of a book known as a scroll, but not so for another form of a book called a codex, which came into use at the end of the first century.

The Codex

A papyrus codex was constructed by folding one or more sheets of papyrus in the middle and sewing them together at the spine. This construction was most advantageous for many reasons. First, it enabled the scribe to write on both sides (most scrolls had writing on one side only), and it facilitated access to particular passages (as opposed to a scroll, which had to be unrolled). A codex also enabled Christians to bind together all four Gospels (or any combination thereof) or all of Paul's Epistles, for instance, and made it easier for any individual or local church to make its own volume of the New Testament or any portion thereof. Christians adopted the codex, just as others did, because it provided the most economical and practical means of publishing the Christian message. To add to the practicality and economy, Christians generally used papyrus codices instead of the more-expensive vellum or parchment. Parchment codices were made for churches during the fourth century and thereafter because churches, no longer persecuted by the Roman government, could afford both to make and to keep such documents.

There were also spiritual reasons for Christians to adopt the codex. First, it gave them a book form that was distinct from that of the Jews, who used scrolls exclusively. Second, it enabled Christians to promote two early Christian volumes in particular: a collection of Paul's Epistles and the four Gospels. Scholars such as T. C. Skeat and Graham Stanton have provided convincing arguments that the Christians' adoption of the codex was motivated by a desire to establish the fourfold Gospel as the authoritative norm for the church.[39]

But during the first century, the separate Gospels were circulated as individual publications. This continued in the following centuries, as well. We can tell this by looking at manuscript evidence, wherein we see individual Gospels. For example, this can be seen in several manuscripts that preserve just the Gospel of John: (1) a second-century papyrus, P66, which was found as a single bound codex of John's Gospel; (2) another second-century manuscript, P106, in which the extant pagination of this manuscript (gamma [number three] on the recto, or right side, and delta [number four] on the verso, or left side), indicates that this was probably a single codex of John's Gospel; (3) a third-century papyrus, P5 (John), in which the extant folio format makes it clear that this was a single Gospel codex; and (4) another third-century papyrus, P39, where the pagination (od [number 74]) on the recto of the extant sheet and the large sumptuous calligraphy indicate that this was a single-Gospel codex of John.[†]

Early Gospel collections are found in the following second- and third-century manuscripts:

1. P4+P64+P67 (three papyri of one codex), a second-century manuscript that contains Matthew and Luke and that perhaps originally had all four Gospels.[40]

2. P45 (Chester Beatty Papyrus I), an early third-century manuscript with Matthew, Mark, Luke, and John, as well as Acts.

3. P75 (P. Bodmer XIV–XV), a late second-century codex that contains Luke and John and that may have originally had Matthew and Mark.

4. P53 (P. Michigan 6652), a third-century manuscript that preserves portions of Matthew and Acts. The two fragments were found together; they were part of a codex containing the four Gospels and the book of Acts or else just Matthew and Acts.

5. 0171, a third-century manuscript that contains portions of Matthew and Luke.

Gospel collections (exclusive of any other books) continue in the subsequent centuries, as is evidenced by codex W (the Freer Gospels—all four, ca. A.D. 400), codex N (fifth century), codex Q (fifth century), codex T (fifth century), 042 (sixth century), 043 (sixth century), 067 (sixth century), 070 (sixth century), 078 (sixth century), 087 (sixth century), and 083 (sixth to seventh centuries).

This documentation shows that the Gospels in the second century were being circulated both as individual books and as collected books. The same pattern happened in the third century. By the fourth century, it is likely that

---

[†]A note on the numbering system: A papyrus is numbered with a capital *p*. A number immediately preceded by "P" indicates a numbered New Testament papyrus manuscript. A number preceded by "P." (capital *p* with a period) indicates all other papyri.

most church codices contained all four Gospels. Such is the case for Codex Sinaiticus, Codex Vaticanus, and the Freer Gospels.

Significantly, not one codex manuscript has been discovered that contains Matthew, Mark, Luke, or John bound together with any other Gospel. Some manuscripts include the *Shepherd of Hermas* or the *Epistle of Clement,* as in Codex Sinaiticus. But not one codex has any of the other Gospels! This tells us that the four Gospels, and only the four Gospels, were held in high esteem by the early Christians. The collection of the four Gospels shows that these works were considered canonized Scripture early in the history of the church. Since the collections were made for use in church meetings, these were the writings that the Christians deemed worthy of apostolic status—that is, they were the writings that formulated the truths of the faith.

The Canon

The collection of various books by the Christian churches for use in worship was an inadvertent way of canonizing them. There is evidence that within thirty years of the apostle Paul's death (A.D. 60s), all the Pauline letters (excluding the Pastoral Epistles) were collected and used in the major churches. It is true that the authority of some of the smaller letters of Paul (as well as those of Peter and John) were being questioned in some quarters for perhaps another fifty years, but this was due to uncertainty about their authorship only in those particular locales. And this, in fact, demonstrates that acceptance was not being imposed by the actions of councils or powerful bishops but was rather happening spontaneously, through a natural response of those who had learned the facts about authorship. In those places where the churches were uncertain about the authorship or apostolic approval of certain books, acceptance was slower.

According to early church writers, the criteria of the selection of New Testament books for use in Christian worship revolved around their "apostolicity." In other words, like those books of the Old Testament, these books were collected and preserved by local churches in the continuing process of their worship and need for authoritative guidance for Christian living. The formation of the canon was a process, rather than an event, and it took several hundred years to reach finality in all parts of the Roman Empire. Local canons were the basis for comparison, and out of them eventually emerged the general canon that exists in Christendom today.

We know that the Gospels and the major epistles of Paul were "canonized" in the minds of many Christians as early as A.D. 90–100; that is, the four Gospels and Paul's Epistles were deemed to be Scripture worthy to be read in church. In fact, in Peter's second Epistle, he puts Paul's letters in the same category as "Scriptures."[41] We also know that the church fathers of the second century had a high regard for what is now the canonical New Testament text. Indeed, a study of the writings of the first five outstanding church fathers (all writing before A.D. 150)—namely, Clement, Ignatius, Papias, Justin Martyr, and Polycarp—indicates that they used the New Testament writings with the same or nearly the same sacred regard that they attributed to the Old Testament writings. All were considered Scripture. During the second half of the second century, more apostolic fathers were affirming that the New Testament writings were Scripture. This is especially evident in the writings of Irenaeus, who affirmed a fourfold Gospel text.

The twenty-seven books now included in the New Testament canon were first given notice (as far as we know) in what is called the Muratorian Canon, a document dated A.D. 170. An eighth-century copy of this document was discovered and published in 1740 by the librarian L. A. Muratori. The text names twenty-two books of the New Testament, including the four Gospels. The manuscript is mutilated at both ends, but the remaining text makes it evident that Matthew and Mark were included in the now-missing part. The fragment begins with Luke and John (calling the latter the fourth Gospel) and cites Acts, thirteen Pauline letters, Jude, 1 John, 2 John, and Revelation as books that could be read in the church.

As time went on, numerous other Christians commented directly or showed implicitly what books they accepted as authoritative. Irenaeus was privileged to have begun his Christian training under Polycarp, who was a disciple of apostles. Then, as a presbyter in Lyons, Iranaeus had association with Bishop Pothinus, whose own background also included contact with first-generation Christians. Irenaeus quotes from almost all the New Testament on the basis of its authority and asserts that the apostles were endowed with power from on high. They were, he says, "fully informed concerning all things, and had a perfect knowledge . . . having indeed all in equal measure and each one singly the Gospel of God." Irenaeus reveals his trust in the four Gospels when he says, "The Word . . . gave us the Gospel in a fourfold shape, but held together by one Spirit." [42] In addition to the Gospels, he makes reference also to Acts, 1 Peter, 1 John, all the letters of Paul except Philemon, and the book of Revelation.

In the third century, many Christian scholars—such as Hippolytus, Novatian, Tertullian, Cyprian, Clement of Alexandria, Origen, and Dionysius—affirmed a fourfold, fixed Gospel text. These writers also affirmed the canonical status of most of the twenty-seven books of the New Testament, even while recording doubts about such books as 2 Peter, Jude, 2 John, 3 John, and Revelation.

In the beginning of the fourth century, Eusebius was the chief proponent of establishing the four Gospels and other recognized books as comprising the New Testament canon. But it was in the middle of the fourth century that the development of the canon came to its culmination with the Festal Letter for Easter (A.D. 367). Here, Athanasius of Alexandria included information designed to eliminate once and for all the use of certain apocryphal books. This letter, with its admonition, "Let no one add to these; let nothing be taken away" (an allusion to Revelation 22:18-19), provides the earliest extant document that specifies the twenty-seven books without qualification. At the close of the century, the Council of Carthage (A.D. 397) decreed that "aside from the canonical Scriptures nothing is to be read in church under the name of Divine Scriptures." This decree also listed the twenty-seven books of the New Testament, as we have them today.

CHAPTER 2

Exploring the Religious Context

As we set out to consider the writing of the Gospels of Jesus, we can benefit from a brief survey of what the religious and philosophical culture of the Mediterranean world was like during the time of their composition. This era (roughly from the first to third centuries A.D.) saw the development of not only Christianity and its literature but also Rabbinic Judaism, various forms of Gnosticism with its literature, and several widespread pagan mystery cults. These did not develop out of thin air; rather, they were additions to the Hellenistic culture that had arrived with Alexander the Great some three hundred years earlier. The schools of various Greek philosophers and the religious cults of numerous ancient deities from Greece, Egypt, Persia, Babylon, and elsewhere were already known in the region, and their overall influence was felt.

The Hellenistic world during this period was a variegated tunic of cultural and religious identity. A person living in a big city in Asia Minor, for example, probably interacted regularly with people from several of the different religious and philosophical groups we discuss on the pages that follow. Understanding the basic tenets of these religions and philosophies is very helpful in evaluating the various perspectives people brought to their reading of the many Gospels of Jesus that circulated in the first three centuries of the common era.

CLASSICAL RELIGIONS AND PHILOSOPHIES

For centuries before Alexander conquered the Mediterranean world, uniting it in an increasingly Hellenistic culture, the classical religions of its various cultures were being practiced. In Greece and Rome, this meant the pantheon of gods, topped by Zeus (Jupiter, to the Romans). Babylon and Egypt also featured pantheons, including the likes of Marduk, Bel, Ra, and Isis. Although Persia may have officially adopted Zoroastrianism—with its one good god, Ahura Mazda—as the state religion, Zoroaster's views appear to have been reshaped by later priests to include animal sacrifice and other cultic features from the earlier polytheistic religions and even to accommodate multiple deities.[1] In Canaan and Syria, the gods Baal, Mot, Astarte, and Anat were prominent figures that formed a similar polytheistic background. Israelite religion, with its monotheistic emphasis on the true and living God, Yahweh, often struggled to maintain its unity and purity in this context. Later, with the Jews' return to Judah from their exile in Babylon and through the work of priestly figures such as Ezra, Judaism, on the whole, became faithful to its monotheistic principle and was increasingly centered around the Torah.[2] Virtually every religion gloried in its temples and called for sacrifices, holidays, and other rites.

Under the Roman Empire, the Greco-Roman religions and philosophies would come to have greater influence than those of the Eastern cultures. Increasingly in the Greco-Roman world, rulers would come to be honored as divine (as they had long been in the Eastern cultures). And there were always elements of unsystematized personal religion and superstition—such as oracles, spells, and astrology—that were practiced along with the classical religions. Even so, a person's religion would still be categorized in fairly communal and classical terms.

After Alexander, however, a general sense of individualism increased throughout the Mediterranean world. People became more likely to sacrifice to particular local or personal gods than to simply venerate the heads of the old pantheons. Interest in mystery religions, such as the cult of Isis and the Eleusinian mysteries, increased and broadened. Among the educated, first in Greece and Rome and then throughout the Hellenistic world, the philosophical schools increasingly came to replace the classical religious formulations and began to function as a religion. These sometimes rejected the old beliefs and gods and sometimes reinterpreted them, offering new moral and spiritual direction.

Skepticism

There were, for example, the Skeptics, who were blandly negative in thought and conservative in practice. This philosophy, which was not widely popular, questioned the other schools, preferring to suspend judgment on most issues. Its conclusions about life were pragmatic: To live by societal norms whatever one's particular society was the way to go.

Eclecticism

On the other end of that spectrum was Eclecticism, which allowed one to choose a little from each philosophy, as one liked. The underlying idea was that all the philosophical schools were basically in agreement. In general, this idea increasingly influenced the philosophers of all the schools as time wore on, and favorable quotation of or borrowing from one philosophical school by another grew increasingly common.

Cynicism

There were also the Cynics, whose school had gained a bad reputation from the numerous deadbeats and hucksters who affiliated themselves with it to gain alms. This principle of living simply and as nature intended (rather than as society dictates) and its tradition of living as poor itinerant preachers eventually drove its most extreme members to an ascetic lifestyle. Ironically, this lifestyle included activities calculated to bring the scorn of the community, such as sexual acts in public spaces and the use of obscene and inflammatory language. Cynics were known for their boldness, even shamelessness, in public speech and their value of apathy and the freedom from societal constraints that went with it. They argued against determinism, and some were monotheists.

A later, more moderate Cynic was Dio Chrysostum (A.D. 40–ca. 112). In his day he sought to distinguish true Cynics from "the imposters"[3] and seems to have steered a course between Cynicism and Stoicism.

Stoicism

As a contemporary philosophy of Cynicism, Stoicism had been influenced early on by that movement but also had a strong interest in virtue. For the Stoic, virtue stood as the one possession that could never be supplanted or stolen. People's sure ability to attain and sustain virtue was the foundation that could steady society against the fears and disturbances that plague it as a whole; and this, in the view of the Stoics, was the self-liberation that had been sought by Greek philosophy in general. This fear was not merely personal, incidental fear, but all disturbances as a broader societal dilemma. The Stoics had a more unified view of the unseen world than the Cynics; they asserted that spiritual essence and hard matter interpenetrate everything. Thus, they believed that God was in everything (a form of pantheism), with the cosmos as a giant, interconnected living body. The Stoics also believed in a cyclical view of history, in which the world is periodically recreated from fire. This belief reflected their acceptance of Heraclitus's teaching regarding the four elements in which fire turns to air; air, to water; water, to earth; and earth again to fire.

By the first century, writers such as Seneca and Epictetus, followed by Marcus Aurelius in the second century, were expressing updated versions of the Stoic view, many of which are similar to moral views espoused in the New Testament. They even used some specific vocabulary similar to that found in the

New Testament. Nonetheless, the metaphysical ideas of the Stoics remained founded in pantheistic thought. Furthermore, they pursued self-liberation, thus offering a very different worldview from the Judeo-Christian one.

Epicureanism

Far from the unbridled hedonism we might associate it with today, Epicureanism actually had concerns similar to those of Stoicism. Epicurus, its founder, sought to guide everyone to tranquility and peace. He advocated the pursuit of friendship, contentment, and the balanced and proper use of the mind to arrive at this. Here, rather than a cold call to duty and virtue (as with the Stoics), one would find a call to peacefully enjoy the good things available in life. Educated people in the Hellenistic world often gravitated to either Stoicism or Epicureanism.[4] The Epicureans believed that the world was material (made of particles and space), eternal (having had no creation), and indestructible. Though they did believe in gods, they did not believe these deities ever intervened in the world. They were often called atheists by other philosophical schools because, for the most part, they gave up traditional religious observance. Lucretius (94–55 B.C.), a Roman, and Diogenes of Oinoanda (ca. A.D. 200), a Greek, are two later Epicureans, showing the endurance and broad appeal of this school.

Neopythagoreanism

A more obscure philosophy, Neopythagoreanism is nevertheless of particular importance to the period during which the many Gospels were written. This is due both to some key cosmological ideas that became part of Gnosticism and to the biography of Apollonius of Tyana, who lived in the first century A.D. The *Life of Apollonius* was written by Flavius Philostratus (A.D. 170–249); it is often noted for its parallels to the presentation of Jesus in the canonical Gospels.

Neopythagoreanism was a revival and expansion of the ideas of Greek philosopher and mathematician Pythagoras. Centuries earlier, Pythagoras had observed that the universe functions according to mathematical laws; he had gone on to consider the other possible meanings of numbers. The Neopythagoreans revived these ideas and speculated further on the secret and magical meanings of numbers. They were a more isolated group and were often linked with magical practices. Their teachings included special interest in the stars and in a chain of intermediate demons between God and humankind. In addition, many think the Neopythagoreans are the primary source of the idea that the material world is evil. These last two features would appear later in the gnostic writings as well, as the recently published *Gospel of Judas* demonstrates.

17

Middle Platonism

Middle Platonism was a philosophy that, as its name suggests, derived from the earlier teachings of Plato and descended from his Academy. Its ideas are in evidence from the first century B.C. to the second century A.D., appearing first in Alexandria, Egypt. The study of Plato and Aristotle was revived, and their teachings regained prominence.[5] The effects of this interest can be seen in writings of Philo of Alexandria and of Christian apologists such as Justin Martyr and Clement of Alexandria. In addition, some of the revived ideas made their way into Gnosticism.

As mentioned previously, Eclecticism had an increasing influence on the various philosophical schools. Middle Platonism was thus "Platonism influenced by Stoic ethics, Aristotelian logic, and Neopythagorean metaphysics and religion."[6] It viewed God as the "supreme mind" and believed that a "world soul" is what brings the entire universe to life. These philosophers embraced Plato's teachings about the distinct dualism of the body and soul, matter and spirit. Some followed the Neopythagoreans in asserting that matter is evil, though not all did. They began to return to their religious traditions, seeking to reconcile them with philosophical teachings. Middle Platonism was broad enough in its framework to be adaptable to and have an influence on all kinds of religion, from paganism to Judaism to Christianity.

Neoplatonism

After Middle Platonism, an important change occurred in the third century A.D. with Plotinus (A.D. 205–270), the father of Neoplatonism. Although much of Middle Platonism was inherited by the new system, in Neoplatonism, God "the One" transcended both spirit and matter and encompassed existence and nonexistence. Thus, Plato's dualism remains, but it is expressed within a framework of essential unity. This highest "principle" (God) had never intervened in the cosmos, but it "emanated" other principles, resulting in a chain of emanations that led to material reality. With beliefs similar to pantheism, Plotinus viewed each person as a microcosm of the divine emanations, with potential for greater connection to them. We will see a similar cosmological structure in Gnosticism (seen also in the Neopythagoreans), but Plotinus opposed the Gnostics because he held that nothing, not even matter, is evil in its essence.

Neoplatonism also brought elements of mysticism and theology to its philosophy. In its thought, salvation meant achieving union with the source of all being, which could be achieved by asceticism and contemplation. It was said that Plotinus had four such ecstatic experiences. Neoplatonism could be considered an integration and a distillation of the philosophies that preceded it, and it was the last real intellectual force that confronted the church before the ascendance of the Byzantine Empire.

HELLENISM, JUDAISM, AND THE MACCABEES

With the conquest of Alexander came the influence of these Greco-Roman religions and philosophies, but due to Alexander's general appreciation of the other major cultures (especially that of Persia, the prior world power and great foe of Greece), an atmosphere was created for wide-ranging religious discussion and practice in many places throughout his empire. Thus, we may argue that Alexander himself was the proto-Hellenist; his attitude and policies embodied and propagated Hellenism. After Alexander's death in 323 B.C., his kingdom was divided by four of his generals, who soon took to quarreling and warring with each other. During this period, the Seleucid kings pressed the Jews to immediately become more Hellenized.[7] Hence, one finds marked resistance to Hellenism from within the Jewish community in Judea. A scene from the apocryphal book of 1 Maccabees shows the intensity of the struggle by these Jews to retain their religious and cultural identity against the Hellenistic influence:

> And the [Seleucid] king sent letters by messengers to Jerusalem and the cities of Judah; he directed them to follow customs strange to the land, to forbid burnt offerings and sacrifices and drink offerings in the sanctuary, to profane sabbaths and feasts, to defile the sanctuary and the priests, to build altars and sacred precincts and shrines for idols, to sacrifice swine and unclean animals, and to leave their sons uncircumcised. They were to make themselves abominable by everything unclean and profane, so that they should forget the law and change all the ordinances. "And whoever does not obey the command of the king shall die." [. . .] But many in Israel stood firm and were resolved in their hearts not to eat unclean food. They chose to die rather than to be defiled by food or to profane the holy covenant; and they did die.[8]

It was this situation that led to the Maccabean revolt and ultimately to a temporary measure of independence for the Jews:

> Then the king's officers who were enforcing the apostasy came to the city of Modein to make them offer sacrifice. . . . But Mattathias [father of Judas Maccabee] answered and said in a loud voice: "Even if all the nations that live under the rule of the king obey him, and have chosen to do his commandments, departing each one from the religion of his fathers, yet I and my sons and my brothers will live by

the covenant of our fathers. Far be it from us to desert the law and the ordinances. We will not obey the king's words by turning aside from our religion to the right hand or to the left." When he had finished speaking these words, a Jew came forward in the sight of all to offer sacrifice upon the altar in Modein, according to the king's command. When Mattathias saw it, he burned with zeal and his heart was stirred. He gave vent to righteous anger; he ran and killed him upon the altar. At the same time he killed the king's officer who was forcing them to sacrifice, and he tore down the altar. Thus he burned with zeal for the law, as Phinehas did against Zimri the son of Salu [Numbers 25]. Then Mattathias cried out in the city with a loud voice, saying: "Let every one who is zealous for the law and supports the covenant come out with me!" And he and his sons fled to the hills and left all that they had in the city.[9]

Not every Jew became part of this Maccabean movement—not even every Jew in Palestine. Among these other Jews, various degrees of Hellenistic thought and culture influenced their concept of Israel's religion. For Jews who had lived in the diaspora of exiles for generations, many small decisions had already been made, community by community, that negotiated a way to remain Jewish in their new lands, far from Jerusalem.

Some Jews probably forsook Judaism for all practical purposes. Of those who did not, some felt compelled to travel to Jerusalem to worship at the Temple, while others did not. While some kept the teachings of the Torah as rigorously as they could in their new lands, others were increasingly influenced by the various philosophies already discussed and developed the tendency to harmonize traditional teachings with newfound ones. Some presented biblical ideas in philosophical terms or reinterpreted biblical ideas to mesh better with the current philosophy.

Philo of Alexandria is the preeminent example of this. Without forsaking his Jewish identity or adopting multiple gods, he brought together the Bible and the ideas of Middle Platonism. His presentation offered a reconception of Judaism that appealed to philosophers and educated, Hellenized Jews of his time. While Philo asserted that more was needed than the observance of the outward forms of the Law and that one must pursue its deeper meaning via allegory, he remained an apologist for Judaism throughout his lifetime.[10]

Other trends in Jewish thought and writing were apocalypticism and, to a much lesser degree, mysticism. Apocalyptic writing focused on the revelation of secret knowledge, often with an eye to the distant future, and often incorporated visions. Mysticism was the quest for an experience of communion with the divine (typically ecstatic), usually sought via contemplation.

In the personal and secret nature of the two ideas there is overlap, and one can find elements of both in a book such as *3 Enoch*.

But, in contrast to apocalyptic literature, the earliest Jewish mystical writings are much less certain in their dating, and Kabbalah, the widely known Jewish mysticism of today, was a medieval development. Thought in both of these areas typically took biblical themes and passages as its starting point and then borrowed imagery from throughout the Greco-Roman world. The major example we have of a separate sect with literature reflecting this seems to be the Qumran community, which is the subject of ongoing study.[11]

MYSTERY RELIGIONS

The mystery religions were those into which a person was required to be initiated by a secret rite before being allowed to participate. This concept seems to have originated in Greece, but many of the Eastern religions that entered the Mediterranean in the Hellenistic period also adopted such rites. Generally, a person initiated into such a cult was thought to have the special protection of their particular divinity, something shared by the small group of which they were a member. Many of these groups never flourished beyond the locale where they started, often not even allowing people from beyond the near vicinity to participate, but some expanded throughout the Roman world. Little in the way of moral teaching or doctrinal emphases was passed on from these groups. Rather, myths and symbolic secret rites were dominant. We will briefly mention just a few of the prominent mystery religions of the time.

By the time of Roman rule and during the writing of the Gospels, the Eleusinian mysteries had risen to fame, gaining appeal with people all over the Mediterranean. But because a person had to travel to Eleusis, Greece, to be initiated to the mysteries (for a fee), the group did not spread as widely as some others did. There were actually three degrees of initiation, the secret rites of which remain secret to this day, though some of the public happenings—such as feasts, sacrifices, and proclamations—have been recorded. Also, cult myths were not kept secret. This can be seen in the case of the Eleusinian mysteries, as revealed in the "Homeric Hymn to Demeter."

This myth explains how Demeter, the goddess of grain, came to Eleusis in disguise, apparently to gain a child to replace her daughter, whom Hades had kidnapped. Her true identity, however, ultimately came out, her plan failed, and the Eleusinians built her a temple. She then taught the family of the local king the mysteries that could assure happy immortality. Meanwhile, Zeus intervened to return Demeter's daughter from Hades, at which point Demeter returned to Mount Olympus.

The mysteries of Dionysus (also known as Bacchus) were not confined to any locality and therefore spread much more widely than the Eleusinian mysteries. They were practiced all over Asia Minor and Greece, even in Egypt and Italy. Dionysus was revered as the god who had given wine to humanity. Dionysian celebrations, featuring fasting to the point of delirium followed by orgiastic and ecstatic behavior, are known from classical times, but in Hellenistic times, the mysteries were added. Due to such behaviors, the spread of this religion was opposed early on by both Greek and Roman authorities, but their opposition eventually gave way to its practice under state control. Some of the implements used in the initiation rites are known, but their exact meanings remain debated. Overall, it seems that the mysteries offered the hope of a joyous afterlife and portrayed life there in terms of the revelry of a Dionysian celebration.

The ancient Egyptian deity Isis, usually associated with Osiris and Horus, came to the fore in Hellenistic times. She was identified with Demeter (of the Eleusinian mysteries), and her adherents claimed she was the only real goddess, with all other goddesses being simply other manifestations of her. The depiction of Isis became more Greek but still retained some Egyptian features. She was not the only Egyptian deity to become the focus of a mystery cult but was the most popular of them. Her cult, which most often included the worship of Sarapis, a savior god, was loved by some and hated by others. The inclusion of animal forms, which was natural in Egypt, repulsed the Greeks; but the wisdom of ancient Egypt was undeniable and admired by all. As a mother-goddess, Isis was essentially credited with all the achievements of human civilization. Adherents looked to her for protection, for freedom from control by fate and magic, and for the hope of bliss after death. In the cult of Isis, there were not only priests and initiates to the mysteries but also general followers who could attend many of the ceremonies.

It was into this broad mix of philosophical and religious belief and practice that the gospel of Jesus was spread at the hands of his apostles. And it is in this context that we also find Gnosticism and its interactions with the ideas of the time, including Christianity.

CHAPTER 3

What Is Gnosticism?

RECENT INTEREST IN THE GNOSTICS AND THEIR TEACHINGS

In discussions of the early church and the canon, numerous groups that were eventually deemed heretical inevitably come up. The Gnostics and their writings are no exception, and we often hear the term *Christian* applied to them. The "Christianity" of the Gnostics was discredited by the early church fathers on the basis of apostolic tradition, but recent publicity has presented Gnosticism for consideration again. The situation leaves many wondering, *What do the Gnostics offer us today? Why are they so popular of late? And how valid is it to portray them as Christian?*

Of course, one reason for the recent interest in Gnosticism is the increased availability of its teachings and writings, with the publication of gnostic works in formats that appeal to the masses, including various documentaries on television. This phenomenon of sudden appearance often gives the impression that a great mystery is being revealed—perhaps a truth that was hidden for thousands of years. In fact, the interest in Gnosticism is sort of a "retro" trend. The majority of extant gnostic works have long been available to modern scholars but generated little interest among the public. A parallel development, for example, is the expanded interest in the Bhagavad Gita (along with other religious and philosophical writings from the East) in America during the 1960s. It was not that the Gita had been lost, concealed, or even left untranslated for the thousands of years prior. Rather, cultural events and contemporary spiritual aspirations combined to bring the Gita to a more prominent place in American thought and culture.

Another reason for the current interest in the Gnostics is the manner in which they are presented. As should become evident here, they sometimes appear to be more—or less—than they actually were. Nevertheless, they have become a symbol in the public eye of certain contemporary values.

THE GAPS IN OUR UNDERSTANDING

Modern enthusiasm for the Gnostics is frequently based on either an incomplete understanding of their beliefs or on a quick acceptance of them without thought to what they fully imply. Thus, one frequently encounters a domesticated idea of Gnosticism today that is really used only as a symbol for a current agenda. Later in this chapter we will discuss some aspects of the gnostic worldview at greater length, but here we will simply mention a few things in brief to show the importance of recognizing the cultural and ideological gap that stands between Christians and Gnostics of the early centuries A.D.

The gap is evident, for example, in the fact that the Gnostics were dualistic, considering matter itself—including every physical body or structure, living or not—to be the product of an evil being. This is why we find statements such as the following:

> And the wellspring of the demons that are in all the body is divided in four: heat, cold, wetness, dryness. And the mother of them all is matter.[1]

> Ignorance of the Father brought about agitation and fear . . . like a dense fog so that no one was able to see. Because of this, error became strong and vainly made material [hylic] substance, not knowing the truth.[2]

Working alongside matter, participating in its evil, illusory, imprisoning nature, was scorned as tantamount to worshiping a false god (often called Yaldabaoth or Demiurge). Consider, then, the implications this notion would have for those who protect wildlife, perform CPR, or even plant a garden. At best, these actions would be understood to have little or no connection to the higher spiritual reality. At worst, one might argue that those who would do such things are so blindly bound to matter that they serve the wicked Demiurge without knowing it. The *Gospel of Judas* speaks this way of the disciples (except Judas):

> The disciples said to him, "Master, why are you laughing at our prayer of thanksgiving? We have done what is right." He answered and said to them, "I am not laughing at you. You are not doing this because of your own will but because it is through this that your god will be praised."[3]

In context, Jesus is saying here that his disciples' prayers were honoring the base god who created matter, whom they had unwittingly worshiped all along. Many gnostic groups equated the God of the Old Testament with a Demiurge figure: Saklas, Yaldabaoth, and Samael[4] were all names for this figure.†

---

† *Saklas* is generally understood to mean "fool."

The human attachment to matter was designed by Demiurge and other lower gods for their own benefit. To follow this impulse was to buy into the illusion of *being* and to doom oneself to perish with it at the ultimate demise of Demiurge. This radical divorce of spirit from body or matter would sit well with very few Westerners today, particularly those of an environmentalist or industrialist bent.

The further outworking of this idea was that the *hylic*[5]—the material being, a person who embraced matter and had no aspirations to *gnosis*—was essentially an illusion; he had never truly been (in a spiritual sense) and never would be. He had no spirit (*pneuma*) with which to transcend the material world and was simply part of the material emanation of Demiurge, an emanation that would ultimately dissipate, leaving only the spiritual. There is no hope for the hylic because that which is only matter cannot receive salvation. The pneumatic, on the other hand, was free from fate—free from the control of Demiurge and able to transcend the material world. In fact, the spiritual essence itself was taken to be incorruptible and was predestined to be "saved" in this sense.[6] Somewhere in between these two were the psychics, animated souls who could attain a sort of intermediate salvation surviving beyond matter but not attaining spiritual fullness.[7]

THE GNOSTICS AS A MODERN SYMBOL

Despite this gap between first-century gnostic thinking and most contemporary thought, the Gnostics now appear as a banner for a number of things, especially modern mysticism, feminism, and the application of the name *Christian* to diverse (and unorthodox) doctrines and spiritualities in the Christian church. These latter two ideas miss the mark historically, however, which illuminates the fact that Gnosticism is often made a rhetorical pawn in service of various current agendas. The Gnostics do represent mysticism well, however, and they are rightly seen as a symbol for it.

The Gnostics and Feminism

Those who remember Marshall Applewhite and the Heaven's Gate cult probably remember primarily their association with UFOs, the Hale-Bopp comet, and the thirty-nine identical suicides that brought the group to an end in 1997. But perhaps few remember one of the bizarre details: Applewhite and some of his male disciples had themselves castrated. The group's members also wore unisex hairstyles and clothing. This was all part of the hope that they would reach an androgynous "Level above Human" after being released from their bodies.[8] The group's tragic and self-inflicted demise has made it unlikely that it should ever be hailed as heroically feminist, but its beliefs in regard to gender closely mirror gnostic ideas. Though not via suicide or in conjunction with any ideas about UFOs, the Gnostics also sought to transcend and be released from their human bodies, and they saw androgyny as a part of that higher existence. Feminism was not a gnostic value—androgyny was.

For this reason, the gnostic texts do not regard either physical masculinity or femininity as sacred. So we find statements like the following:

> Simon Peter said to them, "Let Mary leave us, because women are not worthy of life." Jesus said, "Look, I shall lead her so that I will make her male in order that she also may become a living spirit, resembling you males. For every woman who makes herself male will enter the kingdom of heaven."[9]

> Flee from the madness and bondage of femininity, and choose for yourselves the salvation of masculinity.[10]

> The Lord said, "Pray in the place where there is no woman." Matthew said, "Pray in the place where there is [no woman]," he tells us, meaning, "Destroy the works of femininity," not because there is any other (manner of) [birth], but because they will cease [giving birth].[11]

Taken out of context, these quotations almost make Gnosticism seem like a club for men only, but the point of these gnostic teachings on femininity was not that women were inherently evil; as mentioned earlier, androgyny would generally have been preferred over either gender. This is a more accurate understanding of the meaning of saying #114 in the *Gospel of Thomas*. Femininity, however, was used to represent the illusory material world and its trappings, including sexuality. In the quotes above, the ideas of finding salvation in masculinity or in the cessation of birth are tied to the end of the material world and the continuation of the spiritual.

The Gnostics as Mystics

Mysticism, or subjective spirituality, is a larger trend within which Gnosticism fits well. The Gnostics are far from being the originators of mysticism, but they are good representatives of it. As will be seen in the discussion of the gnostic worldview below, a single gnostic worldview is hard to pin down. This is largely due to the subjective nature of this kind of spirituality. Few people know of the last surviving ancient gnostic sect, the Mandaeans,[12] who live today in southern Iraq and southern Iran. Even fewer have any plans to make a pilgrimage and experience their worship.[13] Further, we never hear about the Mandaeans in the news today, and none of the scholars frequently consulted by the media seem to be seeking to hear from this gnostic group. This is not surprising, though. No single gnostic group, such as the Mandaeans, really has the universal appeal of the broader "spirituality" movement. Furthermore, the Mandaeans speak of Jesus as the "false" or "lying" Messiah (though they honor John the Baptist),[14] a fact that lends little support to the idea that Gnosticism offers another "Christian" path.

The appeal to develop one's own spirituality (or even in some cases one's own religion) is strong in Western culture. Many people feel that the only genuine spirituality is one they create for themselves. Spiritually, we are part pioneer spirit and part pragmatic flesh. Happy to set out on our own journey of self-discovery, we seek simply what works for us. In this, there are parallels to Gnosticism—not in any specific or cosmological beliefs, but in the concept of inner knowledge as the path to spirituality and "salvation," however one defines it. The Gnostics are a legitimate symbol for this type of spirituality, but they are only one of many proponents, which also include Buddhism and even atheism.[15] Because this kind of spirituality is more subjective than objective, relying on individual experience, it represents a clear departure from traditional Jewish and early Christian faith, which was directly tied to objective doctrines and moral standards.[16] In the context of contemporary discussion, this naturally brings us to the question, In what sense, if any, were the Gnostics Christian?

The Gnostics as Christian

Christian Gnostics were "Christian" in the sense that they agreed that a messiah had appeared and that something new, some divine intervention, was afoot. The discussion of the gnostic worldview below will show, however, that it is better to understand Christian Gnosticism as borrowing the Christian narrative about Jesus for its own myth and abandoning its original Jewish context. So, there is a broad sense in which "Christian" may be applicable to some gnostic groups, but one should note that Gnostics did not universally think of themselves as Christian. A given sect might have considered itself more or less Christian, but the view of Jesus as the flesh-and-blood Messiah was rarely central in gnostic theology and was almost always separated from the spiritual Christ.[17]

Valentinus is an example of a gnostic teacher who identified himself with the Christian church to such a degree that he went to Rome and may have even hoped to be chosen as bishop of the church there around A.D. 140. He was not appointed, however, and some of his presuppositions about Creation and Christ were likely the reason for this.[18] It is generally agreed that he wrote the *Gospel of Truth*. This work does speak of Christ and the Cross, but its greater focus is on achieving acquaintance (gnosis) with God as the means of salvation—that is, discovering God within oneself.[19]

While Valentinus's continued involvement with the church at Rome seems to indicate that he accepted the church's central teachings about the death and resurrection of Jesus, what we find in his writings is an allegorical expansion on the early church's beliefs about the life of Christ colored by Platonism and the gnostic myth of origins. Some thirty years before this time, Ignatius had already warned Christians about variances from the apostolic tradition.[20] It is no surprise, then, that the *Gospel of Truth* (perhaps the most "Christian" of the Gnostic Gospels), was not canonized. While Valentinus's Gnosticism is arguably Christian in some senses, we should not forget that he is on the far end of a spectrum that stretches to include much that is not Christian in the least.

The wide array of ideas in gnostic thought and the sect's willingness to incorporate virtually any spiritual figure is evident in the codices found at Nag Hammadi. These writings don't represent any one particular brand of Gnosticism, but all sorts. There are pseudo-Christian writings, pseudo-Jewish writings, and pseudo-pagan works all present. There is even a book called *Zōstrianos,* claimed to be the work of Zoroaster.

Gnosticism's teachings are diverse because of its mystic nature, and little is known about actual gnostic practice (perhaps because it was also nonuniform). This being the case, the Gnostics can easily become either everyone's scapegoat or everyone's hero. So today we find that the myth of the Gnostics is more powerful than the historical Gnostics' myths. That is, most of the old doctrines of the Gnostics hold little appeal, but the narrative that has been forged about the Gnostics as a marginalized and persecuted group of devout Christians who upheld values strikingly similar to those of enlightened moderns does hold great appeal. It is empathetic and empowering for those who feel their views or practices have been unjustly condemned by modern churches.

We should remember, however, that the current myth appeals primarily to its own subjective analysis of historical data, filling in many gaps along the way. The more we understand about actual gnostic teachings, the more we can see how they contrast with the earliest church traditions and understand why Gnostic Gospels were not included in any orthodox canon.

THE GNOSTIC WORLDVIEW

Before beginning this discussion, we should point out that the idea of a single "gnostic worldview" can be a bit misleading. The term *gnostic* was originally used by one particular sect of gnostic Christians in reference to themselves, but it is now commonly applied to many different sects that emphasized *gnosis* (Greek for "knowledge") or were influenced by the ideas of Gnosticism—the Valentinians and the Manichaeans, for example. As we've mentioned, various gnostic sects adopted different teachings and imagery. These sects were sometimes more Christian, sometimes more Jewish,[21] sometimes more pagan, and sometimes more of something else, such as Zoroastrianism and Buddhism. As a consequence, there is not a single set of doctrines that fit all the varieties of Gnosticism, though all do share some features in common. These more common features are the ones of greatest interest to our discussion.

It is unknown exactly when Gnosticism first formed, but its ideas certainly underwent much development in the context of pagan beliefs, Judaism, and Christianity. Though no Gnostic Gospels appear earlier than the middle of the second century, the type of philosophy and speculation that characterize Gnosticism are found in the teachings of Plato (especially *Timaeus*), Philo Judaeus (ca. 30 B.C.–A.D. 45), and others. Even if the Gnostics had not yet taken a name for themselves, many of their foundational ideas were already around during Jesus' ministry—there was at least a "proto-gnostic" current of thought. The canonical Gospels, the earliest record of Jesus' teachings (as discussed in chapter 1), seem to give no record of his interacting with proto-gnostic teachings. Only John, the latest of the four Gospels, is regularly examined in regard to its relationship to proto-gnostic ideas. Although the Gospel of John contains similar vocabulary to that of proto-gnostic circles and appears to contain no direct refutation of gnostic teachings, still John presents ideas that are counter to those of Gnosticism. For example, he depicts a very physical resurrection of Jesus,[22] a genuine equation of Jesus with the Christ,[23] and an emphasis on faith and obedience rather than knowledge[24]—ideas that are counter to Gnostic teachings. Among the Epistles of the New Testament, Colossians and 1 John particularly show apostolic reactions against proto-gnostic ideas. Colossians was written around A.D. 60, showing that at least by this time some local churches were in contact with proto-gnostic teachings.

Kabbalism

Because of its associations with mysticism and Judaism, Gnosticism is sometimes associated with Kabbalah, mystic Jewish teachings. The earliest developments in Kabbalah were not until A.D. 600 in Babylon—centuries after the early church and the Gnostics presented their teachings. The best-known book of the Kabbalists, the *Zohar,* was not written until A.D. 1300. Kabbalah does show the influence of gnostic ideas as a later development, and methodologically, it does make use of allegory, as did Philo of Alexandria; however, to read its ideas as representative of Judaism or Jewish mysticism during the time of Gnosticism and the early church would be unwarranted.

It should also be said that although gnostic teachings often make reference to Jesus as well as to other Christian and Jewish figures, they do so primarily to express a philosophical worldview—not to recount history, but to create myth as a means of understanding or "knowing" reality. It is partially for this reason that so few scholars give any historical credence to the Gnostic Gospels when it comes to information about the actual lives of Jesus and his apostles. Another reason is the later date of the gnostic writings; none of the apostles were alive to contribute, verify, or dispute any of the facts by the time the Gnostic Gospels were composed. In fact, it seems unlikely that the Gnostics themselves would have seen a defense of the historical veracity of their Gospels over the four Gospels as inherently beneficial. One gets the sense from some of their writings that they looked askance at the early church and its effort to preserve apostolic, verifiable history.[25]

Dualism

One foundational aspect of the gnostic worldview, derived from Plato's philosophy, was dualism. The idea here was that the world was conceived in pairs of opposing forces. For the Gnostic, this meant that body and matter were evil, while the spirit was good. There were two opposing gods: an evil, matter-creating god (often called Saklas or Yaldabaoth and equated with the biblical God of Genesis) and the hidden god of pure spirit. The Jewish worldview, however, valued matter, and most Jews looked forward to a resurrection. It saw humanity not as spirit trapped in material bodies but as a unity of soul and body.[26] Jesus—a Jew—speaks favorably of physical resurrection in the New Testament, as do Peter, Paul, John, and others. Given the cultural context of the apostles and the early church, which began in Jerusalem, it is almost certain that all the believers there looked forward to a physical resurrection before even hearing Jesus' teaching on the subject. This was not because they had missed Jesus' point and failed to attain higher knowledge, but because their view of the world, like Jesus' teaching, was founded on the idea that a good and all-powerful God created humans as physical and spiritual beings and called that creation "very good."[27] The bottom line is that early Christianity, like orthodox Christianity today, is too Hebraic in its outlook—too closely connected to the Old Testament revelation—to accept dualistic gnostic ideas as an accurate representation of reality or revelation.

Gnostic-Christian Divergence

Because of the historical distance, it is easy to fall into the habit of thinking that Jesus and the apostles formulated most Christian doctrines from scratch—a creation *ex nihilo,* as it were. This is not the case. The teachings of Jesus are those of a Palestine Jew; as such, they imply a shared frame of reference with other prominent rabbis of the era, such as Hillel and Shammai, and bear little resemblance to the philosophizing of Philo Judaeus and other speculative thinkers. Jesus revealed truth directly from God, but he did so in a context where clear reception of his message relied on a generally shared understanding of the world as conceived by Palestinian Judaism. Thus, the church's orthodoxy was founded upon its traditional Jewish roots. That is not to say it was identical, but the idea of a Judeo-Christian worldview emerged precisely because of the high degree of overlap.

When the earliest Christians encountered proto-gnostic ideas, they simply recognized them as pagan and continued in the way of Jesus' teachings. The later entry of gnostic-Christian teachings into the church was naturally regarded as suspicious by most Christians, simply on the basis of the vastly different understanding of the person of God and of the nature of reality, sin, salvation, and the Messiah. It became evident that the Gnostics were not fundamentally Christian—they did not believe in the Messiah that had been promised by the matter-creating God of the Torah and the prophets; they did not celebrate release from the guilt of sin and the hope of a restored creation. Instead, the Gnostics embraced the dissolution of creation, along with all matter, and rejected the God of the Jews in favor of another god. They sought salvation by another gospel, another christ.[28] The Gnostics remained marginal because most early Christians sensed an entirely different "plotline" in their teachings, not an emphasis on different themes from the same "novel."

This different "plotline" is evident in that while the early church continued to affirm the record of Genesis about God creating the earth and humans being tempted and bringing sin into the world through their disobedience, parallel gnostic teachings took a very different direction. In the *Hypostasis of the Archons*,[29] for instance, there was a wide array of gods; the God who claimed to be the only true God and who created the world was evil, acting in ignorant blindness.[30] After the creation, this god was sent to the abyss.[31] The Fall was then orchestrated by higher spiritual beings;[32] the creation of woman was the work of lower evil beings and took away Adam's spiritual essence.[33] The tempting serpent was a spiritual instructor for the humans,[34] and Adam and Eve produced a child after Seth named Norea, who turned out to be the spiritual hope for future generations.[35]

So inherently different was gnostic thought that it was equally at home using a Jewish, Christian, or pagan framework. The works of Hermes Trismegistus, such as Poimandres and Asclepius, are pagan in character, showing much influence from Plato, with perhaps a hint of acquaintance with Jewish thought. Nonetheless, they demonstrate a general solidarity with gnostic thought, so much so that in the sixth century, they appear to have been erroneously associated with the Valentinians, who were Christian Gnostics.[36] It should not surprise us, then, that it was not only the Christian church that recognized gnostic ideas as divergent from its earliest central teachings. Before the time of the church, there is evidence that some Hellenistic Jews may have been divided over proto-gnostic (or perhaps simply pagan) teachings, prompting Philo to speak against some brands of Jewish philosophy[37] and resulting in other warnings that allude to gnostic-sounding teachings.[38] And later in the period of the early church, the pagan philosopher Plotinus (A.D. 205–270) wrote against the Gnostics in his *Enneads,* though his ideas were similar to theirs in many ways and he himself was a mystic. But interestingly, among writers who opposed Christianity, such as Lucian and Celsus,[39] both writing in the A.D. 170s, we do not find any repudiation of gnostic ideas, only of orthodox Christian ones. Again this seems to indicate either the marginal nature of Gnosticism in relation to Christianity or the ability, even of outsiders, to distinguish between the two groups.

BORROWED CLOTHING

In a number of ways, then, the term *Christian Gnostic* is oxymoronic and would have been perceived that way, or at least as syncretistic, from its inception. It is not a term like *Coptic Christian* or *Protestant Christian.* It is rather like *Hindu Christian.* What made Christian Gnostics "Christian" was their positive reference to Jesus Christ and his death and resurrection—though this does not figure equally in all Christian Gnostic writings. But the actual content of their discussion of Christ's life, work, and teachings shows that the resemblance to other Christians was due mainly to borrowing from the Christian movement and adapting some of its teachings and characters to clothe their own beliefs.

This approach is like the use of the saints in Santeria or in Haitian voodoo—little attention is given to the peculiarities of the Christian message, but holy figures are adopted and assimilated into the existing worldview—and also to New Age spirituality, which generally recognizes Jesus as significant but not foundational to its beliefs about God and salvation. The Gnostics' use of this approach is evident, for example, in their insistence that the God of the Old Testament is not the God Jesus referred to as Father and that the Son of God, as a spiritual being, could not have taken on any material form. The result is that though God, Jesus, Adam, and Eve are mentioned in gnostic literature, the stories and characters are altered from their earliest historical forms to fit with a non-Jewish, non-Christian worldview.

VIEW OF SALVATION

With their alternate vision of the nature of creation and spiritual reality, it is not surprising that the Gnostics arrived at a different concept of salvation from that of the early church. This is one of the chief distinctions between gnostic and truly Christian theology. In gnostic thought, sin was generally associated with ignorance or forgetfulness and was located ultimately in the divine realm—among those beings responsible for creating and trying to control matter—rather than in humans, who were more or less victims, creatures trapped in the material world. Thus, the *Gospel of Thomas* does not even bother to speak of sin, and when the *Gospel of Truth* approaches this concept, it speaks of it in terms of ignorance[40] and forgetfulness.[41] Though some gnostic sects seem to have recognized a more traditional concept of sin,[42] they all portrayed special spiritual knowledge as the solution to this problem.

Salvation, then, was attained by special knowledge, and it was a salvation from the oppression of matter and spiritual ignorance. As the *Apocryphon of John* says, "[A soul] attains salvation and therefore is not cast into flesh again."[43] The gnosis (knowledge) itself was salvation—to know oneself, to know the mysteries of the spiritual realm, to reach enlightenment and enter the *pleroma,* or "fullness." As mentioned earlier, it was generally understood that people fell into one of the three spiritual categories—pneumatic (spiritual), psychic (those with spiritual potential), and hylic (material, lacking spiritual potential)—salvation often being rendered inevitable or irrevocably beyond reach. This is observed in the words spoken to the pneumatic Norea in the *Hypostasis of the Archons*:

> You, together with your offspring, belong to the primeval parent; from above, out of incorruptible light, their souls are come. Thus the authorities [beings that created matter] cannot approach them because of the spirit of truth present within them; and all who have become acquainted with this way exist immortal in the midst of dying mankind.[44]

The souls of the spiritual or pneumatics had come from the spiritual realm and would return—they were immortal from the start. Others were "dying mankind." And the psychics (not mentioned in the passage above) might yet attain an existence outside of matter, but it would not be in the "fullness."

VIEW OF JESUS CHRIST

Many gnostic sects did speak about Jesus the Messiah (that is, the Christ). But because of their basic myth of origins, they had inherently different ideas about redemption, and their conception of the person and purpose of the Christ was radically different from that of the earliest Christians. Perhaps the contrast is most visible when considering the Crucifixion. In some cases, such as in the

Gospel of Thomas, the crucifixion of Christ plays no role at all; it simply is not a significant part of Jesus' purpose. While a few gnostic works do tie the death of Jesus to the revelation of the spiritual or divine, his death is more readily seen as a vain attempt by evil spirits to keep him from imparting knowledge to his followers rather than as an essential act for salvation.

Rather, according to gnostic writings, one encounters the real god (not the creator God)[45] in Christ and encounters Christ within oneself; and this acquaintance, or knowledge (gnosis), accomplishes salvation. So the role of Christ is not a mediator or sacrifice for humans whose sin has angered their Creator; rather, it is to save spiritual beings from the creator of matter (and even from matter itself) by means of special knowledge. For example, the *Gospel of Truth* speaks of Christ as "the Word, who is spoken of as 'savior': for that is the term for the work that he was to accomplish to ransom those who had fallen ignorant of the father."[46] In keeping with the idea that knowledge is the key to salvation, we find Jesus frequently imparting secret knowledge (or the path to secret knowledge) in gnostic literature:

> Jesus said, "If you produce what is in you, what you have will save you. If you do not have what is in you, what you do not have will kill you."[47]

> [. . .] The kingdom of heaven is inside of you. And it is outside of you. When you have become acquainted with yourselves, then you will be recognized. And you will understand that it is you who are children of the living father.[48]

> Jesus said, "[Come] that I may teach you about [secrets] no person [has] ever seen. [. . .]" Adam was in the first radiant cloud that no angel has ever seen among all those called "God." He [49] [. . .] that [. . .] the image [. . .] and after the likeness of [this] angel. He made the incorruptible [generation] of Seth appear [. . .] the twelve [. . .] the twenty-four [. . .]. He made seventy-two luminaries appear in the incorruptible generation, in accordance with the will of the Spirit. The seventy-two luminaries themselves made three hundred sixty luminaries appear in the incorruptible generation, in accordance with the will of the Spirit, that their number should be five for each. "The twelve aeons of the twelve luminaries constitute their father, with six heavens for each aeon, so that there are seventy-two heavens for the seventy-two luminaries, and for each [50] [of them five] firmaments, [for a total of] three hundred sixty [firmaments . . .]."[49]

The synoptic Gospels agree that Jesus Christ's basic message has to do with the Kingdom of God, and they summarize the core of that message similarly, calling for repentance and declaring that the Kingdom of Heaven (or Kingdom of God) is near.[50] This message is, then, invariably expanded in terms of moral implications[51] and of realization.[52] Humble, repentant faith is emphasized as the requirement for entrance into the Kingdom,[53] which consists of both physical and spiritual components.[54] As is hinted in the quotes from the *Gospel of Thomas* above, the gnostic concept of the Kingdom was entirely interior and more closely tied to special knowledge than to one's trust in Christ and consequent repentance.

However, on the basis of their Jewish heritage the earliest Christians saw the Kingdom both as interior and as exterior—as spiritual and as physical.[55] Christians and Gnostics did share a sense of alienation from the world that fit into their respective concepts of the Kingdom of Heaven. But for Christians, the alienation was from a world system driven by rebellion against its Creator, whereas the Gnostics' alienation was from the world as a material entity, the product of an errant spiritual being. These two concepts of the Kingdom in contrast to the world resulted in very different stances on the importance of morality.

MORALITY

For Christians, morality was an indispensable outworking of the Kingdom; its standards, a divine revelation. For Gnostics, morality, as commonly conceived, applied only to the material world and was a product of the wicked rulers who created matter. It was of little consequence to the spiritual.

Accordingly, gnostic writings spend little or no time prescribing moral behavior (or condemning immoral behavior). In this they are notably different from Judaism, showing instead their similarity to earlier pagan religions in the Hellenistic world, where "morality was not closely associated with religion. . . . For the most part one's codes of conduct were derived from one's national customs or from the ethical teachings of the philosophical schools. . . . The wedding of Ethics and religious belief, based on divine revelation, was one of the important strengths of Judaism and Christianity in the ancient world."[56] Hence, Gnostics might be ascetic, moderate, or quite sensual, depending on their philosophical conclusions about how best to subvert the material world and the powers that created it. Most seem to have chosen asceticism. In any case, for the pneumatic this choice was of only minor consequence because to be pneumatic was to be free from fate, destined to reach the *pleroma,* or "fullness."

On the other hand, the Torah, the foundation of Jewish belief, is quite concerned with ethics, and it directly ties human morality to belief and worship. Leviticus 19:1–20:8 is a good example of this. The passage opens and closes with a call to holiness based on the Lord's holiness, but it does not consist merely of rules for ritual purity before God in the Temple. Rather, it addresses ethical relationships between people in all areas—at home, in public, at work, in the marketplace.[57] In closing, this section of Leviticus emphasizes the connection between belief and practice: "Keep all my decrees by putting them into practice, for I am the LORD who makes you holy."[58] The prophets, pointing back to the Torah, also tied the moral to the religious. Isaiah 1:15-17, for example, connects God's refusal to hear the people's prayers not to ritual impurity but unethical practice.

The earliest church maintained its Jewish roots, and even when Judaism and Christianity became increasingly separate, Christians maintained their Jewish heritage through their Scriptures and worldview. This included having moral standards that were directly connected to their beliefs. In keeping with this, 1 Peter 1:14-16 speaks of obedience to God and then cites the command from Leviticus to be holy because the Lord is holy. Peter then goes on to speak of the practical morality that results from believing the gospel. The cosmological ideas inherent in the prayer that God's will be done "on earth as it is in heaven" also bespeak this heritage and would have irked any gnostic believer.[59] The rejection of these earliest and central beliefs separated Gnosticism and Christianity from the beginning. Though outsiders might have taken references to the Christ as indicating that the groups were similar, the participants in each group quickly recognized each other as following a very different messiah.

GNOSTIC TEACHINGS AND THE EARLY CHURCH

In the early chapters of this book, we saw that the manuscripts and traditions for the four Gospels predate all others. We also saw that most local churches widely read and began grouping together the four Gospels while reading various other "Gospels" sporadically, attempting to assess their value. This process finally climaxed with Athanasius's Festal Letter (A.D. 367), which lists the New Testament canon as it stands today, as well as the decrees of the Council of Carthage (A.D. 397). But recent questions regarding the early church and its canon make one wonder, *Why did gnostic works not thrive or gain wide acceptance in the church? Was it a matter of unfair church judgments and heavily enforced decrees? Or were there factors that made the Gnostics a marginal group from the start?*

The recently popularized conception is that the Gnostics were a prominent group of Christians, though of a different theological stripe, who were driven out of the originally "diverse" movement of Christianity. This oversimplification is often used to point to the supposed conspiratorial nature of the church. While history shows there clearly were church leaders denouncing the teachings of the Gnostics, an honest assessment does not turn up evidence that Gnosticism was a popular Christian idea that was accepted at one time and conspiratorially repudiated later. The first half of this chapter has taken a look at the Gnostics' beliefs and teachings; these are the primary reason why these groups could not thrive under the prevailing worldview of the early church. In a world of early church fish, the Gnostics were ducks—the two groups were near each other but never could school together for obvious reasons.

In contemporary dialogue, one often gets the message that the early church clandestinely suppressed the Gnostics and by its conspiracy nearly stamped them out of existence. To be sure, the church did reach a consensus affirming its original orthodoxy and did make its stance against the Gnostics clear. But the early church never had any real power to "stamp out" the Gnostics or the diversity of the cultures in which it found itself. It could only seek to guard the truth within its own membership.[60] This being the case, we find that before his conversion Augustine was able to regularly attend meetings of the Manichaeans in A.D. 373—decades after Constantine—in spite of the ties of Augustine's mother to Christianity.[61] What follows is an annotated list of some different gnostic groups, a number of which survived well past the time of the early church and its recognition of an orthodox canon.

Some Gnostic Groups

EARLY OR PROTO-GNOSTICS
This is a category that describes the earliest gnostic sects. These were varied and include those that primarily developed in the context of Hellenistic Judaism before the time of Christianity.

CERINTHIANS
This was a school led by Cerinthus (died ca. A.D. 100), an opponent of the apostle John mentioned in Eusebius's *Ecclesiastical History* 3.28.1-6.[62]

CLASSIC GNOSTICS
Though it was not the earliest, this group is labeled "classic" because it is the group that actually called itself gnostic. Other groups were typically known by their founders' names and were referred to as gnostic on the basis of a general resemblance to the teachings of this group, particularly a shared emphasis on mystical knowledge.

VALENTINIANS
This school of gnostic thinking was founded by Valentinus, who was active in Rome around A.D. 140.

MANICHAEANS

Mani (A.D. 215–276), who was regarded by the group as a prophet in succession to Zoroaster, Buddha, Hermes, and Christ, founded this sect. Augustine of Hippo made this sect famous when he joined it in A.D. 373, before his conversion to Christianity in A.D. 387.

CATHARI

The Greek name of this group means "the pure." It was an offshoot of Manichaeism that spread from the Balkans to England. The Cathari were known for rigid asceticism.

ALBIGENSIANS

The Albigensians were a group derived from the Cathari who were found in southern France. This group disappeared in the thirteenth century under political and religious domination.

BOGOMILS

This was also a group derived from the Cathari. They were found in Bulgaria and the Balkans from the tenth to the fifteenth centuries.

MANDAEANS

The Mandaeans were a sect thought to have originated in Syria and Palestine in the second century and currently surviving in parts of Iran and Iraq.

We sometimes think of the early church and its "bishops" in terms of modern institutions, hierarchies, and policies. But it was not until A.D. 381 (the First Council of Constantinople) that a central, enforceable decree was made to define orthodoxy. The Nicene Council (A.D. 325) had indeed made some significant decrees, but it was still the responsibility of local churches and regional bishops to enforce them. The earlier canon lists were likewise the product of local efforts and broader consultation, not of a central church government. What began as a grassroots movement to establish and verify the apostolic teaching was finally given a clear, unified voice through the debates and decrees of the early councils.

Perhaps a better model for the period of the development of the canon, as well as the exclusion of gnostic teachings, is the very first recorded church council, the Council of Jerusalem.[63] There the church met, expressed and evaluated opposing views, and arrived at a position. Nonetheless, Paul, who was one of the original messengers of the Jerusalem Council's decree regarding Gentile Christians,[64] would spend years—perhaps the rest of his life—attempting to ensure that churches understood and followed the apostolic decree.

There was no easy enforcement of this decree—no funds to withhold, no government legislation to appeal to, no majority large enough to bring social pressure to bear. There was simply the message, preached with passion, and the appeal to apostolic authority for its authenticity. It is this tradition that the early church followed, enduring various persecutions from the Roman government, identifying various false teachings in its midst, and working to faithfully transmit the message of Jesus and his apostles.

The earliest and most broadly circulated early evidence for the Christian message was Paul's Epistles. Groups of Christians throughout the Roman world apparently agreed on the basic tenets Paul taught and began to bind his works in codices that did not include gnostic works. These letters affirm Jesus, the physical human being, as the Messiah, as the Son of God, and as having physically died and risen again. They also proclaim the Christian hope of a physical resurrection and the continuity of Christian faith with the Jewish Scriptures in both physical and spiritual terms. A church relying on these writings as faithful apostolic witness to the message of Christ would have noticed the conflict between its teachings and those of the gnostic writings.[65]

Local churches were circulating Paul's letters by A.D. 100–110 at the latest, possibly earlier. These were generally written before the canonical Gospels and make plain statements about the human nature of the Messiah/Son of God/Jesus and the physical reality of his death and resurrection as essential to the Christian gospel.[66] Churches already accepting these letters (which were widely circulated, unlike the gnostic literature) would have naturally rejected the gnostic message of their own accord. If we must blame someone for throwing the Gnostics out of the church, we should blame Paul, not Irenaeus.

But in reality, it is more accurate to say that the churches themselves were already confessing a gospel message that was in contradiction to Gnosticism, so when Gnosticism came along, the church disagreed with it and did not consider it Christian. After the deaths of Paul and the other apostles, we find the church still embracing the Christian gospel. Around A.D. 110, we read from the church father Ignatius an affirmation of these teachings:

> Stop your ears, therefore, when any one speaks to you at variance with Jesus Christ, the Son of God, who was descended from David, and was also of Mary; who was truly begotten of God and of the Virgin, but not after the same manner. For indeed God and man are not the same. He truly assumed a body; for "the Word was made flesh," and

lived upon earth without sin. [. . .] He did in reality both eat and drink. He was crucified and died under Pontius Pilate. He really, and not merely in appearance, was crucified, and died.[67]

Ignatius's statement predates the activity of Valentinus and Marcion in Rome. The doctrinal concerns he expresses can be traced back to Paul and the canonical Gospels, and in his writings Ignatius even quotes from the Gospel of Matthew. He is not merely reacting to false teachings but is reaffirming the original gospel message. In this message, the church could not permit change. By A.D. 175–200, Clement of Alexandria was already able to refer to "the commands of both the old and the new covenants,"[68] a reference that seems to imply an understanding of Christian teaching as codified. And in that same time period, Irenaeus, bishop of Lyons, was writing his *Against Heresies*. Among other things, Irenaeus was reacting to Gnosticism and to Marcion's assertion of a canon that rejected the Hebrew Scriptures. But Irenaeus's responses did not offer a new definition of Christianity; they simply reiterated what Paul and Ignatius and others had said before him, this time in a new context of debate.

The result of the circulation of Paul's writings and the statements made by church leaders was that the claim that the Gnostics were sundry Christians—a little different in their thinking but still Christians—was transparently false to other Christians in their vicinity. Their claims and beliefs were so different upon examination that no positive label could make up the difference. The situation is similar to the American two-party political system in that regard: It would be like a candidate labeled as a Republican giving a campaign speech about how she hopes to expand government services, implementing state-funded health care for all U.S. citizens and expanding welfare programs by means of an "affordable" tax increase. She might get some votes from people who didn't hear her speech and merely saw *Republican* next to her name on Election Day, but no Republican who actually listened to her message would consider her a Republican. There is diversity in both the Democratic and the Republican parties, but only to a certain extent.

The early church was, however, diverse in another important sense, and it is one we should not forget: It was diverse in ethnicity and in many nonessential practices. Jews, Palestinians, Ethiopians, Greeks, and Romans are all recorded as joining the flock—the invitation was offered to whoever would believe.[69] Christians might or might not be circumcised.

They might or might not eat meat. No set liturgy or language for church services was mandated in the orthodox canon. The book of Revelation envisions a multitude of Christians "from every nation and tribe and people and language" worshiping together.[70] Paul's statement in Galatians 3:28 also makes this point about gender and social status: "There is no longer Jew or Gentile, slave or free, male and female. For you are all one in Christ Jesus."

Some scholars and historians assert that "proto-orthodox" theology defined itself primarily as what Gnosticism was not—thus portraying orthodox Christianity as a reactionary trend that took over the early church and eventually evicted the Gnostics as heretics. In light of our discussion above concerning the essentially Jewish worldview of the early Christian message and its perpetuation by the likes of Paul, Ignatius, and Irenaeus, this view should be rejected. It is more accurate to understand Christianity as defining itself in terms of realized, messianic Judaism—what Paul and the earliest Gospels proclaimed. Its core beliefs predated even proto-Gnosticism. As such, the Gnostics did not pass from a period of acceptance in the church at large to a period of rejection and condemnation. As their various teachings became known to the church, they were rejected locally and then on a larger scale.

One may object that the early church would have tolerated these teachings, citing evidence that Christian writers also borrowed from Greek philosophy and other sources. (In Acts 17:23, 28, even Paul appeals to a local inscription and poetic quotes.) But it is still impossible to get away from the fact that the greatest source of Christian teaching remained the Hebrew Scriptures, as traditionally understood. And most of the philosophy that is borrowed is shaped to fit with apostolic doctrine, not the other way around. Some contrasts with Gnosticism are evident in early-church creeds, but this is natural because the purpose of the creeds was to express Christian beliefs in a contemporary fashion, answering some of the charges raised by other worldviews.

Irenaeus and other church leaders are sometimes painted as bitter and politically ambitious individuals, intent on driving people they didn't like out of the otherwise peaceful and diverse church. The historical context, however, alters the coloration of such portraits. Take Irenaeus as an example: At the time he wrote *Against Heresies,* he had recently taken the post of Pothinus, bishop of Lyons, who at age ninety was tortured to death in a prison with the support of the Romans. His death was only part of a larger, intense persecution of Christians in Lyons and Vienne, during which Christians were brutally killed and apparently mocked for their belief in the resurrection.[71] The literature of the martyrs and the background of the time make it hard to accept the idea that there was a political agenda at work in the church leaders' continual claim to and refinement of their historic faith. They were considered the heretics in the world in which they lived.

It is also sometimes suggested that the Gnostics were just some of many

Christians in the early church who were fond of allegorical interpretation or who experienced heavenly visions—part of an overall trend toward diversity. The Christian theologian Origen (ca. A.D. 185–254) and the book of Revelation are often cited in this regard. This is again taken as an indication that it was a small, authoritarian group in later church history that did away with the Gnostics and their allegory.

While the church may have debated the validity of allegorical interpretation, it was not simply on the basis of this methodology that gnostic ideas were rejected. One should note that in spite of Origen's love of allegory and even his departure from tradition on a few doctrines, he didn't set his allegorical interpretations in opposition to the plain, unallegorized message of the gospel—he accepted the apostolic tradition.[72] The Gnostics, however, insisted on the superiority of their understanding in contradiction to the plain meaning of the sacred texts and the predestined salvation of those who had attained special knowledge—a clear departure from the apostles' call to repent, claim Jesus as Lord, and rest in the grace of God.

The concept of a vision of Christ or of an angel, such as John recounts in the book of Revelation, was not foreign to most early Christians. A well-known and early example was Paul's encounter on the road to Damascus.[73] But even from the earliest times, there was an objective framework within which to evaluate such subjective experiences. In Galatians, probably written before A.D. 50, Paul spoke of the potential of angelic visions—these were not condemned as such, but if the angels' message was at odds with the gospel, it had to be rejected.[74] So the claim of a heavenly vision, alone, would not have been the reason for rejecting a gnostic writing, but the content of the vision would have been examined. This is in keeping with the principle of Deuteronomy 13:1-5, which teaches that prophets' visions and teachings are to be examined for their correspondence to previous revelation, no matter what signs accompany them.

Understanding the historical and theological link between Judaism and orthodox Christianity sheds new light on the proposition that the early church was conspiratorial in its rejection of gnostic teachings. There was nothing secret about Christianity's links to Judaism—for decades Christians had been known by most as a sect of Judaism. The statements of the church leaders against Gnosticism, then, are somewhat predictable and amount to a consensus rather than a conspiracy.

When the justices of the United States Supreme Court vote, their consensus is not regarded as a conspiracy. They are chosen precisely to uphold the Constitution by their consensus and are not regarded (except by marginal groups in American society) as pursuing some clandestine agenda. The consensus of early Christian leaders that the "Gnostic" Gospels were not in keeping with the earliest gospel message was no secret vendetta against Gnostics; it was an honest assessment of gnostic teaching in light of the oral tradition (or precedent) of the apostles and the content of the earliest Christian writings. The Gnostics were simply judged "unconstitutional." It should be remembered that many other groups besides the Gnostics were also deemed not Christian on this same basis.[75]

Just as any American can read the Constitution and make sense of the Supreme Court decisions to strike down unconstitutional laws, so any Christian can read the Gospels and Paul's Epistles and see the obvious contradictions to the core of the Christian message in the gnostic scriptures that make these teachings unchristian. A person's disagreement with such a consensus does not make the consensus a conspiracy—especially not with the modern connotations of the word.

In review, when the church entered the scene, many of the pagan ideas of Gnosticism (even if not Gnosticism itself) were already there, but the Christian message was founded on Palestinian Judaism and the teachings of Jesus, a Jew who claimed to be the Messiah. The church's early response to gnostic ideas was consistent and maintained the major aspects of the Jewish worldview. If Gnostics entered the church, it was by a way other than the "gate of the sheepfold,"[76] and the church simply continued its early response.

The fact that church teachings were only later called orthodoxy does not mean that the beliefs of orthodoxy were invented or chosen at a given point in time. Rather, the core beliefs had existed all along, and periphery beliefs and areas of doctrine were later clarified in detail. The formation of the church's canon was a slow process, not one centralized act designed to stamp out Gnosticism. Rather, it rested in the general pattern of agreement that developed through dialogue between the local churches.

The early church recognized divine revelation in the life and teaching of Jesus Christ. It also recognized in the apostles the accurate testimony to that teaching[77] and consequently recognized divine revelation in certain writings that could be traced to the apostles and other disciples who had been contemporaries of Jesus. The recognition of divine inspiration must come before the listing of such writings that proclaim their special status as canonical, and lists of canonical writings are not necessary to the recognition of this special status.

For example, there is no record of Jesus and other rabbis debating the inspiration of the Law and the Prophets—they simply cited them as inspired—yet the Jewish canon was not formally declared until around A.D. 90 at Jamnia. So also with the New Testament, Christians recognized divine revelation, though no public declaration of canon was made until much later. Canonical books were not immediately recognized via one litmus test and then strategically declared in. Various qualities were recognized on a more nuanced scale, and only the works that best fit the criteria could be regarded as worthy of canonization. Thus, the Muratorian Fragment speaks of some works, such as the *Shepherd of Hermas,* that were considered appropriate for private reading, but not for public worship. And later, Eusebius[78] speaks of works in four categories: accepted, disputed, spurious (to be disregarded), and heretical.

Thus, in the stage before any formal canonical development, there were the Law and the Prophets (the Hebrew Scriptures), which Christ and Christians continued to regard as inspired.[79] Next, the life and work of Jesus happened according to the Scriptures.[80] And Jesus' teachings and sayings were considered divine revelation and were preserved by his disciples. This was an important task of all good disciples. As *Pirqe Aboth* 2:10 states, they should be like "plastered cisterns" that retain every drop of water put in them.[†] At this time, the apostles were also still alive and perpetuating the message as Jesus had taught it. They already recognized certain works as being inspired, like the Hebrew Scriptures were.[81]

After all the apostles had died, local churches and the early church fathers—especially the latter—continued to measure new teachings against the apostolic standard. Because some gnostic or proto-gnostic teachers claimed a link to apostolic authority (as Valentinus and Basilides did), the churches sought to find the greatest agreement among apostolic traditions. Claims to apostolically derived teaching were then evaluated in terms of their correspondence and fit with the broad and already accepted teachings of the apostles. The canonical Gospels were often quoted by the church fathers in this period, showing their general acceptance.[82]

Around the time of Marcion, the development of a canon became more important because he challenged the validity of the Jewish Scriptures for Christianity—an idea that conflicted with all apostolic teaching and even Jesus' own words. To implement his ideal for a canon apart from Jewish Scriptures, Marcion systematically removed references to the Old Testament in Luke's and Paul's writings.[83] The majority of churches rejected this move by Marcion, recognizing its departure from the Old Testament and from the teaching of the apostles. But the question had been raised: Which books do we agree are inspired? The discussion resulted in various lists, some of which are extant. These lists give us a window into the development of the canon. Notably, no gnostic writing appears on these lists.[84] Much is often made of the fact that in the Syrian church the canon was not officially accepted until

---

[†] *Pirqe Aboth,* written in the early centuries A.D., is a portion of the Mishnah, the rabbinic record of Jewish oral law.

the sixth century. But this only pertains to some books. Agreement on the majority of the books occurred much earlier.

HIGHLIGHTS IN NEW TESTAMENT CANONICAL DEVELOPMENT

Marcion's Canon (ca. A.D. 140)	Includes Luke (heavily edited), Galatians, 1–2 Corinthians, 1–2 Thessalonians, *Laodiceans* (this was probably Ephesians or a pseudepigraphal work[85]), Colossians, Philemon, and Philippians (Tertullian, *Contra Marcion* 5), all edited by Marcion.
Justin Martyr (ca. A.D. 150)	Talks about public readings of early apostolic writings (*Apology* 1.67) and quoted from the four canonical Gospels to the exclusion of all others.
Irenaeus (ca. A.D. 180)	Gives a discussion of canonical books that includes everything now considered canonical except Hebrews, James, Philemon, 2 Peter, 3 John, Jude. He also supported *1 Clement* and the *Shepherd of Hermas* as canonical.[86]
The Muratorian Fragment (ca. A.D. 200)	Includes as canonical everything except Hebrews, James, 1–2 Peter, 3 John; this document also specifies *Wisdom*, the *Apocalypse of Peter*, and the *Shepherd of Hermas* as edifying, but for private use by Christians, not church use.
Origen (A.D. 185–254)	Wrote commentaries on many books, affirmed all the canonical books, but held some as of lower quality: 2 Peter, 2 John, 3 John, and James. He outright rejected some gnostic works, such as the *Gospel of Thomas*.
Nicene Council (A.D. 325)	Surprisingly, the issue of canon was apparently not discussed at any length, and no list was made.
Eusebius (ca. A.D. 320–340)	All except James, 2 Peter, 2–3 John, and Jude are accepted by him; but these along with Revelation and the *Gospel of the Nazaraeans* (also known as the *Gospel of the Hebrews*) are disputed by others (*History* 3.24-25). He reports that the *Shepherd of Hermas* and the *Apocalypse of Peter* (among other books) are rejected and mentions the *Gospel of Thomas* and a few others as "heretical."

HIGHLIGHTS IN NEW TESTAMENT
CANONICAL DEVELOPMENT *(Continued)*

Athanasius's Festal Letter (A.D. 367)	Accepts only the 27 books of the New Testament as canonical.
Syriac Peshitta (late fourth century)	Includes everything except 2 Peter, 2 John, 3 John, Jude, and Revelation.[†]
Council of Carthage (A.D. 397)	Published a list in agreement with Athanasius.

[†]The development of the canon in the Syriac church was slower due to its relative cultural and linguistic isolation. These shorter, general Epistles and the book of Revelation were later included in the Syriac (Philoxenus's version [A.D. 508] and Harkel's version [A.D. 616]).

TOPIC	GENERAL CHRISTIAN PERSPECTIVE	GENERAL GNOSTIC "CHRISTIAN" PERSPECTIVE
Yahweh (the Creator spoken of in Gen 1:1)	The eternal, almighty, good God who covenanted to bless Abraham and his descendants, and through them, all humanity.	An intermediate, misguided (or malicious) divinity whose deeds will ultimately be thwarted and whose relationship with humanity is self-serving and deceptive.
The physical world	The normal and intended dwelling place for humanity, good in its essential creation, but now marred through human wrongdoing.	An inherently wrong creation which holds humanity's inherent spiritual goodness captive so that it may be exploited by the creator god.
Jesus the Messiah	The Messiah and Jesus are one and the same person, most assuredly human and also recognized as divine (though various explanations of the way these two natures coexist were formulated).	The Messiah and Jesus are two separate beings, one a human and the other a spiritual being from a realm higher than the creator god whose spiritual essence would not permit being fully joined to matter.
The Crucifixion	The one person, Jesus the Messiah, died via Roman crucifixion and rose from the grave.	Jesus the man may have died by crucifixion, but the Christ, the Messiah, could not suffer this fate (various explanations of the Messiah's evasion of the crucifixion were formulated).
Salvation	Salvation consists in being restored to a proper relationship with God, which culminates in a physical resurrection to eternal life at the restoration of the earth to its perfect state. This is accomplished by aligning oneself with the Messiah through faith in him and his teaching.	Salvation consists in discovering an inner spiritual nature that allows one to escape the material world and enter the higher metaphysical realms. This is accomplished by gaining special knowledge (gnosis).

CHAPTER 4

Discovering the Evidence

In the last century, an amazing number of ancient manuscripts have been discovered, thousands of which are portions of the Bible, as well as other writings that could be called spiritual texts (otherwise known as noncanonical writings). Many of the biblical manuscripts are texts of the four Gospels, and several of these are very early—dating to the early second century, which means they originated less than fifty years from the time the original Gospels were written! No other book of ancient literature can boast this number of manuscripts so close to the dates the originals were written.

The purpose of this chapter is to familiarize the reader with the most significant sites of discovery and the variety of manuscripts discovered in those locations, whether they are canonical writings of Scripture, noncanonical writings, or other spiritual writings. At the top of the list are five places, four in Egypt and one in Israel. The sites in Egypt are Oxyrhynchus, Aphroditopolis, Nag Hammadi, and Dishna; the site in Israel is Qumran, overlooking the Dead Sea. Magnificent manuscript discoveries have come from each of these sites.

OXYRHYNCHUS, EGYPT

This site is quite significant, though it has not received as much press as Qumran, where the Dead Sea Scrolls were discovered. Thousands and thousands of manuscripts were discovered in Oxyrhynchus, jump-starting a new era in manuscript studies.

On January 11, 1897, B. P. Grenfell and A. S. Hunt started excavating Oxyrhynchus, which is 120 miles south of Cairo. Excavators searched in tombs, cemeteries, monasteries, and church buildings, but they did not find papyri in these places, as they originally expected. Rather, they found them in ancient rubbish heaps.[1] Grenfell and Hunt's choice of the ancient rubbish heap at Oxyrhynchus was fortuitous, for it yielded the largest cache of papyri ever discovered. They made new finds of papyrus fragments almost continuously, day after day and week after week, until they ceased operations in 1907. After Grenfell and Hunt stopped their operation, the Italian Exploration Society continued work there from 1910 to 1913 and from 1927 to 1934.

This site yielded volumes of papyrus fragments containing all sorts of written material (literature, business and legal contracts, letters, and so forth), along with several biblical manuscripts. Nearly half of the 116 New Testament papyrus manuscripts now known came from Oxyrhynchus. Of the fifty Oxyrhynchus papyri, about half were published between 1898 and 1940. These include the papyri named as follows: P1, P5, P9, P10, P13, P15, P16, P17, -P18, P20, P21, P22, P23, -P24, P27, P28, P29, P30, P35, -P36, P39, P48.

In addition to the twenty-five New Testament papyri they published in the early part of the last century, they gave us another twenty-five in the second part of the century: P51, P65, P69, P70, P71, P77, P78, P90, and P100 through P116.[2] These last seventeen were released in the late 1990s. Some of the more significant Oxyrhynchus papyri are as follows: P1 (Matthew 1), P5 (John 1; 16), P13 (Hebrews 2–5; 10–12), P22 (John 15–16), P77 (Matthew 23), P90 (John 18), P104 (Matthew 21), P115 (Revelation 3–12).

Several of the Oxyrhynchus papyri are quite early and accurate. They are as follows:

> P1 (Matthew 1), ca. A.D. 200
> P5 (John 1; 16), early third century
> P13 (Hebrews 2–5; 10–12), early third century
> P20 (James 2–3), early third century
> P22 (John 15–16), third century
> P30 (1 Thessalonians 4–5; 2 Thessalonians 1), early third century
> P49+65 (Ephesians 4–5; 1 Thessalonians 1–2), third century
> P70 (Matthew 2–3; 11–12; 24), third century
> P77 (Matthew 23), second century
> P90 (John 18), second century
> P100 (James 3–5), third century
> P101 (Matthew 3–4), third century
> P104 (Matthew 21), early second century
> P106 (John 1), third century
> P107 (John 17), ca. 200
> P108 (John 17), ca. 200
> P109 (John 21), ca. 200
> P115 (Revelation 3–12), early third century[3]

Several Greek Old Testament manuscripts were discovered at Oxyrhynchus, as well. We know that these manuscripts were produced by Christians and read by Christians because they are codices and/or contain nomina sacra (i.e., divine names written in special lexical forms).[4] Two of the more significant manuscripts, because of their early date, are P. Oxyrhynchus 656 (Genesis), second century; P. Oxyrhynchus 1074 (Exodus), also second century. Other Oxyrhynchus manuscripts have the following books: Genesis (1166, 1167, 1225), Exodus (1075), Leviticus (1351), Joshua (1168), Job (1163), and Psalms (1226, 1352, 1779).

In addition to the canonical books, the Oxyrhynchus papyri include *Tobit* (P. Oxy. 1594), *6 Ezra* (P. Oxy. 1010), the popular *Shepherd of Hermas* (P. Oxy. 5, 404, 1172+3526, 1599, 1828, 3527, 3528), the *Didache* (P. Oxy. 1782), the *Gospel of Thomas* (P. Oxy. 1, 654, 655), *Sophia of Jesus Christ* (P. Oxy. 1081), the *Gospel of Peter* (P. Oxy. 2929), some unidentified noncanonical Gospels (P. Oxy. 840, 1224, 2949), the *Gospel of Mary* (P. Oxy. 3525), the *Acts of Paul* (P. Oxy. 6, 1602), the *Acts of Peter* (P. Oxy. 849), and the *Acts of John* (P. Oxy. 850).

The Oxyrhynchus Manuscripts give us a window into the kind of books Christians were reading in the second, third, and fourth centuries. They were reading primarily canonical Greek Old and New Testament books—but also books that did not get accepted into the canon, especially the *Shepherd of Hermas*.

APHRODITOPOLIS, EGYPT: THE CHESTER BEATTY MANUSCRIPTS

In 1931, the *London Times* announced an amazing discovery of biblical manuscripts. Twelve manuscripts were found in a Coptic graveyard, stowed away in jars—eight books of the Old Testament and three of the New Testament, nearly all of them complete. It is generally believed that the manuscripts came from the ruins of an ancient church or monastery—perhaps in Aphroditopolis (modern Atfih). These manuscripts were likely hidden during the persecution under Diocletian (A.D. 303). The eight manuscripts containing portions of the Greek translation of the Old Testament are as follows: two manuscripts of Genesis (one from the third century, another from the fourth), one of Numbers and Deuteronomy (early second century), one of Ezekiel and Esther (third century), one of Isaiah (third century), one of Jeremiah (late second century), one of Daniel (third century), and one of the apocryphal Ecclesiasticus (fourth century).

The three Greek New Testament manuscripts that, according to bedouin oral tradition, are said to be found in the Coptic graveyard were the earliest manuscripts to contain large portions of the New Testament text. The first manuscript, P45 (ca. A.D. 200), is a codex of the four Gospels and Acts; the second, P46 (second century), is a codex of the Pauline Epistles; and the third, P47 (third century), is a codex of Revelation. A dealer from Cairo sold the manuscript P46 in different batches to two different parties—mining magnate Alfred Chester Beatty and the University of Michigan. P45 and P47 are also in the Beatty collection.

One of the most significant codices among the collection from Aphroditopolis is P46, which I have studied in person on four separate visits to the University of Michigan, and which I have dated to the middle second century on the basis of very extensive research.[5] This is an early second-century collection in one codex of all of Paul's major Epistles. As such, it tells us that Christians were collecting Paul's Epistles for church circulation at about the same time Christians were collecting the four Gospels for church reading. These were the two major collections of Scripture that second-century Christians possessed. There were no such collections of any other writings.

NAG HAMMADI, EGYPT: THE NAG HAMMADI MANUSCRIPTS

Around 1945, a group of Egyptian peasant farmers near modern Nag Hammadi inadvertently dug into a grave of the ancient village known as Shenesit-Chenoboskeia and unearthed a jar containing thirteen books, nine of which were largely complete, and fifteen fragments of works. This find was the library of an ancient gnostic sect and contained all or parts of fifty-one different gnostic writings—all but two of which had never come into modern scholars' hands before. Now called the Nag Hammadi or Chenoboskion texts, these works were the first modern find of original gnostic literature. All are believed to be Coptic translations of earlier Greek originals.

The Nag Hammadi Manuscripts are a collection of twelve Coptic codices containing fifty-two tractates (or documents), six of which are duplicates. They were originally thirteen codices; one volume was smuggled out of Egypt and finally purchased in 1952 by the Jung Institute.[6] That volume, Codex I (also called the Jung Codex because it is now owned by the Jung Institute in Vienna) is unique among the original thirteen works because it is in Sub-Achmimic Coptic, while the rest of the works are in the more usual Sahidic Coptic. Codex I contains five works, two of which are the *Gospel of Thomas* and the *Gospel of Truth.*

The Nag Hammadi collection is now housed in the Coptic Museum in Cairo. Its documents can be divided into several categories:

1. Gnostic Texts with Christian Orientation

In this category, the documents that have received considerable attention are the *Gospel of Thomas,* which is a series of 114 sayings and is thought by some scholars to be a source for the sayings in the canonical Gospels of Matthew and Luke; the *Gospel of Truth,* which some scholars have thought came from the pen of the well-known heretic Valentinus; the *Gospel of Philip,* which contains a unique series of logia related to gnostic sacraments; and the *Apocryphon of John,* which has close affinities to the theories of the Ophites and Sethians as described by the heresiologs, and which provides a full-scale primary source for the Syrian gnostic reinterpretation of the Garden of Eden story. Some of the other documents in this category that show indisputable signs of Christian influence on Gnosticism are the *Treatise on the Resurrection,* the several apocalypses of Peter and James, the *Book of Thomas the Contender,* and *Melchizedek.*

2. Gnostic Texts with Less Than Clear Christian Orientation

Some scholars have considered that these texts suggest a pre-Christian Gnosticism, but such a conclusion does not seem to be fully substantiated. *Eugnostos the Blessed* is the document usually cited in this matter and is frequently viewed as an undeveloped stage of the more Christianized form of the text known for some time as the *Sophia of Jesus Christ.* Even the so-called pre-Christian *Eugnostos,* however, seems to bear unmistakable signs of being related to the Alexandrian school of Christian writings and has been found to contain some allusions to the New Testament. The *Paraphrase of Shem* is another document frequently assigned to this category. Its references to baptism and the Redeemer, however, may be the result of a reinterpretation of Christian views and may reflect the conflict between the church and the Gnostics. Other documents in the library usually assigned to this category are the *Apocalypse of Adam,* the *Three Steles of Seth,* and the *Thunder.*

3. Non-Gnostic, Christian Documents

There are also several non-gnostic, yet noncanonical, Christian documents in the library that include the *Acts of Peter and the Twelve,* the *Sentences of Sextus,* and the *Teachings of Silvanus.*

4. Miscellaneous Documents

There are several documents that are neither Christian nor technically Gnostic but that were probably read with great interest by the gnostic scribes. Of particular note are the hermetic treatises that are Egyptian in orientation but contain a less radical dualism than is evident in typical gnostic literature. Hermetic literature has long been known by scholars through the publication of a hermetic library known as the *Corpus Hermeticum* (the English translation is known as *Thrice Great Hermes*). The first tractate, "Poimandres," is probably of the greatest interest to biblical students because of its rather positive view of creation and its interesting parallels with theological ideas such as "light" and "life" in the fourth Gospel.

QUMRAN, ISRAEL: THE DEAD SEA SCROLLS

In 1947 and 1948, the year Israel regained its national independence, there was a phenomenal discovery. A bedouin shepherd boy found scrolls in a cave west of the Dead Sea. These scrolls, known as the Dead Sea Scrolls, are dated between 100 B.C. and A.D. 100. They are nearly a thousand years earlier than any of the Masoretic text, which is the collection of manuscripts in the Jewish canon, preserved by the Masoretes in the seventh through the tenth centuries A.D. The Dead Sea Scrolls contain significant portions of the Old Testament—every book except Esther is represented. The largest portions come from the Pentateuch, which is the first five books of the Old Testament (especially Deuteronomy, twenty-five manuscripts in all); from the major Prophets (especially Isaiah, eighteen manuscripts); and from Psalms (twenty-seven manuscripts). The Dead Sea Scrolls also have portions of the Septuagint, a Greek version of the Jewish Scriptures; the Targums, an Aramaic translation of the Old Testament; some apocryphal fragments; and a commentary on Habakkuk. The scribes who made these scrolls were members of a community of ascetic Jews who lived in Qumran from the third century B.C. to the first century A.D.

Because of the importance of the initial discovery of the Dead Sea Scrolls, both archaeologists and bedouins continued their search for more manuscripts. Early in 1949, G. Lankester Harding, director of antiquities for the Kingdom of Jordan, and Roland G. de Vaux, of the Dominic Ecole Biblique in Jerusalem, excavated the cave where the initial discovery was made. This cave has been designated *cave one*—or *1Q,* according to the Qumran cave-naming system. Several hundred caves were explored the same year.

So far, eleven caves in the Wadi Qumran have yielded treasures. Almost six hundred manuscripts have been recovered, about two hundred of which are biblical material. The fragments number between fifty thousand and sixty thousand pieces. About 85 percent of the fragments are leather; the other 15 percent are papyrus. The fact that most of the manuscripts are leather contributed to their preservation. Probably the cave next in importance to cave one is cave four (4Q), which has yielded about forty thousand fragments of four hundred different manuscripts, one hundred of which are biblical.

Many sectarian scrolls peculiar to the religious community that lived at Qumran were also found. They furnish historical background on the nature of pre-Christian Judaism and help fill in the gaps of intertestamental history. One of the scrolls, the *Damascus Document,* had originally turned up in Cairo, but manuscripts of it have now been found at Qumran. The *Manual of Discipline* was one of the seven scrolls from cave one. Fragmentary manuscripts of it have been found in other caves. The document gives the group's entrance requirements, as well as regulations governing life in the Qumran community. The *Thanksgiving Hymns* includes some thirty hymns, probably composed by one individual.

There were also some commentaries on different books of the Old Testament. The *Habakkuk Commentary* was a copy of the first two chapters of Habakkuk in Hebrew accompanied by a verse-by-verse commentary. The commentary gives many details about an apocalyptic figure called the "Teacher of Righteousness" who is persecuted by a wicked priest.

A unique discovery was made in cave three (3Q) in 1952. It was a scroll of copper, measuring about eight feet long and a foot wide. Because of its brittleness, it was not opened until 1966, and then it could only be opened by cutting it into strips. It contained an inventory of some sixty locations where treasures of gold, silver, and incense were hidden, though archaeologists have not been able to find any of the cache. That list of treasures, perhaps from the Jerusalem Temple, may have been stored in the cave by Zealots[7] during their struggle with the Romans in A.D. 66–70.

During the Six-Day War, in June 1967, Yigael Yadin of the Hebrew University acquired a Qumran document called the Temple Scroll. That scroll measures twenty-eight feet and is the longest scroll found in the Qumran area to date. A major portion of it is devoted to statutes of the kings and matters of defense. It also describes sacrificial feasts and rules of cleanliness. Almost half of the scroll gives detailed instructions for building a future temple, supposedly revealed by God to the scroll's author.

Two manuscripts from cave seven (7Q) have received a lot of attention because some scholars identified them as portions of the New Testament. In *Los Papiros Griegos de la Cueva 7 de Qumran,* Jose O'Callaghan identified the first manuscript, called 7Q4, as preserving a portion of 1 Timothy 3:16–4:3. The manuscript consists of two small fragments—five partial lines on one and one partial line on another. Other scholars have identified it as belonging to *1 Enoch* 103; G. W. Nebe considered it a portion of *1 Enoch* 103:3.[8] Both reconstructions, though problematic, can work—that for 1 Timothy 3:16–4:3 and that for *1 Enoch* 103:3. But since the *1 Enoch* reconstruction does not take into account the second, smaller fragment of 7Q4 (which must be considered as contiguous text), and the 1 Timothy reconstruction does, then the 1 Timothy reconstruction stands on more solid ground. Its date has never been in question: It must be before A.D. 68 because the manuscript was found in 7Q in Qumran—and the Qumran caves were abandoned in that year.

The second manuscript, 7Q5, is considered by O'Callaghan to be a portion of Mark 6:52-53.[9] Some well-known papyrologists also recognized that this fragment preserves a portion of Mark's Gospel. Orsolina Montevecchi, author of *La Papirologia,* a standard text in papyrology, has accepted this identification and stated that 7Q5 should be given a papyrus number in the Gregory-Aland list of New Testament papyri.[10] The eminent papyrologist Herbert Hunger also supports Marcan identification for 7Q5,[11] as does Sergio Daris.[12] However, many other scholars are not convinced, primarily because there are problems with the reconstruction of the text. Nonetheless, those who have tried to identify this text as belonging to other biblical passages have failed. For example, Victoria Spottorno has attempted to identify it with the Greek text of Zechariah 7:4-5, but her argument is less convincing than that advocating Marcan identification.[13]

It could very well be that 7Q5 is Mark 6:52-53, especially in light of the papyrological opinion registered by such eminent scholars as O'Callaghan, Montevecchi, and Hunger. If 7Q4 and 7Q5 are New Testament manuscripts, there is no doubt that they belong to the first century. As such, they provide the earliest witnesses to the New Testament, and no one could ever again say that the New Testament was composed in the second century. However, I cannot discount the possibility that this fragment is an original piece of unknown writing or is a copy of some other work unknown to us. In this light, I think it is fair to list it as "unclassified"[14] or as "possibly Mark 6:52-53," in the case of 7Q5.

DISHNA, EGYPT: THE DISHNA PAPERS

The most significant discovery of biblical manuscripts after the Dead Sea Scrolls is that of the Dishna Papers, several of which are known as the Bodmer biblical papyri and a few of which are also in the Chester Beatty collection. James Robinson, an expert in the Nag Hammadi Manuscripts, was able to pinpoint the place of discovery, which had not been previously revealed by those who found the manuscripts. The Bodmer biblical papyri were discovered in 1952 in close proximity to where the Nag Hammadi codices had been found, north of Luxor, along the Nile River. They are also called the Dishna Papers, as they were found in Jabal Abu Manna, which is located just north of the Dishna Plain, near the town of Dishna, seven and a half miles east of Jabal al-Tarif.

It is quite likely that all these manuscripts were part of a library of a Pachomian monastery. Within a few miles of Jabal Abu Manna, in Faw Qibli, lie the ruins of the ancient basilica of Pachomius (A.D. 287–346), who brought monasticism to the area around A.D. 320. By the time of his death, there were thousands of monks in eleven monasteries within a radius of sixty miles along the Nile River. A century later there were nearly fifty thousand monks in the area.

As part of their daily regimen, these monks read and memorized the Scriptures—especially the New Testament and Psalms. Pachomius himself took an active role in this practice: He read the Scriptures aloud to his first congregation. Because Pachomius knew both Coptic and Greek (as did other monks in his monasteries), some of the monks must have read the Scriptures in both languages. More monks read Coptic than Greek. With the passage of time, beginning in the fifth century, almost all read only Coptic. Because the library in the Pachomian monastery could not have started until after A.D. 320, all earlier manuscripts—especially the New Testament papyri—must have been produced in other *scriptoria,* or monastic copying rooms (probably in Alexandria), and given to the library.

Most of these manuscripts were purchased by Martin Bodmer, founder of the Bodmer Library of World Literature, from a dealer in Cairo, Egypt, in the 1950s and 1960s. Chester Beatty, of Dublin, Ireland, also collected some manuscripts. Those collections of biblical and spiritual writings are as follows:

The Bodmer Manuscripts

GREEK: BIBLICAL WRITINGS

1. II, Gospel of John (P66)

2. VII–IX, 1 and 2 Peter, Jude (P72), and Psalms 33 and 34

3. XIV–XV, Luke and John (P75)

4. XVII, Acts, James, 1 and 2 Peter, Jude (P74, seventh century). This manuscript did not come from the same find as the rest of the manuscripts.

5. XXIV, Psalms 17–118

6. XLVI, Daniel

GREEK: CHRISTIAN WRITINGS

1. V, *Gospel of the Nativity of Mary*

2. X–XII, the *Apocryphal Correspondence between Paul and the Corinthians, Odes of Solomon,* liturgical hymn, *Apology of Phileas*

3. XIII, *Homily of Melitus*

4. XLV–XLVI, *Susanna and Moral Exhortations*

5. XXIX–XXXVIII, Codex Visionum

Coptic: Biblical and Christian Writings

1. III, John and Genesis

2. VI, Proverbs

3. XVI, Exodus

4. XVIII, Deuteronomy

5. XIX, Matthew and Romans

6. XXI, Joshua (a collection divided with Beatty)

7. XXII, Jeremiah 40–52, Lamentations, *Epistle of Jeremy*, Baruch (a collection divided with the University of Mississippi)

8. XXIII, Isaiah 47–66

9. XL, Song of Songs

10. XLI, *Acts of Paul*

11. XLII, 2 Corinthians

12. XLIII, *Apocryphon* (unidentified)

13. XLIV, Daniel

Chester Beatty Manuscripts

Greek

1. Greek Grammar, Greco-Latin Lexicon on Romans, 2 Corinthians, Galatians, Ephesians

2. Psalms 72–88 (P. Beatty XIII)

3. Psalms 2, 26, 31 (P. Beatty XIV)

4. Legal Documents from Panopolis

Coptic

1. The *Apocalypse of Elijah* (P. Beatty 2018)

Manuscripts in Other Collections

1. Melito of Sardis On the Passover, 2 Maccabees 5:27–7:41, 1 Peter, Jonah, homily or hymn (Crosby-Schoyen Codex)

2. Scholia to the Odyssey (P. Colon inv. 906)

3. Achilleus Tatios (P. Colon inv. 901)

4. A philosophical treatise (P. Colon inv. 903)

5. Cicero's In Catilinam, Psalmus Responsorius, Greek liturgical text, Alcestis—all in Latin except Greek liturgical text (P. Barcinonenses 149–161 and P. Duke inv. L)

6. Luke, John, Mark in Sahidic Coptic (P. Palau Ribes 181–183)

Some of the Greek manuscripts listed above date to the second century (P66, P75, Bodmer Papyri X–XII), but most of the Greek manuscripts are from the third and fourth centuries. The Coptic manuscripts date from the fourth century to the seventh century. The four important New Testament papyri in this collection are P66 (ca. A.D. 150, containing almost all of John), P72 (third century, having all of 1 and 2 Peter and Jude), P74 (ca. A.D. 600, containing Acts and the general Epistles), and P75 (ca. A.D. 175–200, containing large parts of Luke 3—John 15). P66, one of the earliest texts of John, is very helpful in establishing the original wording of the fourth Gospel. But, far and away, P75 is the best manuscript. It is one of the greatest discoveries of all time for the Gospels because it presents a text of Luke and John that is so very close to the original wording.[15]

A WORD ABOUT COPIES

The natural charge raised against copies is that faithfulness to original wording cannot be determined where an original no longer exists. This is a complicated matter, and one difficult to address in the brief space we have in this context since the purpose of this book is not to defend textual criticism but to present the many Gospels and their backgrounds. Simply put, there are indeed ways to determine the faithfulness of a manuscript copy to its *original.*

The assumption of Textual critics is that scribes were attempting to produce faithful copies of original works and not to be inventive. Wherever they might have made an error or been inventive, the testimony of other manuscripts, of which there are a plethora for the New Testament, will expose it. In the previously mentioned case, P75 does have a few inventive, singular readings; we know this because 1,000-plus manuscripts do not all have the same reading. But for the most part, P75 is remarkably reliable—and we know this by technical comparison with thousands of other manuscripts.[16]

CONCLUSIONS

Of all the spiritual writings discovered in the past one hundred years, the vast majority are canonical books of the Bible, whether from the Old Testament or the New Testament. An overview of the discoveries of four different sites in Egypt, as well as that of the Dead Sea Scrolls, is extremely significant. It reveals that Christians in Oxyrhynchus from the second to the fifth centuries were reading primarily Greek New Testament canonical books (fifty-five manuscripts found in total); some Old Testament manuscripts (fifteen manuscripts); and some noncanonical books, the favorite of which was the *Shepherd of Hermas* (seven manuscripts). As for noncanonical Gospels, there are three fragments of the *Gospel of Thomas,* one of the *Sophia of Jesus Christ,* one of the *Gospel of Mary,* and three unknown Gospels (which, as far as can be told from the fragments, are orthodox).

The manuscripts discovered in Aphroditopolis tell us that one monk in the third century read only canonical books of the Bible, one of which was a Gospel-plus-Acts codex (P45).

The discoveries of the Dishna Papers in the library of a Pachomian monastery a few kilometers from Jabal Abu Manna show that the monks in the third and fourth centuries read a vast array of canonical Greek biblical books and Coptic translations of biblical books, whether from the Old Testament or the New. There are nearly forty separate manuscripts, including the significant collection of Luke, John, and Mark. The monks were also reading some apocryphal works (nine in all), only one of which is an apocryphal Gospel: the *Gospel of the Nativity of Mary.*

A few miles away from an orthodox Christian monastery, near Nag Hammadi, lies Chenoboskeia, where a peasant unearthed a jar containing thirteen books and fifteen fragments of works. This was the library of an ancient gnostic sect and contained all or parts of fifty-one different gnostic writings. Not one canonical book was part of this library.

Thus, we have two extremes: a find in Aphroditopolis of all canonical books, and a find in Chenoboskeia of all noncanonical books. In between these extremes we have the finds of Christian reading material in Oxyrhynchus and Jabal Abu Manna, wherein the great majority is canonical, with a minority of noncanonical books.

These two sites most likely depict the normal situation among Christians in the second to fourth centuries. Most were reading the canonical Gospels and other books of the New Testament, and a few were also reading noncanonical Gospels. No powerful church authority had banned the noncanonical Gospels; they were still being read. But most Christians preferred the four Gospels. The gnostic sect at Nag Hammadi was exceptional; it seems that they purposely rejected canonical books. The fact that these noncanonical Gospels are not found elsewhere also suggests that almost all the known Gnostic Gospels were used by a local group; whereas the four Gospels have been found in many sites, which suggests their universality.

What we see in these various sites in Egypt provides a big picture for the Gospels in particular. The extant Greek manuscripts of canonical Gospels dated from the second to sixth centuries number no less than one hundred! Yet there are but a few manuscripts for some of the noncanonical Gospels, such as the *Gospel of Thomas,* the *Gospel of Mary,* and the *Gospel of Peter.*

PART II

Examining *the* Evidence

THE HARDEST CASES a detective has to face are those in which there are multiple possible interpretations of the evidence at hand. Rather than reaching a hasty conclusion, an investigator must take time to truly weigh the evidence, to examine it closely. This part of the book gives you the chance to do just that, with the translated texts of the many Gospels themselves. So now, with the tools and background information you've been given in Part I, you will be better able to understand what you are reading as you look closely at the various and sometimes cryptic Gospels available to modern scholars.

With this full look at the texts, you'll be getting more information than is usually provided by scholars and pundits in their comments on news shows and documentaries. Whatever your conclusion, you'll be able to weigh a much broader base of evidence. As you do so, remember that such variables as dates, locations, and the spectrum of worldviews all play a role in understanding the evidence.

CHAPTER 5

The Four Canonical Gospels

W hat was it in the process of the formation of the canon that indicated the four Gospels' superiority to all others? Why did these particular works rise to the top and come to be considered the authoritative testimony to the life of Jesus? In this chapter we'll look at the historical facts available regarding the date of composition and authorship for each of the four Gospels, including what significant manuscripts are available. It will be seen that the four Gospels are the only Gospels we have that were written as eyewitness accounts of Jesus' ministry, and only these four were composed in the first century. In addition, we will see that the four Gospels have far earlier and greater manuscript support than any other writing that claims to be a Gospel. We'll discuss these topics as they apply to the four Gospels generally and then look at the specific data for Matthew, Mark, Luke, and John.

AUTHORSHIP

First, it must be stated that authors' names typically did not appear on ancient books. It was assumed that the readers of a particular book would know its author. Some time after the publication of a book, an author's name was attached to it, especially when it was shelved in a library. For example, in the famous Alexandrian Library, tags with title and author were attached to each scroll, which was stored in its own space—much like a post office box—so that librarians could readily find a particular volume. Some of these tags have been preserved; one scroll, for example, has a tag indicating that it is Pindar's odes.

Second, ancient literature did not have a date of publication. Official documents would usually be dated, but literature would not. Thus, historians have had to try to determine publication dates based on other attenuating historical data—such as the author's birth and death dates, the author's position or occupation at the time of writing, statements in the work itself that give clues concerning dates, and comments about the work written by others.

With respect to pseudepigrapha, which refers to written works erroneously ascribed to particular writers, it is interesting to note that some of them include the "pseudo" name at the beginning or end of the document (e.g., the

Gospel of Thomas at Nag Hammadi and the *Gospel of Judas*). To those familiar with ancient literature, this is a sure sign of inauthenticity. As for the four Gospels, they retained the tradition of the first century: None had the author's name written in the book. Consequently, scholars throughout the centuries have been able to discern the authorship of each Gospel based only on the testimonies of those who lived close to the time of the apostles.

The earliest testimony comes from Papias, a scholarly historian who collected oral and written traditions about Jesus. Most of what we know about Papias comes from Eusebius's famous work, *Ecclesiastical History*.[1] Papias's comments about the Gospel writers are sometimes dated around A.D. 140. However, other scholars argue that his comments actually could be as much as thirty years earlier because Papias was connected to Polycarp, Ignatius, and Clement of Rome (each of whom was alive at the end of the first century) and because Eusebius's discussion about Papias precedes mention of Emperor Trajan's persecution of Christians, occurring in A.D. 110. Furthermore, Papias claimed that what he said went back to John, also moving the source of the information back one generation from his report.

So Papias's remarks about the Gospel writers were likely made at the end of the first century or the beginning of the second. He was the earliest person we know of to identify the apostle Matthew as the author of the first Gospel, Mark (writing for Peter) as the author of the second Gospel, and the apostle John as the author of the fourth Gospel. Presumably, he also identified Luke, but there is no account of this.

DATES OF WRITING

Though the date for each Gospel varies, all of them are dated within the second half of the first century. Matthew has been dated between A.D. 65 and 85; Mark, between the early A.D. 50s and 65; Luke, between the early A.D. 60s and 80s; and John, between the A.D. 60s and 90s. Though there will be some disagreement in the standard commentaries on the four Gospels about which decade in the first century a book was written, nearly all will place the time of writing in the first century. By contrast, not one noncanonical Gospel has been dated earlier than the second century. The significance of this is that only the four Gospels were written during the apostolic age—that is, while the apostles were still alive and ministering. Other Gospels were written after this time.

THE MANUSCRIPTS OF THE GOSPELS

Since the original compositions of the various New Testament books are not extant, we must rely on copies for recovering the original text. New Testament scholars have a great advantage over scholars trying to reconstruct the texts of classical works in the number of manuscripts available to them.

According to current tabulations of New Testament manuscripts, there are 116 papyrus manuscripts, 257 uncial manuscripts, and 2,795 minuscule[†] manuscripts.[2] There are also 2,200 Greek lectionaries. In total, there are over 5,350 manuscript copies or portions of the Greek New Testament. By comparison, Homer's *Iliad,* the greatest of all Greek classical works, is extant in about 650 manuscripts; and Euripides' tragedies exist in about 330 manuscripts. The numbers on all the other works of Greek literature are much smaller. Furthermore, it must be said that the gap in time between the original composition and the next surviving manuscript is far less for the New Testament writings than for any other work in Greek literature. The lapse for most classical Greek works is from eight hundred to one thousand years, whereas the lapse for many books in the New Testament is around one hundred years. Several of the Gospel manuscripts are among the earliest and most faithful copies; these include P1, P4, P64+67, P66, P75, as well as Codex Vaticanus and Codex Sinaiticus. (See Preface for further discussion on this issue.)

THE GOSPEL OF MATTHEW

Author

Though the first Gospel is anonymous, it is clear that it was ascribed to Matthew the apostle by the end of the first century A.D. Patristic tradition agrees with this ascription. Eusebius's *Ecclesiastical History* (fourth century A.D.) cites Papias (early second century A.D.),[3] Clement of Alexandria (early third century A.D.),[4] and Origen (mid-third century A.D.),[5] all of whom stated that the apostle Matthew was the author of the first Gospel. The words of Irenaeus (late second century A.D.) agree as well.[6]

Eusebius cites Papias to the effect that "Matthew collected the oracles [*logia,* sayings of and about Jesus] in the Hebrew language [*Hebraidi dialekto*] and each one interpreted [*hermeneusen*] them as best he could."[7] This probably means that Matthew had collected Jesus' sayings in Hebrew and then translated them into Greek as he wrote the Gospel. The expression *each one* could mean that each Gospel writer did the same.

Date

It is very likely that there are allusions to Matthew in Ignatius (late first/early second century A.D.) and in the *Didache* (early second century A.D.). When these allusions are taken in conjunction with Papias's testimony, it seems clear that Matthew's Gospel was well known by the early second century. Accordingly, the Gospel must have been written by the turn of the first century A.D. at the latest. The current scholarly consensus places Matthew's origin in the A.D. 80s or 90s.

[†] See glossary.

However, if one accepts the patristic testimony to apostolic authorship, the date would probably need to be set earlier. For example, Irenaeus thought Matthew wrote his Gospel during Peter's and Paul's lifetimes. (See standard commentaries on Matthew for further discussion about the date of composition.)

Manuscripts

There are twenty early papyrus manuscripts containing portions of Matthew. In order of date, from earliest to latest, these include the following:

P104 (Matthew 21), early second century
P64+67 (Matthew 3; 5; 26), late second century
P77 (Matthew 23), late second century
P103 (Matthew 13–14), second century
P1 (Matthew 1), early third century[8]
P45 (Matthew 20–21; 25–26), early third century
P37 (Matthew 26), third century
P70 (Matthew 2–3; 11–12; 24), third century
P101 (Matthew 3), third century
P102 (Matthew 4), late third century
P110 (Matthew 10), late third century
P53 (Matthew 26), late third century
P86 (Matthew 5), third/fourth centuries
P35 (Matthew 25), third/fourth centuries
P25 (Matthew 18–19), fourth century
P62 (Matthew 11), fourth century
P71 (Matthew 19), fourth century
P19 (Matthew 10–11), fourth century
P21 (Matthew 12), fourth century

It is noteworthy that Matthew has four manuscripts dating to the second century. This not only affirms a first-century date for Matthew but also gives some copies of text that may be only a few generations removed from the autograph (original).

More than twenty uncial manuscripts contain complete or nearly complete texts of Matthew. Among these manuscripts are the following:

Aleph, B (fourth century)
C, D, W, O, Z (fifth century)
042, 043 (sixth century)
0211 (seventh century)
L (eighth century)
K, M, U, 037, 038 (ninth century)
G and S (tenth century)

MATTHEW

CHAPTER 1

The Ancestors of Jesus the Messiah

This is a record of the ancestors of Jesus the Messiah, a descendant of David* and of Abraham:

2 Abraham was the father of Isaac.
Isaac was the father of Jacob.
Jacob was the father of Judah and his brothers.

3 Judah was the father of Perez and Zerah (whose mother was Tamar).
Perez was the father of Hezron.
Hezron was the father of Ram.*

4 Ram was the father of Amminadab.
Amminadab was the father of Nahshon.
Nahshon was the father of Salmon.

5 Salmon was the father of Boaz (whose mother was Rahab).
Boaz was the father of Obed (whose mother was Ruth).
Obed was the father of Jesse.

6 Jesse was the father of King David.
David was the father of Solomon (whose mother was Bathsheba, the widow of Uriah).

7 Solomon was the father of Rehoboam.
Rehoboam was the father of Abijah.
Abijah was the father of Asa.*

8 Asa was the father of Jehoshaphat.
Jehoshaphat was the father of Jehoram.*
Jehoram was the father* of Uzziah.

9 Uzziah was the father of Jotham.
Jotham was the father of Ahaz.
Ahaz was the father of Hezekiah.

10 Hezekiah was the father of Manasseh.
Manasseh was the father of Amon.*
Amon was the father of Josiah.

11 Josiah was the father of Jehoiachin* and his brothers (born at the time of the exile to Babylon).

12 After the Babylonian exile:
Jehoiachin was the father of Shealtiel.

1:1 Greek *Jesus the Messiah, son of David.*   1:3 Greek *Aram,* a variant spelling of Ram; also in 1:4. See 1 Chr 2:9-10.   1:7 Greek *Asaph,* a variant spelling of Asa; also in 1:8. See 1 Chr 3:10.   1:8a Greek *Joram,* a variant spelling of Jehoram; also in 1:8b. See 1 Kgs 22:50 and note at 1 Chr 3:11.   1:8b Or *ancestor;* also in 1:11.   1:10 Greek *Amos,* a variant spelling of Amon; also in 1:10b. See 1 Chr 3:14.   1:11 Greek *Jeconiah,* a variant spelling of Jehoiachin; also in 1:12. See 2 Kgs 24:6 and note at 1 Chr 3:16.

Shealtiel was the father of Zerubbabel.
13 Zerubbabel was the father of Abiud.
Abiud was the father of Eliakim.
Eliakim was the father of Azor.
14 Azor was the father of Zadok.
Zadok was the father of Akim.
Akim was the father of Eliud.
15 Eliud was the father of Eleazar.
Eleazar was the father of Matthan.
Matthan was the father of Jacob.
16 Jacob was the father of Joseph, the husband of Mary.
Mary gave birth to Jesus, who is called the Messiah.

17All those listed above include fourteen generations from Abraham to David, fourteen from David to the Babylonian exile, and fourteen from the Babylonian exile to the Messiah.

The Birth of Jesus the Messiah

18This is how Jesus the Messiah was born. His mother, Mary, was engaged to be married to Joseph. But before the marriage took place, while she was still a virgin, she became pregnant through the power of the Holy Spirit. 19Joseph, her fiancé, was a good man and did not want to disgrace her publicly, so he decided to break the engagement* quietly.

20As he considered this, an angel of the Lord appeared to him in a dream. "Joseph, son of David," the angel said, "do not be afraid to take Mary as your wife. For the child within her was conceived by the Holy Spirit. 21And she will have a son, and you are to name him Jesus,* for he will save his people from their sins."

22All of this occurred to fulfill the Lord's message through his prophet:

23"Look! The virgin will conceive a child!
She will give birth to a son,
and they will call him Immanuel,*
which means 'God is with us.'"

24When Joseph woke up, he did as the angel of the Lord commanded and took Mary as his wife. 25But he did not have sexual relations with her until her son was born. And Joseph named him Jesus.

CHAPTER 2

Visitors from the East

Jesus was born in Bethlehem in Judea, during the reign of King Herod. About that time some wise men* from eastern lands arrived in Jerusalem, asking, 2"Where is

---

1:19 Greek *to divorce her.*   **1:21** *Jesus* means "The LORD saves."   **1:23** Isa 7:14; 8:8, 10 (Greek version).   **2:1** Or *royal astrologers;* Greek reads *magi;* also in 2:7, 16.

the newborn king of the Jews? We saw his star as it rose,* and we have come to worship him."

³King Herod was deeply disturbed when he heard this, as was everyone in Jerusalem. ⁴He called a meeting of the leading priests and teachers of religious law and asked, "Where is the Messiah supposed to be born?"

⁵"In Bethlehem in Judea," they said, "for this is what the prophet wrote:

6   'And you, O Bethlehem in the land of Judah,
        are not least among the ruling cities* of Judah,
    for a ruler will come from you
        who will be the shepherd for my people Israel.'*"

⁷Then Herod called for a private meeting with the wise men, and he learned from them the time when the star first appeared. ⁸Then he told them, "Go to Bethlehem and search carefully for the child. And when you find him, come back and tell me so that I can go and worship him, too!"

⁹After this interview the wise men went their way. And the star they had seen in the east guided them to Bethlehem. It went ahead of them and stopped over the place where the child was. ¹⁰When they saw the star, they were filled with joy! ¹¹They entered the house and saw the child with his mother, Mary, and they bowed down and worshiped him. Then they opened their treasure chests and gave him gifts of gold, frankincense, and myrrh.

¹²When it was time to leave, they returned to their own country by another route, for God had warned them in a dream not to return to Herod.

The Escape to Egypt

¹³After the wise men were gone, an angel of the Lord appeared to Joseph in a dream. "Get up! Flee to Egypt with the child and his mother," the angel said. "Stay there until I tell you to return, because Herod is going to search for the child to kill him."

¹⁴That night Joseph left for Egypt with the child and Mary, his mother, ¹⁵and they stayed there until Herod's death. This fulfilled what the Lord had spoken through the prophet: "I called my Son out of Egypt."*

¹⁶Herod was furious when he realized that the wise men had outwitted him. He sent soldiers to kill all the boys in and around Bethlehem who were two years old and under, based on the wise men's report of the star's first appearance. ¹⁷Herod's brutal action fulfilled what God had spoken through the prophet Jeremiah:

18   "A cry was heard in Ramah—
        weeping and great mourning.
    Rachel weeps for her children,
        refusing to be comforted,
        for they are dead."*

2:2 Or *star in the east.*   **2:6a** Greek *the rulers.*   **2:6b** Mic 5:2; 2 Sam 5:2.   **2:15** Hos 11:1.   **2:18** Jer 31:15.

The Return to Nazareth

[19]When Herod died, an angel of the Lord appeared in a dream to Joseph in Egypt. [20]"Get up!" the angel said. "Take the child and his mother back to the land of Israel, because those who were trying to kill the child are dead."

[21]So Joseph got up and returned to the land of Israel with Jesus and his mother. [22]But when he learned that the new ruler of Judea was Herod's son Archelaus, he was afraid to go there. Then, after being warned in a dream, he left for the region of Galilee. [23]So the family went and lived in a town called Nazareth. This fulfilled what the prophets had said: "He will be called a Nazarene."

CHAPTER 3

John the Baptist Prepares the Way

In those days John the Baptist came to the Judean wilderness and began preaching. His message was, [2]"Repent of your sins and turn to God, for the Kingdom of Heaven is near.*" [3]The prophet Isaiah was speaking about John when he said,

"He is a voice shouting in the wilderness,
'Prepare the way for the LORD's coming!
    Clear the road for him!'"*

[4]John's clothes were woven from coarse camel hair, and he wore a leather belt around his waist. For food he ate locusts and wild honey. [5]People from Jerusalem and from all of Judea and all over the Jordan Valley went out to see and hear John. [6]And when they confessed their sins, he baptized them in the Jordan River.

[7]But when he saw many Pharisees and Sadducees coming to watch him baptize,* he denounced them. "You brood of snakes!" he exclaimed. "Who warned you to flee God's coming wrath? [8]Prove by the way you live that you have repented of your sins and turned to God. [9]Don't just say to each other, 'We're safe, for we are descendants of Abraham.' That means nothing, for I tell you, God can create children of Abraham from these very stones. [10]Even now the ax of God's judgment is poised, ready to sever the roots of the trees. Yes, every tree that does not produce good fruit will be chopped down and thrown into the fire.

[11]"I baptize with* water those who repent of their sins and turn to God. But someone is coming soon who is greater than I am—so much greater that I'm not worthy even to be his slave and carry his sandals. He will baptize you with the Holy Spirit and with fire.* [12]He is ready to separate the chaff from the wheat with his winnowing fork. Then he will clean up the threshing area, gathering the wheat into his barn but burning the chaff with never-ending fire."

3:2 Or *has come*, or *is coming soon.*　**3:3** Isa 40:3 (Greek version).　**3:7** Or *coming to be baptized.*　**3:11a** Or *in.*
3:11b Or *in the Holy Spirit and in fire.*

The Baptism of Jesus

¹³Then Jesus went from Galilee to the Jordan River to be baptized by John. ¹⁴But John tried to talk him out of it. "I am the one who needs to be baptized by you," he said, "so why are you coming to me?"

¹⁵But Jesus said, "It should be done, for we must carry out all that God requires.*" So John agreed to baptize him.

¹⁶After his baptism, as Jesus came up out of the water, the heavens were opened* and he saw the Spirit of God descending like a dove and settling on him. ¹⁷And a voice from heaven said, "This is my dearly loved Son, who brings me great joy."

CHAPTER 4

The Temptation of Jesus

Then Jesus was led by the Spirit into the wilderness to be tempted there by the devil. ²For forty days and forty nights he fasted and became very hungry.

³During that time the devil* came and said to him, "If you are the Son of God, tell these stones to become loaves of bread."

⁴But Jesus told him, "No! The Scriptures say,

'People do not live by bread alone,
but by every word that comes from the mouth of God.'*"

⁵Then the devil took him to the holy city, Jerusalem, to the highest point of the Temple, ⁶and said, "If you are the Son of God, jump off! For the Scriptures say,

'He will order his angels to protect you.
And they will hold you up with their hands
so you won't even hurt your foot on a stone.'*"

⁷Jesus responded, "The Scriptures also say, 'You must not test the LORD your God.'*"

⁸Next the devil took him to the peak of a very high mountain and showed him all the kingdoms of the world and their glory. ⁹"I will give it all to you," he said, "if you will kneel down and worship me."

¹⁰"Get out of here, Satan," Jesus told him. "For the Scriptures say,

'You must worship the LORD your God
and serve only him.'*"

¹¹Then the devil went away, and angels came and took care of Jesus.

The Ministry of Jesus Begins

¹²When Jesus heard that John had been arrested, he left Judea and returned to Galilee. ¹³He went first to Nazareth, then left there and moved to Capernaum, beside

---

3:15 Or *for we must fulfill all righteousness.*   **3:16** Some manuscripts read *opened to him.*   **4:3** Greek *the tempter.*
4:4 Deut 8:3.   **4:6** Ps 91:11-12.   **4:7** Deut 6:16.   **4:10** Deut 6:13.

the Sea of Galilee, in the region of Zebulun and Naphtali. [14]This fulfilled what God said through the prophet Isaiah:

[15] "In the land of Zebulun and of Naphtali,
    beside the sea, beyond the Jordan River,
    in Galilee where so many Gentiles live,
[16] the people who sat in darkness
    have seen a great light.
And for those who lived in the land where death casts its shadow,
    a light has shined."*

[17]From then on Jesus began to preach, "Repent of your sins and turn to God, for the Kingdom of Heaven is near.*"

The First Disciples
[18]One day as Jesus was walking along the shore of the Sea of Galilee, he saw two brothers—Simon, also called Peter, and Andrew—throwing a net into the water, for they fished for a living. [19]Jesus called out to them, "Come, follow me, and I will show you how to fish for people!" [20]And they left their nets at once and followed him.

[21]A little farther up the shore he saw two other brothers, James and John, sitting in a boat with their father, Zebedee, repairing their nets. And he called them to come, too. [22]They immediately followed him, leaving the boat and their father behind.

Crowds Follow Jesus
[23]Jesus traveled throughout the region of Galilee, teaching in the synagogues and announcing the Good News about the Kingdom. And he healed every kind of disease and illness. [24]News about him spread as far as Syria, and people soon began bringing to him all who were sick. And whatever their sickness or disease, or if they were demon possessed or epileptic or paralyzed—he healed them all. [25]Large crowds followed him wherever he went—people from Galilee, the Ten Towns,* Jerusalem, from all over Judea, and from east of the Jordan River.

CHAPTER 5

The Sermon on the Mount
One day as he saw the crowds gathering, Jesus went up on the mountainside and sat down. His disciples gathered around him, [2]and he began to teach them.

The Beatitudes
[3] "God blesses those who are poor and realize their need for him,*
    for the Kingdom of Heaven is theirs.
[4] God blesses those who mourn,
    for they will be comforted.

4:15-16 Isa 9:1-2 (Greek version).   4:17 Or *has come,* or *is coming soon.*   4:25 Greek *Decapolis.*   5:3 Greek *poor in spirit.*

⁵ God blesses those who are humble,
    for they will inherit the whole earth.
⁶ God blesses those who hunger and thirst for justice,*
    for they will be satisfied.
⁷ God blesses those who are merciful,
    for they will be shown mercy.
⁸ God blesses those whose hearts are pure,
    for they will see God.
⁹ God blesses those who work for peace,
    for they will be called the children of God.
¹⁰ God blesses those who are persecuted for doing right,
    for the Kingdom of Heaven is theirs.

¹¹ "God blesses you when people mock you and persecute you and lie about you* and say all sorts of evil things against you because you are my followers. ¹²Be happy about it! Be very glad! For a great reward awaits you in heaven. And remember, the ancient prophets were persecuted in the same way.

Teaching about Salt and Light

¹³ "You are the salt of the earth. But what good is salt if it has lost its flavor? Can you make it salty again? It will be thrown out and trampled underfoot as worthless.

¹⁴ "You are the light of the world—like a city on a hilltop that cannot be hidden. ¹⁵No one lights a lamp and then puts it under a basket. Instead, a lamp is placed on a stand, where it gives light to everyone in the house. ¹⁶In the same way, let your good deeds shine out for all to see, so that everyone will praise your heavenly Father.

Teaching about the Law

¹⁷ "Don't misunderstand why I have come. I did not come to abolish the law of Moses or the writings of the prophets. No, I came to accomplish their purpose. ¹⁸I tell you the truth, until heaven and earth disappear, not even the smallest detail of God's law will disappear until its purpose is achieved. ¹⁹So if you ignore the least commandment and teach others to do the same, you will be called the least in the Kingdom of Heaven. But anyone who obeys God's laws and teaches them will be called great in the Kingdom of Heaven.

²⁰ "But I warn you—unless your righteousness is better than the righteousness of the teachers of religious law and the Pharisees, you will never enter the Kingdom of Heaven!

Teaching about Anger

²¹ "You have heard that our ancestors were told, 'You must not murder. If you commit murder, you are subject to judgment.'* ²²But I say, if you are even angry with someone,* you are subject to judgment! If you call someone an idiot,* you

---

5:6 Or *for righteousness.*　**5:11** Some manuscripts do not include *and lie about you.*　**5:21** Exod 20:13; Deut 5:17. **5:22a** Some manuscripts add *without cause.*　**5:22b** Greek uses an Aramaic term of contempt: *If you say to your brother, 'Raca.'*

are in danger of being brought before the court. And if you curse someone,* you are in danger of the fires of hell.*

²³"So if you are presenting a sacrifice* at the altar in the Temple and you suddenly remember that someone has something against you, ²⁴leave your sacrifice there at the altar. Go and be reconciled to that person. Then come and offer your sacrifice to God.

²⁵"When you are on the way to court with your adversary, settle your differences quickly. Otherwise, your accuser may hand you over to the judge, who will hand you over to an officer, and you will be thrown into prison. ²⁶And if that happens, you surely won't be free again until you have paid the last penny.*

Teaching about Adultery

²⁷"You have heard the commandment that says, 'You must not commit adultery.'* ²⁸But I say, anyone who even looks at a woman with lust has already committed adultery with her in his heart. ²⁹So if your eye—even your good eye*—causes you to lust, gouge it out and throw it away. It is better for you to lose one part of your body than for your whole body to be thrown into hell. ³⁰And if your hand—even your stronger hand*—causes you to sin, cut it off and throw it away. It is better for you to lose one part of your body than for your whole body to be thrown into hell.

Teaching about Divorce

³¹"You have heard the law that says, 'A man can divorce his wife by merely giving her a written notice of divorce.'* ³²But I say that a man who divorces his wife, unless she has been unfaithful, causes her to commit adultery. And anyone who marries a divorced woman also commits adultery.

Teaching about Vows

³³"You have also heard that our ancestors were told, 'You must not break your vows; you must carry out the vows you make to the LORD.'* ³⁴But I say, do not make any vows! Do not say, 'By heaven!' because heaven is God's throne. ³⁵And do not say, 'By the earth!' because the earth is his footstool. And do not say, 'By Jerusalem!' for Jerusalem is the city of the great King. ³⁶Do not even say, 'By my head!' for you can't turn one hair white or black. ³⁷Just say a simple, 'Yes, I will,' or 'No, I won't.' Anything beyond this is from the evil one.

Teaching about Revenge

³⁸"You have heard the law that says the punishment must match the injury: 'An eye for an eye, and a tooth for a tooth.'* ³⁹But I say, do not resist an evil person! If someone slaps you on the right cheek, offer the other cheek also. ⁴⁰If you are sued in court and your shirt is taken from you, give your coat, too. ⁴¹If a soldier demands

---

5:22c Greek *if you say, 'You fool.'*   5:22d Greek *Gehenna;* also in 5:29, 30.   5:23 Greek *gift;* also in 5:24.
5:26 Greek *the last kodrantes* [i.e., quadrans].   5:27 Exod 20:14; Deut 5:18.   5:29 Greek *your right eye.*
5:30 Greek *your right hand.*   5:31 Deut 24:1.   5:33 Num 30:2.   5:38 Greek *the law that says: 'An eye for an eye and a tooth for a tooth.'* Exod 21:24; Lev 24:20; Deut 19:21.

that you carry his gear for a mile,* carry it two miles. ⁴²Give to those who ask, and don't turn away from those who want to borrow.

Teaching about Love for Enemies

⁴³"You have heard the law that says, 'Love your neighbor'* and hate your enemy. ⁴⁴But I say, love your enemies!* Pray for those who persecute you! ⁴⁵In that way, you will be acting as true children of your Father in heaven. For he gives his sunlight to both the evil and the good, and he sends rain on the just and the unjust alike. ⁴⁶If you love only those who love you, what reward is there for that? Even corrupt tax collectors do that much. ⁴⁷If you are kind only to your friends,* how are you different from anyone else? Even pagans do that. ⁴⁸But you are to be perfect, even as your Father in heaven is perfect.

CHAPTER 6

Teaching about Giving to the Needy

"Watch out! Don't do your good deeds publicly, to be admired by others, for you will lose the reward from your Father in heaven. ²When you give to someone in need, don't do as the hypocrites do—blowing trumpets in the synagogues and streets to call attention to their acts of charity! I tell you the truth, they have received all the reward they will ever get. ³But when you give to someone in need, don't let your left hand know what your right hand is doing. ⁴Give your gifts in private, and your Father, who sees everything, will reward you.

Teaching about Prayer and Fasting

⁵"When you pray, don't be like the hypocrites who love to pray publicly on street corners and in the synagogues where everyone can see them. I tell you the truth, that is all the reward they will ever get. ⁶But when you pray, go away by yourself, shut the door behind you, and pray to your Father in private. Then your Father, who sees everything, will reward you.

⁷"When you pray, don't babble on and on as people of other religions do. They think their prayers are answered merely by repeating their words again and again. ⁸Don't be like them, for your Father knows exactly what you need even before you ask him! ⁹Pray like this:

> Our Father in heaven,
>   may your name be kept holy.
> ¹⁰ May your Kingdom come soon.
> May your will be done on earth,
>   as it is in heaven.
> ¹¹ Give us today the food we need,*

5:41 Greek *milion* [4,854 feet or 1,478 meters]. **5:43** Lev 19:18. **5:44** Some manuscripts add *Bless those who curse you. Do good to those who hate you.* Compare Luke 6:27-28. **5:47** Greek *your brothers.* **6:11** Or *Give us today our food for the day;* or *Give us today our food for tomorrow.*

¹² and forgive us our sins,
>
> as we have forgiven those who sin against us.

¹³ And don't let us yield to temptation,*
>
> but rescue us from the evil one.*

¹⁴"If you forgive those who sin against you, your heavenly Father will forgive you. ¹⁵But if you refuse to forgive others, your Father will not forgive your sins.

¹⁶"And when you fast, don't make it obvious, as the hypocrites do, for they try to look miserable and disheveled so people will admire them for their fasting. I tell you the truth, that is the only reward they will ever get. ¹⁷But when you fast, comb your hair and wash your face. ¹⁸Then no one will notice that you are fasting, except your Father, who knows what you do in private. And your Father, who sees everything, will reward you.

Teaching about Money and Possessions

¹⁹"Don't store up treasures here on earth, where moths eat them and rust destroys them, and where thieves break in and steal. ²⁰Store your treasures in heaven, where moths and rust cannot destroy, and thieves do not break in and steal. ²¹Wherever your treasure is, there the desires of your heart will also be.

²²"Your eye is a lamp that provides light for your body. When your eye is good, your whole body is filled with light. ²³But when your eye is bad, your whole body is filled with darkness. And if the light you think you have is actually darkness, how deep that darkness is!

²⁴"No one can serve two masters. For you will hate one and love the other; you will be devoted to one and despise the other. You cannot serve both God and money.

²⁵"That is why I tell you not to worry about everyday life—whether you have enough food and drink, or enough clothes to wear. Isn't life more than food, and your body more than clothing? ²⁶Look at the birds. They don't plant or harvest or store food in barns, for your heavenly Father feeds them. And aren't you far more valuable to him than they are? ²⁷Can all your worries add a single moment to your life?

²⁸"And why worry about your clothing? Look at the lilies of the field and how they grow. They don't work or make their clothing, ²⁹yet Solomon in all his glory was not dressed as beautifully as they are. ³⁰And if God cares so wonderfully for wildflowers that are here today and thrown into the fire tomorrow, he will certainly care for you. Why do you have so little faith?

³¹"So don't worry about these things, saying, 'What will we eat? What will we drink? What will we wear?' ³²These things dominate the thoughts of unbelievers, but your heavenly Father already knows all your needs. ³³Seek the Kingdom of God* above all else, and live righteously, and he will give you everything you need.

³⁴"So don't worry about tomorrow, for tomorrow will bring its own worries. Today's trouble is enough for today.

6:13a Or *And keep us from being tested.*   **6:13b** Or *from evil.* Some manuscripts add *For yours is the kingdom and the power and the glory forever. Amen.*   **6:33** Some manuscripts do not include *of God.*

CHAPTER 7

Do Not Judge Others
"Do not judge others, and you will not be judged. ²For you will be treated as you treat others.* The standard you use in judging is the standard by which you will be judged.*

³"And why worry about a speck in your friend's eye* when you have a log in your own? ⁴How can you think of saying to your friend,* 'Let me help you get rid of that speck in your eye,' when you can't see past the log in your own eye? ⁵Hypocrite! First get rid of the log in your own eye; then you will see well enough to deal with the speck in your friend's eye.

⁶"Don't waste what is holy on people who are unholy.* Don't throw your pearls to pigs! They will trample the pearls, then turn and attack you.

Effective Prayer
⁷"Keep on asking, and you will receive what you ask for. Keep on seeking, and you will find. Keep on knocking, and the door will be opened to you. ⁸For everyone who asks, receives. Everyone who seeks, finds. And to everyone who knocks, the door will be opened.

⁹"You parents—if your children ask for a loaf of bread, do you give them a stone instead? ¹⁰Or if they ask for a fish, do you give them a snake? Of course not! ¹¹So if you sinful people know how to give good gifts to your children, how much more will your heavenly Father give good gifts to those who ask him.

The Golden Rule
¹²"Do to others whatever you would like them to do to you. This is the essence of all that is taught in the law and the prophets.

The Narrow Gate
¹³"You can enter God's Kingdom only through the narrow gate. The highway to hell* is broad, and its gate is wide for the many who choose that way. ¹⁴But the gateway to life is very narrow and the road is difficult, and only a few ever find it.

The Tree and Its Fruit
¹⁵"Beware of false prophets who come disguised as harmless sheep but are really vicious wolves. ¹⁶You can identify them by their fruit, that is, by the way they act. Can you pick grapes from thornbushes, or figs from thistles? ¹⁷A good tree produces good fruit, and a bad tree produces bad fruit. ¹⁸A good tree can't produce bad fruit, and a bad tree can't produce good fruit. ¹⁹So every tree that does not produce good fruit is chopped down and thrown into the fire. ²⁰Yes, just as you can identify a tree by its fruit, so you can identify people by their actions.

7:2a Or *For God will judge you as you judge others.*　　**7:2b** Or *The measure you give will be the measure you get back.*
7:3 Greek *your brother's eye;* also in 7:5.　　**7:4** Greek *your brother.*　　**7:6** Greek *Don't give the sacred to dogs.*
7:13 Greek *The road that leads to destruction.*

True Disciples

²¹"Not everyone who calls out to me, 'Lord! Lord!' will enter the Kingdom of Heaven. Only those who actually do the will of my Father in heaven will enter. ²²On judgment day many will say to me, 'Lord! Lord! We prophesied in your name and cast out demons in your name and performed many miracles in your name.' ²³But I will reply, 'I never knew you. Get away from me, you who break God's laws.'

Building on a Solid Foundation

²⁴"Anyone who listens to my teaching and follows it is wise, like a person who builds a house on solid rock. ²⁵Though the rain comes in torrents and the flood-waters rise and the winds beat against that house, it won't collapse because it is built on bedrock. ²⁶But anyone who hears my teaching and doesn't obey it is foolish, like a person who builds a house on sand. ²⁷When the rains and floods come and the winds beat against that house, it will collapse with a mighty crash."

²⁸When Jesus had finished saying these things, the crowds were amazed at his teaching, ²⁹for he taught with real authority—quite unlike their teachers of religious law.

CHAPTER 8

Jesus Heals a Man with Leprosy

Large crowds followed Jesus as he came down the mountainside. ²Suddenly, a man with leprosy approached him and knelt before him. "Lord," the man said, "if you are willing, you can heal me and make me clean."

³Jesus reached out and touched him. "I am willing," he said. "Be healed!" And instantly the leprosy disappeared. ⁴Then Jesus said to him, "Don't tell anyone about this. Instead, go to the priest and let him examine you. Take along the offering required in the law of Moses for those who have been healed of leprosy.* This will be a public testimony that you have been cleansed."

The Faith of a Roman Officer

⁵When Jesus returned to Capernaum, a Roman officer* came and pleaded with him, ⁶"Lord, my young servant* lies in bed, paralyzed and in terrible pain."

⁷Jesus said, "I will come and heal him."

⁸But the officer said, "Lord, I am not worthy to have you come into my home. Just say the word from where you are, and my servant will be healed. ⁹I know this because I am under the authority of my superior officers, and I have authority over my soldiers. I only need to say, 'Go,' and they go, or 'Come,' and they come. And if I say to my slaves, 'Do this,' they do it."

¹⁰When Jesus heard this, he was amazed. Turning to those who were following him, he said, "I tell you the truth, I haven't seen faith like this in all Israel! ¹¹And I tell you this, that many Gentiles will come from all over the world—from east and

---

8:4 See Lev 14:2-32.   **8:5** Greek *a centurion;* similarly in 8:8, 13.   **8:6** Or *child;* also in 8:13.

west—and sit down with Abraham, Isaac, and Jacob at the feast in the Kingdom of Heaven. [12]But many Israelites—those for whom the Kingdom was prepared—will be thrown into outer darkness, where there will be weeping and gnashing of teeth."

[13]Then Jesus said to the Roman officer, "Go back home. Because you believed, it has happened." And the young servant was healed that same hour.

Jesus Heals Many People

[14]When Jesus arrived at Peter's house, Peter's mother-in-law was sick in bed with a high fever. [15]But when Jesus touched her hand, the fever left her. Then she got up and prepared a meal for him.

[16]That evening many demon-possessed people were brought to Jesus. He cast out the evil spirits with a simple command, and he healed all the sick. [17]This fulfilled the word of the Lord through the prophet Isaiah, who said,

"He took our sicknesses
    and removed our diseases."*

The Cost of Following Jesus

[18]When Jesus saw the crowd around him, he instructed his disciples to cross to the other side of the lake.

[19]Then one of the teachers of religious law said to him, "Teacher, I will follow you wherever you go."

[20]But Jesus replied, "Foxes have dens to live in, and birds have nests, but the Son of Man* has no place even to lay his head."

[21]Another of his disciples said, "Lord, first let me return home and bury my father."

[22]But Jesus told him, "Follow me now. Let the spiritually dead bury their own dead.*"

Jesus Calms the Storm

[23]Then Jesus got into the boat and started across the lake with his disciples. [24]Suddenly, a fierce storm struck the lake, with waves breaking into the boat. But Jesus was sleeping. [25]The disciples went and woke him up, shouting, "Lord, save us! We're going to drown!"

[26]Jesus responded, "Why are you afraid? You have so little faith!" Then he got up and rebuked the wind and waves, and suddenly there was a great calm.

[27]The disciples were amazed. "Who is this man?" they asked. "Even the winds and waves obey him!"

Jesus Heals Two Demon-Possessed Men

[28]When Jesus arrived on the other side of the lake, in the region of the Gadarenes,* two men who were possessed by demons met him. They lived in a cemetery and were so violent that no one could go through that area.

8:17 Isa 53:4.   **8:20** "Son of Man" is a title Jesus used for himself.   **8:22** Greek *Let the dead bury their own dead.*
8:28 Other manuscripts read *Gerasenes;* still others read *Gergesenes.* Compare Mark 5:1; Luke 8:26.

²⁹They began screaming at him, "Why are you interfering with us, Son of God? Have you come here to torture us before God's appointed time?"

³⁰There happened to be a large herd of pigs feeding in the distance. ³¹So the demons begged, "If you cast us out, send us into that herd of pigs."

³²"All right, go!" Jesus commanded them. So the demons came out of the men and entered the pigs, and the whole herd plunged down the steep hillside into the lake and drowned in the water.

³³The herdsmen fled to the nearby town, telling everyone what happened to the demon-possessed men. ³⁴Then the entire town came out to meet Jesus, but they begged him to go away and leave them alone.

CHAPTER 9

Jesus Heals a Paralyzed Man

Jesus climbed into a boat and went back across the lake to his own town. ²Some people brought to him a paralyzed man on a mat. Seeing their faith, Jesus said to the paralyzed man, "Be encouraged, my child! Your sins are forgiven."

³But some of the teachers of religious law said to themselves, "That's blasphemy! Does he think he's God?"

⁴Jesus knew* what they were thinking, so he asked them, "Why do you have such evil thoughts in your hearts? ⁵Is it easier to say 'Your sins are forgiven,' or 'Stand up and walk'? ⁶So I will prove to you that the Son of Man* has the authority on earth to forgive sins." Then Jesus turned to the paralyzed man and said, "Stand up, pick up your mat, and go home!"

⁷And the man jumped up and went home! ⁸Fear swept through the crowd as they saw this happen. And they praised God for sending a man with such great authority.*

Jesus Calls Matthew

⁹As Jesus was walking along, he saw a man named Matthew sitting at his tax collector's booth. "Follow me and be my disciple," Jesus said to him. So Matthew got up and followed him.

¹⁰Later, Matthew invited Jesus and his disciples to his home as dinner guests, along with many tax collectors and other disreputable sinners. ¹¹But when the Pharisees saw this, they asked his disciples, "Why does your teacher eat with such scum?*"

¹²When Jesus heard this, he said, "Healthy people don't need a doctor— sick people do." ¹³Then he added, "Now go and learn the meaning of this Scripture: 'I want you to show mercy, not offer sacrifices.'* For I have come to call not those who think they are righteous, but those who know they are sinners."

9:4 Some manuscripts read *saw.*   **9:6** "Son of Man" is a title Jesus used for himself.   **9:8** Greek *for giving such authority to human beings.*   **9:11** Greek *with tax collectors and sinners?*   **9:13** Hos 6:6 (Greek version).

A Discussion about Fasting

[14]One day the disciples of John the Baptist came to Jesus and asked him, "Why don't your disciples fast* like we do and the Pharisees do?"

[15]Jesus replied, "Do wedding guests mourn while celebrating with the groom? Of course not. But someday the groom will be taken away from them, and then they will fast.

[16]"Besides, who would patch old clothing with new cloth? For the new patch would shrink and rip away from the old cloth, leaving an even bigger tear than before.

[17]"And no one puts new wine into old wineskins. For the old skins would burst from the pressure, spilling the wine and ruining the skins. New wine is stored in new wineskins so that both are preserved."

Jesus Heals in Response to Faith

[18]As Jesus was saying this, the leader of a synagogue came and knelt before him. "My daughter has just died," he said, "but you can bring her back to life again if you just come and lay your hand on her."

[19]So Jesus and his disciples got up and went with him. [20]Just then a woman who had suffered for twelve years with constant bleeding came up behind him. She touched the fringe of his robe, [21]for she thought, "If I can just touch his robe, I will be healed."

[22]Jesus turned around, and when he saw her he said, "Daughter, be encouraged! Your faith has made you well." And the woman was healed at that moment.

[23]When Jesus arrived at the official's home, he saw the noisy crowd and heard the funeral music. [24]"Get out!" he told them. "The girl isn't dead; she's only asleep." But the crowd laughed at him. [25]After the crowd was put outside, however, Jesus went in and took the girl by the hand, and she stood up! [26]The report of this miracle swept through the entire countryside.

Jesus Heals the Blind

[27]After Jesus left the girl's home, two blind men followed along behind him, shouting, "Son of David, have mercy on us!"

[28]They went right into the house where he was staying, and Jesus asked them, "Do you believe I can make you see?"

"Yes, Lord," they told him, "we do."

[29]Then he touched their eyes and said, "Because of your faith, it will happen." [30]Then their eyes were opened, and they could see! Jesus sternly warned them, "Don't tell anyone about this." [31]But instead, they went out and spread his fame all over the region.

[32]When they left, a demon-possessed man who couldn't speak was brought to Jesus. [33]So Jesus cast out the demon, and then the man began to speak. The crowds were amazed. "Nothing like this has ever happened in Israel!" they exclaimed.

[34]But the Pharisees said, "He can cast out demons because he is empowered by the prince of demons."

9:14 Some manuscripts read *fast often.*

The Need for Workers

[35]Jesus traveled through all the towns and villages of that area, teaching in the synagogues and announcing the Good News about the Kingdom. And he healed every kind of disease and illness. [36]When he saw the crowds, he had compassion on them because they were confused and helpless, like sheep without a shepherd. [37]He said to his disciples, "The harvest is great, but the workers are few. [38]So pray to the Lord who is in charge of the harvest; ask him to send more workers into his fields."

CHAPTER 10

Jesus Sends Out the Twelve Apostles

Jesus called his twelve disciples together and gave them authority to cast out evil* spirits and to heal every kind of disease and illness. [2]Here are the names of the twelve apostles:

first, Simon (also called Peter),
then Andrew (Peter's brother),
James (son of Zebedee),
John (James's brother),
[3] Philip,
Bartholomew,
Thomas,
Matthew (the tax collector),
James (son of Alphaeus),
Thaddaeus,*
[4] Simon (the zealot*),
Judas Iscariot (who later betrayed him).

[5]Jesus sent out the twelve apostles with these instructions: "Don't go to the Gentiles or the Samaritans, [6]but only to the people of Israel—God's lost sheep. [7]Go and announce to them that the Kingdom of Heaven is near.* [8]Heal the sick, raise the dead, cure those with leprosy, and cast out demons. Give as freely as you have received!

[9]"Don't take any money in your money belts—no gold, silver, or even copper coins. [10]Don't carry a traveler's bag with a change of clothes and sandals or even a walking stick. Don't hesitate to accept hospitality, because those who work deserve to be fed.

[11]"Whenever you enter a city or village, search for a worthy person and stay in his home until you leave town. [12]When you enter the home, give it your blessing. [13]If it turns out to be a worthy home, let your blessing stand; if it is not, take back the

---

10:1 Greek *unclean.*   10:3 Other manuscripts read *Lebbaeus;* still others read *Lebbaeus who is called Thaddaeus.*
10:4 Greek *the Cananean,* an Aramaic term for Jewish nationalists.   10:7 Or *has come,* or *is coming soon.*

blessing. ¹⁴If any household or town refuses to welcome you or listen to your message, shake its dust from your feet as you leave. ¹⁵I tell you the truth, the wicked cities of Sodom and Gomorrah will be better off than such a town on the judgment day.

¹⁶"Look, I am sending you out as sheep among wolves. So be as shrewd as snakes and harmless as doves. ¹⁷But beware! For you will be handed over to the courts and will be flogged with whips in the synagogues. ¹⁸You will stand trial before governors and kings because you are my followers. But this will be your opportunity to tell the rulers and other unbelievers about me.* ¹⁹When you are arrested, don't worry about how to respond or what to say. God will give you the right words at the right time. ²⁰For it is not you who will be speaking—it will be the Spirit of your Father speaking through you.

²¹"A brother will betray his brother to death, a father will betray his own child, and children will rebel against their parents and cause them to be killed. ²²And all nations will hate you because you are my followers.* But everyone who endures to the end will be saved. ²³When you are persecuted in one town, flee to the next. I tell you the truth, the Son of Man* will return before you have reached all the towns of Israel.

²⁴"Students* are not greater than their teacher, and slaves are not greater than their master. ²⁵Students are to be like their teacher, and slaves are to be like their master. And since I, the master of the household, have been called the prince of demons,* the members of my household will be called by even worse names!

²⁶"But don't be afraid of those who threaten you. For the time is coming when everything that is covered will be revealed, and all that is secret will be made known to all. ²⁷What I tell you now in the darkness, shout abroad when daybreak comes. What I whisper in your ear, shout from the housetops for all to hear!

²⁸"Don't be afraid of those who want to kill your body; they cannot touch your soul. Fear only God, who can destroy both soul and body in hell.* ²⁹What is the price of two sparrows—one copper coin*? But not a single sparrow can fall to the ground without your Father knowing it. ³⁰And the very hairs on your head are all numbered. ³¹So don't be afraid; you are more valuable to God than a whole flock of sparrows.

³²"Everyone who acknowledges me publicly here on earth, I will also acknowledge before my Father in heaven. ³³But everyone who denies me here on earth, I will also deny before my Father in heaven.

³⁴"Don't imagine that I came to bring peace to the earth! I came not to bring peace, but a sword.

³⁵ 'I have come to set a man against his father,
    a daughter against her mother,
and a daughter-in-law against her mother-in-law.
³⁶   Your enemies will be right in your own household!'*

10:18 Or *But this will be your testimony against the rulers and other unbelievers.* 10:22 Greek *on account of my name.* 10:23 "Son of Man" is a title Jesus used for himself. 10:24 Or *Disciples.* 10:25 Greek *Beelzeboul;* other manuscripts read *Beezeboul;* Latin version reads *Beelzebub.* 10:28 Greek *Gehenna.* 10:29 Greek *one assarion* [i.e., one "as," a Roman coin equal to ¹/₁₆ of a denarius]. 10:35-36 Mic 7:6.

37"If you love your father or mother more than you love me, you are not worthy of being mine; or if you love your son or daughter more than me, you are not worthy of being mine. 38 If you refuse to take up your cross and follow me, you are not worthy of being mine. 39 If you cling to your life, you will lose it; but if you give up your life for me, you will find it.

40"Anyone who receives you receives me, and anyone who receives me receives the Father who sent me. 41 If you receive a prophet as one who speaks for God,* you will be given the same reward as a prophet. And if you receive righteous people because of their righteousness, you will be given a reward like theirs. 42And if you give even a cup of cold water to one of the least of my followers, you will surely be rewarded."

CHAPTER 11

Jesus and John the Baptist

When Jesus had finished giving these instructions to his twelve disciples, he went out to teach and preach in towns throughout the region.

2John the Baptist, who was in prison, heard about all the things the Messiah was doing. So he sent his disciples to ask Jesus, 3"Are you the Messiah we've been expecting,* or should we keep looking for someone else?"

4Jesus told them, "Go back to John and tell him what you have heard and seen—5the blind see, the lame walk, the lepers are cured, the deaf hear, the dead are raised to life, and the Good News is being preached to the poor. 6And tell him, 'God blesses those who do not turn away because of me.*'"

7As John's disciples were leaving, Jesus began talking about him to the crowds. "What kind of man did you go into the wilderness to see? Was he a weak reed, swayed by every breath of wind? 8Or were you expecting to see a man dressed in expensive clothes? No, people with expensive clothes live in palaces. 9Were you looking for a prophet? Yes, and he is more than a prophet. 10John is the man to whom the Scriptures refer when they say,

'Look, I am sending my messenger ahead of you,
    and he will prepare your way before you.'*

11"I tell you the truth, of all who have ever lived, none is greater than John the Baptist. Yet even the least person in the Kingdom of Heaven is greater than he is! 12And from the time John the Baptist began preaching until now, the Kingdom of Heaven has been forcefully advancing,* and violent people are attacking it. 13For before John came, all the prophets and the law of Moses looked forward to this present time. 14And if you are willing to accept what I say, he is Elijah, the one the prophets said would come.* 15Anyone with ears to hear should listen and understand!

10:41 Greek *receive a prophet in the name of a prophet.* 11:3 Greek *Are you the one who is coming?* 11:6 Or *who are not offended by me.* 11:10 Mal 3:1. 11:12 Or *the Kingdom of Heaven has suffered from violence.* 11:14 See Mal 4:5.

[16] "To what can I compare this generation? It is like children playing a game in the public square. They complain to their friends,

[17]   'We played wedding songs,
         and you didn't dance,
      so we played funeral songs,
         and you didn't mourn.'

[18] For John didn't spend his time eating and drinking, and you say, 'He's possessed by a demon.' [19] The Son of Man,* on the other hand, feasts and drinks, and you say, 'He's a glutton and a drunkard, and a friend of tax collectors and other sinners!' But wisdom is shown to be right by its results."

Judgment for the Unbelievers

[20] Then Jesus began to denounce the towns where he had done so many of his miracles, because they hadn't repented of their sins and turned to God. [21] "What sorrow awaits you, Korazin and Bethsaida! For if the miracles I did in you had been done in wicked Tyre and Sidon, their people would have repented of their sins long ago, clothing themselves in burlap and throwing ashes on their heads to show their remorse. [22] I tell you, Tyre and Sidon will be better off on judgment day than you.

[23] "And you people of Capernaum, will you be honored in heaven? No, you will go down to the place of the dead.* For if the miracles I did for you had been done in wicked Sodom, it would still be here today. [24] I tell you, even Sodom will be better off on judgment day than you."

Jesus' Prayer of Thanksgiving

[25] At that time Jesus prayed this prayer: "O Father, Lord of heaven and earth, thank you for hiding these things from those who think themselves wise and clever, and for revealing them to the childlike. [26] Yes, Father, it pleased you to do it this way!

[27] "My Father has entrusted everything to me. No one truly knows the Son except the Father, and no one truly knows the Father except the Son and those to whom the Son chooses to reveal him."

[28] Then Jesus said, "Come to me, all of you who are weary and carry heavy burdens, and I will give you rest. [29] Take my yoke upon you. Let me teach you, because I am humble and gentle at heart, and you will find rest for your souls. [30] For my yoke is easy to bear, and the burden I give you is light."

CHAPTER 12

A Discussion about the Sabbath

At about that time Jesus was walking through some grainfields on the Sabbath. His disciples were hungry, so they began breaking off some heads of grain and eating

11:19 "Son of Man" is a title Jesus used for himself.   11:23 Greek *to Hades.*

them. ²But some Pharisees saw them do it and protested, "Look, your disciples are breaking the law by harvesting grain on the Sabbath."

³Jesus said to them, "Haven't you read in the Scriptures what David did when he and his companions were hungry? ⁴He went into the house of God, and he and his companions broke the law by eating the sacred loaves of bread that only the priests are allowed to eat. ⁵And haven't you read in the law of Moses that the priests on duty in the Temple may work on the Sabbath? ⁶I tell you, there is one here who is even greater than the Temple! ⁷But you would not have condemned my innocent disciples if you knew the meaning of this Scripture: 'I want you to show mercy, not offer sacrifices.'* ⁸For the Son of Man* is Lord, even over the Sabbath!"

Jesus Heals on the Sabbath

⁹Then Jesus went over to their synagogue, ¹⁰where he noticed a man with a deformed hand. The Pharisees asked Jesus, "Does the law permit a person to work by healing on the Sabbath?" (They were hoping he would say yes, so they could bring charges against him.)

¹¹And he answered, "If you had a sheep that fell into a well on the Sabbath, wouldn't you work to pull it out? Of course you would. ¹²And how much more valuable is a person than a sheep! Yes, the law permits a person to do good on the Sabbath."

¹³Then he said to the man, "Hold out your hand." So the man held out his hand, and it was restored, just like the other one! ¹⁴Then the Pharisees called a meeting to plot how to kill Jesus.

Jesus, God's Chosen Servant

¹⁵But Jesus knew what they were planning. So he left that area, and many people followed him. He healed all the sick among them, ¹⁶but he warned them not to reveal who he was. ¹⁷This fulfilled the prophecy of Isaiah concerning him:

18 "Look at my Servant, whom I have chosen.
   He is my Beloved, who pleases me.
 I will put my Spirit upon him,
   and he will proclaim justice to the nations.
19 He will not fight or shout
   or raise his voice in public.
20 He will not crush the weakest reed
   or put out a flickering candle.
   Finally he will cause justice to be victorious.
21 And his name will be the hope
   of all the world."*

Jesus and the Prince of Demons

²²Then a demon-possessed man, who was blind and couldn't speak, was brought to Jesus. He healed the man so that he could both speak and see. ²³The

---

12:7 Hos 6:6 (Greek version).   **12:8** "Son of Man" is a title Jesus used for himself.   **12:18-21** Isa 42:1-4 (Greek version for 42:4).

crowd was amazed and asked, "Could it be that Jesus is the Son of David, the Messiah?"

²⁴But when the Pharisees heard about the miracle, they said, "No wonder he can cast out demons. He gets his power from Satan,* the prince of demons."

²⁵Jesus knew their thoughts and replied, "Any kingdom divided by civil war is doomed. A town or family splintered by feuding will fall apart. ²⁶And if Satan is casting out Satan, he is divided and fighting against himself. His own kingdom will not survive. ²⁷And if I am empowered by Satan, what about your own exorcists? They cast out demons, too, so they will condemn you for what you have said. ²⁸But if I am casting out demons by the Spirit of God, then the Kingdom of God has arrived among you. ²⁹For who is powerful enough to enter the house of a strong man like Satan and plunder his goods? Only someone even stronger—someone who could tie him up and then plunder his house.

³⁰"Anyone who isn't with me opposes me, and anyone who isn't working with me is actually working against me.

³¹"So I tell you, every sin and blasphemy can be forgiven—except blasphemy against the Holy Spirit, which will never be forgiven. ³²Anyone who speaks against the Son of Man can be forgiven, but anyone who speaks against the Holy Spirit will never be forgiven, either in this world or in the world to come.

³³"A tree is identified by its fruit. If a tree is good, its fruit will be good. If a tree is bad, its fruit will be bad. ³⁴You brood of snakes! How could evil men like you speak what is good and right? For whatever is in your heart determines what you say. ³⁵A good person produces good things from the treasury of a good heart, and an evil person produces evil things from the treasury of an evil heart. ³⁶And I tell you this, you must give an account on judgment day for every idle word you speak. ³⁷The words you say will either acquit you or condemn you."

The Sign of Jonah

³⁸One day some teachers of religious law and Pharisees came to Jesus and said, "Teacher, we want you to show us a miraculous sign to prove your authority."

³⁹But Jesus replied, "Only an evil, adulterous generation would demand a miraculous sign; but the only sign I will give them is the sign of the prophet Jonah. ⁴⁰For as Jonah was in the belly of the great fish for three days and three nights, so will the Son of Man be in the heart of the earth for three days and three nights.

⁴¹"The people of Nineveh will stand up against this generation on judgment day and condemn it, for they repented of their sins at the preaching of Jonah. Now someone greater than Jonah is here—but you refuse to repent. ⁴²The queen of Sheba* will also stand up against this generation on judgment day and condemn it, for she came from a distant land to hear the wisdom of Solomon. Now someone greater than Solomon is here—but you refuse to listen.

⁴³"When an evil* spirit leaves a person, it goes into the desert, seeking rest but finding none. ⁴⁴Then it says, 'I will return to the person I came from.' So it returns

---

12:24 Greek *Beelzeboul;* also in 12:27. Other manuscripts read *Beezeboul;* Latin version reads *Beelzebub.*
12:42 Greek *The queen of the south.*   **12:43** Greek *unclean.*

and finds its former home empty, swept, and in order. ⁴⁵Then the spirit finds seven other spirits more evil than itself, and they all enter the person and live there. And so that person is worse off than before. That will be the experience of this evil generation."

The True Family of Jesus

⁴⁶As Jesus was speaking to the crowd, his mother and brothers stood outside, asking to speak to him. ⁴⁷Someone told Jesus, "Your mother and your brothers are outside, and they want to speak to you."*

⁴⁸Jesus asked, "Who is my mother? Who are my brothers?" ⁴⁹Then he pointed to his disciples and said, "Look, these are my mother and brothers. ⁵⁰Anyone who does the will of my Father in heaven is my brother and sister and mother!"

CHAPTER 13

Parable of the Farmer Scattering Seed

Later that same day Jesus left the house and sat beside the lake. ²A large crowd soon gathered around him, so he got into a boat. Then he sat there and taught as the people stood on the shore. ³He told many stories in the form of parables, such as this one:

"Listen! A farmer went out to plant some seeds. ⁴As he scattered them across his field, some seeds fell on a footpath, and the birds came and ate them. ⁵Other seeds fell on shallow soil with underlying rock. The seeds sprouted quickly because the soil was shallow. ⁶But the plants soon wilted under the hot sun, and since they didn't have deep roots, they died. ⁷Other seeds fell among thorns that grew up and choked out the tender plants. ⁸Still other seeds fell on fertile soil, and they produced a crop that was thirty, sixty, and even a hundred times as much as had been planted! ⁹Anyone with ears to hear should listen and understand."

¹⁰His disciples came and asked him, "Why do you use parables when you talk to the people?"

¹¹He replied, "You are permitted to understand the secrets* of the Kingdom of Heaven, but others are not. ¹²To those who listen to my teaching, more understanding will be given, and they will have an abundance of knowledge. But for those who are not listening, even what little understanding they have will be taken away from them. ¹³That is why I use these parables,

For they look, but they don't really see.
They hear, but they don't really listen or understand.

¹⁴This fulfills the prophecy of Isaiah that says,

'When you hear what I say,
you will not understand.

12:47 Some manuscripts do not include verse 47. Compare Mark 3:32 and Luke 8:20.   **13:11** Greek *the mysteries.*

When you see what I do,
you will not comprehend.
15 For the hearts of these people are hardened,
and their ears cannot hear,
and they have closed their eyes—
so their eyes cannot see,
and their ears cannot hear,
and their hearts cannot understand,
and they cannot turn to me
and let me heal them.'*

16"But blessed are your eyes, because they see; and your ears, because they hear. 17I tell you the truth, many prophets and righteous people longed to see what you see, but they didn't see it. And they longed to hear what you hear, but they didn't hear it.

18"Now listen to the explanation of the parable about the farmer planting seeds: 19The seed that fell on the footpath represents those who hear the message about the Kingdom and don't understand it. Then the evil one comes and snatches away the seed that was planted in their hearts. 20The seed on the rocky soil represents those who hear the message and immediately receive it with joy. 21But since they don't have deep roots, they don't last long. They fall away as soon as they have problems or are persecuted for believing God's word. 22The seed that fell among the thorns represents those who hear God's word, but all too quickly the message is crowded out by the worries of this life and the lure of wealth, so no fruit is produced. 23The seed that fell on good soil represents those who truly hear and understand God's word and produce a harvest of thirty, sixty, or even a hundred times as much as had been planted!"

Parable of the Wheat and Weeds
24Here is another story Jesus told: "The Kingdom of Heaven is like a farmer who planted good seed in his field. 25But that night as the workers slept, his enemy came and planted weeds among the wheat, then slipped away. 26When the crop began to grow and produce grain, the weeds also grew.

27"The farmer's workers went to him and said, 'Sir, the field where you planted that good seed is full of weeds! Where did they come from?'

28"'An enemy has done this!' the farmer exclaimed.

"'Should we pull out the weeds?' they asked.

29"'No,' he replied, 'you'll uproot the wheat if you do. 30Let both grow together until the harvest. Then I will tell the harvesters to sort out the weeds, tie them into bundles, and burn them, and to put the wheat in the barn.'"

Parable of the Mustard Seed
31Here is another illustration Jesus used: "The Kingdom of Heaven is like a mustard seed planted in a field. 32It is the smallest of all seeds, but it becomes the largest of garden plants; it grows into a tree, and birds come and make nests in its branches."

13:14-15 Isa 6:9-10 (Greek version).

Parable of the Yeast

³³Jesus also used this illustration: "The Kingdom of Heaven is like the yeast a woman used in making bread. Even though she put only a little yeast in three measures of flour, it permeated every part of the dough."

³⁴Jesus always used stories and illustrations like these when speaking to the crowds. In fact, he never spoke to them without using such parables. ³⁵This fulfilled what God had spoken through the prophet:

"I will speak to you in parables.
I will explain things hidden since the creation of the world.*"

Parable of the Wheat and Weeds Explained

³⁶Then, leaving the crowds outside, Jesus went into the house. His disciples said, "Please explain to us the story of the weeds in the field."

³⁷Jesus replied, "The Son of Man* is the farmer who plants the good seed. ³⁸The field is the world, and the good seed represents the people of the Kingdom. The weeds are the people who belong to the evil one. ³⁹The enemy who planted the weeds among the wheat is the devil. The harvest is the end of the world,* and the harvesters are the angels.

⁴⁰"Just as the weeds are sorted out and burned in the fire, so it will be at the end of the world. ⁴¹The Son of Man will send his angels, and they will remove from his Kingdom everything that causes sin and all who do evil. ⁴²And the angels will throw them into the fiery furnace, where there will be weeping and gnashing of teeth. ⁴³Then the righteous will shine like the sun in their Father's Kingdom. Anyone with ears to hear should listen and understand!

Parables of the Hidden Treasure and the Pearl

⁴⁴"The Kingdom of Heaven is like a treasure that a man discovered hidden in a field. In his excitement, he hid it again and sold everything he owned to get enough money to buy the field.

⁴⁵"Again, the Kingdom of Heaven is like a merchant on the lookout for choice pearls. ⁴⁶When he discovered a pearl of great value, he sold everything he owned and bought it!

Parable of the Fishing Net

⁴⁷"Again, the Kingdom of Heaven is like a fishing net that was thrown into the water and caught fish of every kind. ⁴⁸When the net was full, they dragged it up onto the shore, sat down, and sorted the good fish into crates, but threw the bad ones away. ⁴⁹That is the way it will be at the end of the world. The angels will come and separate the wicked people from the righteous, ⁵⁰throwing the wicked into the fiery furnace, where there will be weeping and gnashing of teeth. ⁵¹Do you understand all these things?"

"Yes," they said, "we do."

13:35 Some manuscripts do not include *of the world.* Ps 78:2.   **13:37** "Son of Man" is a title Jesus used for himself.
13:39 Or *the age;* also in 13:40, 49.

⁵²Then he added, "Every teacher of religious law who becomes a disciple in the Kingdom of Heaven is like a homeowner who brings from his storeroom new gems of truth as well as old."

Jesus Rejected at Nazareth

⁵³When Jesus had finished telling these stories and illustrations, he left that part of the country. ⁵⁴He returned to Nazareth, his hometown. When he taught there in the synagogue, everyone was amazed and said, "Where does he get this wisdom and the power to do miracles?" ⁵⁵Then they scoffed, "He's just the carpenter's son, and we know Mary, his mother, and his brothers—James, Joseph,* Simon, and Judas. ⁵⁶All his sisters live right here among us. Where did he learn all these things?" ⁵⁷And they were deeply offended and refused to believe in him.

Then Jesus told them, "A prophet is honored everywhere except in his own hometown and among his own family." ⁵⁸And so he did only a few miracles there because of their unbelief.

CHAPTER 14

The Death of John the Baptist

When Herod Antipas, the ruler of Galilee,* heard about Jesus, ²he said to his advisers, "This must be John the Baptist raised from the dead! That is why he can do such miracles."

³For Herod had arrested and imprisoned John as a favor to his wife Herodias (the former wife of Herod's brother Philip). ⁴John had been telling Herod, "It is against God's law for you to marry her." ⁵Herod wanted to kill John, but he was afraid of a riot, because all the people believed John was a prophet.

⁶But at a birthday party for Herod, Herodias's daughter performed a dance that greatly pleased him, ⁷so he promised with a vow to give her anything she wanted. ⁸At her mother's urging, the girl said, "I want the head of John the Baptist on a tray!" ⁹Then the king regretted what he had said; but because of the vow he had made in front of his guests, he issued the necessary orders. ¹⁰So John was beheaded in the prison, ¹¹and his head was brought on a tray and given to the girl, who took it to her mother. ¹²Later, John's disciples came for his body and buried it. Then they went and told Jesus what had happened.

Jesus Feeds Five Thousand

¹³As soon as Jesus heard the news, he left in a boat to a remote area to be alone. But the crowds heard where he was headed and followed on foot from many towns. ¹⁴Jesus saw the huge crowd as he stepped from the boat, and he had compassion on them and healed their sick.

¹⁵That evening the disciples came to him and said, "This is a remote place, and

---

13:55 Other manuscripts read *Joses;* still others read *John.*　**14:1** Greek *Herod the tetrarch.* Herod Antipas was a son of King Herod and was ruler over Galilee.

it's already getting late. Send the crowds away so they can go to the villages and buy food for themselves."

[16]But Jesus said, "That isn't necessary—you feed them."

[17]"But we have only five loaves of bread and two fish!" they answered.

[18]"Bring them here," he said. [19]Then he told the people to sit down on the grass. Jesus took the five loaves and two fish, looked up toward heaven, and blessed them. Then, breaking the loaves into pieces, he gave the bread to the disciples, who distributed it to the people. [20]They all ate as much as they wanted, and afterward, the disciples picked up twelve baskets of leftovers. [21]About 5,000 men were fed that day, in addition to all the women and children!

Jesus Walks on Water

[22]Immediately after this, Jesus insisted that his disciples get back into the boat and cross to the other side of the lake, while he sent the people home. [23]After sending them home, he went up into the hills by himself to pray. Night fell while he was there alone.

[24]Meanwhile, the disciples were in trouble far away from land, for a strong wind had risen, and they were fighting heavy waves. [25]About three o'clock in the morning* Jesus came toward them, walking on the water. [26]When the disciples saw him walking on the water, they were terrified. In their fear, they cried out, "It's a ghost!"

[27]But Jesus spoke to them at once. "Don't be afraid," he said. "Take courage. I am here!*"

[28]Then Peter called to him, "Lord, if it's really you, tell me to come to you, walking on the water."

[29]"Yes, come," Jesus said.

So Peter went over the side of the boat and walked on the water toward Jesus. [30]But when he saw the strong* wind and the waves, he was terrified and began to sink. "Save me, Lord!" he shouted.

[31]Jesus immediately reached out and grabbed him. "You have so little faith," Jesus said. "Why did you doubt me?"

[32]When they climbed back into the boat, the wind stopped. [33]Then the disciples worshiped him. "You really are the Son of God!" they exclaimed.

[34]After they had crossed the lake, they landed at Gennesaret. [35]When the people recognized Jesus, the news of his arrival spread quickly throughout the whole area, and soon people were bringing all their sick to be healed. [36]They begged him to let the sick touch at least the fringe of his robe, and all who touched him were healed.

CHAPTER 15

Jesus Teaches about Inner Purity

Some Pharisees and teachers of religious law now arrived from Jerusalem to see Jesus. They asked him, [2]"Why do your disciples disobey our age-old tradition? For they ignore our tradition of ceremonial hand washing before they eat."

14:25 Greek *In the fourth watch of the night.*   **14:27** Or *The 'I AM' is here;* Greek reads *I am.* See Exod 3:14.
14:30 Some manuscripts do not include *strong.*

³Jesus replied, "And why do you, by your traditions, violate the direct commandments of God? ⁴For instance, God says, 'Honor your father and mother,'* and 'Anyone who speaks disrespectfully of father or mother must be put to death.'* ⁵But you say it is all right for people to say to their parents, 'Sorry, I can't help you. For I have vowed to give to God what I would have given to you.' ⁶In this way, you say they don't need to honor their parents.* And so you cancel the word of God for the sake of your own tradition. ⁷You hypocrites! Isaiah was right when he prophesied about you, for he wrote,

⁸ 'These people honor me with their lips,
    but their hearts are far from me.
⁹ Their worship is a farce,
    for they teach man-made ideas as commands from God.'*"

¹⁰Then Jesus called to the crowd to come and hear. "Listen," he said, "and try to understand. ¹¹It's not what goes into your mouth that defiles you; you are defiled by the words that come out of your mouth."

¹²Then the disciples came to him and asked, "Do you realize you offended the Pharisees by what you just said?"

¹³Jesus replied, "Every plant not planted by my heavenly Father will be uprooted, ¹⁴so ignore them. They are blind guides leading the blind, and if one blind person guides another, they will both fall into a ditch."

¹⁵Then Peter said to Jesus, "Explain to us the parable that says people aren't defiled by what they eat."

¹⁶"Don't you understand yet?" Jesus asked. ¹⁷"Anything you eat passes through the stomach and then goes into the sewer. ¹⁸But the words you speak come from the heart—that's what defiles you. ¹⁹For from the heart come evil thoughts, murder, adultery, all sexual immorality, theft, lying, and slander. ²⁰These are what defile you. Eating with unwashed hands will never defile you."

The Faith of a Gentile Woman

²¹Then Jesus left Galilee and went north to the region of Tyre and Sidon. ²²A Gentile* woman who lived there came to him, pleading, "Have mercy on me, O Lord, Son of David! For my daughter is possessed by a demon that torments her severely."

²³But Jesus gave her no reply, not even a word. Then his disciples urged him to send her away. "Tell her to go away," they said. "She is bothering us with all her begging."

²⁴Then Jesus said to the woman, "I was sent only to help God's lost sheep—the people of Israel."

²⁵But she came and worshiped him, pleading again, "Lord, help me!"

15:4a Exod 20:12; Deut 5:16.　**15:4b** Exod 21:17 (Greek version); Lev 20:9 (Greek version).　**15:6** Greek *their father;* other manuscripts read *their father or their mother.*　**15:8-9** Isa 29:13 (Greek version).　**15:22** Greek *Canaanite.*

²⁶Jesus responded, "It isn't right to take food from the children and throw it to the dogs."

²⁷She replied, "That's true, Lord, but even dogs are allowed to eat the scraps that fall beneath their masters' table."

²⁸"Dear woman," Jesus said to her, "your faith is great. Your request is granted." And her daughter was instantly healed.

Jesus Heals Many People

²⁹Jesus returned to the Sea of Galilee and climbed a hill and sat down. ³⁰A vast crowd brought to him people who were lame, blind, crippled, those who couldn't speak, and many others. They laid them before Jesus, and he healed them all. ³¹The crowd was amazed! Those who hadn't been able to speak were talking, the crippled were made well, the lame were walking, and the blind could see again! And they praised the God of Israel.

Jesus Feeds Four Thousand

³²Then Jesus called his disciples and told them, "I feel sorry for these people. They have been here with me for three days, and they have nothing left to eat. I don't want to send them away hungry, or they will faint along the way."

³³The disciples replied, "Where would we get enough food here in the wilderness for such a huge crowd?"

³⁴Jesus asked, "How much bread do you have?"

They replied, "Seven loaves, and a few small fish."

³⁵So Jesus told all the people to sit down on the ground. ³⁶Then he took the seven loaves and the fish, thanked God for them, and broke them into pieces. He gave them to the disciples, who distributed the food to the crowd.

³⁷They all ate as much as they wanted. Afterward, the disciples picked up seven large baskets of leftover food. ³⁸There were 4,000 men who were fed that day, in addition to all the women and children. ³⁹Then Jesus sent the people home, and he got into a boat and crossed over to the region of Magadan.

CHAPTER 16

Leaders Demand a Miraculous Sign

One day the Pharisees and Sadducees came to test Jesus, demanding that he show them a miraculous sign from heaven to prove his authority.

²He replied, "You know the saying, 'Red sky at night means fair weather tomorrow; ³red sky in the morning means foul weather all day.' You know how to interpret the weather signs in the sky, but you don't know how to interpret the signs of the times!* ⁴Only an evil, adulterous generation would demand a miraculous sign, but the only sign I will give them is the sign of the prophet Jonah.*" Then Jesus left them and went away.

16:2-3 Several manuscripts do not include any of the words in 16:2-3 after *He replied.*   16:4 Greek *the sign of Jonah.*

Yeast of the Pharisees and Sadducees

⁵Later, after they crossed to the other side of the lake, the disciples discovered they had forgotten to bring any bread. ⁶"Watch out!" Jesus warned them. "Beware of the yeast of the Pharisees and Sadducees."

⁷At this they began to argue with each other because they hadn't brought any bread. ⁸Jesus knew what they were saying, so he said, "You have so little faith! Why are you arguing with each other about having no bread? ⁹Don't you understand even yet? Don't you remember the 5,000 I fed with five loaves, and the baskets of leftovers you picked up? ¹⁰Or the 4,000 I fed with seven loaves, and the large baskets of leftovers you picked up? ¹¹Why can't you understand that I'm not talking about bread? So again I say, 'Beware of the yeast of the Pharisees and Sadducees.'"

¹²Then at last they understood that he wasn't speaking about the yeast in bread, but about the deceptive teaching of the Pharisees and Sadducees.

Peter's Declaration about Jesus

¹³When Jesus came to the region of Caesarea Philippi, he asked his disciples, "Who do people say that the Son of Man is?"*

¹⁴"Well," they replied, "some say John the Baptist, some say Elijah, and others say Jeremiah or one of the other prophets."

¹⁵Then he asked them, "But who do you say I am?"

¹⁶Simon Peter answered, "You are the Messiah,* the Son of the living God."

¹⁷Jesus replied, "You are blessed, Simon son of John,* because my Father in heaven has revealed this to you. You did not learn this from any human being. ¹⁸Now I say to you that you are Peter (which means 'rock'),* and upon this rock I will build my church, and all the powers of hell* will not conquer it. ¹⁹And I will give you the keys of the Kingdom of Heaven. Whatever you forbid* on earth will be forbidden in heaven, and whatever you permit* on earth will be permitted in heaven."

²⁰Then he sternly warned the disciples not to tell anyone that he was the Messiah.

Jesus Predicts His Death

²¹From then on Jesus* began to tell his disciples plainly that it was necessary for him to go to Jerusalem, and that he would suffer many terrible things at the hands of the elders, the leading priests, and the teachers of religious law. He would be killed, but on the third day he would be raised from the dead.

²²But Peter took him aside and began to reprimand him* for saying such things. "Heaven forbid, Lord," he said. "This will never happen to you!"

²³Jesus turned to Peter and said, "Get away from me, Satan! You are a dangerous trap to me. You are seeing things merely from a human point of view, not from God's."

16:13 "Son of Man" is a title Jesus used for himself.   16:16 Or *the Christ. Messiah* (a Hebrew term) and *Christ* (a Greek term) both mean "the anointed one."   16:17 Greek *Simon bar-Jonah;* see John 1:42; 21:15-17.   16:18a Greek *that you are Peter.*   16:18b Greek *and the gates of Hades.*   16:19a Or *bind,* or *lock.*   16:19b Or *loose,* or *open.*   16:21 Some manuscripts read *Jesus the Messiah.*   16:22 Or *began to correct him.*

²⁴Then Jesus said to his disciples, "If any of you wants to be my follower, you must turn from your selfish ways, take up your cross, and follow me. ²⁵If you try to hang on to your life, you will lose it. But if you give up your life for my sake, you will save it. ²⁶And what do you benefit if you gain the whole world but lose your own soul?* Is anything worth more than your soul? ²⁷For the Son of Man will come with his angels in the glory of his Father and will judge all people according to their deeds. ²⁸And I tell you the truth, some standing here right now will not die before they see the Son of Man coming in his Kingdom."

CHAPTER 17

The Transfiguration
Six days later Jesus took Peter and the two brothers, James and John, and led them up a high mountain to be alone. ²As the men watched, Jesus' appearance was transformed so that his face shone like the sun, and his clothes became as white as light. ³Suddenly, Moses and Elijah appeared and began talking with Jesus.

⁴Peter exclaimed, "Lord, it's wonderful for us to be here! If you want, I'll make three shelters as memorials*—one for you, one for Moses, and one for Elijah."

⁵But even as he spoke, a bright cloud overshadowed them, and a voice from the cloud said, "This is my dearly loved Son, who brings me great joy. Listen to him."
⁶The disciples were terrified and fell face down on the ground.

⁷Then Jesus came over and touched them. "Get up," he said. "Don't be afraid."
⁸And when they looked up, Moses and Elijah were gone, and they saw only Jesus.

⁹As they went back down the mountain, Jesus commanded them, "Don't tell anyone what you have seen until the Son of Man* has been raised from the dead."

¹⁰Then his disciples asked him, "Why do the teachers of religious law insist that Elijah must return before the Messiah comes?*"

¹¹Jesus replied, "Elijah is indeed coming first to get everything ready. ¹²But I tell you, Elijah has already come, but he wasn't recognized, and they chose to abuse him. And in the same way they will also make the Son of Man suffer." ¹³Then the disciples realized he was talking about John the Baptist.

Jesus Heals a Demon-Possessed Boy
¹⁴At the foot of the mountain, a large crowd was waiting for them. A man came and knelt before Jesus and said, ¹⁵"Lord, have mercy on my son. He has seizures and suffers terribly. He often falls into the fire or into the water. ¹⁶So I brought him to your disciples, but they couldn't heal him."

¹⁷Jesus said, "You faithless and corrupt people! How long must I be with you? How long must I put up with you? Bring the boy here to me." ¹⁸Then Jesus rebuked the demon in the boy, and it left him. From that moment the boy was well.

16:26 Or *your self?* also in 16:26b.   **17:4** Greek *three tabernacles.*   **17:9** "Son of Man" is a title Jesus used for himself.
17:10 Greek *that Elijah must come first?*

¹⁹Afterward the disciples asked Jesus privately, "Why couldn't we cast out that demon?"

²⁰"You don't have enough faith," Jesus told them. "I tell you the truth, if you had faith even as small as a mustard seed, you could say to this mountain, 'Move from here to there,' and it would move. Nothing would be impossible.*"

Jesus Again Predicts His Death

²²After they gathered again in Galilee, Jesus told them, "The Son of Man is going to be betrayed into the hands of his enemies. ²³He will be killed, but on the third day he will be raised from the dead." And the disciples were filled with grief.

Payment of the Temple Tax

²⁴On their arrival in Capernaum, the collectors of the Temple tax* came to Peter and asked him, "Doesn't your teacher pay the Temple tax?"

²⁵"Yes, he does," Peter replied. Then he went into the house.

But before he had a chance to speak, Jesus asked him, "What do you think, Peter?* Do kings tax their own people or the people they have conquered?*"

²⁶"They tax the people they have conquered," Peter replied.

"Well, then," Jesus said, "the citizens are free! ²⁷However, we don't want to offend them, so go down to the lake and throw in a line. Open the mouth of the first fish you catch, and you will find a large silver coin.* Take it and pay the tax for both of us."

CHAPTER 18

The Greatest in the Kingdom

About that time the disciples came to Jesus and asked, "Who is greatest in the Kingdom of Heaven?"

²Jesus called a little child to him and put the child among them. ³Then he said, "I tell you the truth, unless you turn from your sins and become like little children, you will never get into the Kingdom of Heaven. ⁴So anyone who becomes as humble as this little child is the greatest in the Kingdom of Heaven.

⁵"And anyone who welcomes a little child like this on my behalf* is welcoming me. ⁶But if you cause one of these little ones who trusts in me to fall into sin, it would be better for you to have a large millstone tied around your neck and be drowned in the depths of the sea.

⁷"What sorrow awaits the world, because it tempts people to sin. Temptations are inevitable, but what sorrow awaits the person who does the tempting. ⁸So if your hand or foot causes you to sin, cut it off and throw it away. It's better to enter eternal life with only one hand or one foot than to be thrown into eternal fire with both of your hands and feet. ⁹And if your eye causes you to sin, gouge it out and

---

17:20 Some manuscripts add verse 21, *But this kind of demon won't leave except by prayer and fasting.* Compare Mark 9:29. **17:24** Greek *the two-drachma [tax];* also in 17:24b. See Exod 30:13-16; Neh 10:32-33. **17:25a** Greek *Simon?* **17:25b** Greek *their sons or others?* **17:27** Greek *a stater* [a Greek coin equivalent to four drachmas]. **18:5** Greek *in my name.*

throw it away. It's better to enter eternal life with only one eye than to have two eyes and be thrown into the fire of hell.*

[10]"Beware that you don't look down on any of these little ones. For I tell you that in heaven their angels are always in the presence of my heavenly Father.*

Parable of the Lost Sheep

[12]"If a man has a hundred sheep and one of them wanders away, what will he do? Won't he leave the ninety-nine others on the hills and go out to search for the one that is lost? [13]And if he finds it, I tell you the truth, he will rejoice over it more than over the ninety-nine that didn't wander away! [14]In the same way, it is not my heavenly Father's will that even one of these little ones should perish.

Correcting Another Believer

[15]"If another believer* sins against you,* go privately and point out the offense. If the other person listens and confesses it, you have won that person back. [16]But if you are unsuccessful, take one or two others with you and go back again, so that everything you say may be confirmed by two or three witnesses. [17]If the person still refuses to listen, take your case to the church. Then if he or she won't accept the church's decision, treat that person as a pagan or a corrupt tax collector.

[18]"I tell you the truth, whatever you forbid* on earth will be forbidden in heaven, and whatever you permit* on earth will be permitted in heaven.

[19]"I also tell you this: If two of you agree here on earth concerning anything you ask, my Father in heaven will do it for you. [20]For where two or three gather together as my followers,* I am there among them."

Parable of the Unforgiving Debtor

[21]Then Peter came to him and asked, "Lord, how often should I forgive someone* who sins against me? Seven times?"

[22]"No, not seven times," Jesus replied, "but seventy times seven!*

[23]"Therefore, the Kingdom of Heaven can be compared to a king who decided to bring his accounts up to date with servants who had borrowed money from him. [24]In the process, one of his debtors was brought in who owed him millions of dollars.* [25]He couldn't pay, so his master ordered that he be sold—along with his wife, his children, and everything he owned—to pay the debt.

[26]"But the man fell down before his master and begged him, 'Please, be patient with me, and I will pay it all.' [27]Then his master was filled with pity for him, and he released him and forgave his debt.

[28]"But when the man left the king, he went to a fellow servant who owed him a few thousand dollars.* He grabbed him by the throat and demanded instant payment.

[29]"His fellow servant fell down before him and begged for a little more time. 'Be

---

18:9 Greek *the Gehenna of fire.*   18:10 Some manuscripts add verse 11, *And the Son of Man came to save those who are lost.* Compare Luke 19:10.   18:15a Greek *If your brother.*   18:15b Some manuscripts do not include *against you.*   18:18a Or *bind,* or *lock.*   18:18b Or *loose,* or *open.*   18:20 Greek *gather together in my name.*   18:21 Greek *my brother.*   18:22 Or *seventy-seven times.*   18:24 Greek *10,000 talents* [375 tons or 340 metric tons of silver].   18:28 Greek *100 denarii.* A denarius was equivalent to a laborer's full day's wage.

patient with me, and I will pay it,' he pleaded. [30]But his creditor wouldn't wait. He had the man arrested and put in prison until the debt could be paid in full.

[31]"When some of the other servants saw this, they were very upset. They went to the king and told him everything that had happened. [32]Then the king called in the man he had forgiven and said, 'You evil servant! I forgave you that tremendous debt because you pleaded with me. [33]Shouldn't you have mercy on your fellow servant, just as I had mercy on you?' [34]Then the angry king sent the man to prison to be tortured until he had paid his entire debt.

[35]"That's what my heavenly Father will do to you if you refuse to forgive your brothers and sisters* from your heart."

CHAPTER 19

Discussion about Divorce and Marriage

When Jesus had finished saying these things, he left Galilee and went down to the region of Judea east of the Jordan River. [2]Large crowds followed him there, and he healed their sick.

[3]Some Pharisees came and tried to trap him with this question: "Should a man be allowed to divorce his wife for just any reason?"

[4]"Haven't you read the Scriptures?" Jesus replied. "They record that from the beginning 'God made them male and female.'* [5]And he said, 'This explains why a man leaves his father and mother and is joined to his wife, and the two are united into one.'* [6]Since they are no longer two but one, let no one split apart what God has joined together."

[7]"Then why did Moses say in the law that a man could give his wife a written notice of divorce and send her away?"* they asked.

[8]Jesus replied, "Moses permitted divorce only as a concession to your hard hearts, but it was not what God had originally intended. [9]And I tell you this, whoever divorces his wife and marries someone else commits adultery—unless his wife has been unfaithful.*"

[10]Jesus' disciples then said to him, "If this is the case, it is better not to marry!"

[11]"Not everyone can accept this statement," Jesus said. "Only those whom God helps. [12]Some are born as eunuchs, some have been made eunuchs by others, and some choose not to marry* for the sake of the Kingdom of Heaven. Let anyone accept this who can."

Jesus Blesses the Children

[13]One day some parents brought their children to Jesus so he could lay his hands on them and pray for them. But the disciples scolded the parents for bothering him.

[14]But Jesus said, "Let the children come to me. Don't stop them! For the Kingdom of Heaven belongs to those who are like these children." [15]And he placed his hands on their heads and blessed them before he left.

18:35 Greek *your brother.*　**19:4** Gen 1:27; 5:2.　**19:5** Gen 2:24.　**19:7** See Deut 24:1.　**19:9** Some manuscripts add *And anyone who marries a divorced woman commits adultery.* Compare Matt 5:32.　**19:12** Greek *and some make themselves eunuchs.*

The Rich Man

[16]Someone came to Jesus with this question: "Teacher,* what good deed must I do to have eternal life?"

[17]"Why ask me about what is good?" Jesus replied. "There is only One who is good. But to answer your question—if you want to receive eternal life, keep* the commandments."

[18]"Which ones?" the man asked.

And Jesus replied: "'You must not murder. You must not commit adultery. You must not steal. You must not testify falsely. [19]Honor your father and mother. Love your neighbor as yourself.'*"

[20]"I've obeyed all these commandments," the young man replied. "What else must I do?"

[21]Jesus told him, "If you want to be perfect, go and sell all your possessions and give the money to the poor, and you will have treasure in heaven. Then come, follow me."

[22]But when the young man heard this, he went away sad, for he had many possessions.

[23]Then Jesus said to his disciples, "I tell you the truth, it is very hard for a rich person to enter the Kingdom of Heaven. [24]I'll say it again—it is easier for a camel to go through the eye of a needle than for a rich person to enter the Kingdom of God!"

[25]The disciples were astounded. "Then who in the world can be saved?" they asked.

[26]Jesus looked at them intently and said, "Humanly speaking, it is impossible. But with God everything is possible."

[27]Then Peter said to him, "We've given up everything to follow you. What will we get?"

[28]Jesus replied, "I assure you that when the world is made new* and the Son of Man* sits upon his glorious throne, you who have been my followers will also sit on twelve thrones, judging the twelve tribes of Israel. [29]And everyone who has given up houses or brothers or sisters or father or mother or children or property, for my sake, will receive a hundred times as much in return and will inherit eternal life. [30]But many who are the greatest now will be least important then, and those who seem least important now will be the greatest then.*

CHAPTER 20

Parable of the Vineyard Workers

"For the Kingdom of Heaven is like the landowner who went out early one morning to hire workers for his vineyard. [2]He agreed to pay the normal daily wage* and sent them out to work.

19:16 Some manuscripts read *Good Teacher.* 19:17 Some manuscripts read *continue to keep.* 19:18-19 Exod 20:12-16; Deut 5:16-20; Lev 19:18. 19:28a Or *in the regeneration.* 19:28b "Son of Man" is a title Jesus used for himself. 19:30 Greek *But many who are first will be last; and the last, first.* 20:2 Greek *a denarius,* the payment for a full day's labor; similarly in 20:9, 10, 13.

³"At nine o'clock in the morning he was passing through the marketplace and saw some people standing around doing nothing. ⁴So he hired them, telling them he would pay them whatever was right at the end of the day. ⁵So they went to work in the vineyard. At noon and again at three o'clock he did the same thing.

⁶"At five o'clock that afternoon he was in town again and saw some more people standing around. He asked them, 'Why haven't you been working today?'

⁷"They replied, 'Because no one hired us.'

"The landowner told them, 'Then go out and join the others in my vineyard.'

⁸"That evening he told the foreman to call the workers in and pay them, beginning with the last workers first. ⁹When those hired at five o'clock were paid, each received a full day's wage. ¹⁰When those hired first came to get their pay, they assumed they would receive more. But they, too, were paid a day's wage. ¹¹When they received their pay, they protested to the owner, ¹²'Those people worked only one hour, and yet you've paid them just as much as you paid us who worked all day in the scorching heat.'

¹³"He answered one of them, 'Friend, I haven't been unfair! Didn't you agree to work all day for the usual wage? ¹⁴Take your money and go. I wanted to pay this last worker the same as you. ¹⁵Is it against the law for me to do what I want with my money? Should you be jealous because I am kind to others?'

¹⁶"So those who are last now will be first then, and those who are first will be last."

Jesus Again Predicts His Death

¹⁷As Jesus was going up to Jerusalem, he took the twelve disciples aside privately and told them what was going to happen to him. ¹⁸"Listen," he said, "we're going up to Jerusalem, where the Son of Man* will be betrayed to the leading priests and the teachers of religious law. They will sentence him to die. ¹⁹Then they will hand him over to the Romans* to be mocked, flogged with a whip, and crucified. But on the third day he will be raised from the dead."

Jesus Teaches about Serving Others

²⁰Then the mother of James and John, the sons of Zebedee, came to Jesus with her sons. She knelt respectfully to ask a favor. ²¹"What is your request?" he asked.

She replied, "In your Kingdom, please let my two sons sit in places of honor next to you, one on your right and the other on your left."

²²But Jesus answered by saying to them, "You don't know what you are asking! Are you able to drink from the bitter cup of suffering I am about to drink?"

"Oh yes," they replied, "we are able!"

²³Jesus told them, "You will indeed drink from my bitter cup. But I have no right to say who will sit on my right or my left. My Father has prepared those places for the ones he has chosen."

²⁴When the ten other disciples heard what James and John had asked, they were indignant. ²⁵But Jesus called them together and said, "You know that the rulers in

---

20:18 "Son of Man" is a title Jesus used for himself.   **20:19** Greek *the Gentiles.*

this world lord it over their people, and officials flaunt their authority over those under them. [26]But among you it will be different. Whoever wants to be a leader among you must be your servant, [27]and whoever wants to be first among you must become your slave. [28]For even the Son of Man came not to be served but to serve others and to give his life as a ransom for many."

Jesus Heals Two Blind Men

[29]As Jesus and the disciples left the town of Jericho, a large crowd followed behind. [30]Two blind men were sitting beside the road. When they heard that Jesus was coming that way, they began shouting, "Lord, Son of David, have mercy on us!"

[31]"Be quiet!" the crowd yelled at them.

But they only shouted louder, "Lord, Son of David, have mercy on us!"

[32]When Jesus heard them, he stopped and called, "What do you want me to do for you?"

[33]"Lord," they said, "we want to see!" [34]Jesus felt sorry for them and touched their eyes. Instantly they could see! Then they followed him.

CHAPTER 21

Jesus' Triumphant Entry

As Jesus and the disciples approached Jerusalem, they came to the town of Bethphage on the Mount of Olives. Jesus sent two of them on ahead. [2]"Go into the village over there," he said. "As soon as you enter it, you will see a donkey tied there, with its colt beside it. Untie them and bring them to me. [3]If anyone asks what you are doing, just say, 'The Lord needs them,' and he will immediately let you take them."

[4]This took place to fulfill the prophecy that said,

5   "Tell the people of Jerusalem,*
          'Look, your King is coming to you.
      He is humble, riding on a donkey—
          riding on a donkey's colt.'"*

[6]The two disciples did as Jesus commanded. [7]They brought the donkey and the colt to him and threw their garments over the colt, and he sat on it.*

[8]Most of the crowd spread their garments on the road ahead of him, and others cut branches from the trees and spread them on the road. [9]Jesus was in the center of the procession, and the people all around him were shouting,

"Praise God* for the Son of David!
      Blessings on the one who comes in the name of the LORD!
      Praise God in highest heaven!"*

21:5a Greek *Tell the daughter of Zion.* Isa 62:11.   **21:5b** Zech 9:9.   **21:7** Greek *over them, and he sat on them.*
21:9a Greek *Hosanna,* an exclamation of praise that literally means "save now"; also in 21:9b, 15.   **21:9b** Pss 118:25-26; 148:1.

[10]The entire city of Jerusalem was in an uproar as he entered. "Who is this?" they asked.

[11]And the crowds replied, "It's Jesus, the prophet from Nazareth in Galilee."

Jesus Clears the Temple

[12]Jesus entered the Temple and began to drive out all the people buying and selling animals for sacrifice. He knocked over the tables of the money changers and the chairs of those selling doves. [13]He said to them, "The Scriptures declare, 'My Temple will be called a house of prayer,' but you have turned it into a den of thieves!"*

[14]The blind and the lame came to him in the Temple, and he healed them. [15]The leading priests and the teachers of religious law saw these wonderful miracles and heard even the children in the Temple shouting, "Praise God for the Son of David."

But the leaders were indignant. [16]They asked Jesus, "Do you hear what these children are saying?"

"Yes," Jesus replied. "Haven't you ever read the Scriptures? For they say, 'You have taught children and infants to give you praise.'*" [17]Then he returned to Bethany, where he stayed overnight.

Jesus Curses the Fig Tree

[18]In the morning, as Jesus was returning to Jerusalem, he was hungry, [19]and he noticed a fig tree beside the road. He went over to see if there were any figs, but there were only leaves. Then he said to it, "May you never bear fruit again!" And immediately the fig tree withered up.

[20]The disciples were amazed when they saw this and asked, "How did the fig tree wither so quickly?"

[21]Then Jesus told them, "I tell you the truth, if you have faith and don't doubt, you can do things like this and much more. You can even say to this mountain, 'May you be lifted up and thrown into the sea,' and it will happen. [22]You can pray for anything, and if you have faith, you will receive it."

The Authority of Jesus Challenged

[23]When Jesus returned to the Temple and began teaching, the leading priests and elders came up to him. They demanded, "By what authority are you doing all these things? Who gave you the right?"

[24]"I'll tell you by what authority I do these things if you answer one question," Jesus replied. [25]"Did John's authority to baptize come from heaven, or was it merely human?"

They talked it over among themselves. "If we say it was from heaven, he will ask us why we didn't believe John. [26]But if we say it was merely human, we'll be mobbed because the people believe John was a prophet." [27]So they finally replied, "We don't know."

And Jesus responded, "Then I won't tell you by what authority I do these things.

21:13 Isa 56:7; Jer 7:11. **21:16** Ps 8:2.

Parable of the Two Sons

28 "But what do you think about this? A man with two sons told the older boy, 'Son, go out and work in the vineyard today.' 29 The son answered, 'No, I won't go,' but later he changed his mind and went anyway. 30 Then the father told the other son, 'You go,' and he said, 'Yes, sir, I will.' But he didn't go.

31 "Which of the two obeyed his father?"

They replied, "The first."*

Then Jesus explained his meaning: "I tell you the truth, corrupt tax collectors and prostitutes will get into the Kingdom of God before you do. 32 For John the Baptist came and showed you the right way to live, but you didn't believe him, while tax collectors and prostitutes did. And even when you saw this happening, you refused to believe him and repent of your sins.

Parable of the Evil Farmers

33 "Now listen to another story. A certain landowner planted a vineyard, built a wall around it, dug a pit for pressing out the grape juice, and built a lookout tower. Then he leased the vineyard to tenant farmers and moved to another country. 34 At the time of the grape harvest, he sent his servants to collect his share of the crop. 35 But the farmers grabbed his servants, beat one, killed one, and stoned another. 36 So the landowner sent a larger group of his servants to collect for him, but the results were the same.

37 "Finally, the owner sent his son, thinking, 'Surely they will respect my son.'

38 "But when the tenant farmers saw his son coming, they said to one another, 'Here comes the heir to this estate. Come on, let's kill him and get the estate for ourselves!' 39 So they grabbed him, dragged him out of the vineyard, and murdered him.

40 "When the owner of the vineyard returns," Jesus asked, "what do you think he will do to those farmers?"

41 The religious leaders replied, "He will put the wicked men to a horrible death and lease the vineyard to others who will give him his share of the crop after each harvest."

42 Then Jesus asked them, "Didn't you ever read this in the Scriptures?

'The stone that the builders rejected
    has now become the cornerstone.
This is the LORD's doing,
    and it is wonderful to see.'*

43 I tell you, the Kingdom of God will be taken away from you and given to a nation that will produce the proper fruit. 44 Anyone who stumbles over that stone will be broken to pieces, and it will crush anyone it falls on.*"

21:29-31 Other manuscripts read *"The second."* In still other manuscripts the first son says "Yes" but does nothing, the second son says "No" but then repents and goes, and the answer to Jesus' question is that the second son obeyed his father. **21:42** Ps 118:22-23. **21:44** This verse is not included in some early manuscripts. Compare Luke 20:18.

⁴⁵When the leading priests and Pharisees heard this parable, they realized he was telling the story against them—they were the wicked farmers. ⁴⁶They wanted to arrest him, but they were afraid of the crowds, who considered Jesus to be a prophet.

CHAPTER 22

Parable of the Great Feast

Jesus also told them other parables. He said, ²"The Kingdom of Heaven can be illustrated by the story of a king who prepared a great wedding feast for his son. ³When the banquet was ready, he sent his servants to notify those who were invited. But they all refused to come!

⁴"So he sent other servants to tell them, 'The feast has been prepared. The bulls and fattened cattle have been killed, and everything is ready. Come to the banquet!' ⁵But the guests he had invited ignored them and went their own way, one to his farm, another to his business. ⁶Others seized his messengers and insulted them and killed them.

⁷"The king was furious, and he sent out his army to destroy the murderers and burn their town. ⁸And he said to his servants, 'The wedding feast is ready, and the guests I invited aren't worthy of the honor. ⁹Now go out to the street corners and invite everyone you see.' ¹⁰So the servants brought in everyone they could find, good and bad alike, and the banquet hall was filled with guests.

¹¹"But when the king came in to meet the guests, he noticed a man who wasn't wearing the proper clothes for a wedding. ¹²'Friend,' he asked, 'how is it that you are here without wedding clothes?' But the man had no reply. ¹³Then the king said to his aides, 'Bind his hands and feet and throw him into the outer darkness, where there will be weeping and gnashing of teeth.'

¹⁴"For many are called, but few are chosen."

Taxes for Caesar

¹⁵Then the Pharisees met together to plot how to trap Jesus into saying something for which he could be arrested. ¹⁶They sent some of their disciples, along with the supporters of Herod, to meet with him. "Teacher," they said, "we know how honest you are. You teach the way of God truthfully. You are impartial and don't play favorites. ¹⁷Now tell us what you think about this: Is it right to pay taxes to Caesar or not?"

¹⁸But Jesus knew their evil motives. "You hypocrites!" he said. "Why are you trying to trap me? ¹⁹Here, show me the coin used for the tax." When they handed him a Roman coin,* ²⁰he asked, "Whose picture and title are stamped on it?"

²¹"Caesar's," they replied.

"Well, then," he said, "give to Caesar what belongs to Caesar, and give to God what belongs to God."

²²His reply amazed them, and they went away.

22:19 Greek *a denarius.*

Discussion about Resurrection

²³That same day Jesus was approached by some Sadducees—religious leaders who say there is no resurrection from the dead. They posed this question: ²⁴"Teacher, Moses said, 'If a man dies without children, his brother should marry the widow and have a child who will carry on the brother's name.'* ²⁵Well, suppose there were seven brothers. The oldest one married and then died without children, so his brother married the widow. ²⁶But the second brother also died, and the third brother married her. This continued with all seven of them. ²⁷Last of all, the woman also died. ²⁸So tell us, whose wife will she be in the resurrection? For all seven were married to her."

²⁹Jesus replied, "Your mistake is that you don't know the Scriptures, and you don't know the power of God. ³⁰For when the dead rise, they will neither marry nor be given in marriage. In this respect they will be like the angels in heaven.

³¹"But now, as to whether there will be a resurrection of the dead—haven't you ever read about this in the Scriptures? Long after Abraham, Isaac, and Jacob had died, God said,* ³²'I am the God of Abraham, the God of Isaac, and the God of Jacob.'* So he is the God of the living, not the dead."

³³When the crowds heard him, they were astounded at his teaching.

The Most Important Commandment

³⁴But when the Pharisees heard that he had silenced the Sadducees with his reply, they met together to question him again. ³⁵One of them, an expert in religious law, tried to trap him with this question: ³⁶"Teacher, which is the most important commandment in the law of Moses?"

³⁷Jesus replied, "'You must love the LORD your God with all your heart, all your soul, and all your mind.'* ³⁸This is the first and greatest commandment. ³⁹A second is equally important: 'Love your neighbor as yourself.'* ⁴⁰The entire law and all the demands of the prophets are based on these two commandments."

Whose Son Is the Messiah?

⁴¹Then, surrounded by the Pharisees, Jesus asked them a question: ⁴²"What do you think about the Messiah? Whose son is he?"

They replied, "He is the son of David."

⁴³Jesus responded, "Then why does David, speaking under the inspiration of the Spirit, call the Messiah 'my Lord'? For David said,

⁴⁴ 'The LORD said to my Lord,
Sit in the place of honor at my right hand
until I humble your enemies beneath your feet.'*

⁴⁵Since David called the Messiah 'my Lord,' how can the Messiah be his son?"

⁴⁶No one could answer him. And after that, no one dared to ask him any more questions.

22:24 Deut 25:5-6. **22:31** Greek *read about this? God said.* **22:32** Exod 3:6. **22:37** Deut 6:5. **22:39** Lev 19:18.
22:44 Ps 110:1.

CHAPTER 23

Jesus Criticizes the Religious Leaders

Then Jesus said to the crowds and to his disciples, ²"The teachers of religious law and the Pharisees are the official interpreters of the law of Moses.* ³So practice and obey whatever they tell you, but don't follow their example. For they don't practice what they teach. ⁴They crush people with unbearable religious demands and never lift a finger to ease the burden.

⁵"Everything they do is for show. On their arms they wear extra wide prayer boxes with Scripture verses inside, and they wear robes with extra long tassels.* ⁶And they love to sit at the head table at banquets and in the seats of honor in the synagogues. ⁷They love to receive respectful greetings as they walk in the market-places, and to be called 'Rabbi.'*

⁸"Don't let anyone call you 'Rabbi,' for you have only one teacher, and all of you are equal as brothers and sisters.* ⁹And don't address anyone here on earth as 'Father,' for only God in heaven is your spiritual Father. ¹⁰And don't let anyone call you 'Teacher,' for you have only one teacher, the Messiah. ¹¹The greatest among you must be a servant. ¹²But those who exalt themselves will be humbled, and those who humble themselves will be exalted.

¹³"What sorrow awaits you teachers of religious law and you Pharisees. Hypocrites! For you shut the door of the Kingdom of Heaven in people's faces. You won't go in yourselves, and you don't let others enter either.*

¹⁵"What sorrow awaits you teachers of religious law and you Pharisees. Hypocrites! For you cross land and sea to make one convert, and then you turn that person into twice the child of hell* you yourselves are!

¹⁶"Blind guides! What sorrow awaits you! For you say that it means nothing to swear 'by God's Temple,' but that it is binding to swear 'by the gold in the Temple.' ¹⁷Blind fools! Which is more important—the gold or the Temple that makes the gold sacred? ¹⁸And you say that to swear 'by the altar' is not binding, but to swear 'by the gifts on the altar' is binding. ¹⁹How blind! For which is more important—the gift on the altar or the altar that makes the gift sacred? ²⁰When you swear 'by the altar,' you are swearing by it and by everything on it. ²¹And when you swear 'by the Temple,' you are swearing by it and by God, who lives in it. ²²And when you swear 'by heaven,' you are swearing by the throne of God and by God, who sits on the throne.

²³"What sorrow awaits you teachers of religious law and you Pharisees. Hypocrites! For you are careful to tithe even the tiniest income from your herb gardens,* but you ignore the more important aspects of the law—justice, mercy, and faith. You should tithe, yes, but do not neglect the more important things. ²⁴Blind guides!

23:2 Greek *and the Pharisees sit in the seat of Moses.* **23:5** Greek *They enlarge their phylacteries and lengthen their tassels.* **23:7** *Rabbi,* from Aramaic, means "master" or "teacher." **23:8** Greek *brothers.* **23:13** Some manuscripts add verse 14, *What sorrow awaits you teachers of religious law and you Pharisees. Hypocrites! You shamelessly cheat widows out of their property and then pretend to be pious by making long prayers in public. Because of this, you will be severely punished.* Compare Mark 12:40 and Luke 20:47. **23:15** Greek *of Gehenna;* also in 23:33. **23:23** Greek *tithe the mint, the dill, and the cumin.*

You strain your water so you won't accidentally swallow a gnat, but you swallow a camel!*

²⁵"What sorrow awaits you teachers of religious law and you Pharisees. Hypocrites! For you are so careful to clean the outside of the cup and the dish, but inside you are filthy—full of greed and self-indulgence! ²⁶You blind Pharisee! First wash the inside of the cup and the dish,* and then the outside will become clean, too.

²⁷"What sorrow awaits you teachers of religious law and you Pharisees. Hypocrites! For you are like whitewashed tombs—beautiful on the outside but filled on the inside with dead people's bones and all sorts of impurity. ²⁸Outwardly you look like righteous people, but inwardly your hearts are filled with hypocrisy and lawlessness.

²⁹"What sorrow awaits you teachers of religious law and you Pharisees. Hypocrites! For you build tombs for the prophets your ancestors killed, and you decorate the monuments of the godly people your ancestors destroyed. ³⁰Then you say, 'If we had lived in the days of our ancestors, we would never have joined them in killing the prophets.'

³¹"But in saying that, you testify against yourselves that you are indeed the descendants of those who murdered the prophets. ³²Go ahead and finish what your ancestors started. ³³Snakes! Sons of vipers! How will you escape the judgment of hell?

³⁴"Therefore, I am sending you prophets and wise men and teachers of religious law. But you will kill some by crucifixion, and you will flog others with whips in your synagogues, chasing them from city to city. ³⁵As a result, you will be held responsible for the murder of all godly people of all time—from the murder of righteous Abel to the murder of Zechariah son of Barachiah, whom you killed in the Temple between the sanctuary and the altar. ³⁶I tell you the truth, this judgment will fall on this very generation.

Jesus Grieves over Jerusalem

³⁷"O Jerusalem, Jerusalem, the city that kills the prophets and stones God's messengers! How often I have wanted to gather your children together as a hen protects her chicks beneath her wings, but you wouldn't let me. ³⁸And now, look, your house is abandoned and desolate.* ³⁹For I tell you this, you will never see me again until you say, 'Blessings on the one who comes in the name of the LORD!'*"

CHAPTER 24

Jesus Foretells the Future

As Jesus was leaving the Temple grounds, his disciples pointed out to him the various Temple buildings. ²But he responded, "Do you see all these buildings? I tell you the truth, they will be completely demolished. Not one stone will be left on top of another!"

³Later, Jesus sat on the Mount of Olives. His disciples came to him privately

---

23:24 See Lev 11:4, 23, where gnats and camels are both forbidden as food.   **23:26** Some manuscripts do not include *and the dish.*   **23:38** Some manuscripts do not include *and desolate.*   **23:39** Ps 118:26.

and said, "Tell us, when will all this happen? What sign will signal your return and the end of the world?*"

⁴Jesus told them, "Don't let anyone mislead you, ⁵for many will come in my name, claiming, 'I am the Messiah.' They will deceive many. ⁶And you will hear of wars and threats of wars, but don't panic. Yes, these things must take place, but the end won't follow immediately. ⁷Nation will go to war against nation, and kingdom against kingdom. There will be famines and earthquakes in many parts of the world. ⁸But all this is only the first of the birth pains, with more to come.

⁹"Then you will be arrested, persecuted, and killed. You will be hated all over the world because you are my followers.* ¹⁰And many will turn away from me and betray and hate each other. ¹¹And many false prophets will appear and will deceive many people. ¹²Sin will be rampant everywhere, and the love of many will grow cold. ¹³But the one who endures to the end will be saved. ¹⁴And the Good News about the Kingdom will be preached throughout the whole world, so that all nations* will hear it; and then the end will come.

¹⁵"The day is coming when you will see what Daniel the prophet spoke about—the sacrilegious object that causes desecration* standing in the Holy Place." (Reader, pay attention!) ¹⁶"Then those in Judea must flee to the hills. ¹⁷A person out on the deck of a roof must not go down into the house to pack. ¹⁸A person out in the field must not return even to get a coat. ¹⁹How terrible it will be for pregnant women and for nursing mothers in those days. ²⁰And pray that your flight will not be in winter or on the Sabbath. ²¹For there will be greater anguish than at any time since the world began. And it will never be so great again. ²²In fact, unless that time of calamity is shortened, not a single person will survive. But it will be shortened for the sake of God's chosen ones.

²³"Then if anyone tells you, 'Look, here is the Messiah,' or 'There he is,' don't believe it. ²⁴For false messiahs and false prophets will rise up and perform great signs and wonders so as to deceive, if possible, even God's chosen ones. ²⁵See, I have warned you about this ahead of time.

²⁶"So if someone tells you, 'Look, the Messiah is out in the desert,' don't bother to go and look. Or, 'Look, he is hiding here,' don't believe it! ²⁷For as the lightning flashes in the east and shines to the west, so it will be when the Son of Man* comes. ²⁸Just as the gathering of vultures shows there is a carcass nearby, so these signs indicate that the end is near.*

²⁹"Immediately after the anguish of those days,

> the sun will be darkened,
>   the moon will give no light,
> the stars will fall from the sky,
>   and the powers in the heavens will be shaken.*

24:3 Or *the age?*   **24:9** Greek *on account of my name.*   **24:14** Or *all peoples.*   **24:15** Greek *the abomination of desolation.* See Dan 9:27; 11:31; 12:11.   **24:27** "Son of Man" is a title Jesus used for himself.   **24:28** Greek *Wherever the carcass is, the vultures gather.*   **24:29** See Isa 13:10; 34:4; Joel 2:10.

³⁰And then at last, the sign that the Son of Man is coming will appear in the heavens, and there will be deep mourning among all the peoples of the earth. And they will see the Son of Man coming on the clouds of heaven with power and great glory.* ³¹And he will send out his angels with the mighty blast of a trumpet, and they will gather his chosen ones from all over the world*—from the farthest ends of the earth and heaven.

³²"Now learn a lesson from the fig tree. When its branches bud and its leaves begin to sprout, you know that summer is near. ³³In the same way, when you see all these things, you can know his return is very near, right at the door. ³⁴I tell you the truth, this generation* will not pass from the scene until all these things take place. ³⁵Heaven and earth will disappear, but my words will never disappear.

³⁶"However, no one knows the day or hour when these things will happen, not even the angels in heaven or the Son himself.* Only the Father knows.

³⁷"When the Son of Man returns, it will be like it was in Noah's day. ³⁸In those days before the flood, the people were enjoying banquets and parties and weddings right up to the time Noah entered his boat. ³⁹People didn't realize what was going to happen until the flood came and swept them all away. That is the way it will be when the Son of Man comes.

⁴⁰"Two men will be working together in the field; one will be taken, the other left. ⁴¹Two women will be grinding flour at the mill; one will be taken, the other left.

⁴²"So you, too, must keep watch! For you don't know what day your Lord is coming. ⁴³Understand this: If a homeowner knew exactly when a burglar was coming, he would keep watch and not permit his house to be broken into. ⁴⁴You also must be ready all the time, for the Son of Man will come when least expected.

⁴⁵"A faithful, sensible servant is one to whom the master can give the responsibility of managing his other household servants and feeding them. ⁴⁶If the master returns and finds that the servant has done a good job, there will be a reward. ⁴⁷I tell you the truth, the master will put that servant in charge of all he owns. ⁴⁸But what if the servant is evil and thinks, 'My master won't be back for a while,' ⁴⁹and he begins beating the other servants, partying, and getting drunk? ⁵⁰The master will return unannounced and unexpected, ⁵¹and he will cut the servant to pieces and assign him a place with the hypocrites. In that place there will be weeping and gnashing of teeth.

CHAPTER 25

Parable of the Ten Bridesmaids

"Then the Kingdom of Heaven will be like ten bridesmaids* who took their lamps and went to meet the bridegroom. ²Five of them were foolish, and five were wise. ³The five who were foolish didn't take enough olive oil for their lamps, ⁴but the other five were wise enough to take along extra oil. ⁵When the bridegroom was delayed, they all became drowsy and fell asleep.

24:30 See Dan 7:13.　24:31 Greek *from the four winds.*　24:34 Or *this age,* or *this nation.*　24:36 Some manuscripts do not include *or the Son himself.*　25:1 Or *virgins;* also in 25:7, 11.

⁶"At midnight they were roused by the shout, 'Look, the bridegroom is coming! Come out and meet him!'

⁷"All the bridesmaids got up and prepared their lamps. ⁸Then the five foolish ones asked the others, 'Please give us some of your oil because our lamps are going out.'

⁹"But the others replied, 'We don't have enough for all of us. Go to a shop and buy some for yourselves.'

¹⁰"But while they were gone to buy oil, the bridegroom came. Then those who were ready went in with him to the marriage feast, and the door was locked. ¹¹Later, when the other five bridesmaids returned, they stood outside, calling, 'Lord! Lord! Open the door for us!'

¹²"But he called back, 'Believe me, I don't know you!'

¹³"So you, too, must keep watch! For you do not know the day or hour of my return.

Parable of the Three Servants

¹⁴"Again, the Kingdom of Heaven can be illustrated by the story of a man going on a long trip. He called together his servants and entrusted his money to them while he was gone. ¹⁵He gave five bags of silver* to one, two bags of silver to another, and one bag of silver to the last—dividing it in proportion to their abilities. He then left on his trip.

¹⁶"The servant who received the five bags of silver began to invest the money and earned five more. ¹⁷The servant with two bags of silver also went to work and earned two more. ¹⁸But the servant who received the one bag of silver dug a hole in the ground and hid the master's money.

¹⁹"After a long time their master returned from his trip and called them to give an account of how they had used his money. ²⁰The servant to whom he had entrusted the five bags of silver came forward with five more and said, 'Master, you gave me five bags of silver to invest, and I have earned five more.'

²¹"The master was full of praise. 'Well done, my good and faithful servant. You have been faithful in handling this small amount, so now I will give you many more responsibilities. Let's celebrate together!*'

²²"The servant who had received the two bags of silver came forward and said, 'Master, you gave me two bags of silver to invest, and I have earned two more.'

²³"The master said, 'Well done, my good and faithful servant. You have been faithful in handling this small amount, so now I will give you many more responsibilities. Let's celebrate together!'

²⁴"Then the servant with the one bag of silver came and said, 'Master, I knew you were a harsh man, harvesting crops you didn't plant and gathering crops you didn't cultivate. ²⁵I was afraid I would lose your money, so I hid it in the earth. Look, here is your money back.'

²⁶"But the master replied, 'You wicked and lazy servant! If you knew I harvested

---

25:15 Greek *talents;* also throughout the story. A talent is equal to 75 pounds or 34 kilograms.　　**25:21** Greek *Enter into the joy of your master* [or *your Lord*]; also in 25:23.

crops I didn't plant and gathered crops I didn't cultivate, ²⁷why didn't you deposit my money in the bank? At least I could have gotten some interest on it.'

²⁸"Then he ordered, 'Take the money from this servant, and give it to the one with the ten bags of silver. ²⁹To those who use well what they are given, even more will be given, and they will have an abundance. But from those who do nothing, even what little they have will be taken away. ³⁰Now throw this useless servant into outer darkness, where there will be weeping and gnashing of teeth.'

The Final Judgment

³¹"But when the Son of Man* comes in his glory, and all the angels with him, then he will sit upon his glorious throne. ³²All the nations* will be gathered in his presence, and he will separate the people as a shepherd separates the sheep from the goats. ³³He will place the sheep at his right hand and the goats at his left.

³⁴"Then the King will say to those on his right, 'Come, you who are blessed by my Father, inherit the Kingdom prepared for you from the creation of the world. ³⁵For I was hungry, and you fed me. I was thirsty, and you gave me a drink. I was a stranger, and you invited me into your home. ³⁶I was naked, and you gave me clothing. I was sick, and you cared for me. I was in prison, and you visited me.'

³⁷"Then these righteous ones will reply, 'Lord, when did we ever see you hungry and feed you? Or thirsty and give you something to drink? ³⁸Or a stranger and show you hospitality? Or naked and give you clothing? ³⁹When did we ever see you sick or in prison and visit you?'

⁴⁰"And the King will say, 'I tell you the truth, when you did it to one of the least of these my brothers and sisters,* you were doing it to me!'

⁴¹"Then the King will turn to those on the left and say, 'Away with you, you cursed ones, into the eternal fire prepared for the devil and his demons.* ⁴²For I was hungry, and you didn't feed me. I was thirsty, and you didn't give me a drink. ⁴³I was a stranger, and you didn't invite me into your home. I was naked, and you didn't give me clothing. I was sick and in prison, and you didn't visit me.'

⁴⁴"Then they will reply, 'Lord, when did we ever see you hungry or thirsty or a stranger or naked or sick or in prison, and not help you?'

⁴⁵"And he will answer, 'I tell you the truth, when you refused to help the least of these my brothers and sisters, you were refusing to help me.'

⁴⁶"And they will go away into eternal punishment, but the righteous will go into eternal life."

CHAPTER 26

The Plot to Kill Jesus

When Jesus had finished saying all these things, he said to his disciples, ²"As you know, Passover begins in two days, and the Son of Man* will be handed over to be crucified."

25:31 "Son of Man" is a title Jesus used for himself.   **25:32** Or *peoples.*   **25:40** Greek *my brothers.*   **25:41** Greek *his angels.*   **26:2** "Son of Man" is a title Jesus used for himself.

³At that same time the leading priests and elders were meeting at the residence of Caiaphas, the high priest, ⁴plotting how to capture Jesus secretly and kill him. ⁵"But not during the Passover celebration," they agreed, "or the people may riot."

Jesus Anointed at Bethany

⁶Meanwhile, Jesus was in Bethany at the home of Simon, a man who had previously had leprosy. ⁷While he was eating,* a woman came in with a beautiful alabaster jar of expensive perfume and poured it over his head.

⁸The disciples were indignant when they saw this. "What a waste!" they said. ⁹"It could have been sold for a high price and the money given to the poor."

¹⁰But Jesus, aware of this, replied, "Why criticize this woman for doing such a good thing to me? ¹¹You will always have the poor among you, but you will not always have me. ¹²She has poured this perfume on me to prepare my body for burial. ¹³I tell you the truth, wherever the Good News is preached throughout the world, this woman's deed will be remembered and discussed."

Judas Agrees to Betray Jesus

¹⁴Then Judas Iscariot, one of the twelve disciples, went to the leading priests ¹⁵and asked, "How much will you pay me to betray Jesus to you?" And they gave him thirty pieces of silver. ¹⁶From that time on, Judas began looking for an opportunity to betray Jesus.

The Last Supper

¹⁷On the first day of the Festival of Unleavened Bread, the disciples came to Jesus and asked, "Where do you want us to prepare the Passover meal for you?"

¹⁸"As you go into the city," he told them, "you will see a certain man. Tell him, 'The Teacher says: My time has come, and I will eat the Passover meal with my disciples at your house.'" ¹⁹So the disciples did as Jesus told them and prepared the Passover meal there.

²⁰When it was evening, Jesus sat down at the table* with the twelve disciples.* ²¹While they were eating, he said, "I tell you the truth, one of you will betray me."

²²Greatly distressed, each one asked in turn, "Am I the one, Lord?"

²³He replied, "One of you who has just eaten from this bowl with me will betray me. ²⁴For the Son of Man must die, as the Scriptures declared long ago. But how terrible it will be for the one who betrays him. It would be far better for that man if he had never been born!"

²⁵Judas, the one who would betray him, also asked, "Rabbi, am I the one?"

And Jesus told him, "You have said it."

²⁶As they were eating, Jesus took some bread and blessed it. Then he broke it in pieces and gave it to the disciples, saying, "Take this and eat it, for this is my body."

²⁷And he took a cup of wine and gave thanks to God for it. He gave it to them and said, "Each of you drink from it, ²⁸for this is my blood, which confirms the

---

26:7 Or *reclining.*   **26:20a** Or *Jesus reclined.*   **26:20b** Some manuscripts read *the Twelve.*

covenant* between God and his people. It is poured out as a sacrifice to forgive the sins of many. ²⁹Mark my words—I will not drink wine again until the day I drink it new with you in my Father's Kingdom."

³⁰Then they sang a hymn and went out to the Mount of Olives.

Jesus Predicts Peter's Denial

³¹On the way, Jesus told them, "Tonight all of you will desert me. For the Scriptures say,

'God will strike* the Shepherd,
and the sheep of the flock will be scattered.'

³²But after I have been raised from the dead, I will go ahead of you to Galilee and meet you there."

³³Peter declared, "Even if everyone else deserts you, I will never desert you."

³⁴Jesus replied, "I tell you the truth, Peter—this very night, before the rooster crows, you will deny three times that you even know me."

³⁵"No!" Peter insisted. "Even if I have to die with you, I will never deny you!" And all the other disciples vowed the same.

Jesus Prays in Gethsemane

³⁶Then Jesus went with them to the olive grove called Gethsemane, and he said, "Sit here while I go over there to pray." ³⁷He took Peter and Zebedee's two sons, James and John, and he became anguished and distressed. ³⁸He told them, "My soul is crushed with grief to the point of death. Stay here and keep watch with me."

³⁹He went on a little farther and bowed with his face to the ground, praying, "My Father! If it is possible, let this cup of suffering be taken away from me. Yet I want your will to be done, not mine."

⁴⁰Then he returned to the disciples and found them asleep. He said to Peter, "Couldn't you watch with me even one hour? ⁴¹Keep watch and pray, so that you will not give in to temptation. For the spirit is willing, but the body is weak!"

⁴²Then Jesus left them a second time and prayed, "My Father! If this cup cannot be taken away* unless I drink it, your will be done." ⁴³When he returned to them again, he found them sleeping, for they couldn't keep their eyes open.

⁴⁴So he went to pray a third time, saying the same things again. ⁴⁵Then he came to the disciples and said, "Go ahead and sleep. Have your rest. But look—the time has come. The Son of Man is betrayed into the hands of sinners. ⁴⁶Up, let's be going. Look, my betrayer is here!"

Jesus Is Betrayed and Arrested

⁴⁷And even as Jesus said this, Judas, one of the twelve disciples, arrived with a crowd of men armed with swords and clubs. They had been sent by the leading priests and elders of the people. ⁴⁸The traitor, Judas, had given them a prearranged

---

26:28 Some manuscripts read *the new covenant.*   26:31 Greek *I will strike.* Zech 13:7.   26:42 Greek *If this cannot pass.*

signal: "You will know which one to arrest when I greet him with a kiss." [49]So Judas came straight to Jesus. "Greetings, Rabbi!" he exclaimed and gave him the kiss.

[50]Jesus said, "My friend, go ahead and do what you have come for."

Then the others grabbed Jesus and arrested him. [51]But one of the men with Jesus pulled out his sword and struck the high priest's slave, slashing off his ear.

[52]"Put away your sword," Jesus told him. "Those who use the sword will die by the sword. [53]Don't you realize that I could ask my Father for thousands* of angels to protect us, and he would send them instantly? [54]But if I did, how would the Scriptures be fulfilled that describe what must happen now?"

[55]Then Jesus said to the crowd, "Am I some dangerous revolutionary, that you come with swords and clubs to arrest me? Why didn't you arrest me in the Temple? I was there teaching every day. [56]But this is all happening to fulfill the words of the prophets as recorded in the Scriptures." At that point, all the disciples deserted him and fled.

Jesus before the Council

[57]Then the people who had arrested Jesus led him to the home of Caiaphas, the high priest, where the teachers of religious law and the elders had gathered. [58]Meanwhile, Peter followed him at a distance and came to the high priest's courtyard. He went in and sat with the guards and waited to see how it would all end.

[59]Inside, the leading priests and the entire high council* were trying to find witnesses who would lie about Jesus, so they could put him to death. [60]But even though they found many who agreed to give false witness, they could not use anyone's testimony. Finally, two men came forward [61]who declared, "This man said, 'I am able to destroy the Temple of God and rebuild it in three days.'"

[62]Then the high priest stood up and said to Jesus, "Well, aren't you going to answer these charges? What do you have to say for yourself?" [63]But Jesus remained silent. Then the high priest said to him, "I demand in the name of the living God—tell us if you are the Messiah, the Son of God."

[64]Jesus replied, "You have said it. And in the future you will see the Son of Man seated in the place of power at God's right hand* and coming on the clouds of heaven."*

[65]Then the high priest tore his clothing to show his horror and said, "Blasphemy! Why do we need other witnesses? You have all heard his blasphemy. [66]What is your verdict?"

"Guilty!" they shouted. "He deserves to die!"

[67]Then they began to spit in Jesus' face and beat him with their fists. And some slapped him, [68]jeering, "Prophesy to us, you Messiah! Who hit you that time?"

Peter Denies Jesus

[69]Meanwhile, Peter was sitting outside in the courtyard. A servant girl came over and said to him, "You were one of those with Jesus the Galilean."

[70]But Peter denied it in front of everyone. "I don't know what you're talking about," he said.

26:53 Greek *twelve legions.*   26:59 Greek *the Sanhedrin.*   26:64a Greek *seated at the right hand of the power.* See Ps 110:1.   26:64b See Dan 7:13.

⁷¹Later, out by the gate, another servant girl noticed him and said to those standing around, "This man was with Jesus of Nazareth.*"

⁷²Again Peter denied it, this time with an oath. "I don't even know the man," he said.

⁷³A little later some of the other bystanders came over to Peter and said, "You must be one of them; we can tell by your Galilean accent."

⁷⁴Peter swore, "A curse on me if I'm lying—I don't know the man!" And immediately the rooster crowed.

⁷⁵Suddenly, Jesus' words flashed through Peter's mind: "Before the rooster crows, you will deny three times that you even know me." And he went away, weeping bitterly.

CHAPTER 27

Judas Hangs Himself

Very early in the morning the leading priests and the elders of the people met again to lay plans for putting Jesus to death. ²Then they bound him, led him away, and took him to Pilate, the Roman governor.

³When Judas, who had betrayed him, realized that Jesus had been condemned to die, he was filled with remorse. So he took the thirty pieces of silver back to the leading priests and the elders. ⁴"I have sinned," he declared, "for I have betrayed an innocent man."

"What do we care?" they retorted. "That's your problem."

⁵Then Judas threw the silver coins down in the Temple and went out and hanged himself.

⁶The leading priests picked up the coins. "It wouldn't be right to put this money in the Temple treasury," they said, "since it was payment for murder."* ⁷After some discussion they finally decided to buy the potter's field, and they made it into a cemetery for foreigners. ⁸That is why the field is still called the Field of Blood. ⁹This fulfilled the prophecy of Jeremiah that says,

"They took* the thirty pieces of silver—
the price at which he was valued by the people of Israel,
¹⁰ and purchased the potter's field,
as the LORD directed.*"

Jesus' Trial before Pilate

¹¹Now Jesus was standing before Pilate, the Roman governor. "Are you the king of the Jews?" the governor asked him.

Jesus replied, "You have said it."

¹²But when the leading priests and the elders made their accusations against him, Jesus remained silent. ¹³"Don't you hear all these charges they are bringing

---

26:71 Or *Jesus the Nazarene.*   27:6 Greek *since it is the price for blood.*   27:9 Or *I took.*   27:9-10 Greek *as the LORD directed me.* Zech 11:12-13; Jer 32:6-9.

against you?" Pilate demanded. [14]But Jesus made no response to any of the charges, much to the governor's surprise.

[15]Now it was the governor's custom each year during the Passover celebration to release one prisoner to the crowd—anyone they wanted. [16]This year there was a notorious prisoner, a man named Barabbas.* [17]As the crowds gathered before Pilate's house that morning, he asked them, "Which one do you want me to release to you—Barabbas, or Jesus who is called the Messiah?" [18](He knew very well that the religious leaders had arrested Jesus out of envy.)

[19]Just then, as Pilate was sitting on the judgment seat, his wife sent him this message: "Leave that innocent man alone. I suffered through a terrible nightmare about him last night."

[20]Meanwhile, the leading priests and the elders persuaded the crowd to ask for Barabbas to be released and for Jesus to be put to death. [21]So the governor asked again, "Which of these two do you want me to release to you?"

The crowd shouted back, "Barabbas!"

[22]Pilate responded, "Then what should I do with Jesus who is called the Messiah?"

They shouted back, "Crucify him!"

[23]"Why?" Pilate demanded. "What crime has he committed?"

But the mob roared even louder, "Crucify him!"

[24]Pilate saw that he wasn't getting anywhere and that a riot was developing. So he sent for a bowl of water and washed his hands before the crowd, saying, "I am innocent of this man's blood. The responsibility is yours!"

[25]And all the people yelled back, "We will take responsibility for his death—we and our children!"*

[26]So Pilate released Barabbas to them. He ordered Jesus flogged with a lead-tipped whip, then turned him over to the Roman soldiers to be crucified.

The Soldiers Mock Jesus

[27]Some of the governor's soldiers took Jesus into their headquarters* and called out the entire regiment. [28]They stripped him and put a scarlet robe on him. [29]They wove thorn branches into a crown and put it on his head, and they placed a reed stick in his right hand as a scepter. Then they knelt before him in mockery and taunted, "Hail! King of the Jews!" [30]And they spit on him and grabbed the stick and struck him on the head with it. [31]When they were finally tired of mocking him, they took off the robe and put his own clothes on him again. Then they led him away to be crucified.

The Crucifixion

[32]Along the way, they came across a man named Simon, who was from Cyrene,* and the soldiers forced him to carry Jesus' cross. [33]And they went out to a place called Golgotha (which means "Place of the Skull"). [34]The soldiers gave him wine mixed with bitter gall, but when he had tasted it, he refused to drink it.

27:16 Some manuscripts read *Jesus Barabbas;* also in 27:17.   **27:25** Greek *"His blood be on us and on our children."*
27:27 Or *into the Praetorium.*   **27:32** *Cyrene* was a city in northern Africa.

³⁵After they had nailed him to the cross, the soldiers gambled for his clothes by throwing dice.* ³⁶Then they sat around and kept guard as he hung there. ³⁷A sign was fastened above Jesus' head, announcing the charge against him. It read: "This is Jesus, the King of the Jews." ³⁸Two revolutionaries* were crucified with him, one on his right and one on his left.

³⁹The people passing by shouted abuse, shaking their heads in mockery. ⁴⁰"Look at you now!" they yelled at him. "You said you were going to destroy the Temple and rebuild it in three days. Well then, if you are the Son of God, save yourself and come down from the cross!"

⁴¹The leading priests, the teachers of religious law, and the elders also mocked Jesus. ⁴²"He saved others," they scoffed, "but he can't save himself! So he is the King of Israel, is he? Let him come down from the cross right now, and we will believe in him! ⁴³He trusted God, so let God rescue him now if he wants him! For he said, 'I am the Son of God.'" ⁴⁴Even the revolutionaries who were crucified with him ridiculed him in the same way.

The Death of Jesus

⁴⁵At noon, darkness fell across the whole land until three o'clock. ⁴⁶At about three o'clock, Jesus called out with a loud voice, *"Eli, Eli,* lema sabachthani?"* which means "My God, my God, why have you abandoned me?"*

⁴⁷Some of the bystanders misunderstood and thought he was calling for the prophet Elijah. ⁴⁸One of them ran and filled a sponge with sour wine, holding it up to him on a reed stick so he could drink. ⁴⁹But the rest said, "Wait! Let's see whether Elijah comes to save him."*

⁵⁰Then Jesus shouted out again, and he released his spirit. ⁵¹At that moment the curtain in the sanctuary of the Temple was torn in two, from top to bottom. The earth shook, rocks split apart, ⁵²and tombs opened. The bodies of many godly men and women who had died were raised from the dead. ⁵³They left the cemetery after Jesus' resurrection, went into the holy city of Jerusalem, and appeared to many people.

⁵⁴The Roman officer* and the other soldiers at the crucifixion were terrified by the earthquake and all that had happened. They said, "This man truly was the Son of God!"

⁵⁵And many women who had come from Galilee with Jesus to care for him were watching from a distance. ⁵⁶Among them were Mary Magdalene, Mary (the mother of James and Joseph), and the mother of James and John, the sons of Zebedee.

The Burial of Jesus

⁵⁷As evening approached, Joseph, a rich man from Arimathea who had become a follower of Jesus, ⁵⁸went to Pilate and asked for Jesus' body. And Pilate issued an order to release it to him. ⁵⁹Joseph took the body and wrapped it in a long sheet of clean linen cloth. ⁶⁰He placed it in his own new tomb, which had been

---

27:35 Greek *by casting lots.* A few late manuscripts add *This fulfilled the word of the prophet: "They divided my garments among themselves and cast lots for my robe."* See Ps 22:18.   **27:38** Or *criminals;* also in 27:44.
27:46a Some manuscripts read *Eloi, Eloi.*   **27:46b** Ps 22:1.   **27:49** Some manuscripts add *And another took a spear and pierced his side, and out flowed water and blood.* Compare John 19:34.   **27:54** Greek *The centurion.*

carved out of the rock. Then he rolled a great stone across the entrance and left. [61] Both Mary Magdalene and the other Mary were sitting across from the tomb and watching.

The Guard at the Tomb

[62] The next day, on the Sabbath,* the leading priests and Pharisees went to see Pilate. [63] They told him, "Sir, we remember what that deceiver once said while he was still alive: 'After three days I will rise from the dead.' [64] So we request that you seal the tomb until the third day. This will prevent his disciples from coming and stealing his body and then telling everyone he was raised from the dead! If that happens, we'll be worse off than we were at first."

[65] Pilate replied, "Take guards and secure it the best you can." [66] So they sealed the tomb and posted guards to protect it.

CHAPTER 28

The Resurrection

Early on Sunday morning,* as the new day was dawning, Mary Magdalene and the other Mary went out to visit the tomb.

[2] Suddenly there was a great earthquake! For an angel of the Lord came down from heaven, rolled aside the stone, and sat on it. [3] His face shone like lightning, and his clothing was as white as snow. [4] The guards shook with fear when they saw him, and they fell into a dead faint.

[5] Then the angel spoke to the women. "Don't be afraid!" he said. "I know you are looking for Jesus, who was crucified. [6] He isn't here! He is risen from the dead, just as he said would happen. Come, see where his body was lying. [7] And now, go quickly and tell his disciples that he has risen from the dead, and he is going ahead of you to Galilee. You will see him there. Remember what I have told you."

[8] The women ran quickly from the tomb. They were very frightened but also filled with great joy, and they rushed to give the disciples the angel's message. [9] And as they went, Jesus met them and greeted them. And they ran to him, grasped his feet, and worshiped him. [10] Then Jesus said to them, "Don't be afraid! Go tell my brothers to leave for Galilee, and they will see me there."

The Report of the Guard

[11] As the women were on their way, some of the guards went into the city and told the leading priests what had happened. [12] A meeting with the elders was called, and they decided to give the soldiers a large bribe. [13] They told the soldiers, "You must say, 'Jesus' disciples came during the night while we were sleeping, and they stole his body.' [14] If the governor hears about it, we'll stand up for you so you won't get in trouble." [15] So the guards accepted the bribe and said what they were told to say. Their story spread widely among the Jews, and they still tell it today.

27:62 Or *On the next day, which is after the Preparation.* **28:1** Greek *After the Sabbath, on the first day of the week.*

The Great Commission

[16]Then the eleven disciples left for Galilee, going to the mountain where Jesus had told them to go. [17]When they saw him, they worshiped him—but some of them doubted!

[18]Jesus came and told his disciples, "I have been given all authority in heaven and on earth. [19]Therefore, go and make disciples of all the nations,* baptizing them in the name of the Father and the Son and the Holy Spirit. [20]Teach these new disciples to obey all the commands I have given you. And be sure of this: I am with you always, even to the end of the age."

28:19 Or *all peoples.*

THE GOSPEL OF MARK

Author

Since the author does not name himself in his book, we need to look at other sources to discover the author of this Gospel. One of the earliest sources comes from Papias, who (as related through Eusebius) claims this:

> Mark, having become the interpreter of Peter, wrote down accurately, though not in order, whatsoever he remembered of the things said or done by Christ. For he neither heard the Lord nor followed him, but afterward, as I said, he followed Peter, who adapted his teaching to the needs of his hearers, but with no intention of giving a connected account of the Lord's discourses, so that Mark committed no error while he thus wrote some things as he remembered them. For he was careful of one thing, not to omit any of the things which he had heard, and not to state any of them falsely.[9]

Sources besides Papias—including the Anti-Marcionite Prologue (ca. A.D. 180), Irenaeus,[10] and Clement of Alexandria,[11] also confirm this identification. Clement is reported to have said this:

> The Gospel according to Mark had this occasion. As Peter had preached the word publicly at Rome, and declared the Gospel by the Spirit, many who were present requested that Mark, who had followed him for a long time and remembered his sayings, should write them out. And having composed the Gospel he gave it to those who had requested it.[12]

Irenaeus wrote that "after their [Peter and Paul's] departure, Mark, the disciple and interpreter of Peter, did also hand down to us in writing what had been preached by Peter." Justin Martyr suggests Mark was connected to Peter; he alludes to Mark 3:16-17 in his *Dialogue with Trypho* (106), commenting on it as "the memoirs of [Peter]."

The title "Mark" probably refers to John Mark, known as an assistant to Peter, Paul, and Barnabas.[13] The name Mark was common, so this conclusion is dependent to some degree on early-church testimony and the association of Mark with both Peter and Paul. However, no good alternative options exist.

Date

Determining the date of Mark's Gospel is somewhat difficult because the external testimony is not in agreement. Irenaeus places the composition after the death of Peter and Paul, a date that would be in the late A.D. 60s,[14] while Clement of Alexandria dates it during Peter and Paul's time in Rome.[15] This could push the date back into the A.D. 50s. If one accepts the testimony tied to Clement of Alexandria that Peter ratified Mark's work, then a date in the late A.D. 50s to mid-60s is possible. A mid- to late-60s date would mean that, although Mark got his material from Peter, he took some time to compile and compose his Gospel. The possibility of a date in the early 60s is good, but one in the mid to late 60s is also possible. In the end, most commentators opt for a date around A.D. 65–70 (see standard commentaries on Mark).

Manuscripts
Mark exists only in a few papyri: P45, P84, and P88.

> P45 (third century A.D.), Mark 4:36–9:31 and 11:27–12:28
> P84 (sixth century A.D.), Mark 2:2-9 and 6:30-41
> P88 (fourth century A.D.), Mark 2:1-26

Complete manuscripts appear in Aleph (to 16:8), A (to 16:20), B (to 16:8), D, and W.

A few manuscripts have been identified as "Caesarean" in the Gospel of Mark. These manuscripts probably came from Origen's text, a text that he took with him from Alexandria to Caesarea and that bears a mixture of so-called "Western" and Alexandrian readings. These witnesses are Codex Koridethi (038); the miniscules 28, 565, 700, f[1], f[13]; the Armenian and Georgian versions; P45; and codex W (in Mark 1:1–5:30).

MARK

CHAPTER 1

John the Baptist Prepares the Way

This is the Good News about Jesus the Messiah, the Son of God.* It began ²just as the prophet Isaiah had written:

"Look, I am sending my messenger ahead of you,
    and he will prepare your way.*
³ He is a voice shouting in the wilderness,
    'Prepare the way for the LORD's coming!
    Clear the road for him!'*"

⁴This messenger was John the Baptist. He was in the wilderness and preached that people should be baptized to show that they had repented of their sins and turned to God to be forgiven. ⁵All of Judea, including all the people of Jerusalem, went out to see and hear John. And when they confessed their sins, he baptized them in the Jordan River. ⁶His clothes were woven from coarse camel hair, and he wore a leather belt around his waist. For food he ate locusts and wild honey.

⁷John announced: "Someone is coming soon who is greater than I am—so much greater that I'm not even worthy to stoop down like a slave and untie the straps of his sandals. ⁸I baptize you with* water, but he will baptize you with the Holy Spirit!"

The Baptism and Temptation of Jesus

⁹One day Jesus came from Nazareth in Galilee, and John baptized him in the Jordan River. ¹⁰As Jesus came up out of the water, he saw the heavens splitting apart and the Holy Spirit descending on him* like a dove. ¹¹And a voice from heaven said, "You are my dearly loved Son, and you bring me great joy."

¹²The Spirit then compelled Jesus to go into the wilderness, ¹³where he was tempted by Satan for forty days. He was out among the wild animals, and angels took care of him.

¹⁴Later on, after John was arrested, Jesus went into Galilee, where he preached God's Good News.* ¹⁵"The time promised by God has come at last!" he announced. "The Kingdom of God is near! Repent of your sins and believe the Good News!"

The First Disciples

¹⁶One day as Jesus was walking along the shore of the Sea of Galilee, he saw Simon* and his brother Andrew throwing a net into the water, for they fished for

---

1:1 Some manuscripts do not include *the Son of God.* 1:2 Mal 3:1. 1:3 Isa 40:3 (Greek version). 1:8 Or *in;* also in 1:8b. 1:10 Or *toward him,* or *into him.* 1:14 Some manuscripts read *the Good News of the Kingdom of God.* 1:16 *Simon* is called "Peter" in 3:16 and thereafter.

a living. [17]Jesus called out to them, "Come, follow me, and I will show you how to fish for people!" [18]And they left their nets at once and followed him.

[19]A little farther up the shore Jesus saw Zebedee's sons, James and John, in a boat repairing their nets. [20]He called them at once, and they also followed him, leaving their father, Zebedee, in the boat with the hired men.

Jesus Casts Out an Evil Spirit

[21]Jesus and his companions went to the town of Capernaum. When the Sabbath day came, he went into the synagogue and began to teach. [22]The people were amazed at his teaching, for he taught with real authority—quite unlike the teachers of religious law.

[23]Suddenly, a man in the synagogue who was possessed by an evil* spirit began shouting, [24]"Why are you interfering with us, Jesus of Nazareth? Have you come to destroy us? I know who you are—the Holy One of God!"

[25]Jesus cut him short. "Be quiet! Come out of the man," he ordered. [26]At that, the evil spirit screamed, threw the man into a convulsion, and then came out of him.

[27]Amazement gripped the audience, and they began to discuss what had happened. "What sort of new teaching is this?" they asked excitedly. "It has such authority! Even evil spirits obey his orders!" [28]The news about Jesus spread quickly throughout the entire region of Galilee.

Jesus Heals Many People

[29]After Jesus left the synagogue with James and John, they went to Simon and Andrew's home. [30]Now Simon's mother-in-law was sick in bed with a high fever. They told Jesus about her right away. [31]So he went to her bedside, took her by the hand, and helped her sit up. Then the fever left her, and she prepared a meal for them.

[32]That evening after sunset, many sick and demon-possessed people were brought to Jesus. [33]The whole town gathered at the door to watch. [34]So Jesus healed many people who were sick with various diseases, and he cast out many demons. But because the demons knew who he was, he did not allow them to speak.

Jesus Preaches in Galilee

[35]Before daybreak the next morning, Jesus got up and went out to an isolated place to pray. [36]Later Simon and the others went out to find him. [37]When they found him, they said, "Everyone is looking for you."

[38]But Jesus replied, "We must go on to other towns as well, and I will preach to them, too. That is why I came." [39]So he traveled throughout the region of Galilee, preaching in the synagogues and casting out demons.

Jesus Heals a Man with Leprosy

[40]A man with leprosy came and knelt in front of Jesus, begging to be healed. "If you are willing, you can heal me and make me clean," he said.

[41]Moved with compassion,* Jesus reached out and touched him. "I am willing,"

1:23 Greek *unclean;* also in 1:26, 27.   1:41 Some manuscripts read *Moved with anger.*

123

he said. "Be healed!" 42Instantly the leprosy disappeared, and the man was healed. 43Then Jesus sent him on his way with a stern warning: 44"Don't tell anyone about this. Instead, go to the priest and let him examine you. Take along the offering required in the law of Moses for those who have been healed of leprosy.* This will be a public testimony that you have been cleansed."

45But the man went and spread the word, proclaiming to everyone what had happened. As a result, large crowds soon surrounded Jesus, and he couldn't publicly enter a town anywhere. He had to stay out in the secluded places, but people from everywhere kept coming to him.

CHAPTER 2

Jesus Heals a Paralyzed Man

When Jesus returned to Capernaum several days later, the news spread quickly that he was back home. 2Soon the house where he was staying was so packed with visitors that there was no more room, even outside the door. While he was preaching God's word to them, 3four men arrived carrying a paralyzed man on a mat. 4They couldn't bring him to Jesus because of the crowd, so they dug a hole through the roof above his head. Then they lowered the man on his mat, right down in front of Jesus. 5Seeing their faith, Jesus said to the paralyzed man, "My child, your sins are forgiven."

6But some of the teachers of religious law who were sitting there thought to themselves, 7"What is he saying? This is blasphemy! Only God can forgive sins!"

8Jesus knew immediately what they were thinking, so he asked them, "Why do you question this in your hearts? 9Is it easier to say to the paralyzed man 'Your sins are forgiven,' or 'Stand up, pick up your mat, and walk'? 10So I will prove to you that the Son of Man* has the authority on earth to forgive sins." Then Jesus turned to the paralyzed man and said, 11"Stand up, pick up your mat, and go home!"

12And the man jumped up, grabbed his mat, and walked out through the stunned onlookers. They were all amazed and praised God, exclaiming, "We've never seen anything like this before!"

Jesus Calls Levi (Matthew)

13Then Jesus went out to the lakeshore again and taught the crowds that were coming to him. 14As he walked along, he saw Levi son of Alphaeus sitting at his tax collector's booth. "Follow me and be my disciple," Jesus said to him. So Levi got up and followed him.

15Later, Levi invited Jesus and his disciples to his home as dinner guests, along with many tax collectors and other disreputable sinners. (There were many people of this kind among Jesus' followers.) 16But when the teachers of religious law who were Pharisees* saw him eating with tax collectors and other sinners, they asked his disciples, "Why does he eat with such scum?*"

1:44 See Lev 14:2-32.   **2:10** "Son of Man" is a title Jesus used for himself.   **2:16a** Greek *the scribes of the Pharisees*. **2:16b** Greek *with tax collectors and sinners?*

[17]When Jesus heard this, he told them, "Healthy people don't need a doctor—sick people do. I have come to call not those who think they are righteous, but those who know they are sinners."

A Discussion about Fasting

[18]Once when John's disciples and the Pharisees were fasting, some people came to Jesus and asked, "Why don't your disciples fast like John's disciples and the Pharisees do?"

[19]Jesus replied, "Do wedding guests fast while celebrating with the groom? Of course not. They can't fast while the groom is with them. [20]But someday the groom will be taken away from them, and then they will fast.

[21]"Besides, who would patch old clothing with new cloth? For the new patch would shrink and rip away from the old cloth, leaving an even bigger tear than before.

[22]"And no one puts new wine into old wineskins. For the wine would burst the wineskins, and the wine and the skins would both be lost. New wine calls for new wineskins."

A Discussion about the Sabbath

[23]One Sabbath day as Jesus was walking through some grainfields, his disciples began breaking off heads of grain to eat. [24]But the Pharisees said to Jesus, "Look, why are they breaking the law by harvesting grain on the Sabbath?"

[25]Jesus said to them, "Haven't you ever read in the Scriptures what David did when he and his companions were hungry? [26]He went into the house of God (during the days when Abiathar was high priest) and broke the law by eating the sacred loaves of bread that only the priests are allowed to eat. He also gave some to his companions."

[27]Then Jesus said to them, "The Sabbath was made to meet the needs of people, and not people to meet the requirements of the Sabbath. [28]So the Son of Man is Lord, even over the Sabbath!"

CHAPTER 3

Jesus Heals on the Sabbath

Jesus went into the synagogue again and noticed a man with a deformed hand. [2]Since it was the Sabbath, Jesus' enemies watched him closely. If he healed the man's hand, they planned to accuse him of working on the Sabbath.

[3]Jesus said to the man with the deformed hand, "Come and stand in front of everyone." [4]Then he turned to his critics and asked, "Does the law permit good deeds on the Sabbath, or is it a day for doing evil? Is this a day to save life or to destroy it?" But they wouldn't answer him.

[5]He looked around at them angrily and was deeply saddened by their hard hearts. Then he said to the man, "Hold out your hand." So the man held out his hand, and it was restored! [6]At once the Pharisees went away and met with the supporters of Herod to plot how to kill Jesus.

Crowds Follow Jesus

[7]Jesus went out to the lake with his disciples, and a large crowd followed him. They came from all over Galilee, Judea, [8]Jerusalem, Idumea, from east of the Jordan River, and even from as far north as Tyre and Sidon. The news about his miracles had spread far and wide, and vast numbers of people came to see him.

[9]Jesus instructed his disciples to have a boat ready so the crowd would not crush him. [10]He had healed many people that day, so all the sick people eagerly pushed forward to touch him. [11]And whenever those possessed by evil* spirits caught sight of him, the spirits would throw them to the ground in front of him shrieking, "You are the Son of God!" [12]But Jesus sternly commanded the spirits not to reveal who he was.

Jesus Chooses the Twelve Apostles

[13]Afterward Jesus went up on a mountain and called out the ones he wanted to go with him. And they came to him. [14]Then he appointed twelve of them and called them his apostles.* They were to accompany him, and he would send them out to preach, [15]giving them authority to cast out demons. [16]These are the twelve he chose:

Simon (whom he named Peter),
[17] James and John (the sons of Zebedee, but Jesus nicknamed them "Sons of Thunder"*),
[18] Andrew,
Philip,
Bartholomew,
Matthew,
Thomas,
James (son of Alphaeus),
Thaddaeus,
Simon (the zealot*),
[19]Judas Iscariot (who later betrayed him).

Jesus and the Prince of Demons

[20]One time Jesus entered a house, and the crowds began to gather again. Soon he and his disciples couldn't even find time to eat. [21]When his family heard what was happening, they tried to take him away. "He's out of his mind," they said.

[22]But the teachers of religious law who had arrived from Jerusalem said, "He's possessed by Satan,* the prince of demons. That's where he gets the power to cast out demons."

[23]Jesus called them over and responded with an illustration. "How can Satan cast out Satan?" he asked. [24]"A kingdom divided by civil war will collapse. [25]Similarly, a family splintered by feuding will fall apart. [26]And if Satan is divided and fights against himself, how can he stand? He would never survive. [27]Let me illustrate this

---

3:11 Greek *unclean;* also in 3:30.　**3:14** Some manuscripts do not include *and called them his apostles.*　**3:17** Greek *whom he named Boanerges, which means Sons of Thunder.*　**3:18** Greek *the Cananean,* an Aramaic term for Jewish nationalists.　**3:22** Greek *Beelzeboul;* other manuscripts read *Beezeboul;* Latin version reads *Beelzebub.*

further. Who is powerful enough to enter the house of a strong man like Satan and plunder his goods? Only someone even stronger—someone who could tie him up and then plunder his house.

²⁸"I tell you the truth, all sin and blasphemy can be forgiven, ²⁹but anyone who blasphemes the Holy Spirit will never be forgiven. This is a sin with eternal consequences." ³⁰He told them this because they were saying, "He's possessed by an evil spirit."

The True Family of Jesus

³¹Then Jesus' mother and brothers came to see him. They stood outside and sent word for him to come out and talk with them. ³²There was a crowd sitting around Jesus, and someone said, "Your mother and your brothers* are outside asking for you."

³³Jesus replied, "Who is my mother? Who are my brothers?" ³⁴Then he looked at those around him and said, "Look, these are my mother and brothers. ³⁵Anyone who does God's will is my brother and sister and mother."

CHAPTER 4

Parable of the Farmer Scattering Seed

Once again Jesus began teaching by the lakeshore. A very large crowd soon gathered around him, so he got into a boat. Then he sat in the boat while all the people remained on the shore. ²He taught them by telling many stories in the form of parables, such as this one:

³"Listen! A farmer went out to plant some seed. ⁴As he scattered it across his field, some of the seed fell on a footpath, and the birds came and ate it. ⁵Other seed fell on shallow soil with underlying rock. The seed sprouted quickly because the soil was shallow. ⁶But the plant soon wilted under the hot sun, and since it didn't have deep roots, it died. ⁷Other seed fell among thorns that grew up and choked out the tender plants so they produced no grain. ⁸Still other seeds fell on fertile soil, and they sprouted, grew, and produced a crop that was thirty, sixty, and even a hundred times as much as had been planted!" ⁹Then he said, "Anyone with ears to hear should listen and understand."

¹⁰Later, when Jesus was alone with the twelve disciples and with the others who were gathered around, they asked him what the parables meant.

¹¹He replied, "You are permitted to understand the secret* of the Kingdom of God. But I use parables for everything I say to outsiders, ¹²so that the Scriptures might be fulfilled:

'When they see what I do,
    they will learn nothing.
When they hear what I say,
    they will not understand.
Otherwise, they will turn to me
    and be forgiven.'*"

3:32 Some manuscripts add *and sisters.*   **4:11** Greek *mystery.*   **4:12** Isa 6:9-10 (Greek version).

[13]Then Jesus said to them, "If you can't understand the meaning of this parable, how will you understand all the other parables? [14]The farmer plants seed by taking God's word to others. [15]The seed that fell on the footpath represents those who hear the message, only to have Satan come at once and take it away. [16]The seed on the rocky soil represents those who hear the message and immediately receive it with joy. [17]But since they don't have deep roots, they don't last long. They fall away as soon as they have problems or are persecuted for believing God's word. [18]The seed that fell among the thorns represents others who hear God's word, [19]but all too quickly the message is crowded out by the worries of this life, the lure of wealth, and the desire for other things, so no fruit is produced. [20]And the seed that fell on good soil represents those who hear and accept God's word and produce a harvest of thirty, sixty, or even a hundred times as much as had been planted!"

Parable of the Lamp

[21]Then Jesus asked them, "Would anyone light a lamp and then put it under a basket or under a bed? Of course not! A lamp is placed on a stand, where its light will shine. [22]For everything that is hidden will eventually be brought into the open, and every secret will be brought to light. [23]Anyone with ears to hear should listen and understand."

[24]Then he added, "Pay close attention to what you hear. The closer you listen, the more understanding you will be given*—and you will receive even more. [25]To those who listen to my teaching, more understanding will be given. But for those who are not listening, even what little understanding they have will be taken away from them."

Parable of the Growing Seed

[26]Jesus also said, "The Kingdom of God is like a farmer who scatters seed on the ground. [27]Night and day, while he's asleep or awake, the seed sprouts and grows, but he does not understand how it happens. [28]The earth produces the crops on its own. First a leaf blade pushes through, then the heads of wheat are formed, and finally the grain ripens. [29]And as soon as the grain is ready, the farmer comes and harvests it with a sickle, for the harvest time has come."

Parable of the Mustard Seed

[30]Jesus said, "How can I describe the Kingdom of God? What story should I use to illustrate it? [31]It is like a mustard seed planted in the ground. It is the smallest of all seeds, [32]but it becomes the largest of all garden plants; it grows long branches, and birds can make nests in its shade."

[33]Jesus used many similar stories and illustrations to teach the people as much as they could understand. [34]In fact, in his public ministry he never taught without using parables; but afterward, when he was alone with his disciples, he explained everything to them.

4:24 Or *The measure you give will be the measure you get back.*

Jesus Calms the Storm

[35]As evening came, Jesus said to his disciples, "Let's cross to the other side of the lake." [36]So they took Jesus in the boat and started out, leaving the crowds behind (although other boats followed). [37]But soon a fierce storm came up. High waves were breaking into the boat, and it began to fill with water.

[38]Jesus was sleeping at the back of the boat with his head on a cushion. The disciples woke him up, shouting, "Teacher, don't you care that we're going to drown?"

[39]When Jesus woke up, he rebuked the wind and said to the waves, "Silence! Be still!" Suddenly the wind stopped, and there was a great calm. [40]Then he asked them, "Why are you afraid? Do you still have no faith?"

[41]The disciples were absolutely terrified. "Who is this man?" they asked each other. "Even the wind and waves obey him!"

CHAPTER 5

Jesus Heals a Demon-Possessed Man

So they arrived at the other side of the lake, in the region of the Gerasenes.* [2]When Jesus climbed out of the boat, a man possessed by an evil* spirit came out from a cemetery to meet him. [3]This man lived among the burial caves and could no longer be restrained, even with a chain. [4]Whenever he was put into chains and shackles—as he often was—he snapped the chains from his wrists and smashed the shackles. No one was strong enough to subdue him. [5]Day and night he wandered among the burial caves and in the hills, howling and cutting himself with sharp stones.

[6]When Jesus was still some distance away, the man saw him, ran to meet him, and bowed low before him. [7]With a shriek, he screamed, "Why are you interfering with me, Jesus, Son of the Most High God? In the name of God, I beg you, don't torture me!" [8]For Jesus had already said to the spirit, "Come out of the man, you evil spirit."

[9]Then Jesus demanded, "What is your name?"

And he replied, "My name is Legion, because there are many of us inside this man." [10]Then the evil spirits begged him again and again not to send them to some distant place.

[11]There happened to be a large herd of pigs feeding on the hillside nearby. [12]"Send us into those pigs," the spirits begged. "Let us enter them." [13]So Jesus gave them permission. The evil spirits came out of the man and entered the pigs, and the entire herd of about 2,000 pigs plunged down the steep hillside into the lake and drowned in the water.

[14]The herdsmen fled to the nearby town and the surrounding countryside, spreading the news as they ran. People rushed out to see what had happened. [15]A crowd soon gathered around Jesus, and they saw the man who had been possessed

---

5:1 Other manuscripts read *Gadarenes;* still others read *Gergesenes.* See Matt 8:28; Luke 8:26.   **5:2** Greek *unclean;* also in 5:8, 13.

by the legion of demons. He was sitting there fully clothed and perfectly sane, and they were all afraid. [16]Then those who had seen what happened told the others about the demon-possessed man and the pigs. [17]And the crowd began pleading with Jesus to go away and leave them alone.

[18]As Jesus was getting into the boat, the man who had been demon possessed begged to go with him. [19]But Jesus said, "No, go home to your family, and tell them everything the Lord has done for you and how merciful he has been." [20]So the man started off to visit the Ten Towns* of that region and began to proclaim the great things Jesus had done for him; and everyone was amazed at what he told them.

Jesus Heals in Response to Faith

[21]Jesus got into the boat again and went back to the other side of the lake, where a large crowd gathered around him on the shore. [22]Then a leader of the local synagogue, whose name was Jairus, arrived. When he saw Jesus, he fell at his feet, [23]pleading fervently with him. "My little daughter is dying," he said. "Please come and lay your hands on her; heal her so she can live."

[24]Jesus went with him, and all the people followed, crowding around him. [25]A woman in the crowd had suffered for twelve years with constant bleeding. [26]She had suffered a great deal from many doctors, and over the years she had spent everything she had to pay them, but she had gotten no better. In fact, she had gotten worse. [27]She had heard about Jesus, so she came up behind him through the crowd and touched his robe. [28]For she thought to herself, "If I can just touch his robe, I will be healed." [29]Immediately the bleeding stopped, and she could feel in her body that she had been healed of her terrible condition.

[30]Jesus realized at once that healing power had gone out from him, so he turned around in the crowd and asked, "Who touched my robe?"

[31]His disciples said to him, "Look at this crowd pressing around you. How can you ask, 'Who touched me?'"

[32]But he kept on looking around to see who had done it. [33]Then the frightened woman, trembling at the realization of what had happened to her, came and fell to her knees in front of him and told him what she had done. [34]And he said to her, "Daughter, your faith has made you well. Go in peace. Your suffering is over."

[35]While he was still speaking to her, messengers arrived from the home of Jairus, the leader of the synagogue. They told him, "Your daughter is dead. There's no use troubling the Teacher now."

[36]But Jesus overheard* them and said to Jairus, "Don't be afraid. Just have faith."

[37]Then Jesus stopped the crowd and wouldn't let anyone go with him except Peter, James, and John (the brother of James). [38]When they came to the home of the synagogue leader, Jesus saw much commotion and weeping and wailing. [39]He went inside and asked, "Why all this commotion and weeping? The child isn't dead; she's only asleep."

5:20 Greek *Decapolis.*   **5:36** Or *ignored.*

⁴⁰The crowd laughed at him. But he made them all leave, and he took the girl's father and mother and his three disciples into the room where the girl was lying. ⁴¹Holding her hand, he said to her, *"Talitha koum,"* which means "Little girl, get up!" ⁴²And the girl, who was twelve years old, immediately stood up and walked around! They were overwhelmed and totally amazed. ⁴³Jesus gave them strict orders not to tell anyone what had happened, and then he told them to give her something to eat.

CHAPTER 6

Jesus Rejected at Nazareth
Jesus left that part of the country and returned with his disciples to Nazareth, his hometown. ²The next Sabbath he began teaching in the synagogue, and many who heard him were amazed. They asked, "Where did he get all this wisdom and the power to perform such miracles?" ³Then they scoffed, "He's just a carpenter, the son of Mary* and the brother of James, Joseph,* Judas, and Simon. And his sisters live right here among us." They were deeply offended and refused to believe in him.

⁴Then Jesus told them, "A prophet is honored everywhere except in his own hometown and among his relatives and his own family." ⁵And because of their unbelief, he couldn't do any miracles among them except to place his hands on a few sick people and heal them. ⁶And he was amazed at their unbelief.

Jesus Sends Out the Twelve Disciples
Then Jesus went from village to village, teaching the people. ⁷And he called his twelve disciples together and began sending them out two by two, giving them authority to cast out evil* spirits. ⁸He told them to take nothing for their journey except a walking stick—no food, no traveler's bag, no money.* ⁹He allowed them to wear sandals but not to take a change of clothes.

¹⁰"Wherever you go," he said, "stay in the same house until you leave town. ¹¹But if any place refuses to welcome you or listen to you, shake its dust from your feet as you leave to show that you have abandoned those people to their fate."

¹²So the disciples went out, telling everyone they met to repent of their sins and turn to God. ¹³And they cast out many demons and healed many sick people, anointing them with olive oil.

The Death of John the Baptist
¹⁴Herod Antipas, the king, soon heard about Jesus, because everyone was talking about him. Some were saying,* "This must be John the Baptist raised from the dead. That is why he can do such miracles." ¹⁵Others said, "He's the prophet Elijah." Still others said, "He's a prophet like the other great prophets of the past."

6:3a Some manuscripts read *He's just the son of the carpenter and of Mary.*   **6:3b** Most manuscripts read *Joses;* see Matt 13:55.   **6:7** Greek *unclean.*   **6:8** Greek *no copper coins in their money belts.*   **6:14** Some manuscripts read *He was saying.*

¹⁶When Herod heard about Jesus, he said, "John, the man I beheaded, has come back from the dead."

¹⁷For Herod had sent soldiers to arrest and imprison John as a favor to Herodias. She had been his brother Philip's wife, but Herod had married her. ¹⁸John had been telling Herod, "It is against God's law for you to marry your brother's wife." ¹⁹So Herodias bore a grudge against John and wanted to kill him. But without Herod's approval she was powerless, ²⁰for Herod respected John; and knowing that he was a good and holy man, he protected him. Herod was greatly disturbed whenever he talked with John, but even so, he liked to listen to him.

²¹Herodias's chance finally came on Herod's birthday. He gave a party for his high government officials, army officers, and the leading citizens of Galilee. ²²Then his daughter, also named Herodias,* came in and performed a dance that greatly pleased Herod and his guests. "Ask me for anything you like," the king said to the girl, "and I will give it to you." ²³He even vowed, "I will give you whatever you ask, up to half my kingdom!"

²⁴She went out and asked her mother, "What should I ask for?"

Her mother told her, "Ask for the head of John the Baptist!"

²⁵So the girl hurried back to the king and told him, "I want the head of John the Baptist, right now, on a tray!"

²⁶Then the king deeply regretted what he had said; but because of the vows he had made in front of his guests, he couldn't refuse her. ²⁷So he immediately sent an executioner to the prison to cut off John's head and bring it to him. The soldier beheaded John in the prison, ²⁸brought his head on a tray, and gave it to the girl, who took it to her mother. ²⁹When John's disciples heard what had happened, they came to get his body and buried it in a tomb.

Jesus Feeds Five Thousand

³⁰The apostles returned to Jesus from their ministry tour and told him all they had done and taught. ³¹Then Jesus said, "Let's go off by ourselves to a quiet place and rest awhile." He said this because there were so many people coming and going that Jesus and his apostles didn't even have time to eat.

³²So they left by boat for a quiet place, where they could be alone. ³³But many people recognized them and saw them leaving, and people from many towns ran ahead along the shore and got there ahead of them. ³⁴Jesus saw the huge crowd as he stepped from the boat, and he had compassion on them because they were like sheep without a shepherd. So he began teaching them many things.

³⁵Late in the afternoon his disciples came to him and said, "This is a remote place, and it's already getting late. ³⁶Send the crowds away so they can go to the nearby farms and villages and buy something to eat."

³⁷But Jesus said, "You feed them."

"With what?" they asked. "We'd have to work for months to earn enough money* to buy food for all these people!"

6:22 Some manuscripts read *the daughter of Herodias herself.*   **6:37** Greek *It would take 200 denarii.* A denarius was equivalent to a laborer's full day's wage.

³⁸"How much bread do you have?" he asked. "Go and find out."

They came back and reported, "We have five loaves of bread and two fish."

³⁹Then Jesus told the disciples to have the people sit down in groups on the green grass. ⁴⁰So they sat down in groups of fifty or a hundred.

⁴¹Jesus took the five loaves and two fish, looked up toward heaven, and blessed them. Then, breaking the loaves into pieces, he kept giving the bread to the disciples so they could distribute it to the people. He also divided the fish for everyone to share. ⁴²They all ate as much as they wanted, ⁴³and afterward, the disciples picked up twelve baskets of leftover bread and fish. ⁴⁴A total of 5,000 men and their families were fed from those loaves!

Jesus Walks on Water

⁴⁵Immediately after this, Jesus insisted that his disciples get back into the boat and head across the lake to Bethsaida, while he sent the people home. ⁴⁶After telling everyone good-bye, he went up into the hills by himself to pray.

⁴⁷Late that night, the disciples were in their boat in the middle of the lake, and Jesus was alone on land. ⁴⁸He saw that they were in serious trouble, rowing hard and struggling against the wind and waves. About three o'clock in the morning* Jesus came toward them, walking on the water. He intended to go past them, ⁴⁹but when they saw him walking on the water, they cried out in terror, thinking he was a ghost. ⁵⁰They were all terrified when they saw him.

But Jesus spoke to them at once. "Don't be afraid," he said. "Take courage! I am here!*" ⁵¹Then he climbed into the boat, and the wind stopped. They were totally amazed, ⁵²for they still didn't understand the significance of the miracle of the loaves. Their hearts were too hard to take it in.

⁵³After they had crossed the lake, they landed at Gennesaret. They brought the boat to shore ⁵⁴and climbed out. The people recognized Jesus at once, ⁵⁵and they ran throughout the whole area, carrying sick people on mats to wherever they heard he was. ⁵⁶Wherever he went—in villages, cities, or the countryside—they brought the sick out to the marketplaces. They begged him to let the sick touch at least the fringe of his robe, and all who touched him were healed.

CHAPTER 7

Jesus Teaches about Inner Purity

One day some Pharisees and teachers of religious law arrived from Jerusalem to see Jesus. ²They noticed that some of his disciples failed to follow the Jewish ritual of hand washing before eating. ³(The Jews, especially the Pharisees, do not eat until they have poured water over their cupped hands,* as required by their ancient traditions. ⁴Similarly, they don't eat anything from the market until they immerse

---

6:48 Greek *About the fourth watch of the night.* 6:50 Or *The 'I AM' is here;* Greek reads *I am.* See Exod 3:14.
7:3 Greek *have washed with the fist.*

their hands* in water. This is but one of many traditions they have clung to—such as their ceremonial washing of cups, pitchers, and kettles.*)

⁵So the Pharisees and teachers of religious law asked him, "Why don't your disciples follow our age-old tradition? They eat without first performing the hand-washing ceremony."

⁶Jesus replied, "You hypocrites! Isaiah was right when he prophesied about you, for he wrote,

'These people honor me with their lips,
     but their hearts are far from me.
⁷   Their worship is a farce,
     for they teach man-made ideas as commands from God.'*

⁸For you ignore God's law and substitute your own tradition."

⁹Then he said, "You skillfully sidestep God's law in order to hold on to your own tradition. ¹⁰For instance, Moses gave you this law from God: 'Honor your father and mother,'* and 'Anyone who speaks disrespectfully of father or mother must be put to death.'* ¹¹But you say it is all right for people to say to their parents, 'Sorry, I can't help you. For I have vowed to give to God what I would have given to you.'* ¹²In this way, you let them disregard their needy parents. ¹³And so you cancel the word of God in order to hand down your own tradition. And this is only one example among many others."

¹⁴Then Jesus called to the crowd to come and hear. "All of you listen," he said, "and try to understand. ¹⁵It's not what goes into your body that defiles you; you are defiled by what comes from your heart.*"

¹⁷Then Jesus went into a house to get away from the crowd, and his disciples asked him what he meant by the parable he had just used. ¹⁸"Don't you understand either?" he asked. "Can't you see that the food you put into your body cannot defile you? ¹⁹Food doesn't go into your heart, but only passes through the stomach and then goes into the sewer." (By saying this, he declared that every kind of food is acceptable in God's eyes.)

²⁰And then he added, "It is what comes from inside that defiles you. ²¹For from within, out of a person's heart, come evil thoughts, sexual immorality, theft, murder, ²²adultery, greed, wickedness, deceit, lustful desires, envy, slander, pride, and foolishness. ²³All these vile things come from within; they are what defile you."

The Faith of a Gentile Woman

²⁴Then Jesus left Galilee and went north to the region of Tyre.* He didn't want anyone to know which house he was staying in, but he couldn't keep it a secret. ²⁵Right away a woman who had heard about him came and fell at his feet. Her little

---

7:4a Some manuscripts read *sprinkle themselves.*   **7:4b** Some manuscripts add *and dining couches.*   **7:7** Isa 29:13 (Greek version).   **7:10a** Exod 20:12; Deut 5:16.   **7:10b** Exod 21:17 (Greek version); Lev 20:9 (Greek version). **7:11** Greek *'What I would have given to you is Corban' (that is, a gift).*   **7:15** Some manuscripts add verse 16, *Anyone with ears to hear should listen and understand.* Compare 4:9, 23.   **7:24** Some manuscripts add *and Sidon.*

girl was possessed by an evil* spirit, ²⁶and she begged him to cast out the demon from her daughter.

Since she was a Gentile, born in Syrian Phoenicia, ²⁷Jesus told her, "First I should feed the children—my own family, the Jews.* It isn't right to take food from the children and throw it to the dogs."

²⁸She replied, "That's true, Lord, but even the dogs under the table are allowed to eat the scraps from the children's plates."

²⁹"Good answer!" he said. "Now go home, for the demon has left your daughter." ³⁰And when she arrived home, she found her little girl lying quietly in bed, and the demon was gone.

Jesus Heals a Deaf Man

³¹Jesus left Tyre and went up to Sidon before going back to the Sea of Galilee and the region of the Ten Towns.* ³²A deaf man with a speech impediment was brought to him, and the people begged Jesus to lay his hands on the man to heal him.

³³Jesus led him away from the crowd so they could be alone. He put his fingers into the man's ears. Then, spitting on his own fingers, he touched the man's tongue. ³⁴Looking up to heaven, he sighed and said, *"Ephphatha,"* which means, "Be opened!" ³⁵Instantly the man could hear perfectly, and his tongue was freed so he could speak plainly!

³⁶Jesus told the crowd not to tell anyone, but the more he told them not to, the more they spread the news. ³⁷They were completely amazed and said again and again, "Everything he does is wonderful. He even makes the deaf to hear and gives speech to those who cannot speak."

CHAPTER 8

Jesus Feeds Four Thousand

About this time another large crowd had gathered, and the people ran out of food again. Jesus called his disciples and told them, ²"I feel sorry for these people. They have been here with me for three days, and they have nothing left to eat. ³If I send them home hungry, they will faint along the way. For some of them have come a long distance."

⁴His disciples replied, "How are we supposed to find enough food to feed them out here in the wilderness?"

⁵Jesus asked, "How much bread do you have?"

"Seven loaves," they replied.

⁶So Jesus told all the people to sit down on the ground. Then he took the seven loaves, thanked God for them, and broke them into pieces. He gave them to his disciples, who distributed the bread to the crowd. ⁷A few small fish were found, too, so Jesus also blessed these and told the disciples to distribute them.

⁸They ate as much as they wanted. Afterward, the disciples picked up seven

---

7:25 Greek *unclean.*   **7:27** Greek *Let the children eat first.*   **7:31** Greek *Decapolis.*

large baskets of leftover food. [9]There were about 4,000 people in the crowd that day, and Jesus sent them home after they had eaten. [10]Immediately after this, he got into a boat with his disciples and crossed over to the region of Dalmanutha.

Pharisees Demand a Miraculous Sign

[11]When the Pharisees heard that Jesus had arrived, they came and started to argue with him. Testing him, they demanded that he show them a miraculous sign from heaven to prove his authority.

[12]When he heard this, he sighed deeply in his spirit and said, "Why do these people keep demanding a miraculous sign? I tell you the truth, I will not give this generation any such sign." [13]So he got back into the boat and left them, and he crossed to the other side of the lake.

Yeast of the Pharisees and Herod

[14]But the disciples had forgotten to bring any food. They had only one loaf of bread with them in the boat. [15]As they were crossing the lake, Jesus warned them, "Watch out! Beware of the yeast of the Pharisees and of Herod."

[16]At this they began to argue with each other because they hadn't brought any bread. [17]Jesus knew what they were saying, so he said, "Why are you arguing about having no bread? Don't you know or understand even yet? Are your hearts too hard to take it in? [18]'You have eyes—can't you see? You have ears—can't you hear?'* Don't you remember anything at all? [19]When I fed the 5,000 with five loaves of bread, how many baskets of leftovers did you pick up afterward?"

"Twelve," they said.

[20]"And when I fed the 4,000 with seven loaves, how many large baskets of leftovers did you pick up?"

"Seven," they said.

[21]"Don't you understand yet?" he asked them.

Jesus Heals a Blind Man

[22]When they arrived at Bethsaida, some people brought a blind man to Jesus, and they begged him to touch the man and heal him. [23]Jesus took the blind man by the hand and led him out of the village. Then, spitting on the man's eyes, he laid his hands on him and asked, "Can you see anything now?"

[24]The man looked around. "Yes," he said, "I see people, but I can't see them very clearly. They look like trees walking around."

[25]Then Jesus placed his hands on the man's eyes again, and his eyes were opened. His sight was completely restored, and he could see everything clearly. [26]Jesus sent him away, saying, "Don't go back into the village on your way home."

Peter's Declaration about Jesus

[27]Jesus and his disciples left Galilee and went up to the villages near Caesarea Philippi. As they were walking along, he asked them, "Who do people say I am?"

8:18 Jer 5:21.

[28]"Well," they replied, "some say John the Baptist, some say Elijah, and others say you are one of the other prophets."

[29]Then he asked them, "But who do you say I am?"

Peter replied, "You are the Messiah.*"

[30]But Jesus warned them not to tell anyone about him.

Jesus Predicts His Death

[31]Then Jesus began to tell them that the Son of Man* must suffer many terrible things and be rejected by the elders, the leading priests, and the teachers of religious law. He would be killed, but three days later he would rise from the dead. [32]As he talked about this openly with his disciples, Peter took him aside and began to reprimand him for saying such things.*

[33]Jesus turned around and looked at his disciples, then reprimanded Peter. "Get away from me, Satan!" he said. "You are seeing things merely from a human point of view, not from God's."

[34]Then, calling the crowd to join his disciples, he said, "If any of you wants to be my follower, you must turn from your selfish ways, take up your cross, and follow me. [35]If you try to hang on to your life, you will lose it. But if you give up your life for my sake and for the sake of the Good News, you will save it. [36]And what do you benefit if you gain the whole world but lose your own soul?* [37]Is anything worth more than your soul? [38]If anyone is ashamed of me and my message in these adulterous and sinful days, the Son of Man will be ashamed of that person when he returns in the glory of his Father with the holy angels."

CHAPTER 9

Jesus went on to say, "I tell you the truth, some standing here right now will not die before they see the Kingdom of God arrive in great power!"

The Transfiguration

[2]Six days later Jesus took Peter, James, and John, and led them up a high mountain to be alone. As the men watched, Jesus' appearance was transformed, [3]and his clothes became dazzling white, far whiter than any earthly bleach could ever make them. [4]Then Elijah and Moses appeared and began talking with Jesus.

[5]Peter exclaimed, "Rabbi, it's wonderful for us to be here! Let's make three shelters as memorials*—one for you, one for Moses, and one for Elijah." [6]He said this because he didn't really know what else to say, for they were all terrified.

[7]Then a cloud overshadowed them, and a voice from the cloud said, "This is

---

8:29 Or *the Christ. Messiah* (a Hebrew term) and *Christ* (a Greek term) both mean "the anointed one."   **8:31** "Son of Man" is a title Jesus used for himself.   **8:32** Or *began to correct him.*   **8:36** Or *your self?* also in 8:37.   **9:5** Greek *three tabernacles.*

my dearly loved Son. Listen to him." [8]Suddenly, when they looked around, Moses and Elijah were gone, and they saw only Jesus with them.

[9]As they went back down the mountain, he told them not to tell anyone what they had seen until the Son of Man* had risen from the dead. [10]So they kept it to themselves, but they often asked each other what he meant by "rising from the dead."

[11]Then they asked him, "Why do the teachers of religious law insist that Elijah must return before the Messiah comes?*"

[12]Jesus responded, "Elijah is indeed coming first to get everything ready. Yet why do the Scriptures say that the Son of Man must suffer greatly and be treated with utter contempt? [13]But I tell you, Elijah has already come, and they chose to abuse him, just as the Scriptures predicted."

Jesus Heals a Demon-Possessed Boy

[14]When they returned to the other disciples, they saw a large crowd surrounding them, and some teachers of religious law were arguing with them. [15]When the crowd saw Jesus, they were overwhelmed with awe, and they ran to greet him.

[16]"What is all this arguing about?" Jesus asked.

[17]One of the men in the crowd spoke up and said, "Teacher, I brought my son so you could heal him. He is possessed by an evil spirit that won't let him talk. [18]And whenever this spirit seizes him, it throws him violently to the ground. Then he foams at the mouth and grinds his teeth and becomes rigid.* So I asked your disciples to cast out the evil spirit, but they couldn't do it."

[19]Jesus said to them,* "You faithless people! How long must I be with you? How long must I put up with you? Bring the boy to me."

[20]So they brought the boy. But when the evil spirit saw Jesus, it threw the child into a violent convulsion, and he fell to the ground, writhing and foaming at the mouth.

[21]"How long has this been happening?" Jesus asked the boy's father.

He replied, "Since he was a little boy. [22]The spirit often throws him into the fire or into water, trying to kill him. Have mercy on us and help us, if you can."

[23]"What do you mean, 'If I can'?" Jesus asked. "Anything is possible if a person believes."

[24]The father instantly cried out, "I do believe, but help me overcome my unbelief!"

[25]When Jesus saw that the crowd of onlookers was growing, he rebuked the evil* spirit. "Listen, you spirit that makes this boy unable to hear and speak," he said. "I command you to come out of this child and never enter him again!"

[26]Then the spirit screamed and threw the boy into another violent convulsion and left him. The boy appeared to be dead. A murmur ran through the crowd as people said, "He's dead." [27]But Jesus took him by the hand and helped him to his feet, and he stood up.

9:9 "Son of Man" is a title Jesus used for himself.   **9:11** Greek *that Elijah must come first?*   **9:18** Or *becomes weak.*   **9:19** Or *said to his disciples.*   **9:25** Greek *unclean.*

²⁸Afterward, when Jesus was alone in the house with his disciples, they asked him, "Why couldn't we cast out that evil spirit?"

²⁹Jesus replied, "This kind can be cast out only by prayer.*"

Jesus Again Predicts His Death

³⁰Leaving that region, they traveled through Galilee. Jesus didn't want anyone to know he was there, ³¹for he wanted to spend more time with his disciples and teach them. He said to them, "The Son of Man is going to be betrayed into the hands of his enemies. He will be killed, but three days later he will rise from the dead." ³²They didn't understand what he was saying, however, and they were afraid to ask him what he meant.

The Greatest in the Kingdom

³³After they arrived at Capernaum and settled in a house, Jesus asked his disciples, "What were you discussing out on the road?" ³⁴But they didn't answer, because they had been arguing about which of them was the greatest. ³⁵He sat down, called the twelve disciples over to him, and said, "Whoever wants to be first must take last place and be the servant of everyone else."

³⁶Then he put a little child among them. Taking the child in his arms, he said to them, ³⁷"Anyone who welcomes a little child like this on my behalf* welcomes me, and anyone who welcomes me welcomes not only me but also my Father who sent me."

Using the Name of Jesus

³⁸John said to Jesus, "Teacher, we saw someone using your name to cast out demons, but we told him to stop because he wasn't in our group."

³⁹"Don't stop him!" Jesus said. "No one who performs a miracle in my name will soon be able to speak evil of me. ⁴⁰Anyone who is not against us is for us. ⁴¹If anyone gives you even a cup of water because you belong to the Messiah, I tell you the truth, that person will surely be rewarded.

⁴²"But if you cause one of these little ones who trusts in me to fall into sin, it would be better for you to be thrown into the sea with a large millstone hung around your neck. ⁴³If your hand causes you to sin, cut it off. It's better to enter eternal life with only one hand than to go into the unquenchable fires of hell* with two hands.* ⁴⁵If your foot causes you to sin, cut it off. It's better to enter eternal life with only one foot than to be thrown into hell with two feet.* ⁴⁷And if your eye causes you to sin, gouge it out. It's better to enter the Kingdom of God with only one eye than to have two eyes and be thrown into hell, ⁴⁸'where the maggots never die and the fire never goes out.'*

⁴⁹"For everyone will be tested with fire.* ⁵⁰Salt is good for seasoning. But if it loses its flavor, how do you make it salty again? You must have the qualities of salt among yourselves and live in peace with each other."

9:29 Some manuscripts read *by prayer and fasting.*   **9:37** Greek *in my name.*   **9:43a** Greek *Gehenna;* also in 9:45, 47.   **9:43b** Some manuscripts add verse 44, *'where the maggots never die and the fire never goes out.'* See 9:48.   **9:45** Some manuscripts add verse 46, *'where the maggots never die and the fire never goes out.'* See 9:48.   **9:48** Isa 66:24.   **9:49** Greek *salted with fire;* other manuscripts add *and every sacrifice will be salted with salt.*

CHAPTER 10

Discussion about Divorce and Marriage

Then Jesus left Capernaum and went down to the region of Judea and into the area east of the Jordan River. Once again crowds gathered around him, and as usual he was teaching them.

²Some Pharisees came and tried to trap him with this question: "Should a man be allowed to divorce his wife?"

³Jesus answered them with a question: "What did Moses say in the law about divorce?"

⁴"Well, he permitted it," they replied. "He said a man can give his wife a written notice of divorce and send her away."*

⁵But Jesus responded, "He wrote this commandment only as a concession to your hard hearts. ⁶But 'God made them male and female'* from the beginning of creation. ⁷'This explains why a man leaves his father and mother and is joined to his wife,* ⁸and the two are united into one.'* Since they are no longer two but one, ⁹let no one split apart what God has joined together."

¹⁰Later, when he was alone with his disciples in the house, they brought up the subject again. ¹¹He told them, "Whoever divorces his wife and marries someone else commits adultery against her. ¹²And if a woman divorces her husband and marries someone else, she commits adultery."

Jesus Blesses the Children

¹³One day some parents brought their children to Jesus so he could touch and bless them. But the disciples scolded the parents for bothering him.

¹⁴When Jesus saw what was happening, he was angry with his disciples. He said to them, "Let the children come to me. Don't stop them! For the Kingdom of God belongs to those who are like these children. ¹⁵I tell you the truth, anyone who doesn't receive the Kingdom of God like a child will never enter it." ¹⁶Then he took the children in his arms and placed his hands on their heads and blessed them.

The Rich Man

¹⁷As Jesus was starting out on his way to Jerusalem, a man came running up to him, knelt down, and asked, "Good Teacher, what must I do to inherit eternal life?"

¹⁸"Why do you call me good?" Jesus asked. "Only God is truly good. ¹⁹But to answer your question, you know the commandments: 'You must not murder. You must not commit adultery. You must not steal. You must not testify falsely. You must not cheat anyone. Honor your father and mother.'*"

²⁰"Teacher," the man replied, "I've obeyed all these commandments since I was young."

²¹Looking at the man, Jesus felt genuine love for him. "There is still one thing you

---

10:4 See Deut 24:1.   **10:6** Gen 1:27; 5:2.   **10:7** Some manuscripts do not include *and is joined to his wife.*
10:7-8 Gen 2:24.   **10:19** Exod 20:12-16; Deut 5:16-20.

haven't done," he told him. "Go and sell all your possessions and give the money to the poor, and you will have treasure in heaven. Then come, follow me."

²²At this the man's face fell, and he went away sad, for he had many possessions.

²³Jesus looked around and said to his disciples, "How hard it is for the rich to enter the Kingdom of God!" ²⁴This amazed them. But Jesus said again, "Dear children, it is very hard* to enter the Kingdom of God. ²⁵In fact, it is easier for a camel to go through the eye of a needle than for a rich person to enter the Kingdom of God!"

²⁶The disciples were astounded. "Then who in the world can be saved?" they asked.

²⁷Jesus looked at them intently and said, "Humanly speaking, it is impossible. But not with God. Everything is possible with God."

²⁸Then Peter began to speak up. "We've given up everything to follow you," he said.

²⁹"Yes," Jesus replied, "and I assure you that everyone who has given up house or brothers or sisters or mother or father or children or property, for my sake and for the Good News, ³⁰will receive now in return a hundred times as many houses, brothers, sisters, mothers, children, and property—along with persecution. And in the world to come that person will have eternal life. ³¹But many who are the greatest now will be least important then, and those who seem least important now will be the greatest then.*"

Jesus Again Predicts His Death

³²They were now on the way up to Jerusalem, and Jesus was walking ahead of them. The disciples were filled with awe, and the people following behind were overwhelmed with fear. Taking the twelve disciples aside, Jesus once more began to describe everything that was about to happen to him. ³³"Listen," he said, "we're going up to Jerusalem, where the Son of Man* will be betrayed to the leading priests and the teachers of religious law. They will sentence him to die and hand him over to the Romans.* ³⁴They will mock him, spit on him, flog him with a whip, and kill him, but after three days he will rise again."

Jesus Teaches about Serving Others

³⁵Then James and John, the sons of Zebedee, came over and spoke to him. "Teacher," they said, "we want you to do us a favor."

³⁶"What is your request?" he asked.

³⁷They replied, "When you sit on your glorious throne, we want to sit in places of honor next to you, one on your right and the other on your left."

³⁸But Jesus said to them, "You don't know what you are asking! Are you able to drink from the bitter cup of suffering I am about to drink? Are you able to be baptized with the baptism of suffering I must be baptized with?"

10:24 Some manuscripts read *very hard for those who trust in riches.*   **10:31** Greek *But many who are first will be last; and the last, first.*   **10:33a** "Son of Man" is a title Jesus used for himself.   **10:33b** Greek *the Gentiles.*

[39]"Oh yes," they replied, "we are able!"

Then Jesus told them, "You will indeed drink from my bitter cup and be baptized with my baptism of suffering. [40]But I have no right to say who will sit on my right or my left. God has prepared those places for the ones he has chosen."

[41]When the ten other disciples heard what James and John had asked, they were indignant. [42]So Jesus called them together and said, "You know that the rulers in this world lord it over their people, and officials flaunt their authority over those under them. [43]But among you it will be different. Whoever wants to be a leader among you must be your servant, [44]and whoever wants to be first among you must be the slave of everyone else. [45]For even the Son of Man came not to be served but to serve others and to give his life as a ransom for many."

Jesus Heals Blind Bartimaeus

[46]Then they reached Jericho, and as Jesus and his disciples left town, a large crowd followed him. A blind beggar named Bartimaeus (son of Timaeus) was sitting beside the road. [47]When Bartimaeus heard that Jesus of Nazareth was nearby, he began to shout, "Jesus, Son of David, have mercy on me!"

[48]"Be quiet!" many of the people yelled at him.

But he only shouted louder, "Son of David, have mercy on me!"

[49]When Jesus heard him, he stopped and said, "Tell him to come here."

So they called the blind man. "Cheer up," they said. "Come on, he's calling you!" [50]Bartimaeus threw aside his coat, jumped up, and came to Jesus.

[51]"What do you want me to do for you?" Jesus asked.

"My rabbi,*" the blind man said, "I want to see!"

[52]And Jesus said to him, "Go, for your faith has healed you." Instantly the man could see, and he followed Jesus down the road.*

CHAPTER 11

Jesus' Triumphant Entry

As Jesus and his disciples approached Jerusalem, they came to the towns of Bethphage and Bethany on the Mount of Olives. Jesus sent two of them on ahead. [2]"Go into that village over there," he told them. "As soon as you enter it, you will see a young donkey tied there that no one has ever ridden. Untie it and bring it here. [3]If anyone asks, 'What are you doing?' just say, 'The Lord needs it and will return it soon.'"

[4]The two disciples left and found the colt standing in the street, tied outside the front door. [5]As they were untying it, some bystanders demanded, "What are you doing, untying that colt?" [6]They said what Jesus had told them to say, and they were permitted to take it. [7]Then they brought the colt to Jesus and threw their garments over it, and he sat on it.

10:51 Greek uses the Hebrew term *Rabboni.*   **10:52** Or *on the way.*

[8] Many in the crowd spread their garments on the road ahead of him, and others spread leafy branches they had cut in the fields. [9] Jesus was in the center of the procession, and the people all around him were shouting,

"Praise God!*
Blessings on the one who comes in the name of the LORD!
[10] Blessings on the coming Kingdom of our ancestor David!
Praise God in highest heaven!"*

[11] So Jesus came to Jerusalem and went into the Temple. After looking around carefully at everything, he left because it was late in the afternoon. Then he returned to Bethany with the twelve disciples.

Jesus Curses the Fig Tree

[12] The next morning as they were leaving Bethany, Jesus was hungry. [13] He noticed a fig tree in full leaf a little way off, so he went over to see if he could find any figs. But there were only leaves because it was too early in the season for fruit. [14] Then Jesus said to the tree, "May no one ever eat your fruit again!" And the disciples heard him say it.

Jesus Clears the Temple

[15] When they arrived back in Jerusalem, Jesus entered the Temple and began to drive out the people buying and selling animals for sacrifices. He knocked over the tables of the money changers and the chairs of those selling doves, [16] and he stopped everyone from using the Temple as a marketplace.* [17] He said to them, "The Scriptures declare, 'My Temple will be called a house of prayer for all nations,' but you have turned it into a den of thieves."*

[18] When the leading priests and teachers of religious law heard what Jesus had done, they began planning how to kill him. But they were afraid of him because the people were so amazed at his teaching.

[19] That evening Jesus and the disciples left* the city.

[20] The next morning as they passed by the fig tree he had cursed, the disciples noticed it had withered from the roots up. [21] Peter remembered what Jesus had said to the tree on the previous day and exclaimed, "Look, Rabbi! The fig tree you cursed has withered and died!"

[22] Then Jesus said to the disciples, "Have faith in God. [23] I tell you the truth, you can say to this mountain, 'May you be lifted up and thrown into the sea,' and it will happen. But you must really believe it will happen and have no doubt in your heart. [24] I tell you, you can pray for anything, and if you believe that you've received it, it will be yours. [25] But when you are praying, first forgive anyone you are holding a grudge against, so that your Father in heaven will forgive your sins, too.*"

11:9 Greek *Hosanna,* an exclamation of praise that literally means "save now"; also in 11:10.   11:9-10 Pss 118:25-26; 148:1.   11:16 Or *from carrying merchandise through the Temple.*   11:17 Isa 56:7; Jer 7:11.   11:19 Greek *they left;* other manuscripts read *he left.*   11:25 Some manuscripts add verse 26, *But if you refuse to forgive, your Father in heaven will not forgive your sins.* Compare Matt 6:15.

The Authority of Jesus Challenged

²⁷Again they entered Jerusalem. As Jesus was walking through the Temple area, the leading priests, the teachers of religious law, and the elders came up to him. ²⁸They demanded, "By what authority are you doing all these things? Who gave you the right to do them?"

²⁹"I'll tell you by what authority I do these things if you answer one question," Jesus replied. ³⁰"Did John's authority to baptize come from heaven, or was it merely human? Answer me!"

³¹They talked it over among themselves. "If we say it was from heaven, he will ask why we didn't believe John. ³²But do we dare say it was merely human?" For they were afraid of what the people would do, because everyone believed that John was a prophet. ³³So they finally replied, "We don't know."

And Jesus responded, "Then I won't tell you by what authority I do these things."

CHAPTER 12

Parable of the Evil Farmers

Then Jesus began teaching them with stories: "A man planted a vineyard. He built a wall around it, dug a pit for pressing out the grape juice, and built a look-out tower. Then he leased the vineyard to tenant farmers and moved to another country. ²At the time of the grape harvest, he sent one of his servants to collect his share of the crop. ³But the farmers grabbed the servant, beat him up, and sent him back empty-handed. ⁴The owner then sent another servant, but they insulted him and beat him over the head. ⁵The next servant he sent was killed. Others he sent were either beaten or killed, ⁶until there was only one left—his son whom he loved dearly. The owner finally sent him, thinking, 'Surely they will respect my son.'

⁷"But the tenant farmers said to one another, 'Here comes the heir to this estate. Let's kill him and get the estate for ourselves!' ⁸So they grabbed him and murdered him and threw his body out of the vineyard.

⁹"What do you suppose the owner of the vineyard will do?" Jesus asked. "I'll tell you—he will come and kill those farmers and lease the vineyard to others. ¹⁰Didn't you ever read this in the Scriptures?

'The stone that the builders rejected
    has now become the cornerstone.
¹¹ This is the LORD's doing,
    and it is wonderful to see.'*"

¹²The religious leaders* wanted to arrest Jesus because they realized he was telling the story against them—they were the wicked farmers. But they were afraid of the crowd, so they left him and went away.

12:10-11 Ps 118:22-23. **12:12** Greek *They.*

Taxes for Caesar

¹³Later the leaders sent some Pharisees and supporters of Herod to trap Jesus into saying something for which he could be arrested. ¹⁴"Teacher," they said, "we know how honest you are. You are impartial and don't play favorites. You teach the way of God truthfully. Now tell us—is it right to pay taxes to Caesar or not? ¹⁵Should we pay them, or shouldn't we?"

Jesus saw through their hypocrisy and said, "Why are you trying to trap me? Show me a Roman coin,* and I'll tell you." ¹⁶When they handed it to him, he asked, "Whose picture and title are stamped on it?"

"Caesar's," they replied.

¹⁷"Well, then," Jesus said, "give to Caesar what belongs to Caesar, and give to God what belongs to God."

His reply completely amazed them.

Discussion about Resurrection

¹⁸Then Jesus was approached by some Sadducees—religious leaders who say there is no resurrection from the dead. They posed this question: ¹⁹"Teacher, Moses gave us a law that if a man dies, leaving a wife without children, his brother should marry the widow and have a child who will carry on the brother's name.* ²⁰Well, suppose there were seven brothers. The oldest one married and then died without children. ²¹So the second brother married the widow, but he also died without children. Then the third brother married her. ²²This continued with all seven of them, and still there were no children. Last of all, the woman also died. ²³So tell us, whose wife will she be in the resurrection? For all seven were married to her."

²⁴Jesus replied, "Your mistake is that you don't know the Scriptures, and you don't know the power of God. ²⁵For when the dead rise, they will neither marry nor be given in marriage. In this respect they will be like the angels in heaven.

²⁶"But now, as to whether the dead will be raised—haven't you ever read about this in the writings of Moses, in the story of the burning bush? Long after Abraham, Isaac, and Jacob had died, God said to Moses,* 'I am the God of Abraham, the God of Isaac, and the God of Jacob.'* ²⁷So he is the God of the living, not the dead. You have made a serious error."

The Most Important Commandment

²⁸One of the teachers of religious law was standing there listening to the debate. He realized that Jesus had answered well, so he asked, "Of all the commandments, which is the most important?"

²⁹Jesus replied, "The most important commandment is this: 'Listen, O Israel! The LORD our God is the one and only LORD. ³⁰And you must love the LORD your God with all your heart, all your soul, all your mind, and all your strength.'* ³¹The second is equally important: 'Love your neighbor as yourself.'* No other commandment is greater than these."

12:15 Greek *a denarius.*   12:19 See Deut 25:5-6.   12:26a Greek *in the story of the bush? God said to him.*
12:26b Exod 3:6.   12:29-30 Deut 6:4-5.   12:31 Lev 19:18.

³²The teacher of religious law replied, "Well said, Teacher. You have spoken the truth by saying that there is only one God and no other. ³³And I know it is important to love him with all my heart and all my understanding and all my strength, and to love my neighbor as myself. This is more important than to offer all of the burnt offerings and sacrifices required in the law."

³⁴Realizing how much the man understood, Jesus said to him, "You are not far from the Kingdom of God." And after that, no one dared to ask him any more questions.

Whose Son Is the Messiah?

³⁵Later, as Jesus was teaching the people in the Temple, he asked, "Why do the teachers of religious law claim that the Messiah is the son of David? ³⁶For David himself, speaking under the inspiration of the Holy Spirit, said,

> 'The LORD said to my Lord,
> Sit in the place of honor at my right hand
>   until I humble your enemies beneath your feet.'*

³⁷Since David himself called the Messiah 'my Lord,' how can the Messiah be his son?" The large crowd listened to him with great delight.

³⁸Jesus also taught: "Beware of these teachers of religious law! For they like to parade around in flowing robes and receive respectful greetings as they walk in the marketplaces. ³⁹And how they love the seats of honor in the synagogues and the head table at banquets. ⁴⁰Yet they shamelessly cheat widows out of their property and then pretend to be pious by making long prayers in public. Because of this, they will be more severely punished."

The Widow's Offering

⁴¹Jesus sat down near the collection box in the Temple and watched as the crowds dropped in their money. Many rich people put in large amounts. ⁴²Then a poor widow came and dropped in two small coins.*

⁴³Jesus called his disciples to him and said, "I tell you the truth, this poor widow has given more than all the others who are making contributions. ⁴⁴For they gave a tiny part of their surplus, but she, poor as she is, has given everything she had to live on."

CHAPTER 13

Jesus Foretells the Future

As Jesus was leaving the Temple that day, one of his disciples said, "Teacher, look at these magnificent buildings! Look at the impressive stones in the walls."

²Jesus replied, "Yes, look at these great buildings. But they will be completely demolished. Not one stone will be left on top of another!"

³Later, Jesus sat on the Mount of Olives across the valley from the Temple. Peter,

---

12:36 Ps 110:1. **12:42** Greek *two lepta, which is a kodrantes* [i.e., a quadrans].

James, John, and Andrew came to him privately and asked him, [4]"Tell us, when will all this happen? What sign will show us that these things are about to be fulfilled?"

[5]Jesus replied, "Don't let anyone mislead you, [6]for many will come in my name, claiming, 'I am the Messiah.'* They will deceive many. [7]And you will hear of wars and threats of wars, but don't panic. Yes, these things must take place, but the end won't follow immediately. [8]Nation will go to war against nation, and kingdom against kingdom. There will be earthquakes in many parts of the world, as well as famines. But this is only the first of the birth pains, with more to come.

[9]"When these things begin to happen, watch out! You will be handed over to the local councils and beaten in the synagogues. You will stand trial before governors and kings because you are my followers. But this will be your opportunity to tell them about me.* [10]For the Good News must first be preached to all nations.* [11]But when you are arrested and stand trial, don't worry in advance about what to say. Just say what God tells you at that time, for it is not you who will be speaking, but the Holy Spirit.

[12]"A brother will betray his brother to death, a father will betray his own child, and children will rebel against their parents and cause them to be killed. [13]And everyone will hate you because you are my followers.* But the one who endures to the end will be saved.

[14]"The day is coming when you will see the sacrilegious object that causes desecration* standing where he* should not be." (Reader, pay attention!) "Then those in Judea must flee to the hills. [15]A person out on the deck of a roof must not go down into the house to pack. [16]A person out in the field must not return even to get a coat. [17]How terrible it will be for pregnant women and for nursing mothers in those days. [18]And pray that your flight will not be in winter. [19]For there will be greater anguish in those days than at any time since God created the world. And it will never be so great again. [20]In fact, unless the Lord shortens that time of calamity, not a single person will survive. But for the sake of his chosen ones he has shortened those days.

[21]"Then if anyone tells you, 'Look, here is the Messiah,' or 'There he is,' don't believe it. [22]For false messiahs and false prophets will rise up and perform signs and wonders so as to deceive, if possible, even God's chosen ones. [23]Watch out! I have warned you about this ahead of time!

[24]"At that time, after the anguish of those days,

the sun will be darkened,
the moon will give no light,
[25] the stars will fall from the sky,
and the powers in the heavens will be shaken.*

[26]Then everyone will see the Son of Man* coming on the clouds with great power and glory.* [27]And he will send out his angels to gather his chosen ones from all over the world*—from the farthest ends of the earth and heaven.

13:6 Greek claiming, 'I am.'   13:9 Or But this will be your testimony against them.   13:10 Or all peoples.
13:13 Greek on account of my name.   13:14a Greek the abomination of desolation. See Dan 9:27; 11:31; 12:11.
13:14b Or it.   13:24-25 See Isa 13:10; 34:4; Joel 2:10.   13:26a "Son of Man" is a title Jesus used for himself.
13:26b See Dan 7:13.   13:27 Greek from the four winds.

²⁸"Now learn a lesson from the fig tree. When its branches bud and its leaves begin to sprout, you know that summer is near. ²⁹In the same way, when you see all these things taking place, you can know that his return is very near, right at the door. ³⁰I tell you the truth, this generation* will not pass from the scene before all these things take place. ³¹Heaven and earth will disappear, but my words will never disappear.

³²"However, no one knows the day or hour when these things will happen, not even the angels in heaven or the Son himself. Only the Father knows. ³³And since you don't know when that time will come, be on guard! Stay alert*!

³⁴"The coming of the Son of Man can be illustrated by the story of a man going on a long trip. When he left home, he gave each of his slaves instructions about the work they were to do, and he told the gatekeeper to watch for his return. ³⁵You, too, must keep watch! For you don't know when the master of the household will return—in the evening, at midnight, before dawn, or at daybreak. ³⁶Don't let him find you sleeping when he arrives without warning. ³⁷I say to you what I say to everyone: Watch for him!"

CHAPTER 14

Jesus Anointed at Bethany

It was now two days before Passover and the Festival of Unleavened Bread. The leading priests and the teachers of religious law were still looking for an opportunity to capture Jesus secretly and kill him. ²"But not during the Passover celebration," they agreed, "or the people may riot."

³Meanwhile, Jesus was in Bethany at the home of Simon, a man who had previously had leprosy. While he was eating,* a woman came in with a beautiful alabaster jar of expensive perfume made from essence of nard. She broke open the jar and poured the perfume over his head.

⁴Some of those at the table were indignant. "Why waste such expensive perfume?" they asked. ⁵"It could have been sold for a year's wages* and the money given to the poor!" So they scolded her harshly.

⁶But Jesus replied, "Leave her alone. Why criticize her for doing such a good thing to me? ⁷You will always have the poor among you, and you can help them whenever you want to. But you will not always have me. ⁸She has done what she could and has anointed my body for burial ahead of time. ⁹I tell you the truth, wherever the Good News is preached throughout the world, this woman's deed will be remembered and discussed."

Judas Agrees to Betray Jesus

¹⁰Then Judas Iscariot, one of the twelve disciples, went to the leading priests to arrange to betray Jesus to them. ¹¹They were delighted when they heard why

---

13:30 Or *this age,* or *this nation.*   **13:33** Some manuscripts add *and pray.*   **14:3** Or *reclining.*   **14:5** Greek *for 300 denarii.* A denarius was equivalent to a laborer's full day's wage.

he had come, and they promised to give him money. So he began looking for an opportunity to betray Jesus.

The Last Supper

¹²On the first day of the Festival of Unleavened Bread, when the Passover lamb is sacrificed, Jesus' disciples asked him, "Where do you want us to go to prepare the Passover meal for you?"

¹³So Jesus sent two of them into Jerusalem with these instructions: "As you go into the city, a man carrying a pitcher of water will meet you. Follow him. ¹⁴At the house he enters, say to the owner, 'The Teacher asks: Where is the guest room where I can eat the Passover meal with my disciples?' ¹⁵He will take you upstairs to a large room that is already set up. That is where you should prepare our meal."

¹⁶So the two disciples went into the city and found everything just as Jesus had said, and they prepared the Passover meal there.

¹⁷In the evening Jesus arrived with the twelve disciples.* ¹⁸As they were at the table* eating, Jesus said, "I tell you the truth, one of you eating with me here will betray me."

¹⁹Greatly distressed, each one asked in turn, "Am I the one?"

²⁰He replied, "It is one of you twelve who is eating from this bowl with me. ²¹For the Son of Man* must die, as the Scriptures declared long ago. But how terrible it will be for the one who betrays him. It would be far better for that man if he had never been born!"

²²As they were eating, Jesus took some bread and blessed it. Then he broke it in pieces and gave it to the disciples, saying, "Take it, for this is my body."

²³And he took a cup of wine and gave thanks to God for it. He gave it to them, and they all drank from it. ²⁴And he said to them, "This is my blood, which confirms the covenant* between God and his people. It is poured out as a sacrifice for many. ²⁵I tell you the truth, I will not drink wine again until the day I drink it new in the Kingdom of God."

²⁶Then they sang a hymn and went out to the Mount of Olives.

Jesus Predicts Peter's Denial

²⁷On the way, Jesus told them, "All of you will desert me. For the Scriptures say,

'God will strike* the Shepherd,
and the sheep will be scattered.'

²⁸But after I am raised from the dead, I will go ahead of you to Galilee and meet you there."

²⁹Peter said to him, "Even if everyone else deserts you, I never will."

³⁰Jesus replied, "I tell you the truth, Peter—this very night, before the rooster crows twice, you will deny three times that you even know me."

14:17 Greek *the Twelve.*   14:18 Or *As they reclined.*   14:21 "Son of Man" is a title Jesus used for himself.
14:24 Some manuscripts read *the new covenant.*   14:27 Greek *I will strike.* Zech 13:7.

³¹"No!" Peter declared emphatically. "Even if I have to die with you, I will never deny you!" And all the others vowed the same.

Jesus Prays in Gethsemane

³²They went to the olive grove called Gethsemane, and Jesus said, "Sit here while I go and pray." ³³He took Peter, James, and John with him, and he became deeply troubled and distressed. ³⁴He told them, "My soul is crushed with grief to the point of death. Stay here and keep watch with me."

³⁵He went on a little farther and fell to the ground. He prayed that, if it were possible, the awful hour awaiting him might pass him by. ³⁶"Abba, Father,"* he cried out, "everything is possible for you. Please take this cup of suffering away from me. Yet I want your will to be done, not mine."

³⁷Then he returned and found the disciples asleep. He said to Peter, "Simon, are you asleep? Couldn't you watch with me even one hour? ³⁸Keep watch and pray, so that you will not give in to temptation. For the spirit is willing, but the body is weak."

³⁹Then Jesus left them again and prayed the same prayer as before. ⁴⁰When he returned to them again, he found them sleeping, for they couldn't keep their eyes open. And they didn't know what to say.

⁴¹When he returned to them the third time, he said, "Go ahead and sleep. Have your rest. But no—the time has come. The Son of Man is betrayed into the hands of sinners. ⁴²Up, let's be going. Look, my betrayer is here!"

Jesus Is Betrayed and Arrested

⁴³And immediately, even as Jesus said this, Judas, one of the twelve disciples, arrived with a crowd of men armed with swords and clubs. They had been sent by the leading priests, the teachers of religious law, and the elders. ⁴⁴The traitor, Judas, had given them a prearranged signal: "You will know which one to arrest when I greet him with a kiss. Then you can take him away under guard." ⁴⁵As soon as they arrived, Judas walked up to Jesus. "Rabbi!" he exclaimed, and gave him the kiss.

⁴⁶Then the others grabbed Jesus and arrested him. ⁴⁷But one of the men with Jesus pulled out his sword and struck the high priest's slave, slashing off his ear.

⁴⁸Jesus asked them, "Am I some dangerous revolutionary, that you come with swords and clubs to arrest me? ⁴⁹Why didn't you arrest me in the Temple? I was there among you teaching every day. But these things are happening to fulfill what the Scriptures say about me."

⁵⁰Then all his disciples deserted him and ran away. ⁵¹One young man following behind was clothed only in a long linen shirt. When the mob tried to grab him, ⁵²he slipped out of his shirt and ran away naked.

Jesus before the Council

⁵³They took Jesus to the high priest's home where the leading priests, the elders, and the teachers of religious law had gathered. ⁵⁴Meanwhile, Peter followed him at a distance and went right into the high priest's courtyard. There he sat with the guards, warming himself by the fire.

14:36 *Abba* is an Aramaic term for "father."

⁵⁵Inside, the leading priests and the entire high council* were trying to find evidence against Jesus, so they could put him to death. But they couldn't find any. ⁵⁶Many false witnesses spoke against him, but they contradicted each other. ⁵⁷Finally, some men stood up and gave this false testimony: ⁵⁸"We heard him say, 'I will destroy this Temple made with human hands, and in three days I will build another, made without human hands.'" ⁵⁹But even then they didn't get their stories straight!

⁶⁰Then the high priest stood up before the others and asked Jesus, "Well, aren't you going to answer these charges? What do you have to say for yourself?" ⁶¹But Jesus was silent and made no reply. Then the high priest asked him, "Are you the Messiah, the Son of the Blessed One?"

⁶²Jesus said, "I AM.* And you will see the Son of Man seated in the place of power at God's right hand* and coming on the clouds of heaven.*"

⁶³Then the high priest tore his clothing to show his horror and said, "Why do we need other witnesses? ⁶⁴You have all heard his blasphemy. What is your verdict?"

"Guilty!" they all cried. "He deserves to die!"

⁶⁵Then some of them began to spit at him, and they blindfolded him and beat him with their fists. "Prophesy to us," they jeered. And the guards slapped him as they took him away.

Peter Denies Jesus

⁶⁶Meanwhile, Peter was in the courtyard below. One of the servant girls who worked for the high priest came by ⁶⁷and noticed Peter warming himself at the fire. She looked at him closely and said, "You were one of those with Jesus of Nazareth.*"

⁶⁸But Peter denied it. "I don't know what you're talking about," he said, and he went out into the entryway. Just then, a rooster crowed.*

⁶⁹When the servant girl saw him standing there, she began telling the others, "This man is definitely one of them!" ⁷⁰But Peter denied it again.

A little later some of the other bystanders confronted Peter and said, "You must be one of them, because you are a Galilean."

⁷¹Peter swore, "A curse on me if I'm lying—I don't know this man you're talking about!" ⁷²And immediately the rooster crowed the second time.

Suddenly, Jesus' words flashed through Peter's mind: "Before the rooster crows twice, you will deny three times that you even know me." And he broke down and wept.

CHAPTER 15

Jesus' Trial before Pilate

Very early in the morning the leading priests, the elders, and the teachers of religious law—the entire high council*—met to discuss their next step. They bound Jesus, led him away, and took him to Pilate, the Roman governor.

14:55 Greek *the Sanhedrin.*   **14:62a** Or *The 'I AM' is here;* or *I am the* LORD. See Exod 3:14.   **14:62b** Greek *at the right hand of the power.* See Ps 110:1.   **14:62c** See Dan 7:13.   **14:67** Or *Jesus the Nazarene.*   **14:68** Some manuscripts do not include *Just then, a rooster crowed.*   **15:1** Greek *the Sanhedrin;* also in 15:43.

[2]Pilate asked Jesus, "Are you the king of the Jews?"

Jesus replied, "You have said it."

[3]Then the leading priests kept accusing him of many crimes, [4]and Pilate asked him, "Aren't you going to answer them? What about all these charges they are bringing against you?" [5]But Jesus said nothing, much to Pilate's surprise.

[6]Now it was the governor's custom each year during the Passover celebration to release one prisoner—anyone the people requested. [7]One of the prisoners at that time was Barabbas, a revolutionary who had committed murder in an uprising. [8]The crowd went to Pilate and asked him to release a prisoner as usual.

[9]"Would you like me to release to you this 'King of the Jews'?" Pilate asked. [10](For he realized by now that the leading priests had arrested Jesus out of envy.) [11]But at this point the leading priests stirred up the crowd to demand the release of Barabbas instead of Jesus. [12]Pilate asked them, "Then what should I do with this man you call the king of the Jews?"

[13]They shouted back, "Crucify him!"

[14]"Why?" Pilate demanded. "What crime has he committed?"

But the mob roared even louder, "Crucify him!"

[15]So to pacify the crowd, Pilate released Barabbas to them. He ordered Jesus flogged with a lead-tipped whip, then turned him over to the Roman soldiers to be crucified.

The Soldiers Mock Jesus

[16]The soldiers took Jesus into the courtyard of the governor's headquarters (called the Praetorium) and called out the entire regiment. [17]They dressed him in a purple robe, and they wove thorn branches into a crown and put it on his head. [18]Then they saluted him and taunted, "Hail! King of the Jews!" [19]And they struck him on the head with a reed stick, spit on him, and dropped to their knees in mock worship. [20]When they were finally tired of mocking him, they took off the purple robe and put his own clothes on him again. Then they led him away to be crucified.

The Crucifixion

[21]A passerby named Simon, who was from Cyrene,* was coming in from the countryside just then, and the soldiers forced him to carry Jesus' cross. (Simon was the father of Alexander and Rufus.) [22]And they brought Jesus to a place called Golgotha (which means "Place of the Skull"). [23]They offered him wine drugged with myrrh, but he refused it.

[24]Then the soldiers nailed him to the cross. They divided his clothes and threw dice* to decide who would get each piece. [25]It was nine o'clock in the morning when they crucified him. [26]A sign announced the charge against him. It read, "The King of the Jews." [27]Two revolutionaries* were crucified with him, one on his right and one on his left.*

15:21 *Cyrene* was a city in northern Africa. **15:24** Greek *cast lots.* See Ps 22:18. **15:27a** Or *Two criminals.*
15:27b Some manuscripts add verse 28, *And the Scripture was fulfilled that said, "He was counted among those who were rebels."* See Isa 53:12; also compare Luke 22:37.

²⁹The people passing by shouted abuse, shaking their heads in mockery. "Ha! Look at you now!" they yelled at him. "You said you were going to destroy the Temple and rebuild it in three days. ³⁰Well then, save yourself and come down from the cross!"

³¹The leading priests and teachers of religious law also mocked Jesus. "He saved others," they scoffed, "but he can't save himself! ³²Let this Messiah, this King of Israel, come down from the cross so we can see it and believe him!" Even the men who were crucified with Jesus ridiculed him.

The Death of Jesus

³³At noon, darkness fell across the whole land until three o'clock. ³⁴Then at three o'clock Jesus called out with a loud voice, *"Eloi, Eloi, lema sabachthani?"* which means "My God, my God, why have you abandoned me?"*

³⁵Some of the bystanders misunderstood and thought he was calling for the prophet Elijah. ³⁶One of them ran and filled a sponge with sour wine, holding it up to him on a reed stick so he could drink. "Wait!" he said. "Let's see whether Elijah comes to take him down!"

³⁷Then Jesus uttered another loud cry and breathed his last. ³⁸And the curtain in the sanctuary of the Temple was torn in two, from top to bottom.

³⁹When the Roman officer* who stood facing him* saw how he had died, he exclaimed, "This man truly was the Son of God!"

⁴⁰Some women were there, watching from a distance, including Mary Magdalene, Mary (the mother of James the younger and of Joseph*), and Salome. ⁴¹They had been followers of Jesus and had cared for him while he was in Galilee. Many other women who had come with him to Jerusalem were also there.

The Burial of Jesus

⁴²This all happened on Friday, the day of preparation,* the day before the Sabbath. As evening approached, ⁴³Joseph of Arimathea took a risk and went to Pilate and asked for Jesus' body. (Joseph was an honored member of the high council, and he was waiting for the Kingdom of God to come.) ⁴⁴Pilate couldn't believe that Jesus was already dead, so he called for the Roman officer and asked if he had died yet. ⁴⁵The officer confirmed that Jesus was dead, so Pilate told Joseph he could have the body. ⁴⁶Joseph bought a long sheet of linen cloth. Then he took Jesus' body down from the cross, wrapped it in the cloth, and laid it in a tomb that had been carved out of the rock. Then he rolled a stone in front of the entrance. ⁴⁷Mary Magdalene and Mary the mother of Joseph saw where Jesus' body was laid.

CHAPTER 16

The Resurrection

Saturday evening, when the Sabbath ended, Mary Magdalene, Mary the mother of James, and Salome went out and purchased burial spices so they could anoint Jesus'

15:34 Ps 22:1. **15:39a** Greek *the centurion;* similarly in 15:44, 45. **15:39b** Some manuscripts add *heard his cry and.* **15:40** Greek *Joses;* also in 15:47. See Matt 27:56. **15:42** Greek *It was the day of preparation.*

body. [2]Very early on Sunday morning,* just at sunrise, they went to the tomb. [3]On the way they were asking each other, "Who will roll away the stone for us from the entrance to the tomb?" [4]But as they arrived, they looked up and saw that the stone, which was very large, had already been rolled aside.

[5]When they entered the tomb, they saw a young man clothed in a white robe sitting on the right side. The women were shocked, [6]but the angel said, "Don't be alarmed. You are looking for Jesus of Nazareth,* who was crucified. He isn't here! He is risen from the dead! Look, this is where they laid his body. [7]Now go and tell his disciples, including Peter, that Jesus is going ahead of you to Galilee. You will see him there, just as he told you before he died."

[8]The women fled from the tomb, trembling and bewildered, and they said nothing to anyone because they were too frightened.*

[*Shorter Ending of Mark*]

Then they briefly reported all this to Peter and his companions. Afterward Jesus himself sent them out from east to west with the sacred and unfailing message of salvation that gives eternal life. Amen.

[*Longer Ending of Mark*]

[9]After Jesus rose from the dead early on Sunday morning, the first person who saw him was Mary Magdalene, the woman from whom he had cast out seven demons. [10]She went to the disciples, who were grieving and weeping, and told them what had happened. [11]But when she told them that Jesus was alive and she had seen him, they didn't believe her.

[12]Afterward he appeared in a different form to two of his followers who were walking from Jerusalem into the country. [13]They rushed back to tell the others, but no one believed them.

[14]Still later he appeared to the eleven disciples as they were eating together. He rebuked them for their stubborn unbelief because they refused to believe those who had seen him after he had been raised from the dead.*

[15]And then he told them, "Go into all the world and preach the Good News to everyone. [16]Anyone who believes and is baptized will be saved. But anyone who refuses to believe will be condemned. [17]These miraculous signs will accompany those who believe: They will cast out demons in my name, and they will speak in new languages.* [18]They will be able to handle snakes with safety, and if they drink

---

16:2 Greek *on the first day of the week;* also in 16:9.   **16:6** Or *Jesus the Nazarene.*   **16:8** The most reliable early manuscripts of the Gospel of Mark end at verse 8. Other manuscripts include various endings to the Gospel. A few include both the "shorter ending" and the "longer ending." The majority of manuscripts include the "longer ending" immediately after verse 8.   **16:14** Some early manuscripts add: *And they excused themselves, saying, "This age of lawlessness and unbelief is under Satan, who does not permit God's truth and power to conquer the evil [unclean] spirits. Therefore, reveal your justice now." This is what they said to Christ. And Christ replied to them, "The period of years of Satan's power has been fulfilled, but other dreadful things will happen soon. And I was handed over to death for those who have sinned, so that they may return to the truth and sin no more, and so they may inherit the spiritual, incorruptible, and righteous glory in heaven."*   **16:17** Or *new tongues;* some manuscripts do not include *new.*

anything poisonous, it won't hurt them. They will be able to place their hands on the sick, and they will be healed."

[19]When the Lord Jesus had finished talking with them, he was taken up into heaven and sat down in the place of honor at God's right hand. [20]And the disciples went everywhere and preached, and the Lord worked through them, confirming what they said by many miraculous signs.

THE GOSPEL OF LUKE

Author

Though Luke's Gospel doesn't name its author, most scholars today acknowledge Luke as the author of both the third Gospel and the book of Acts. Luke's authorship of the third Gospel is reckoned by the facts that the same author wrote both the third Gospel and Acts (compare Luke 1:1-4 with Acts 1:1-2). The two books show no marked differences in style or vocabulary, so the two books appear to be by the same author, as they purport; and the style and vocabulary of Acts seem to harmonize well with the Gospel of Luke, pointing strongly to a single writer as the author of both books. The book of Acts uses the first person plural ("we") in chapter 16 and thereafter. These "'we' passages" indicate that the author was a participant in the action and a traveling companion of the apostle Paul.[16]

There was a strong and persistent tradition in the early church that Luke wrote the third Gospel and the book of Acts. This view receives support from the Muratorian Fragment (which reflects the view of the church in Rome around A.D. 170–190); from Irenaeus, bishop of Lyons around 185; and later from the influential church leaders Eusebius and Jerome.

Luke was the beloved physician and traveling companion of the apostle Paul.[17] Paul valued the help and support of Luke as a trusted confidante and aide.

Date

The dating of Luke must involve the book of Acts, which is the sequel of a two-part work, Luke-Acts. Paul's ministry dominates the second half of Acts, and the last quarter of the text is occupied with Paul's trip to Rome as a prisoner awaiting trial. However, Acts ends without telling us the outcome of Paul's trial, leading some to argue that the trial had not taken place by the time Acts was written. Based on this view, Acts, and possibly Luke-Acts, is dated in the early A.D. 60s.

However, Luke called attention to the fact that other Gospel accounts had preceded his,[18] and almost certainly Mark's Gospel was one of these sources. The generally accepted date for Mark's Gospel is in the mid-to-late 60s (see page 120). Thus, acknowledging that Luke probably used Mark in the composition of his Gospel, most scholars opt for a date for Luke-Acts after the destruction of Jerusalem in A.D. 70. The story of the early church in Acts, it is argued, was carried only to about A.D. 62 because that was a natural point to end Luke's account of the unhindered spread of the gospel (Acts 28:31).

Manuscripts

There are several early manuscripts of the Gospel of Luke, including manuscripts P4 and P75—both from the second century—which are extremely early and remarkably good copies of the Greek text of Luke. Manuscripts of the second and third centuries include the following:

> P4 (Luke 1–6)[19]
> P45 (Luke 6; 9–14)
> P69 (Luke 22)
> P75 (Luke 3–24)
> P111 (Luke 17)
> 0171 (Luke 22)

There are more than fifteen uncial manuscripts from the fourth to the tenth centuries that contain complete or nearly complete texts of Luke. Among them are the following:

> Aleph and B (fourth century)
> C, D, and W (fifth century)
> P and 040 (sixth century)
> L (eighth century)
> K, M, U, and V (ninth century)
> S (tenth century)

Two other important manuscripts for Luke are Q and T of the fifth century, even though each of these extant manuscripts contains less than half of Luke.

LUKE

CHAPTER 1

Introduction

Many people have set out to write accounts about the events that have been fulfilled among us. ²They used the eyewitness reports circulating among us from the early disciples.* ³Having carefully investigated everything from the beginning, I also have decided to write a careful account for you, most honorable Theophilus, ⁴so you can be certain of the truth of everything you were taught.

The Birth of John the Baptist Foretold

⁵When Herod was king of Judea, there was a Jewish priest named Zechariah. He was a member of the priestly order of Abijah, and his wife, Elizabeth, was also from the priestly line of Aaron. ⁶Zechariah and Elizabeth were righteous in God's eyes, careful to obey all of the Lord's commandments and regulations. ⁷They had no children because Elizabeth was unable to conceive, and they were both very old.

⁸One day Zechariah was serving God in the Temple, for his order was on duty that week. ⁹As was the custom of the priests, he was chosen by lot to enter the sanctuary of the Lord and burn incense. ¹⁰While the incense was being burned, a great crowd stood outside, praying.

¹¹While Zechariah was in the sanctuary, an angel of the Lord appeared to him, standing to the right of the incense altar. ¹²Zechariah was shaken and overwhelmed with fear when he saw him. ¹³But the angel said, "Don't be afraid, Zechariah! God has heard your prayer. Your wife, Elizabeth, will give you a son, and you are to name him John. ¹⁴You will have great joy and gladness, and many will rejoice at his birth, ¹⁵for he will be great in the eyes of the Lord. He must never touch wine or other alcoholic drinks. He will be filled with the Holy Spirit, even before his birth.* ¹⁶And he will turn many Israelites to the Lord their God. ¹⁷He will be a man with the spirit and power of Elijah. He will prepare the people for the coming of the Lord. He will turn the hearts of the fathers to their children,* and he will cause those who are rebellious to accept the wisdom of the godly."

¹⁸Zechariah said to the angel, "How can I be sure this will happen? I'm an old man now, and my wife is also well along in years."

¹⁹Then the angel said, "I am Gabriel! I stand in the very presence of God. It was he who sent me to bring you this good news! ²⁰But now, since you didn't believe what I said, you will be silent and unable to speak until the child is born. For my words will certainly be fulfilled at the proper time."

²¹Meanwhile, the people were waiting for Zechariah to come out of the sanctuary, wondering why he was taking so long. ²²When he finally did come out, he

---

1:2 Greek *from those who from the beginning were servants of the word.*   1:15 Or *even from birth.*   1:17 See Mal 4:5-6.

couldn't speak to them. Then they realized from his gestures and his silence that he must have seen a vision in the sanctuary.

[23]When Zechariah's week of service in the Temple was over, he returned home. [24]Soon afterward his wife, Elizabeth, became pregnant and went into seclusion for five months. [25]"How kind the Lord is!" she exclaimed. "He has taken away my disgrace of having no children."

The Birth of Jesus Foretold

[26]In the sixth month of Elizabeth's pregnancy, God sent the angel Gabriel to Nazareth, a village in Galilee, [27]to a virgin named Mary. She was engaged to be married to a man named Joseph, a descendant of King David. [28]Gabriel appeared to her and said, "Greetings, favored woman! The Lord is with you!*"

[29]Confused and disturbed, Mary tried to think what the angel could mean. [30]"Don't be afraid, Mary," the angel told her, "for you have found favor with God! [31]You will conceive and give birth to a son, and you will name him Jesus. [32]He will be very great and will be called the Son of the Most High. The Lord God will give him the throne of his ancestor David. [33]And he will reign over Israel* forever; his Kingdom will never end!"

[34]Mary asked the angel, "But how can this happen? I am a virgin."

[35]The angel replied, "The Holy Spirit will come upon you, and the power of the Most High will overshadow you. So the baby to be born will be holy, and he will be called the Son of God. [36]What's more, your relative Elizabeth has become pregnant in her old age! People used to say she was barren, but she has conceived a son and is now in her sixth month. [37]For nothing is impossible with God.*"

[38]Mary responded, "I am the Lord's servant. May everything you have said about me come true." And then the angel left her.

Mary Visits Elizabeth

[39]A few days later Mary hurried to the hill country of Judea, to the town [40]where Zechariah lived. She entered the house and greeted Elizabeth. [41]At the sound of Mary's greeting, Elizabeth's child leaped within her, and Elizabeth was filled with the Holy Spirit.

[42]Elizabeth gave a glad cry and exclaimed to Mary, "God has blessed you above all women, and your child is blessed. [43]Why am I so honored, that the mother of my Lord should visit me? [44]When I heard your greeting, the baby in my womb jumped for joy. [45]You are blessed because you believed that the Lord would do what he said."

The Magnificat: Mary's Song of Praise

[46]Mary responded,

"Oh, how my soul praises the Lord.
[47] How my spirit rejoices in God my Savior!

1:28 Some manuscripts add *Blessed are you among women.*   **1:33** Greek *over the house of Jacob.*   **1:37** Some manuscripts read *For the word of God will never fail.*

48 For he took notice of his lowly servant girl,
    and from now on all generations will call me blessed.
49 For the Mighty One is holy,
    and he has done great things for me.
50 He shows mercy from generation to generation
    to all who fear him.
51 His mighty arm has done tremendous things!
    He has scattered the proud and haughty ones.
52 He has brought down princes from their thrones
    and exalted the humble.
53 He has filled the hungry with good things
    and sent the rich away with empty hands.
54 He has helped his servant Israel
    and remembered to be merciful.
55 For he made this promise to our ancestors,
    to Abraham and his children forever."

56Mary stayed with Elizabeth about three months and then went back to her own home.

The Birth of John the Baptist

57When it was time for Elizabeth's baby to be born, she gave birth to a son. 58And when her neighbors and relatives heard that the Lord had been very merciful to her, everyone rejoiced with her.

59When the baby was eight days old, they all came for the circumcision ceremony. They wanted to name him Zechariah, after his father. 60But Elizabeth said, "No! His name is John!"

61"What?" they exclaimed. "There is no one in all your family by that name." 62So they used gestures to ask the baby's father what he wanted to name him. 63He motioned for a writing tablet, and to everyone's surprise he wrote, "His name is John." 64Instantly Zechariah could speak again, and he began praising God.

65Awe fell upon the whole neighborhood, and the news of what had happened spread throughout the Judean hills. 66Everyone who heard about it reflected on these events and asked, "What will this child turn out to be?" For the hand of the Lord was surely upon him in a special way.

Zechariah's Prophecy

67Then his father, Zechariah, was filled with the Holy Spirit and gave this prophecy:

68 "Praise the Lord, the God of Israel,
    because he has visited and redeemed his people.
69 He has sent us a mighty Savior*
    from the royal line of his servant David,
70 just as he promised
    through his holy prophets long ago.

1:69 Greek *has raised up a horn of salvation for us.*

71 Now we will be saved from our enemies
    and from all who hate us.
72 He has been merciful to our ancestors
    by remembering his sacred covenant—
73 the covenant he swore with an oath
    to our ancestor Abraham.
74 We have been rescued from our enemies
    so we can serve God without fear,
75 in holiness and righteousness
    for as long as we live.

76 "And you, my little son,
    will be called the prophet of the Most High,
    because you will prepare the way for the Lord.
77 You will tell his people how to find salvation
    through forgiveness of their sins.
78 Because of God's tender mercy,
    the morning light from heaven is about to break upon us,*
79 to give light to those who sit in darkness and in the shadow of death,
    and to guide us to the path of peace."

80 John grew up and became strong in spirit. And he lived in the wilderness until he began his public ministry to Israel.

CHAPTER 2

The Birth of Jesus

At that time the Roman emperor, Augustus, decreed that a census should be taken throughout the Roman Empire. 2(This was the first census taken when Quirinius was governor of Syria.) 3All returned to their own ancestral towns to register for this census. 4And because Joseph was a descendant of King David, he had to go to Bethlehem in Judea, David's ancient home. He traveled there from the village of Nazareth in Galilee. 5He took with him Mary, his fiancée, who was now obviously pregnant.

6And while they were there, the time came for her baby to be born. 7She gave birth to her first child, a son. She wrapped him snugly in strips of cloth and laid him in a manger, because there was no lodging available for them.

The Shepherds and Angels

8That night there were shepherds staying in the fields nearby, guarding their flocks of sheep. 9Suddenly, an angel of the Lord appeared among them, and the radiance of the Lord's glory surrounded them. They were terrified, 10but the angel reassured them. "Don't be afraid!" he said. "I bring you good news that will bring great joy to all people. 11The Savior—yes, the Messiah, the Lord—has been born today in

---

1:78 Or *the Morning Light from Heaven is about to visit us.*

Bethlehem, the city of David! [12]And you will recognize him by this sign: You will find a baby wrapped snugly in strips of cloth, lying in a manger."

[13]Suddenly, the angel was joined by a vast host of others—the armies of heaven—praising God and saying,

[14] "Glory to God in highest heaven,
        and peace on earth to those with whom God is pleased."

[15]When the angels had returned to heaven, the shepherds said to each other, "Let's go to Bethlehem! Let's see this thing that has happened, which the Lord has told us about."

[16]They hurried to the village and found Mary and Joseph. And there was the baby, lying in the manger. [17]After seeing him, the shepherds told everyone what had happened and what the angel had said to them about this child. [18]All who heard the shepherds' story were astonished, [19]but Mary kept all these things in her heart and thought about them often. [20]The shepherds went back to their flocks, glorifying and praising God for all they had heard and seen. It was just as the angel had told them.

Jesus Is Presented in the Temple

[21]Eight days later, when the baby was circumcised, he was named Jesus, the name given him by the angel even before he was conceived.

[22]Then it was time for their purification offering, as required by the law of Moses after the birth of a child; so his parents took him to Jerusalem to present him to the Lord. [23]The law of the Lord says, "If a woman's first child is a boy, he must be dedicated to the LORD."* [24]So they offered the sacrifice required in the law of the Lord—"either a pair of turtledoves or two young pigeons."*

The Prophecy of Simeon

[25]At that time there was a man in Jerusalem named Simeon. He was righteous and devout and was eagerly waiting for the Messiah to come and rescue Israel. The Holy Spirit was upon him [26]and had revealed to him that he would not die until he had seen the Lord's Messiah. [27]That day the Spirit led him to the Temple. So when Mary and Joseph came to present the baby Jesus to the Lord as the law required, [28]Simeon was there. He took the child in his arms and praised God, saying,

[29] "Sovereign Lord, now let your servant die in peace,
        as you have promised.
[30] I have seen your salvation,
[31]   which you have prepared for all people.
[32] He is a light to reveal God to the nations,
        and he is the glory of your people Israel!"

[33]Jesus' parents were amazed at what was being said about him. [34]Then Simeon blessed them, and he said to Mary, the baby's mother, "This child is destined to cause many in Israel to fall, but he will be a joy to many others. He has been sent

---

2:23 Exod 13:2.   **2:24** Lev 12:8.

THE FOUR CANONICAL GOSPELS—LUKE

as a sign from God, but many will oppose him. ³⁵As a result, the deepest thoughts of many hearts will be revealed. And a sword will pierce your very soul."

The Prophecy of Anna

³⁶Anna, a prophet, was also there in the Temple. She was the daughter of Phanuel from the tribe of Asher, and she was very old. Her husband died when they had been married only seven years. ³⁷Then she lived as a widow to the age of eighty-four.* She never left the Temple but stayed there day and night, worshiping God with fasting and prayer. ³⁸She came along just as Simeon was talking with Mary and Joseph, and she began praising God. She talked about the child to everyone who had been waiting expectantly for God to rescue Jerusalem.

³⁹When Jesus' parents had fulfilled all the requirements of the law of the Lord, they returned home to Nazareth in Galilee. ⁴⁰There the child grew up healthy and strong. He was filled with wisdom, and God's favor was on him.

Jesus Speaks with the Teachers

⁴¹Every year Jesus' parents went to Jerusalem for the Passover festival. ⁴²When Jesus was twelve years old, they attended the festival as usual. ⁴³After the celebration was over, they started home to Nazareth, but Jesus stayed behind in Jerusalem. His parents didn't miss him at first, ⁴⁴because they assumed he was among the other travelers. But when he didn't show up that evening, they started looking for him among their relatives and friends.

⁴⁵When they couldn't find him, they went back to Jerusalem to search for him there. ⁴⁶Three days later they finally discovered him in the Temple, sitting among the religious teachers, listening to them and asking questions. ⁴⁷All who heard him were amazed at his understanding and his answers.

⁴⁸His parents didn't know what to think. "Son," his mother said to him, "why have you done this to us? Your father and I have been frantic, searching for you everywhere."

⁴⁹"But why did you need to search?" he asked. "Didn't you know that I must be in my Father's house?"* ⁵⁰But they didn't understand what he meant.

⁵¹Then he returned to Nazareth with them and was obedient to them. And his mother stored all these things in her heart.

⁵²Jesus grew in wisdom and in stature and in favor with God and all the people.

CHAPTER 3

John the Baptist Prepares the Way

It was now the fifteenth year of the reign of Tiberius, the Roman emperor. Pontius Pilate was governor over Judea; Herod Antipas was ruler* over Galilee; his brother Philip was ruler* over Iturea and Traconitis; Lysanias was ruler over Abilene.

2:37 Or *She had been a widow for eighty-four years.*   2:49 Or *"Didn't you realize that I should be involved with my Father's affairs?"*   3:1a Greek *Herod was tetrarch.* Herod Antipas was a son of King Herod.   3:1b Greek *tetrarch;* also in 3:1c.

²Annas and Caiaphas were the high priests. At this time a message from God came to John son of Zechariah, who was living in the wilderness. ³Then John went from place to place on both sides of the Jordan River, preaching that people should be baptized to show that they had repented of their sins and turned to God to be forgiven. ⁴Isaiah had spoken of John when he said,

"He is a voice shouting in the wilderness,
'Prepare the way for the LORD's coming!
 Clear the road for him!
⁵ The valleys will be filled,
 and the mountains and hills made level.
The curves will be straightened,
 and the rough places made smooth.
⁶ And then all people will see
 the salvation sent from God.'"*

⁷When the crowds came to John for baptism, he said, "You brood of snakes! Who warned you to flee God's coming wrath? ⁸Prove by the way you live that you have repented of your sins and turned to God. Don't just say to each other, 'We're safe, for we are descendants of Abraham.' That means nothing, for I tell you, God can create children of Abraham from these very stones. ⁹Even now the ax of God's judgment is poised, ready to sever the roots of the trees. Yes, every tree that does not produce good fruit will be chopped down and thrown into the fire."

¹⁰The crowds asked, "What should we do?"

¹¹John replied, "If you have two shirts, give one to the poor. If you have food, share it with those who are hungry."

¹²Even corrupt tax collectors came to be baptized and asked, "Teacher, what should we do?"

¹³He replied, "Collect no more taxes than the government requires."

¹⁴"What should we do?" asked some soldiers.

John replied, "Don't extort money or make false accusations. And be content with your pay."

¹⁵Everyone was expecting the Messiah to come soon, and they were eager to know whether John might be the Messiah. ¹⁶John answered their questions by saying, "I baptize you with* water; but someone is coming soon who is greater than I am—so much greater that I'm not even worthy to be his slave and untie the straps of his sandals. He will baptize you with the Holy Spirit and with fire.* ¹⁷He is ready to separate the chaff from the wheat with his winnowing fork. Then he will clean up the threshing area, gathering the wheat into his barn but burning the chaff with never-ending fire." ¹⁸John used many such warnings as he announced the Good News to the people.

¹⁹John also publicly criticized Herod Antipas, the ruler of Galilee,* for marrying Herodias, his brother's wife, and for many other wrongs he had done. ²⁰So Herod put John in prison, adding this sin to his many others.

3:4-6 Isa 40:3-5 (Greek version).   **3:16a** Or *in.*   **3:16b** Or *in the Holy Spirit and in fire.*   **3:19** Greek *Herod the tetrarch.*

The Baptism of Jesus

[21] One day when the crowds were being baptized, Jesus himself was baptized. As he was praying, the heavens opened, [22] and the Holy Spirit, in bodily form, descended on him like a dove. And a voice from heaven said, "You are my dearly loved Son, and you bring me great joy.*"

The Ancestors of Jesus

[23] Jesus was about thirty years old when he began his public ministry.

Jesus was known as the son of Joseph.
Joseph was the son of Heli.
[24] Heli was the son of Matthat.
Matthat was the son of Levi.
Levi was the son of Melki.
Melki was the son of Jannai.
Jannai was the son of Joseph.
[25] Joseph was the son of Mattathias.
Mattathias was the son of Amos.
Amos was the son of Nahum.
Nahum was the son of Esli.
Esli was the son of Naggai.
[26] Naggai was the son of Maath.
Maath was the son of Mattathias.
Mattathias was the son of Semein.
Semein was the son of Josech.
Josech was the son of Joda.
[27] Joda was the son of Joanan.
Joanan was the son of Rhesa.
Rhesa was the son of Zerubbabel.
Zerubbabel was the son of Shealtiel.
Shealtiel was the son of Neri.
[28] Neri was the son of Melki.
Melki was the son of Addi.
Addi was the son of Cosam.
Cosam was the son of Elmadam.
Elmadam was the son of Er.
[29] Er was the son of Joshua.
Joshua was the son of Eliezer.
Eliezer was the son of Jorim.
Jorim was the son of Matthat.
Matthat was the son of Levi.
[30] Levi was the son of Simeon.
Simeon was the son of Judah.
Judah was the son of Joseph.

3:22 Some manuscripts read *my Son, and today I have become your Father.*

Joseph was the son of Jonam.
Jonam was the son of Eliakim.
³¹ Eliakim was the son of Melea.
Melea was the son of Menna.
Menna was the son of Mattatha.
Mattatha was the son of Nathan.
Nathan was the son of David.
³² David was the son of Jesse.
Jesse was the son of Obed.
Obed was the son of Boaz.
Boaz was the son of Salmon.*
Salmon was the son of Nahshon.
³³ Nahshon was the son of Amminadab.
Amminadab was the son of Admin.
Admin was the son of Arni.*
Arni was the son of Hezron.
Hezron was the son of Perez.
Perez was the son of Judah.
³⁴ Judah was the son of Jacob.
Jacob was the son of Isaac.
Isaac was the son of Abraham.
Abraham was the son of Terah.
Terah was the son of Nahor.
³⁵ Nahor was the son of Serug.
Serug was the son of Reu.
Reu was the son of Peleg.
Peleg was the son of Eber.
Eber was the son of Shelah.
³⁶ Shelah was the son of Cainan.
Cainan was the son of Arphaxad.
Arphaxad was the son of Shem.
Shem was the son of Noah.
Noah was the son of Lamech.
³⁷ Lamech was the son of Methuselah.
Methuselah was the son of Enoch.
Enoch was the son of Jared.
Jared was the son of Mahalalel.
Mahalalel was the son of Kenan.
³⁸ Kenan was the son of Enosh.*
Enosh was the son of Seth.
Seth was the son of Adam.
Adam was the son of God.

3:32 Greek *Sala,* a variant spelling of Salmon; also in 3:32b. See Ruth 4:22.   **3:33** Some manuscripts read *Amminadab was the son of Aram. Arni* and *Aram* are alternate spellings of Ram. See 1 Chr 2:9-10.   **3:38** Greek *Enos,* a variant spelling of Enosh; also in 3:38b. See Gen 5:6.

CHAPTER 4

The Temptation of Jesus

Then Jesus, full of the Holy Spirit, returned from the Jordan River. He was led by the Spirit in the wilderness,* ²where he was tempted by the devil for forty days. Jesus ate nothing all that time and became very hungry.

³Then the devil said to him, "If you are the Son of God, tell this stone to become a loaf of bread."

⁴But Jesus told him, "No! The Scriptures say, 'People do not live by bread alone.'*"

⁵Then the devil took him up and revealed to him all the kingdoms of the world in a moment of time. ⁶"I will give you the glory of these kingdoms and authority over them," the devil said, "because they are mine to give to anyone I please. ⁷I will give it all to you if you will worship me."

⁸Jesus replied, "The Scriptures say,

'You must worship the LORD your God
    and serve only him.'*"

⁹Then the devil took him to Jerusalem, to the highest point of the Temple, and said, "If you are the Son of God, jump off! ¹⁰For the Scriptures say,

'He will order his angels to protect and guard you.
¹¹   And they will hold you up with their hands
        so you won't even hurt your foot on a stone.'*"

¹²Jesus responded, "The Scriptures also say, 'You must not test the LORD your God.'*"

¹³When the devil had finished tempting Jesus, he left him until the next opportunity came.

Jesus Rejected at Nazareth

¹⁴Then Jesus returned to Galilee, filled with the Holy Spirit's power. Reports about him spread quickly through the whole region. ¹⁵He taught regularly in their synagogues and was praised by everyone.

¹⁶When he came to the village of Nazareth, his boyhood home, he went as usual to the synagogue on the Sabbath and stood up to read the Scriptures. ¹⁷The scroll of Isaiah the prophet was handed to him. He unrolled the scroll and found the place where this was written:

¹⁸   "The Spirit of the LORD is upon me,
        for he has anointed me to bring Good News to the poor.
    He has sent me to proclaim that captives will be released,
        that the blind will see,

4:1 Some manuscripts read *into the wilderness.*   4:4 Deut 8:3.   4:8 Deut 6:13.   4:10-11 Ps 91:11-12.
4:12 Deut 6:16.

that the oppressed will be set free,

19   and that the time of the LORD's favor has come.*"

²⁰He rolled up the scroll, handed it back to the attendant, and sat down. All eyes in the synagogue looked at him intently. ²¹Then he began to speak to them. "The Scripture you've just heard has been fulfilled this very day!"

²²Everyone spoke well of him and was amazed by the gracious words that came from his lips. "How can this be?" they asked. "Isn't this Joseph's son?"

²³Then he said, "You will undoubtedly quote me this proverb: 'Physician, heal yourself'—meaning, 'Do miracles here in your hometown like those you did in Capernaum.' ²⁴But I tell you the truth, no prophet is accepted in his own hometown.

²⁵"Certainly there were many needy widows in Israel in Elijah's time, when the heavens were closed for three and a half years, and a severe famine devastated the land. ²⁶Yet Elijah was not sent to any of them. He was sent instead to a foreigner—a widow of Zarephath in the land of Sidon. ²⁷And there were many lepers in Israel in the time of the prophet Elisha, but the only one healed was Naaman, a Syrian."

²⁸When they heard this, the people in the synagogue were furious. ²⁹Jumping up, they mobbed him and forced him to the edge of the hill on which the town was built. They intended to push him over the cliff, ³⁰but he passed right through the crowd and went on his way.

Jesus Casts Out a Demon

³¹Then Jesus went to Capernaum, a town in Galilee, and taught there in the synagogue every Sabbath day. ³²There, too, the people were amazed at his teaching, for he spoke with authority.

³³Once when he was in the synagogue, a man possessed by a demon—an evil* spirit—began shouting at Jesus, ³⁴"Go away! Why are you interfering with us, Jesus of Nazareth? Have you come to destroy us? I know who you are—the Holy One of God!"

³⁵Jesus cut him short. "Be quiet! Come out of the man," he ordered. At that, the demon threw the man to the floor as the crowd watched; then it came out of him without hurting him further.

³⁶Amazed, the people exclaimed, "What authority and power this man's words possess! Even evil spirits obey him, and they flee at his command!" ³⁷The news about Jesus spread through every village in the entire region.

Jesus Heals Many People

³⁸After leaving the synagogue that day, Jesus went to Simon's home, where he found Simon's mother-in-law very sick with a high fever. "Please heal her," everyone begged. ³⁹Standing at her bedside, he rebuked the fever, and it left her. And she got up at once and prepared a meal for them.

⁴⁰As the sun went down that evening, people throughout the village brought sick family members to Jesus. No matter what their diseases were, the touch of his

4:18-19 Or *and to proclaim the acceptable year of the LORD.* Isa 61:1-2 (Greek version); 58:6.   **4:33** Greek *unclean;* also in 4:36.

hand healed every one. [41]Many were possessed by demons; and the demons came out at his command, shouting, "You are the Son of God!" But because they knew he was the Messiah, he rebuked them and refused to let them speak.

Jesus Continues to Preach

[42]Early the next morning Jesus went out to an isolated place. The crowds searched everywhere for him, and when they finally found him, they begged him not to leave them. [43]But he replied, "I must preach the Good News of the Kingdom of God in other towns, too, because that is why I was sent." [44]So he continued to travel around, preaching in synagogues throughout Judea.*

CHAPTER 5

The First Disciples

One day as Jesus was preaching on the shore of the Sea of Galilee,* great crowds pressed in on him to listen to the word of God. [2]He noticed two empty boats at the water's edge, for the fishermen had left them and were washing their nets. [3]Stepping into one of the boats, Jesus asked Simon,* its owner, to push it out into the water. So he sat in the boat and taught the crowds from there.

[4]When he had finished speaking, he said to Simon, "Now go out where it is deeper, and let down your nets to catch some fish."

[5]"Master," Simon replied, "we worked hard all last night and didn't catch a thing. But if you say so, I'll let the nets down again." [6]And this time their nets were so full of fish they began to tear! [7]A shout for help brought their partners in the other boat, and soon both boats were filled with fish and on the verge of sinking.

[8]When Simon Peter realized what had happened, he fell to his knees before Jesus and said, "Oh, Lord, please leave me—I'm too much of a sinner to be around you." [9]For he was awestruck by the number of fish they had caught, as were the others with him. [10]His partners, James and John, the sons of Zebedee, were also amazed.

Jesus replied to Simon, "Don't be afraid! From now on you'll be fishing for people!" [11]And as soon as they landed, they left everything and followed Jesus.

Jesus Heals a Man with Leprosy

[12]In one of the villages, Jesus met a man with an advanced case of leprosy. When the man saw Jesus, he bowed with his face to the ground, begging to be healed. "Lord," he said, "if you are willing, you can heal me and make me clean."

[13]Jesus reached out and touched him. "I am willing," he said. "Be healed!" And instantly the leprosy disappeared. [14]Then Jesus instructed him not to tell anyone what had happened. He said, "Go to the priest and let him examine you. Take along the offering required in the law of Moses for those who have been healed of leprosy.* This will be a public testimony that you have been cleansed."

4:44 Some manuscripts read *Galilee*.   **5:1** Greek *Lake Gennesaret,* another name for the Sea of Galilee.   **5:3** *Simon* is called "Peter" in 6:14 and thereafter.   **5:14** See Lev 14:2-32.

[15] But despite Jesus' instructions, the report of his power spread even faster, and vast crowds came to hear him preach and to be healed of their diseases. [16] But Jesus often withdrew to the wilderness for prayer.

Jesus Heals a Paralyzed Man

[17] One day while Jesus was teaching, some Pharisees and teachers of religious law were sitting nearby. (It seemed that these men showed up from every village in all Galilee and Judea, as well as from Jerusalem.) And the Lord's healing power was strongly with Jesus.

[18] Some men came carrying a paralyzed man on a sleeping mat. They tried to take him inside to Jesus, [19] but they couldn't reach him because of the crowd. So they went up to the roof and took off some tiles. Then they lowered the sick man on his mat down into the crowd, right in front of Jesus. [20] Seeing their faith, Jesus said to the man, "Young man, your sins are forgiven."

[21] But the Pharisees and teachers of religious law said to themselves, "Who does he think he is? That's blasphemy! Only God can forgive sins!"

[22] Jesus knew what they were thinking, so he asked them, "Why do you question this in your hearts? [23] Is it easier to say 'Your sins are forgiven,' or 'Stand up and walk'? [24] So I will prove to you that the Son of Man* has the authority on earth to forgive sins." Then Jesus turned to the paralyzed man and said, "Stand up, pick up your mat, and go home!"

[25] And immediately, as everyone watched, the man jumped up, picked up his mat, and went home praising God. [26] Everyone was gripped with great wonder and awe, and they praised God, exclaiming, "We have seen amazing things today!"

Jesus Calls Levi (Matthew)

[27] Later, as Jesus left the town, he saw a tax collector named Levi sitting at his tax collector's booth. "Follow me and be my disciple," Jesus said to him. [28] So Levi got up, left everything, and followed him.

[29] Later, Levi held a banquet in his home with Jesus as the guest of honor. Many of Levi's fellow tax collectors and other guests also ate with them. [30] But the Pharisees and their teachers of religious law complained bitterly to Jesus' disciples, "Why do you eat and drink with such scum?*"

[31] Jesus answered them, "Healthy people don't need a doctor—sick people do. [32] I have come to call not those who think they are righteous, but those who know they are sinners and need to repent."

A Discussion about Fasting

[33] One day some people said to Jesus, "John the Baptist's disciples fast and pray regularly, and so do the disciples of the Pharisees. Why are your disciples always eating and drinking?"

[34] Jesus responded, "Do wedding guests fast while celebrating with the groom? Of course not. [35] But someday the groom will be taken away from them, and then they will fast."

5:24 "Son of Man" is a title Jesus used for himself.   **5:30** Greek *with tax collectors and sinners?*

³⁶Then Jesus gave them this illustration: "No one tears a piece of cloth from a new garment and uses it to patch an old garment. For then the new garment would be ruined, and the new patch wouldn't even match the old garment.

³⁷"And no one puts new wine into old wineskins. For the new wine would burst the wineskins, spilling the wine and ruining the skins. ³⁸New wine must be stored in new wineskins. ³⁹But no one who drinks the old wine seems to want the new wine. 'The old is just fine,' they say."

CHAPTER 6

A Discussion about the Sabbath

One Sabbath day as Jesus was walking through some grainfields, his disciples broke off heads of grain, rubbed off the husks in their hands, and ate the grain. ²But some Pharisees said, "Why are you breaking the law by harvesting grain on the Sabbath?"

³Jesus replied, "Haven't you read in the Scriptures what David did when he and his companions were hungry? ⁴He went into the house of God and broke the law by eating the sacred loaves of bread that only the priests can eat. He also gave some to his companions." ⁵And Jesus added, "The Son of Man* is Lord, even over the Sabbath."

Jesus Heals on the Sabbath

⁶On another Sabbath day, a man with a deformed right hand was in the synagogue while Jesus was teaching. ⁷The teachers of religious law and the Pharisees watched Jesus closely. If he healed the man's hand, they planned to accuse him of working on the Sabbath.

⁸But Jesus knew their thoughts. He said to the man with the deformed hand, "Come and stand in front of everyone." So the man came forward. ⁹Then Jesus said to his critics, "I have a question for you. Does the law permit good deeds on the Sabbath, or is it a day for doing evil? Is this a day to save life or to destroy it?"

¹⁰He looked around at them one by one and then said to the man, "Hold out your hand." So the man held out his hand, and it was restored! ¹¹At this, the enemies of Jesus were wild with rage and began to discuss what to do with him.

Jesus Chooses the Twelve Apostles

¹²One day soon afterward Jesus went up on a mountain to pray, and he prayed to God all night. ¹³At daybreak he called together all of his disciples and chose twelve of them to be apostles. Here are their names:

¹⁴ Simon (whom he named Peter),
   Andrew (Peter's brother),
   James,
   John,
   Philip,
   Bartholomew,

6:5 "Son of Man" is a title Jesus used for himself.

¹⁵ Matthew,
Thomas,
James (son of Alphaeus),
Simon (who was called the zealot),
¹⁶ Judas (son of James),
Judas Iscariot (who later betrayed him).

Crowds Follow Jesus

¹⁷When they came down from the mountain, the disciples stood with Jesus on a large, level area, surrounded by many of his followers and by the crowds. There were people from all over Judea and from Jerusalem and from as far north as the seacoasts of Tyre and Sidon. ¹⁸They had come to hear him and to be healed of their diseases; and those troubled by evil* spirits were healed. ¹⁹Everyone tried to touch him, because healing power went out from him, and he healed everyone.

The Beatitudes

²⁰Then Jesus turned to his disciples and said,

"God blesses you who are poor,
for the Kingdom of God is yours.
²¹ God blesses you who are hungry now,
for you will be satisfied.
God blesses you who weep now,
for in due time you will laugh.

²²What blessings await you when people hate you and exclude you and mock you and curse you as evil because you follow the Son of Man. ²³When that happens, be happy! Yes, leap for joy! For a great reward awaits you in heaven. And remember, their ancestors treated the ancient prophets that same way.

Sorrows Foretold

²⁴ "What sorrow awaits you who are rich,
for you have your only happiness now.
²⁵ What sorrow awaits you who are fat and prosperous now,
for a time of awful hunger awaits you.
What sorrow awaits you who laugh now,
for your laughing will turn to mourning and sorrow.
²⁶ What sorrow awaits you who are praised by the crowds,
for their ancestors also praised false prophets.

Love for Enemies

²⁷"But to you who are willing to listen, I say, love your enemies! Do good to those who hate you. ²⁸Bless those who curse you. Pray for those who hurt you. ²⁹If someone slaps you on one cheek, offer the other cheek also. If someone demands your coat,

---

6:18 Greek *unclean.*

offer your shirt also. ³⁰Give to anyone who asks; and when things are taken away from you, don't try to get them back. ³¹Do to others as you would like them to do to you.

³²"If you love only those who love you, why should you get credit for that? Even sinners love those who love them! ³³And if you do good only to those who do good to you, why should you get credit? Even sinners do that much! ³⁴And if you lend money only to those who can repay you, why should you get credit? Even sinners will lend to other sinners for a full return.

³⁵"Love your enemies! Do good to them. Lend to them without expecting to be repaid. Then your reward from heaven will be very great, and you will truly be acting as children of the Most High, for he is kind to those who are unthankful and wicked. ³⁶You must be compassionate, just as your Father is compassionate.

Do Not Judge Others

³⁷"Do not judge others, and you will not be judged. Do not condemn others, or it will all come back against you. Forgive others, and you will be forgiven. ³⁸Give, and you will receive. Your gift will return to you in full—pressed down, shaken together to make room for more, running over, and poured into your lap. The amount you give will determine the amount you get back.*"

³⁹Then Jesus gave the following illustration: "Can one blind person lead another? Won't they both fall into a ditch? ⁴⁰Students* are not greater than their teacher. But the student who is fully trained will become like the teacher.

⁴¹"And why worry about a speck in your friend's eye* when you have a log in your own? ⁴²How can you think of saying, 'Friend,* let me help you get rid of that speck in your eye,' when you can't see past the log in your own eye? Hypocrite! First get rid of the log in your own eye; then you will see well enough to deal with the speck in your friend's eye.

The Tree and Its Fruit

⁴³"A good tree can't produce bad fruit, and a bad tree can't produce good fruit. ⁴⁴A tree is identified by its fruit. Figs are never gathered from thornbushes, and grapes are not picked from bramble bushes. ⁴⁵A good person produces good things from the treasury of a good heart, and an evil person produces evil things from the treasury of an evil heart. What you say flows from what is in your heart.

Building on a Solid Foundation

⁴⁶"So why do you keep calling me 'Lord, Lord!' when you don't do what I say? ⁴⁷I will show you what it's like when someone comes to me, listens to my teaching, and then follows it. ⁴⁸It is like a person building a house who digs deep and lays the foundation on solid rock. When the floodwaters rise and break against that house, it stands firm because it is well built. ⁴⁹But anyone who hears and doesn't obey is like a person who builds a house without a foundation. When the floods sweep down against that house, it will collapse into a heap of ruins."

6:38 Or *The measure you give will be the measure you get back.*   **6:40** Or *Disciples.*   **6:41** Greek *your brother's eye;* also in 6:42.   **6:42** Greek *Brother.*

CHAPTER 7

The Faith of a Roman Officer

When Jesus had finished saying all this to the people, he returned to Capernaum. [2]At that time the highly valued slave of a Roman officer* was sick and near death. [3]When the officer heard about Jesus, he sent some respected Jewish elders to ask him to come and heal his slave. [4]So they earnestly begged Jesus to help the man. "If anyone deserves your help, he does," they said, [5]"for he loves the Jewish people and even built a synagogue for us."

[6]So Jesus went with them. But just before they arrived at the house, the officer sent some friends to say, "Lord, don't trouble yourself by coming to my home, for I am not worthy of such an honor. [7]I am not even worthy to come and meet you. Just say the word from where you are, and my servant will be healed. [8]I know this because I am under the authority of my superior officers, and I have authority over my soldiers. I only need to say, 'Go,' and they go, or 'Come,' and they come. And if I say to my slaves, 'Do this,' they do it."

[9]When Jesus heard this, he was amazed. Turning to the crowd that was following him, he said, "I tell you, I haven't seen faith like this in all Israel!" [10]And when the officer's friends returned to his house, they found the slave completely healed.

Jesus Raises a Widow's Son

[11]Soon afterward Jesus went with his disciples to the village of Nain, and a large crowd followed him. [12]A funeral procession was coming out as he approached the village gate. The young man who had died was a widow's only son, and a large crowd from the village was with her. [13]When the Lord saw her, his heart overflowed with compassion. "Don't cry!" he said. [14]Then he walked over to the coffin and touched it, and the bearers stopped. "Young man," he said, "I tell you, get up." [15]Then the dead boy sat up and began to talk! And Jesus gave him back to his mother.

[16]Great fear swept the crowd, and they praised God, saying, "A mighty prophet has risen among us," and "God has visited his people today." [17]And the news about Jesus spread throughout Judea and the surrounding countryside.

Jesus and John the Baptist

[18]The disciples of John the Baptist told John about everything Jesus was doing. So John called for two of his disciples, [19]and he sent them to the Lord to ask him, "Are you the Messiah we've been expecting,* or should we keep looking for someone else?"

[20]John's two disciples found Jesus and said to him, "John the Baptist sent us to ask, 'Are you the Messiah we've been expecting, or should we keep looking for someone else?'"

[21]At that very time, Jesus cured many people of their diseases, illnesses, and evil spirits, and he restored sight to many who were blind. [22]Then he told John's

---

7:2 Greek *a centurion;* similarly in 7:6. **7:19** Greek *Are you the one who is coming?* Also in 7:20.

disciples, "Go back to John and tell him what you have seen and heard—the blind see, the lame walk, the lepers are cured, the deaf hear, the dead are raised to life, and the Good News is being preached to the poor. ²³And tell him, 'God blesses those who do not turn away because of me.*'"

²⁴After John's disciples left, Jesus began talking about him to the crowds. "What kind of man did you go into the wilderness to see? Was he a weak reed, swayed by every breath of wind? ²⁵Or were you expecting to see a man dressed in expensive clothes? No, people who wear beautiful clothes and live in luxury are found in palaces. ²⁶Were you looking for a prophet? Yes, and he is more than a prophet. ²⁷John is the man to whom the Scriptures refer when they say,

> 'Look, I am sending my messenger ahead of you,
>   and he will prepare your way before you.'*

²⁸I tell you, of all who have ever lived, none is greater than John. Yet even the least person in the Kingdom of God is greater than he is!"

²⁹When they heard this, all the people—even the tax collectors—agreed that God's way was right,* for they had been baptized by John. ³⁰But the Pharisees and experts in religious law rejected God's plan for them, for they had refused John's baptism.

³¹"To what can I compare the people of this generation?" Jesus asked. "How can I describe them? ³²They are like children playing a game in the public square. They complain to their friends,

> 'We played wedding songs,
>   and you didn't dance,
> so we played funeral songs,
>   and you didn't weep.'

³³For John the Baptist didn't spend his time eating bread or drinking wine, and you say, 'He's possessed by a demon.' ³⁴The Son of Man,* on the other hand, feasts and drinks, and you say, 'He's a glutton and a drunkard, and a friend of tax collectors and other sinners!' ³⁵But wisdom is shown to be right by the lives of those who follow it.*"

Jesus Anointed by a Sinful Woman

³⁶One of the Pharisees asked Jesus to have dinner with him, so Jesus went to his home and sat down to eat.* ³⁷When a certain immoral woman from that city heard he was eating there, she brought a beautiful alabaster jar filled with expensive perfume. ³⁸Then she knelt behind him at his feet, weeping. Her tears fell on his feet, and she wiped them off with her hair. Then she kept kissing his feet and putting perfume on them.

³⁹When the Pharisee who had invited him saw this, he said to himself, "If this man were a prophet, he would know what kind of woman is touching him. She's a sinner!"

7:23 Or *who are not offended by me.*   7:27 Mal 3:1.   7:29 Or *praised God for his justice.*   7:34 "Son of Man" is a title Jesus used for himself.   7:35 Or *But wisdom is justified by all her children.*   7:36 Or *and reclined.*

40Then Jesus answered his thoughts. "Simon," he said to the Pharisee, "I have something to say to you."

"Go ahead, Teacher," Simon replied.

41Then Jesus told him this story: "A man loaned money to two people— 500 pieces of silver* to one and 50 pieces to the other. 42But neither of them could repay him, so he kindly forgave them both, canceling their debts. Who do you suppose loved him more after that?"

43Simon answered, "I suppose the one for whom he canceled the larger debt."

"That's right," Jesus said. 44Then he turned to the woman and said to Simon, "Look at this woman kneeling here. When I entered your home, you didn't offer me water to wash the dust from my feet, but she has washed them with her tears and wiped them with her hair. 45You didn't greet me with a kiss, but from the time I first came in, she has not stopped kissing my feet. 46You neglected the courtesy of olive oil to anoint my head, but she has anointed my feet with rare perfume.

47"I tell you, her sins—and they are many—have been forgiven, so she has shown me much love. But a person who is forgiven little shows only little love." 48Then Jesus said to the woman, "Your sins are forgiven."

49The men at the table said among themselves, "Who is this man, that he goes around forgiving sins?"

50And Jesus said to the woman, "Your faith has saved you; go in peace."

CHAPTER 8

Women Who Followed Jesus

Soon afterward Jesus began a tour of the nearby towns and villages, preaching and announcing the Good News about the Kingdom of God. He took his twelve disciples with him, 2along with some women who had been cured of evil spirits and diseases. Among them were Mary Magdalene, from whom he had cast out seven demons; 3Joanna, the wife of Chuza, Herod's business manager; Susanna; and many others who were contributing from their own resources to support Jesus and his disciples.

Parable of the Farmer Scattering Seed

4One day Jesus told a story in the form of a parable to a large crowd that had gathered from many towns to hear him: 5"A farmer went out to plant his seed. As he scattered it across his field, some seed fell on a footpath, where it was stepped on, and the birds ate it. 6Other seed fell among rocks. It began to grow, but the plant soon wilted and died for lack of moisture. 7Other seed fell among thorns that grew up with it and choked out the tender plants. 8Still other seed fell on fertile soil. This seed grew and produced a crop that was a hundred times as much as had been planted!" When he had said this, he called out, "Anyone with ears to hear should listen and understand."

9His disciples asked him what this parable meant. 10He replied, "You are permit-

---

7:41 Greek *500 denarii.* A denarius was equivalent to a laborer's full day's wage.

ted to understand the secrets* of the Kingdom of God. But I use parables to teach the others so that the Scriptures might be fulfilled:

'When they look, they won't really see.
When they hear, they won't understand.'*

[11] "This is the meaning of the parable: The seed is God's word. [12] The seeds that fell on the footpath represent those who hear the message, only to have the devil come and take it away from their hearts and prevent them from believing and being saved. [13] The seeds on the rocky soil represent those who hear the message and receive it with joy. But since they don't have deep roots, they believe for a while, then they fall away when they face temptation. [14] The seeds that fell among the thorns represent those who hear the message, but all too quickly the message is crowded out by the cares and riches and pleasures of this life. And so they never grow into maturity. [15] And the seeds that fell on the good soil represent honest, good-hearted people who hear God's word, cling to it, and patiently produce a huge harvest.

Parable of the Lamp

[16] "No one lights a lamp and then covers it with a bowl or hides it under a bed. A lamp is placed on a stand, where its light can be seen by all who enter the house. [17] For all that is secret will eventually be brought into the open, and everything that is concealed will be brought to light and made known to all.

[18] "So pay attention to how you hear. To those who listen to my teaching, more understanding will be given. But for those who are not listening, even what they think they understand will be taken away from them."

The True Family of Jesus

[19] Then Jesus' mother and brothers came to see him, but they couldn't get to him because of the crowd. [20] Someone told Jesus, "Your mother and your brothers are outside, and they want to see you."

[21] Jesus replied, "My mother and my brothers are all those who hear God's word and obey it."

Jesus Calms the Storm

[22] One day Jesus said to his disciples, "Let's cross to the other side of the lake." So they got into a boat and started out. [23] As they sailed across, Jesus settled down for a nap. But soon a fierce storm came down on the lake. The boat was filling with water, and they were in real danger.

[24] The disciples went and woke him up, shouting, "Master, Master, we're going to drown!"

When Jesus woke up, he rebuked the wind and the raging waves. Suddenly the storm stopped and all was calm. [25] Then he asked them, "Where is your faith?"

The disciples were terrified and amazed. "Who is this man?" they asked each other. "When he gives a command, even the wind and waves obey him!"

8:10a Greek *mysteries*.   **8:10b** Isa 6:9 (Greek version).

Jesus Heals a Demon-Possessed Man

²⁶So they arrived in the region of the Gerasenes,* across the lake from Galilee. ²⁷As Jesus was climbing out of the boat, a man who was possessed by demons came out to meet him. For a long time he had been homeless and naked, living in a cemetery outside the town.

²⁸As soon as he saw Jesus, he shrieked and fell down in front of him. Then he screamed, "Why are you interfering with me, Jesus, Son of the Most High God? Please, I beg you, don't torture me!" ²⁹For Jesus had already commanded the evil* spirit to come out of him. This spirit had often taken control of the man. Even when he was placed under guard and put in chains and shackles, he simply broke them and rushed out into the wilderness, completely under the demon's power.

³⁰Jesus demanded, "What is your name?"

"Legion," he replied, for he was filled with many demons. ³¹The demons kept begging Jesus not to send them into the bottomless pit.*

³²There happened to be a large herd of pigs feeding on the hillside nearby, and the demons begged him to let them enter into the pigs.

So Jesus gave them permission. ³³Then the demons came out of the man and entered the pigs, and the entire herd plunged down the steep hillside into the lake and drowned.

³⁴When the herdsmen saw it, they fled to the nearby town and the surrounding countryside, spreading the news as they ran. ³⁵People rushed out to see what had happened. A crowd soon gathered around Jesus, and they saw the man who had been freed from the demons. He was sitting at Jesus' feet, fully clothed and perfectly sane, and they were all afraid. ³⁶Then those who had seen what happened told the others how the demon-possessed man had been healed. ³⁷And all the people in the region of the Gerasenes begged Jesus to go away and leave them alone, for a great wave of fear swept over them.

So Jesus returned to the boat and left, crossing back to the other side of the lake. ³⁸The man who had been freed from the demons begged to go with him. But Jesus sent him home, saying, ³⁹"No, go back to your family, and tell them everything God has done for you." So he went all through the town proclaiming the great things Jesus had done for him.

Jesus Heals in Response to Faith

⁴⁰On the other side of the lake the crowds welcomed Jesus, because they had been waiting for him. ⁴¹Then a man named Jairus, a leader of the local synagogue, came and fell at Jesus' feet, pleading with him to come home with him. ⁴²His only daughter,* who was about twelve years old, was dying.

As Jesus went with him, he was surrounded by the crowds. ⁴³A woman in the crowd had suffered for twelve years with constant bleeding,* and she could find no

---

8:26 Other manuscripts read *Gadarenes;* still others read *Gergesenes;* also in 8:37. See Matt 8:28; Mark 5:1.
8:29 Greek *unclean.* **8:31** Or *the abyss,* or *the underworld.* **8:42** Or *His only child, a daughter.* **8:43** Some manuscripts add *having spent everything she had on doctors.*

cure. ⁴⁴Coming up behind Jesus, she touched the fringe of his robe. Immediately, the bleeding stopped.

⁴⁵"Who touched me?" Jesus asked.

Everyone denied it, and Peter said, "Master, this whole crowd is pressing up against you."

⁴⁶But Jesus said, "Someone deliberately touched me, for I felt healing power go out from me." ⁴⁷When the woman realized that she could not stay hidden, she began to tremble and fell to her knees in front of him. The whole crowd heard her explain why she had touched him and that she had been immediately healed. ⁴⁸"Daughter," he said to her, "your faith has made you well. Go in peace."

⁴⁹While he was still speaking to her, a messenger arrived from the home of Jairus, the leader of the synagogue. He told him, "Your daughter is dead. There's no use troubling the Teacher now."

⁵⁰But when Jesus heard what had happened, he said to Jairus, "Don't be afraid. Just have faith, and she will be healed."

⁵¹When they arrived at the house, Jesus wouldn't let anyone go in with him except Peter, John, James, and the little girl's father and mother. ⁵²The house was filled with people weeping and wailing, but he said, "Stop the weeping! She isn't dead; she's only asleep."

⁵³But the crowd laughed at him because they all knew she had died. ⁵⁴Then Jesus took her by the hand and said in a loud voice, "My child, get up!" ⁵⁵And at that moment her life* returned, and she immediately stood up! Then Jesus told them to give her something to eat. ⁵⁶Her parents were overwhelmed, but Jesus insisted that they not tell anyone what had happened.

CHAPTER 9

Jesus Sends Out the Twelve Disciples

One day Jesus called together his twelve disciples* and gave them power and authority to cast out all demons and to heal all diseases. ²Then he sent them out to tell everyone about the Kingdom of God and to heal the sick. ³"Take nothing for your journey," he instructed them. "Don't take a walking stick, a traveler's bag, food, money,* or even a change of clothes. ⁴Wherever you go, stay in the same house until you leave town. ⁵And if a town refuses to welcome you, shake its dust from your feet as you leave to show that you have abandoned those people to their fate."

⁶So they began their circuit of the villages, preaching the Good News and healing the sick.

Herod's Confusion

⁷When Herod Antipas, the ruler of Galilee,* heard about everything Jesus was doing, he was puzzled. Some were saying that John the Baptist had been raised

---

8:55 Or *her spirit.*   9:1 Greek *the Twelve;* other manuscripts read *the twelve apostles.*   9:3 Or *silver coins.*
9:7 Greek *Herod the tetrarch.* Herod Antipas was a son of King Herod and was ruler over Galilee.

from the dead. [8]Others thought Jesus was Elijah or one of the other prophets risen from the dead.

[9]"I beheaded John," Herod said, "so who is this man about whom I hear such stories?" And he kept trying to see him.

Jesus Feeds Five Thousand

[10]When the apostles returned, they told Jesus everything they had done. Then he slipped quietly away with them toward the town of Bethsaida. [11]But the crowds found out where he was going, and they followed him. He welcomed them and taught them about the Kingdom of God, and he healed those who were sick.

[12]Late in the afternoon the twelve disciples came to him and said, "Send the crowds away to the nearby villages and farms, so they can find food and lodging for the night. There is nothing to eat here in this remote place."

[13]But Jesus said, "You feed them."

"But we have only five loaves of bread and two fish," they answered. "Or are you expecting us to go and buy enough food for this whole crowd?" [14]For there were about 5,000 men there.

Jesus replied, "Tell them to sit down in groups of about fifty each." [15]So the people all sat down. [16]Jesus took the five loaves and two fish, looked up toward heaven, and blessed them. Then, breaking the loaves into pieces, he kept giving the bread and fish to the disciples so they could distribute it to the people. [17]They all ate as much as they wanted, and afterward, the disciples picked up twelve baskets of leftovers!

Peter's Declaration about Jesus

[18]One day Jesus left the crowds to pray alone. Only his disciples were with him, and he asked them, "Who do people say I am?"

[19]"Well," they replied, "some say John the Baptist, some say Elijah, and others say you are one of the other ancient prophets risen from the dead."

[20]Then he asked them, "But who do you say I am?"

Peter replied, "You are the Messiah* sent from God!"

Jesus Predicts His Death

[21]Jesus warned his disciples not to tell anyone who he was. [22]"The Son of Man* must suffer many terrible things," he said. "He will be rejected by the elders, the leading priests, and the teachers of religious law. He will be killed, but on the third day he will be raised from the dead."

[23]Then he said to the crowd, "If any of you wants to be my follower, you must turn from your selfish ways, take up your cross daily, and follow me. [24]If you try to hang on to your life, you will lose it. But if you give up your life for my sake, you will save it. [25]And what do you benefit if you gain the whole world but are yourself lost or destroyed? [26]If anyone is ashamed of me and my message, the Son of Man will be ashamed of that person when he returns in his glory and in the glory of the

---

9:20 Or *the Christ. Messiah* (a Hebrew term) and *Christ* (a Greek term) both mean "the anointed one."   **9:22** "Son of Man" is a title Jesus used for himself.

Father and the holy angels. [27] I tell you the truth, some standing here right now will not die before they see the Kingdom of God."

The Transfiguration

[28] About eight days later Jesus took Peter, John, and James up on a mountain to pray. [29] And as he was praying, the appearance of his face was transformed, and his clothes became dazzling white. [30] Suddenly, two men, Moses and Elijah, appeared and began talking with Jesus. [31] They were glorious to see. And they were speaking about his exodus from this world, which was about to be fulfilled in Jerusalem.

[32] Peter and the others had fallen asleep. When they woke up, they saw Jesus' glory and the two men standing with him. [33] As Moses and Elijah were starting to leave, Peter, not even knowing what he was saying, blurted out, "Master, it's wonderful for us to be here! Let's make three shelters as memorials*—one for you, one for Moses, and one for Elijah." [34] But even as he was saying this, a cloud overshadowed them, and terror gripped them as the cloud covered them.

[35] Then a voice from the cloud said, "This is my Son, my Chosen One.* Listen to him." [36] When the voice finished, Jesus was there alone. They didn't tell anyone at that time what they had seen.

Jesus Heals a Demon-Possessed Boy

[37] The next day, after they had come down the mountain, a large crowd met Jesus. [38] A man in the crowd called out to him, "Teacher, I beg you to look at my son, my only child. [39] An evil spirit keeps seizing him, making him scream. It throws him into convulsions so that he foams at the mouth. It batters him and hardly ever leaves him alone. [40] I begged your disciples to cast out the spirit, but they couldn't do it."

[41] Jesus said, "You faithless and corrupt people! How long must I be with you and put up with you?" Then he said to the man, "Bring your son here."

[42] As the boy came forward, the demon knocked him to the ground and threw him into a violent convulsion. But Jesus rebuked the evil* spirit and healed the boy. Then he gave him back to his father. [43] Awe gripped the people as they saw this majestic display of God's power.

Jesus Again Predicts His Death

While everyone was marveling at everything he was doing, Jesus said to his disciples, [44] "Listen to me and remember what I say. The Son of Man is going to be betrayed into the hands of his enemies." [45] But they didn't know what he meant. Its significance was hidden from them, so they couldn't understand it, and they were afraid to ask him about it.

The Greatest in the Kingdom

[46] Then his disciples began arguing about which of them was the greatest. [47] But Jesus knew their thoughts, so he brought a little child to his side. [48] Then he said to

---

9:33 Greek *three tabernacles.* **9:35** Some manuscripts read *This is my dearly loved Son.* **9:42** Greek *unclean.*

them, "Anyone who welcomes a little child like this on my behalf* welcomes me, and anyone who welcomes me also welcomes my Father who sent me. Whoever is the least among you is the greatest."

Using the Name of Jesus

⁴⁹John said to Jesus, "Master, we saw someone using your name to cast out demons, but we told him to stop because he isn't in our group."

⁵⁰But Jesus said, "Don't stop him! Anyone who is not against you is for you."

Opposition from Samaritans

⁵¹As the time drew near for him to ascend to heaven, Jesus resolutely set out for Jerusalem. ⁵²He sent messengers ahead to a Samaritan village to prepare for his arrival. ⁵³But the people of the village did not welcome Jesus because he was on his way to Jerusalem. ⁵⁴When James and John saw this, they said to Jesus, "Lord, should we call down fire from heaven to burn them up*?" ⁵⁵But Jesus turned and rebuked them.* ⁵⁶So they went on to another village.

The Cost of Following Jesus

⁵⁷As they were walking along, someone said to Jesus, "I will follow you wherever you go."

⁵⁸But Jesus replied, "Foxes have dens to live in, and birds have nests, but the Son of Man has no place even to lay his head."

⁵⁹He said to another person, "Come, follow me."

The man agreed, but he said, "Lord, first let me return home and bury my father."

⁶⁰But Jesus told him, "Let the spiritually dead bury their own dead!* Your duty is to go and preach about the Kingdom of God."

⁶¹Another said, "Yes, Lord, I will follow you, but first let me say good-bye to my family."

⁶²But Jesus told him, "Anyone who puts a hand to the plow and then looks back is not fit for the Kingdom of God."

CHAPTER 10

Jesus Sends Out His Disciples

The Lord now chose seventy-two* other disciples and sent them ahead in pairs to all the towns and places he planned to visit. ²These were his instructions to them: "The harvest is great, but the workers are few. So pray to the Lord who is in charge of the harvest; ask him to send more workers into his fields. ³Now go, and remember that I am sending you out as lambs among wolves. ⁴Don't take any money with you, nor a traveler's bag, nor an extra pair of sandals. And don't stop to greet anyone on the road.

⁵"Whenever you enter someone's home, first say, 'May God's peace be on this

---

9:48 Greek *in my name.*   **9:54** Some manuscripts add *as Elijah did.*   **9:55** Some manuscripts add an expanded conclusion to verse 55 and an additional sentence in verse 56: *And he said, "You don't realize what your hearts are like.* ⁵⁶*For the Son of Man has not come to destroy people's lives, but to save them."*   **9:60** Greek *Let the dead bury their own dead.*   **10:1** Some manuscripts read *seventy;* also in 10:17.

house.' [6]If those who live there are peaceful, the blessing will stand; if they are not, the blessing will return to you. [7]Don't move around from home to home. Stay in one place, eating and drinking what they provide. Don't hesitate to accept hospitality, because those who work deserve their pay.

[8]"If you enter a town and it welcomes you, eat whatever is set before you. [9]Heal the sick, and tell them, 'The Kingdom of God is near you now.' [10]But if a town refuses to welcome you, go out into its streets and say, [11]'We wipe even the dust of your town from our feet to show that we have abandoned you to your fate. And know this—the Kingdom of God is near!' [12]I assure you, even wicked Sodom will be better off than such a town on judgment day.

[13]"What sorrow awaits you, Korazin and Bethsaida! For if the miracles I did in you had been done in wicked Tyre and Sidon, their people would have repented of their sins long ago, clothing themselves in burlap and throwing ashes on their heads to show their remorse. [14]Yes, Tyre and Sidon will be better off on judgment day than you. [15]And you people of Capernaum, will you be honored in heaven? No, you will go down to the place of the dead.*"

[16]Then he said to the disciples, "Anyone who accepts your message is also accepting me. And anyone who rejects you is rejecting me. And anyone who rejects me is rejecting God, who sent me."

[17]When the seventy-two disciples returned, they joyfully reported to him, "Lord, even the demons obey us when we use your name!"

[18]"Yes," he told them, "I saw Satan fall from heaven like lightning! [19]Look, I have given you authority over all the power of the enemy, and you can walk among snakes and scorpions and crush them. Nothing will injure you. [20]But don't rejoice because evil spirits obey you; rejoice because your names are registered in heaven."

Jesus' Prayer of Thanksgiving

[21]At that same time Jesus was filled with the joy of the Holy Spirit, and he said, "O Father, Lord of heaven and earth, thank you for hiding these things from those who think themselves wise and clever, and for revealing them to the childlike. Yes, Father, it pleased you to do it this way.

[22]"My Father has entrusted everything to me. No one truly knows the Son except the Father, and no one truly knows the Father except the Son and those to whom the Son chooses to reveal him."

[23]Then when they were alone, he turned to the disciples and said, "Blessed are the eyes that see what you have seen. [24]I tell you, many prophets and kings longed to see what you see, but they didn't see it. And they longed to hear what you hear, but they didn't hear it."

The Most Important Commandment

[25]One day an expert in religious law stood up to test Jesus by asking him this question: "Teacher, what should I do to inherit eternal life?"

[26]Jesus replied, "What does the law of Moses say? How do you read it?"

10:15 Greek *to Hades.*

27The man answered, "'You must love the LORD your God with all your heart, all your soul, all your strength, and all your mind.' And, 'Love your neighbor as yourself.'"*

28"Right!" Jesus told him. "Do this and you will live!"

29The man wanted to justify his actions, so he asked Jesus, "And who is my neighbor?"

Parable of the Good Samaritan

30Jesus replied with a story: "A Jewish man was traveling from Jerusalem down to Jericho, and he was attacked by bandits. They stripped him of his clothes, beat him up, and left him half dead beside the road.

31"By chance a priest came along. But when he saw the man lying there, he crossed to the other side of the road and passed him by. 32A Temple assistant* walked over and looked at him lying there, but he also passed by on the other side.

33"Then a despised Samaritan came along, and when he saw the man, he felt compassion for him. 34Going over to him, the Samaritan soothed his wounds with olive oil and wine and bandaged them. Then he put the man on his own donkey and took him to an inn, where he took care of him. 35The next day he handed the innkeeper two silver coins,* telling him, 'Take care of this man. If his bill runs higher than this, I'll pay you the next time I'm here.'

36"Now which of these three would you say was a neighbor to the man who was attacked by bandits?" Jesus asked.

37The man replied, "The one who showed him mercy."

Then Jesus said, "Yes, now go and do the same."

Jesus Visits Martha and Mary

38As Jesus and the disciples continued on their way to Jerusalem, they came to a certain village where a woman named Martha welcomed him into her home. 39Her sister, Mary, sat at the Lord's feet, listening to what he taught. 40But Martha was distracted by the big dinner she was preparing. She came to Jesus and said, "Lord, doesn't it seem unfair to you that my sister just sits here while I do all the work? Tell her to come and help me."

41But the Lord said to her, "My dear Martha, you are worried and upset over all these details! 42There is only one thing worth being concerned about. Mary has discovered it, and it will not be taken away from her."

CHAPTER 11

Teaching about Prayer

Once Jesus was in a certain place praying. As he finished, one of his disciples came to him and said, "Lord, teach us to pray, just as John taught his disciples."

10:27 Deut 6:5; Lev 19:18.   10:32 Greek *A Levite.*   10:35 Greek *two denarii.* A denarius was equivalent to a laborer's full day's wage.

²Jesus said, "This is how you should pray:*

"Father, may your name be kept holy.
May your Kingdom come soon.
3   Give us each day the food we need,*
4   and forgive us our sins,
        as we forgive those who sin against us.
And don't let us yield to temptation.*"

⁵Then, teaching them more about prayer, he used this story: "Suppose you went to a friend's house at midnight, wanting to borrow three loaves of bread. You say to him, ⁶'A friend of mine has just arrived for a visit, and I have nothing for him to eat.' ⁷And suppose he calls out from his bedroom, 'Don't bother me. The door is locked for the night, and my family and I are all in bed. I can't help you.' ⁸But I tell you this—though he won't do it for friendship's sake, if you keep knocking long enough, he will get up and give you whatever you need because of your shameless persistence.*

⁹"And so I tell you, keep on asking, and you will receive what you ask for. Keep on seeking, and you will find. Keep on knocking, and the door will be opened to you. ¹⁰For everyone who asks, receives. Everyone who seeks, finds. And to everyone who knocks, the door will be opened.

¹¹"You fathers—if your children ask* for a fish, do you give them a snake instead? ¹²Or if they ask for an egg, do you give them a scorpion? Of course not! ¹³So if you sinful people know how to give good gifts to your children, how much more will your heavenly Father give the Holy Spirit to those who ask him."

Jesus and the Prince of Demons

¹⁴One day Jesus cast out a demon from a man who couldn't speak, and when the demon was gone, the man began to speak. The crowds were amazed, ¹⁵but some of them said, "No wonder he can cast out demons. He gets his power from Satan,* the prince of demons." ¹⁶Others, trying to test Jesus, demanded that he show them a miraculous sign from heaven to prove his authority.

¹⁷He knew their thoughts, so he said, "Any kingdom divided by civil war is doomed. A family splintered by feuding will fall apart. ¹⁸You say I am empowered by Satan. But if Satan is divided and fighting against himself, how can his kingdom survive? ¹⁹And if I am empowered by Satan, what about your own exorcists? They cast out demons, too, so they will condemn you for what you have said. ²⁰But if I am casting out demons by the power of God,* then the Kingdom of God has arrived among you. ²¹For when a strong man like Satan is fully armed and guards his palace, his possessions are safe—²²until someone even stronger attacks and overpowers him, strips him of his weapons, and carries off his belongings.

11:2 Some manuscripts add additional phrases from the Lord's Prayer as it reads in Matt 6:9-13.   11:3 Or *Give us each day our food for the day;* or *Give us each day our food for tomorrow.*   11:4 Or *And keep us from being tested.*   11:8 Or *in order to avoid shame,* or *so his reputation won't be damaged.*   11:11 Some manuscripts add *for bread, do you give them a stone? Or [if they ask].*   11:15 Greek *Beelzeboul;* also in 11:18, 19. Other manuscripts read *Beezeboul;* Latin version reads *Beelzebub.*   11:20 Greek *by the finger of God.*

²³"Anyone who isn't with me opposes me, and anyone who isn't working with me is actually working against me.

²⁴"When an evil* spirit leaves a person, it goes into the desert, searching for rest. But when it finds none, it says, 'I will return to the person I came from.' ²⁵So it returns and finds that its former home is all swept and in order. ²⁶Then the spirit finds seven other spirits more evil than itself, and they all enter the person and live there. And so that person is worse off than before."

²⁷As he was speaking, a woman in the crowd called out, "God bless your mother—the womb from which you came, and the breasts that nursed you!"

²⁸Jesus replied, "But even more blessed are all who hear the word of God and put it into practice."

The Sign of Jonah

²⁹As the crowd pressed in on Jesus, he said, "This evil generation keeps asking me to show them a miraculous sign. But the only sign I will give them is the sign of Jonah. ³⁰What happened to him was a sign to the people of Nineveh that God had sent him. What happens to the Son of Man* will be a sign to these people that he was sent by God.

³¹"The queen of Sheba* will stand up against this generation on judgment day and condemn it, for she came from a distant land to hear the wisdom of Solomon. Now someone greater than Solomon is here—but you refuse to listen. ³²The people of Nineveh will also stand up against this generation on judgment day and condemn it, for they repented of their sins at the preaching of Jonah. Now someone greater than Jonah is here—but you refuse to repent.

Receiving the Light

³³"No one lights a lamp and then hides it or puts it under a basket.* Instead, a lamp is placed on a stand, where its light can be seen by all who enter the house.

³⁴"Your eye is a lamp that provides light for your body. When your eye is good, your whole body is filled with light. But when it is bad, your body is filled with darkness. ³⁵Make sure that the light you think you have is not actually darkness. ³⁶If you are filled with light, with no dark corners, then your whole life will be radiant, as though a floodlight were filling you with light."

Jesus Criticizes the Religious Leaders

³⁷As Jesus was speaking, one of the Pharisees invited him home for a meal. So he went in and took his place at the table.* ³⁸His host was amazed to see that he sat down to eat without first performing the hand-washing ceremony required by Jewish custom. ³⁹Then the Lord said to him, "You Pharisees are so careful to clean the outside of the cup and the dish, but inside you are filthy—full of greed and wickedness! ⁴⁰Fools! Didn't God make the inside as well as the outside? ⁴¹So clean the inside by giving gifts to the poor, and you will be clean all over.

11:24 Greek *unclean.*   **11:30** "Son of Man" is a title Jesus used for himself.   **11:31** Greek *The queen of the south.*
11:33 Some manuscripts do not include *or puts it under a basket.*   **11:37** Or *and reclined.*

⁴²"What sorrow awaits you Pharisees! For you are careful to tithe even the tiniest income from your herb gardens,* but you ignore justice and the love of God. You should tithe, yes, but do not neglect the more important things.

⁴³"What sorrow awaits you Pharisees! For you love to sit in the seats of honor in the synagogues and receive respectful greetings as you walk in the marketplaces. ⁴⁴Yes, what sorrow awaits you! For you are like hidden graves in a field. People walk over them without knowing the corruption they are stepping on."

⁴⁵"Teacher," said an expert in religious law, "you have insulted us, too, in what you just said."

⁴⁶"Yes," said Jesus, "what sorrow also awaits you experts in religious law! For you crush people with unbearable religious demands, and you never lift a finger to ease the burden. ⁴⁷What sorrow awaits you! For you build monuments for the prophets your own ancestors killed long ago. ⁴⁸But in fact, you stand as witnesses who agree with what your ancestors did. They killed the prophets, and you join in their crime by building the monuments! ⁴⁹This is what God in his wisdom said about you:* 'I will send prophets and apostles to them, but they will kill some and persecute the others.'

⁵⁰"As a result, this generation will be held responsible for the murder of all God's prophets from the creation of the world—⁵¹from the murder of Abel to the murder of Zechariah, who was killed between the altar and the sanctuary. Yes, it will certainly be charged against this generation.

⁵²"What sorrow awaits you experts in religious law! For you remove the key to knowledge from the people. You don't enter the Kingdom yourselves, and you prevent others from entering."

⁵³As Jesus was leaving, the teachers of religious law and the Pharisees became hostile and tried to provoke him with many questions. ⁵⁴They wanted to trap him into saying something they could use against him.

CHAPTER 12

A Warning against Hypocrisy

Meanwhile, the crowds grew until thousands were milling about and stepping on each other. Jesus turned first to his disciples and warned them, "Beware of the yeast of the Pharisees—their hypocrisy. ²The time is coming when everything that is covered up will be revealed, and all that is secret will be made known to all. ³Whatever you have said in the dark will be heard in the light, and what you have whispered behind closed doors will be shouted from the housetops for all to hear!

⁴"Dear friends, don't be afraid of those who want to kill your body; they cannot do any more to you after that. ⁵But I'll tell you whom to fear. Fear God, who has the power to kill you and then throw you into hell.* Yes, he's the one to fear.

11:42 Greek *tithe the mint, the rue, and every herb.*   11:49 Greek *Therefore, the wisdom of God said.*   12:5 Greek *Gehenna.*

⁶"What is the price of five sparrows—two copper coins*? Yet God does not forget a single one of them. ⁷And the very hairs on your head are all numbered. So don't be afraid; you are more valuable to God than a whole flock of sparrows.

⁸"I tell you the truth, everyone who acknowledges me publicly here on earth, the Son of Man* will also acknowledge in the presence of God's angels. ⁹But anyone who denies me here on earth will be denied before God's angels. ¹⁰Anyone who speaks against the Son of Man can be forgiven, but anyone who blasphemes the Holy Spirit will not be forgiven.

¹¹"And when you are brought to trial in the synagogues and before rulers and authorities, don't worry about how to defend yourself or what to say, ¹²for the Holy Spirit will teach you at that time what needs to be said."

Parable of the Rich Fool

¹³Then someone called from the crowd, "Teacher, please tell my brother to divide our father's estate with me."

¹⁴Jesus replied, "Friend, who made me a judge over you to decide such things as that?" ¹⁵Then he said, "Beware! Guard against every kind of greed. Life is not measured by how much you own."

¹⁶Then he told them a story: "A rich man had a fertile farm that produced fine crops. ¹⁷He said to himself, 'What should I do? I don't have room for all my crops.' ¹⁸Then he said, 'I know! I'll tear down my barns and build bigger ones. Then I'll have room enough to store all my wheat and other goods. ¹⁹And I'll sit back and say to myself, "My friend, you have enough stored away for years to come. Now take it easy! Eat, drink, and be merry!"'

²⁰"But God said to him, 'You fool! You will die this very night. Then who will get everything you worked for?'

²¹"Yes, a person is a fool to store up earthly wealth but not have a rich relationship with God."

Teaching about Money and Possessions

²²Then, turning to his disciples, Jesus said, "That is why I tell you not to worry about everyday life—whether you have enough food to eat or enough clothes to wear. ²³For life is more than food, and your body more than clothing. ²⁴Look at the ravens. They don't plant or harvest or store food in barns, for God feeds them. And you are far more valuable to him than any birds! ²⁵Can all your worries add a single moment to your life? ²⁶And if worry can't accomplish a little thing like that, what's the use of worrying over bigger things?

²⁷"Look at the lilies and how they grow. They don't work or make their clothing, yet Solomon in all his glory was not dressed as beautifully as they are. ²⁸And if God cares so wonderfully for flowers that are here today and thrown into the fire tomorrow, he will certainly care for you. Why do you have so little faith?

²⁹"And don't be concerned about what to eat and what to drink. Don't worry about such things. ³⁰These things dominate the thoughts of unbelievers all over

---

12:6 Greek *two assaria* [Roman coins equal to ¹/₁₆ of a denarius].   **12:8** "Son of Man" is a title Jesus used for himself.

the world, but your Father already knows your needs. [31]Seek the Kingdom of God above all else, and he will give you everything you need.

[32]"So don't be afraid, little flock. For it gives your Father great happiness to give you the Kingdom.

[33]"Sell your possessions and give to those in need. This will store up treasure for you in heaven! And the purses of heaven never get old or develop holes. Your treasure will be safe; no thief can steal it and no moth can destroy it. [34]Wherever your treasure is, there the desires of your heart will also be.

Be Ready for the Lord's Coming

[35]"Be dressed for service and keep your lamps burning, [36]as though you were waiting for your master to return from the wedding feast. Then you will be ready to open the door and let him in the moment he arrives and knocks. [37]The servants who are ready and waiting for his return will be rewarded. I tell you the truth, he himself will seat them, put on an apron, and serve them as they sit and eat! [38]He may come in the middle of the night or just before dawn.* But whenever he comes, he will reward the servants who are ready.

[39]"Understand this: If a homeowner knew exactly when a burglar was coming, he would not permit his house to be broken into. [40]You also must be ready all the time, for the Son of Man will come when least expected."

[41]Peter asked, "Lord, is that illustration just for us or for everyone?"

[42]And the Lord replied, "A faithful, sensible servant is one to whom the master can give the responsibility of managing his other household servants and feeding them. [43]If the master returns and finds that the servant has done a good job, there will be a reward. [44]I tell you the truth, the master will put that servant in charge of all he owns. [45]But what if the servant thinks, 'My master won't be back for a while,' and he begins beating the other servants, partying, and getting drunk? [46]The master will return unannounced and unexpected, and he will cut the servant in pieces and banish him with the unfaithful.

[47]"And a servant who knows what the master wants, but isn't prepared and doesn't carry out those instructions, will be severely punished. [48]But someone who does not know, and then does something wrong, will be punished only lightly. When someone has been given much, much will be required in return; and when someone has been entrusted with much, even more will be required.

Jesus Causes Division

[49]"I have come to set the world on fire, and I wish it were already burning! [50]I have a terrible baptism of suffering ahead of me, and I am under a heavy burden until it is accomplished. [51]Do you think I have come to bring peace to the earth? No, I have come to divide people against each other! [52]From now on families will be split apart, three in favor of me, and two against—or two in favor and three against.

[53] 'Father will be divided against son
          and son against father;

12:38 Greek *in the second or third watch.*

mother against daughter
    and daughter against mother;
and mother-in-law against daughter-in-law
    and daughter-in-law against mother-in-law.'*"

54Then Jesus turned to the crowd and said, "When you see clouds beginning to form in the west, you say, 'Here comes a shower.' And you are right. 55When the south wind blows, you say, 'Today will be a scorcher.' And it is. 56You fools! You know how to interpret the weather signs of the earth and sky, but you don't know how to interpret the present times.

57"Why can't you decide for yourselves what is right? 58When you are on the way to court with your accuser, try to settle the matter before you get there. Otherwise, your accuser may drag you before the judge, who will hand you over to an officer, who will throw you into prison. 59And if that happens, you won't be free again until you have paid the very last penny.*"

CHAPTER 13

A Call to Repentance
About this time Jesus was informed that Pilate had murdered some people from Galilee as they were offering sacrifices at the Temple. 2"Do you think those Galileans were worse sinners than all the other people from Galilee?" Jesus asked. "Is that why they suffered? 3Not at all! And you will perish, too, unless you repent of your sins and turn to God. 4And what about the eighteen people who died when the tower in Siloam fell on them? Were they the worst sinners in Jerusalem? 5No, and I tell you again that unless you repent, you will perish, too."

Parable of the Barren Fig Tree
6Then Jesus told this story: "A man planted a fig tree in his garden and came again and again to see if there was any fruit on it, but he was always disappointed. 7Finally, he said to his gardener, 'I've waited three years, and there hasn't been a single fig! Cut it down. It's just taking up space in the garden.'

8"The gardener answered, 'Sir, give it one more chance. Leave it another year, and I'll give it special attention and plenty of fertilizer. 9If we get figs next year, fine. If not, then you can cut it down.'"

Jesus Heals on the Sabbath
10One Sabbath day as Jesus was teaching in a synagogue, 11he saw a woman who had been crippled by an evil spirit. She had been bent double for eighteen years and was unable to stand up straight. 12When Jesus saw her, he called her over and said, "Dear woman, you are healed of your sickness!" 13Then he touched her, and instantly she could stand straight. How she praised God!

12:53 Mic 7:6.   **12:59** Greek *last lepton* [the smallest Jewish coin].

[14]But the leader in charge of the synagogue was indignant that Jesus had healed her on the Sabbath day. "There are six days of the week for working," he said to the crowd. "Come on those days to be healed, not on the Sabbath."

[15]But the Lord replied, "You hypocrites! Each of you works on the Sabbath day! Don't you untie your ox or your donkey from its stall on the Sabbath and lead it out for water? [16]This dear woman, a daughter of Abraham, has been held in bondage by Satan for eighteen years. Isn't it right that she be released, even on the Sabbath?"

[17]This shamed his enemies, but all the people rejoiced at the wonderful things he did.

Parable of the Mustard Seed

[18]Then Jesus said, "What is the Kingdom of God like? How can I illustrate it? [19]It is like a tiny mustard seed that a man planted in a garden; it grows and becomes a tree, and the birds make nests in its branches."

Parable of the Yeast

[20]He also asked, "What else is the Kingdom of God like? [21]It is like the yeast a woman used in making bread. Even though she put only a little yeast in three measures of flour, it permeated every part of the dough."

The Narrow Door

[22]Jesus went through the towns and villages, teaching as he went, always pressing on toward Jerusalem. [23]Someone asked him, "Lord, will only a few be saved?"

He replied, [24]"Work hard to enter the narrow door to God's Kingdom, for many will try to enter but will fail. [25]When the master of the house has locked the door, it will be too late. You will stand outside knocking and pleading, 'Lord, open the door for us!' But he will reply, 'I don't know you or where you come from.' [26]Then you will say, 'But we ate and drank with you, and you taught in our streets.' [27]And he will reply, 'I tell you, I don't know you or where you come from. Get away from me, all you who do evil.'

[28]"There will be weeping and gnashing of teeth, for you will see Abraham, Isaac, Jacob, and all the prophets in the Kingdom of God, but you will be thrown out. [29]And people will come from all over the world—from east and west, north and south—to take their places in the Kingdom of God. [30]And note this: Some who seem least important now will be the greatest then, and some who are the greatest now will be least important then.*"

Jesus Grieves over Jerusalem

[31]At that time some Pharisees said to him, "Get away from here if you want to live! Herod Antipas wants to kill you!"

[32]Jesus replied, "Go tell that fox that I will keep on casting out demons and healing people today and tomorrow; and the third day I will accomplish my purpose. [33]Yes, today, tomorrow, and the next day I must proceed on my way. For it wouldn't do for a prophet of God to be killed except in Jerusalem!

13:30 Greek *Some are last who will be first, and some are first who will be last.*

³⁴"O Jerusalem, Jerusalem, the city that kills the prophets and stones God's messengers! How often I have wanted to gather your children together as a hen protects her chicks beneath her wings, but you wouldn't let me. ³⁵And now, look, your house is abandoned. And you will never see me again until you say, 'Blessings on the one who comes in the name of the LORD!'*"

CHAPTER 14

Jesus Heals on the Sabbath
One Sabbath day Jesus went to eat dinner in the home of a leader of the Pharisees, and the people were watching him closely. ²There was a man there whose arms and legs were swollen.* ³Jesus asked the Pharisees and experts in religious law, "Is it permitted in the law to heal people on the Sabbath day, or not?" ⁴When they refused to answer, Jesus touched the sick man and healed him and sent him away. ⁵Then he turned to them and said, "Which of you doesn't work on the Sabbath? If your son* or your cow falls into a pit, don't you rush to get him out?" ⁶Again they could not answer.

Jesus Teaches about Humility
⁷When Jesus noticed that all who had come to the dinner were trying to sit in the seats of honor near the head of the table, he gave them this advice: ⁸"When you are invited to a wedding feast, don't sit in the seat of honor. What if someone who is more distinguished than you has also been invited? ⁹The host will come and say, 'Give this person your seat.' Then you will be embarrassed, and you will have to take whatever seat is left at the foot of the table!

¹⁰"Instead, take the lowest place at the foot of the table. Then when your host sees you, he will come and say, 'Friend, we have a better place for you!' Then you will be honored in front of all the other guests. ¹¹For those who exalt themselves will be humbled, and those who humble themselves will be exalted."

¹²Then he turned to his host. "When you put on a luncheon or a banquet," he said, "don't invite your friends, brothers, relatives, and rich neighbors. For they will invite you back, and that will be your only reward. ¹³Instead, invite the poor, the crippled, the lame, and the blind. ¹⁴Then at the resurrection of the righteous, God will reward you for inviting those who could not repay you."

Parable of the Great Feast
¹⁵Hearing this, a man sitting at the table with Jesus exclaimed, "What a blessing it will be to attend a banquet* in the Kingdom of God!"

¹⁶Jesus replied with this story: "A man prepared a great feast and sent out many invitations. ¹⁷When the banquet was ready, he sent his servant to tell the guests, 'Come, the banquet is ready.' ¹⁸But they all began making excuses. One said, 'I have just bought a field and must inspect it. Please excuse me.' ¹⁹Another said, 'I have just

---

13:35 Ps 118:26. **14:2** Or *who had dropsy.* **14:5** Some manuscripts read *donkey.* **14:15** Greek *to eat bread.*

bought five pairs of oxen, and I want to try them out. Please excuse me.' [20]Another said, 'I now have a wife, so I can't come.'

[21]"The servant returned and told his master what they had said. His master was furious and said, 'Go quickly into the streets and alleys of the town and invite the poor, the crippled, the blind, and the lame.' [22]After the servant had done this, he reported, 'There is still room for more.' [23]So his master said, 'Go out into the country lanes and behind the hedges and urge anyone you find to come, so that the house will be full. [24]For none of those I first invited will get even the smallest taste of my banquet.'"

The Cost of Being a Disciple

[25]A large crowd was following Jesus. He turned around and said to them, [26]"If you want to be my disciple, you must hate everyone else by comparison—your father and mother, wife and children, brothers and sisters—yes, even your own life. Otherwise, you cannot be my disciple. [27]And if you do not carry your own cross and follow me, you cannot be my disciple.

[28]"But don't begin until you count the cost. For who would begin construction of a building without first calculating the cost to see if there is enough money to finish it? [29]Otherwise, you might complete only the foundation before running out of money, and then everyone would laugh at you. [30]They would say, 'There's the person who started that building and couldn't afford to finish it!'

[31]"Or what king would go to war against another king without first sitting down with his counselors to discuss whether his army of 10,000 could defeat the 20,000 soldiers marching against him? [32]And if he can't, he will send a delegation to discuss terms of peace while the enemy is still far away. [33]So you cannot become my disciple without giving up everything you own.

[34]"Salt is good for seasoning. But if it loses its flavor, how do you make it salty again? [35]Flavorless salt is good neither for the soil nor for the manure pile. It is thrown away. Anyone with ears to hear should listen and understand!"

CHAPTER 15

Parable of the Lost Sheep

Tax collectors and other notorious sinners often came to listen to Jesus teach. [2]This made the Pharisees and teachers of religious law complain that he was associating with such sinful people—even eating with them!

[3]So Jesus told them this story: [4]"If a man has a hundred sheep and one of them gets lost, what will he do? Won't he leave the ninety-nine others in the wilderness and go to search for the one that is lost until he finds it? [5]And when he has found it, he will joyfully carry it home on his shoulders. [6]When he arrives, he will call together his friends and neighbors, saying, 'Rejoice with me because I have found my lost sheep.' [7]In the same way, there is more joy in heaven over one lost sinner who repents and returns to God than over ninety-nine others who are righteous and haven't strayed away!

Parable of the Lost Coin

[8]"Or suppose a woman has ten silver coins* and loses one. Won't she light a lamp and sweep the entire house and search carefully until she finds it? [9]And when she finds it, she will call in her friends and neighbors and say, 'Rejoice with me because I have found my lost coin.' [10]In the same way, there is joy in the presence of God's angels when even one sinner repents."

Parable of the Lost Son

[11]To illustrate the point further, Jesus told them this story: "A man had two sons. [12]The younger son told his father, 'I want my share of your estate now before you die.' So his father agreed to divide his wealth between his sons.

[13]"A few days later this younger son packed all his belongings and moved to a distant land, and there he wasted all his money in wild living. [14]About the time his money ran out, a great famine swept over the land, and he began to starve. [15]He persuaded a local farmer to hire him, and the man sent him into his fields to feed the pigs. [16]The young man became so hungry that even the pods he was feeding the pigs looked good to him. But no one gave him anything.

[17]"When he finally came to his senses, he said to himself, 'At home even the hired servants have food enough to spare, and here I am dying of hunger! [18]I will go home to my father and say, "Father, I have sinned against both heaven and you, [19]and I am no longer worthy of being called your son. Please take me on as a hired servant."'

[20]"So he returned home to his father. And while he was still a long way off, his father saw him coming. Filled with love and compassion, he ran to his son, embraced him, and kissed him. [21]His son said to him, 'Father, I have sinned against both heaven and you, and I am no longer worthy of being called your son.*'

[22]"But his father said to the servants, 'Quick! Bring the finest robe in the house and put it on him. Get a ring for his finger and sandals for his feet. [23]And kill the calf we have been fattening. We must celebrate with a feast, [24]for this son of mine was dead and has now returned to life. He was lost, but now he is found.' So the party began.

[25]"Meanwhile, the older son was in the fields working. When he returned home, he heard music and dancing in the house, [26]and he asked one of the servants what was going on. [27]'Your brother is back,' he was told, 'and your father has killed the fattened calf. We are celebrating because of his safe return.'

[28]"The older brother was angry and wouldn't go in. His father came out and begged him, [29]but he replied, 'All these years I've slaved for you and never once refused to do a single thing you told me to. And in all that time you never gave me even one young goat for a feast with my friends. [30]Yet when this son of yours comes back after squandering your money on prostitutes, you celebrate by killing the fattened calf!'

[31]"His father said to him, 'Look, dear son, you have always stayed by me, and everything I have is yours. [32]We had to celebrate this happy day. For your brother was dead and has come back to life! He was lost, but now he is found!'"

15:8 Greek *ten drachmas.* A drachma was the equivalent of a full day's wage. **15:21** Some manuscripts add *Please take me on as a hired servant.*

CHAPTER 16

Parable of the Shrewd Manager

Jesus told this story to his disciples: "There was a certain rich man who had a manager handling his affairs. One day a report came that the manager was wasting his employer's money. ²So the employer called him in and said, 'What's this I hear about you? Get your report in order, because you are going to be fired.'

³"The manager thought to himself, 'Now what? My boss has fired me. I don't have the strength to dig ditches, and I'm too proud to beg. ⁴Ah, I know how to ensure that I'll have plenty of friends who will give me a home when I am fired.'

⁵"So he invited each person who owed money to his employer to come and discuss the situation. He asked the first one, 'How much do you owe him?' ⁶The man replied, 'I owe him 800 gallons of olive oil.' So the manager told him, 'Take the bill and quickly change it to 400 gallons.*'

⁷"'And how much do you owe my employer?' he asked the next man. 'I owe him 1,000 bushels of wheat,' was the reply. 'Here,' the manager said, 'take the bill and change it to 800 bushels.*'

⁸"The rich man had to admire the dishonest rascal for being so shrewd. And it is true that the children of this world are more shrewd in dealing with the world around them than are the children of the light. ⁹Here's the lesson: Use your worldly resources to benefit others and make friends. Then, when your earthly possessions are gone, they will welcome you to an eternal home.*

¹⁰"If you are faithful in little things, you will be faithful in large ones. But if you are dishonest in little things, you won't be honest with greater responsibilities. ¹¹And if you are untrustworthy about worldly wealth, who will trust you with the true riches of heaven? ¹²And if you are not faithful with other people's things, why should you be trusted with things of your own?

¹³"No one can serve two masters. For you will hate one and love the other; you will be devoted to one and despise the other. You cannot serve both God and money."

¹⁴The Pharisees, who dearly loved their money, heard all this and scoffed at him. ¹⁵Then he said to them, "You like to appear righteous in public, but God knows your hearts. What this world honors is detestable in the sight of God.

¹⁶"Until John the Baptist, the law of Moses and the messages of the prophets were your guides. But now the Good News of the Kingdom of God is preached, and everyone is eager to get in.* ¹⁷But that doesn't mean that the law has lost its force. It is easier for heaven and earth to disappear than for the smallest point of God's law to be overturned.

¹⁸"For example, a man who divorces his wife and marries someone else commits adultery. And anyone who marries a woman divorced from her husband commits adultery."

16:6 Greek *100 baths . . . 50 [baths].*   16:7 Greek *100 korous . . . 80 [korous].*   16:9 Or *you will be welcomed into eternal homes.*   16:16 Or *everyone is urged to enter in.*

Parable of the Rich Man and Lazarus

¹⁹Jesus said, "There was a certain rich man who was splendidly clothed in purple and fine linen and who lived each day in luxury. ²⁰At his gate lay a poor man named Lazarus who was covered with sores. ²¹As Lazarus lay there longing for scraps from the rich man's table, the dogs would come and lick his open sores.

²²"Finally, the poor man died and was carried by the angels to be with Abraham.* The rich man also died and was buried, ²³and his soul went to the place of the dead.* There, in torment, he saw Abraham in the far distance with Lazarus at his side.

²⁴"The rich man shouted, 'Father Abraham, have some pity! Send Lazarus over here to dip the tip of his finger in water and cool my tongue. I am in anguish in these flames.'

²⁵"But Abraham said to him, 'Son, remember that during your lifetime you had everything you wanted, and Lazarus had nothing. So now he is here being comforted, and you are in anguish. ²⁶And besides, there is a great chasm separating us. No one can cross over to you from here, and no one can cross over to us from there.'

²⁷"Then the rich man said, 'Please, Father Abraham, at least send him to my father's home. ²⁸For I have five brothers, and I want him to warn them so they don't end up in this place of torment.'

²⁹"But Abraham said, 'Moses and the prophets have warned them. Your brothers can read what they wrote.'

³⁰"The rich man replied, 'No, Father Abraham! But if someone is sent to them from the dead, then they will repent of their sins and turn to God.'

³¹"But Abraham said, 'If they won't listen to Moses and the prophets, they won't listen even if someone rises from the dead.'"

CHAPTER 17

Teachings about Forgiveness and Faith

One day Jesus said to his disciples, "There will always be temptations to sin, but what sorrow awaits the person who does the tempting! ²It would be better to be thrown into the sea with a millstone hung around your neck than to cause one of these little ones to fall into sin. ³So watch yourselves!

"If another believer* sins, rebuke that person; then if there is repentance, forgive. ⁴Even if that person wrongs you seven times a day and each time turns again and asks forgiveness, you must forgive."

⁵The apostles said to the Lord, "Show us how to increase our faith."

⁶The Lord answered, "If you had faith even as small as a mustard seed, you could say to this mulberry tree, 'May you be uprooted and thrown into the sea,' and it would obey you!

⁷"When a servant comes in from plowing or taking care of sheep, does his master say, 'Come in and eat with me'? ⁸No, he says, 'Prepare my meal, put on your apron, and serve me while I eat. Then you can eat later.' ⁹And does the master

---

16:22 Greek *into Abraham's bosom.*   **16:23** Greek *to Hades.*   **17:3** Greek *If your brother.*

thank the servant for doing what he was told to do? Of course not. [10]In the same way, when you obey me you should say, 'We are unworthy servants who have simply done our duty.'"

Ten Healed of Leprosy

[11]As Jesus continued on toward Jerusalem, he reached the border between Galilee and Samaria. [12]As he entered a village there, ten lepers stood at a distance, [13]crying out, "Jesus, Master, have mercy on us!"

[14]He looked at them and said, "Go show yourselves to the priests."* And as they went, they were cleansed of their leprosy.

[15]One of them, when he saw that he was healed, came back to Jesus, shouting, "Praise God!" [16]He fell to the ground at Jesus' feet, thanking him for what he had done. This man was a Samaritan.

[17]Jesus asked, "Didn't I heal ten men? Where are the other nine? [18]Has no one returned to give glory to God except this foreigner?" [19]And Jesus said to the man, "Stand up and go. Your faith has healed you.*"

The Coming of the Kingdom

[20]One day the Pharisees asked Jesus, "When will the Kingdom of God come?"

Jesus replied, "The Kingdom of God can't be detected by visible signs.* [21]You won't be able to say, 'Here it is!' or 'It's over there!' For the Kingdom of God is already among you.*"

[22]Then he said to his disciples, "The time is coming when you will long to see the day when the Son of Man returns,* but you won't see it. [23]People will tell you, 'Look, there is the Son of Man,' or 'Here he is,' but don't go out and follow them. [24]For as the lightning flashes and lights up the sky from one end to the other, so it will be on the day when the Son of Man comes. [25]But first the Son of Man must suffer terribly* and be rejected by this generation.

[26]"When the Son of Man returns, it will be like it was in Noah's day. [27]In those days, the people enjoyed banquets and parties and weddings right up to the time Noah entered his boat and the flood came and destroyed them all.

[28]"And the world will be as it was in the days of Lot. People went about their daily business—eating and drinking, buying and selling, farming and building— [29]until the morning Lot left Sodom. Then fire and burning sulfur rained down from heaven and destroyed them all. [30]Yes, it will be 'business as usual' right up to the day when the Son of Man is revealed. [31]On that day a person out on the deck of a roof must not go down into the house to pack. A person out in the field must not return home. [32]Remember what happened to Lot's wife! [33]If you cling to your life, you will lose it, and if you let your life go, you will save it. [34]That night two people will be asleep in one bed; one will be taken, the other left. [35]Two women will be grinding flour together at the mill; one will be taken, the other left.*"

17:14 See Lev 14:2-32.   17:19 Or *Your faith has saved you.*   17:20 Or *by your speculations.*   17:21 Or *is within you,* or *is in your grasp.*   17:22 Or *long for even one day with the Son of Man.* "Son of Man" is a title Jesus used for himself.   17:25 Or *suffer many things.*   17:35 Some manuscripts add verse 36, *Two men will be working in the field; one will be taken, the other left.* Compare Matt 24:40.

³⁷"Where will this happen, Lord?"* the disciples asked.

Jesus replied, "Just as the gathering of vultures shows there is a carcass nearby, so these signs indicate that the end is near."*

CHAPTER 18

Parable of the Persistent Widow

One day Jesus told his disciples a story to show that they should always pray and never give up. ²"There was a judge in a certain city," he said, "who neither feared God nor cared about people. ³A widow of that city came to him repeatedly, saying, 'Give me justice in this dispute with my enemy.' ⁴The judge ignored her for a while, but finally he said to himself, 'I don't fear God or care about people, ⁵but this woman is driving me crazy. I'm going to see that she gets justice, because she is wearing me out with her constant requests!'"

⁶Then the Lord said, "Learn a lesson from this unjust judge. ⁷Even he rendered a just decision in the end. So don't you think God will surely give justice to his chosen people who cry out to him day and night? Will he keep putting them off? ⁸I tell you, he will grant justice to them quickly! But when the Son of Man* returns, how many will he find on the earth who have faith?"

Parable of the Pharisee and Tax Collector

⁹Then Jesus told this story to some who had great confidence in their own righteousness and scorned everyone else: ¹⁰"Two men went to the Temple to pray. One was a Pharisee, and the other was a despised tax collector. ¹¹The Pharisee stood by himself and prayed this prayer*: 'I thank you, God, that I am not a sinner like everyone else. For I don't cheat, I don't sin, and I don't commit adultery. I'm certainly not like that tax collector! ¹²I fast twice a week, and I give you a tenth of my income.'

¹³"But the tax collector stood at a distance and dared not even lift his eyes to heaven as he prayed. Instead, he beat his chest in sorrow, saying, 'O God, be merciful to me, for I am a sinner.' ¹⁴I tell you, this sinner, not the Pharisee, returned home justified before God. For those who exalt themselves will be humbled, and those who humble themselves will be exalted."

Jesus Blesses the Children

¹⁵One day some parents brought their little children to Jesus so he could touch and bless them. But when the disciples saw this, they scolded the parents for bothering him.

¹⁶Then Jesus called for the children and said to the disciples, "Let the children come to me. Don't stop them! For the Kingdom of God belongs to those who are like these children. ¹⁷I tell you the truth, anyone who doesn't receive the Kingdom of God like a child will never enter it."

17:37a Greek *"Where, Lord?"*   **17:37b** Greek *"Wherever the carcass is, the vultures gather."*   **18:8** "Son of Man" is a title Jesus used for himself.   **18:11** Some manuscripts read *stood and prayed this prayer to himself.*

The Rich Man

[18]Once a religious leader asked Jesus this question: "Good Teacher, what should I do to inherit eternal life?"

[19]"Why do you call me good?" Jesus asked him. "Only God is truly good. [20]But to answer your question, you know the commandments: 'You must not commit adultery. You must not murder. You must not steal. You must not testify falsely. Honor your father and mother.'*"

[21]The man replied, "I've obeyed all these commandments since I was young."

[22]When Jesus heard his answer, he said, "There is still one thing you haven't done. Sell all your possessions and give the money to the poor, and you will have treasure in heaven. Then come, follow me."

[23]But when the man heard this he became very sad, for he was very rich.

[24]When Jesus saw this,* he said, "How hard it is for the rich to enter the Kingdom of God! [25]In fact, it is easier for a camel to go through the eye of a needle than for a rich person to enter the Kingdom of God!"

[26]Those who heard this said, "Then who in the world can be saved?"

[27]He replied, "What is impossible for people is possible with God."

[28]Peter said, "We've left our homes to follow you."

[29]"Yes," Jesus replied, "and I assure you that everyone who has given up house or wife or brothers or parents or children, for the sake of the Kingdom of God, [30]will be repaid many times over in this life, and will have eternal life in the world to come."

Jesus Again Predicts His Death

[31]Taking the twelve disciples aside, Jesus said, "Listen, we're going up to Jerusalem, where all the predictions of the prophets concerning the Son of Man will come true. [32]He will be handed over to the Romans,* and he will be mocked, treated shamefully, and spit upon. [33]They will flog him with a whip and kill him, but on the third day he will rise again."

[34]But they didn't understand any of this. The significance of his words was hidden from them, and they failed to grasp what he was talking about.

Jesus Heals a Blind Beggar

[35]As Jesus approached Jericho, a blind beggar was sitting beside the road. [36]When he heard the noise of a crowd going past, he asked what was happening. [37]They told him that Jesus the Nazarene* was going by. [38]So he began shouting, "Jesus, Son of David, have mercy on me!"

[39]"Be quiet!" the people in front yelled at him.

But he only shouted louder, "Son of David, have mercy on me!"

[40]When Jesus heard him, he stopped and ordered that the man be brought to him. As the man came near, Jesus asked him, [41]"What do you want me to do for you?"

"Lord," he said, "I want to see!"

18:20 Exod 20:12-16; Deut 5:16-20.   **18:24** Some manuscripts read *When Jesus saw how sad the man was.*
18:32 Greek *the Gentiles.*   **18:37** Or *Jesus of Nazareth.*

⁴²And Jesus said, "All right, receive your sight! Your faith has healed you." ⁴³Instantly the man could see, and he followed Jesus, praising God. And all who saw it praised God, too.

CHAPTER 19

Jesus and Zacchaeus

Jesus entered Jericho and made his way through the town. ²There was a man there named Zacchaeus. He was the chief tax collector in the region, and he had become very rich. ³He tried to get a look at Jesus, but he was too short to see over the crowd. ⁴So he ran ahead and climbed a sycamore-fig tree beside the road, for Jesus was going to pass that way.

⁵When Jesus came by, he looked up at Zacchaeus and called him by name. "Zacchaeus!" he said. "Quick, come down! I must be a guest in your home today."

⁶Zacchaeus quickly climbed down and took Jesus to his house in great excitement and joy. ⁷But the people were displeased. "He has gone to be the guest of a notorious sinner," they grumbled.

⁸Meanwhile, Zacchaeus stood before the Lord and said, "I will give half my wealth to the poor, Lord, and if I have cheated people on their taxes, I will give them back four times as much!"

⁹Jesus responded, "Salvation has come to this home today, for this man has shown himself to be a true son of Abraham. ¹⁰For the Son of Man* came to seek and save those who are lost."

Parable of the Ten Servants

¹¹The crowd was listening to everything Jesus said. And because he was nearing Jerusalem, he told them a story to correct the impression that the Kingdom of God would begin right away. ¹²He said, "A nobleman was called away to a distant empire to be crowned king and then return. ¹³Before he left, he called together ten of his servants and divided among them ten pounds of silver,* saying, 'Invest this for me while I am gone.' ¹⁴But his people hated him and sent a delegation after him to say, 'We do not want him to be our king.'

¹⁵"After he was crowned king, he returned and called in the servants to whom he had given the money. He wanted to find out what their profits were. ¹⁶The first servant reported, 'Master, I invested your money and made ten times the original amount!'

¹⁷"'Well done!' the king exclaimed. 'You are a good servant. You have been faithful with the little I entrusted to you, so you will be governor of ten cities as your reward.'

¹⁸"The next servant reported, 'Master, I invested your money and made five times the original amount.'

19:10 "Son of Man" is a title Jesus used for himself.   **19:13** Greek *ten minas;* one mina was worth about three months' wages.

[19] "'Well done!' the king said. 'You will be governor over five cities.'

[20] "But the third servant brought back only the original amount of money and said, 'Master, I hid your money and kept it safe. [21] I was afraid because you are a hard man to deal with, taking what isn't yours and harvesting crops you didn't plant.'

[22] "'You wicked servant!' the king roared. 'Your own words condemn you. If you knew that I'm a hard man who takes what isn't mine and harvests crops I didn't plant, [23] why didn't you deposit my money in the bank? At least I could have gotten some interest on it.'

[24] "Then, turning to the others standing nearby, the king ordered, 'Take the money from this servant, and give it to the one who has ten pounds.'

[25] "'But, master,' they said, 'he already has ten pounds!'

[26] "'Yes,' the king replied, 'and to those who use well what they are given, even more will be given. But from those who do nothing, even what little they have will be taken away. [27] And as for these enemies of mine who didn't want me to be their king—bring them in and execute them right here in front of me.'"

Jesus' Triumphant Entry

[28] After telling this story, Jesus went on toward Jerusalem, walking ahead of his disciples. [29] As he came to the towns of Bethphage and Bethany on the Mount of Olives, he sent two disciples ahead. [30] "Go into that village over there," he told them. "As you enter it, you will see a young donkey tied there that no one has ever ridden. Untie it and bring it here. [31] If anyone asks, 'Why are you untying that colt?' just say, 'The Lord needs it.'"

[32] So they went and found the colt, just as Jesus had said. [33] And sure enough, as they were untying it, the owners asked them, "Why are you untying that colt?"

[34] And the disciples simply replied, "The Lord needs it." [35] So they brought the colt to Jesus and threw their garments over it for him to ride on.

[36] As he rode along, the crowds spread out their garments on the road ahead of him. [37] When he reached the place where the road started down the Mount of Olives, all of his followers began to shout and sing as they walked along, praising God for all the wonderful miracles they had seen.

[38] "Blessings on the King who comes in the name of the LORD!
Peace in heaven, and glory in highest heaven!"*

[39] But some of the Pharisees among the crowd said, "Teacher, rebuke your followers for saying things like that!"

[40] He replied, "If they kept quiet, the stones along the road would burst into cheers!"

Jesus Weeps over Jerusalem

[41] But as he came closer to Jerusalem and saw the city ahead, he began to weep. [42] "How I wish today that you of all people would understand the way to peace. But now it is too late, and peace is hidden from your eyes. [43] Before long your enemies

---

19:38 Pss 118:26; 148:1.

will build ramparts against your walls and encircle you and close in on you from every side. [44]They will crush you into the ground, and your children with you. Your enemies will not leave a single stone in place, because you did not accept your opportunity for salvation."

Jesus Clears the Temple
[45]Then Jesus entered the Temple and began to drive out the people selling animals for sacrifices. [46]He said to them, "The Scriptures declare, 'My Temple will be a house of prayer,' but you have turned it into a den of thieves."*

[47]After that, he taught daily in the Temple, but the leading priests, the teachers of religious law, and the other leaders of the people began planning how to kill him. [48]But they could think of nothing, because all the people hung on every word he said.

CHAPTER 20

The Authority of Jesus Challenged
One day as Jesus was teaching the people and preaching the Good News in the Temple, the leading priests, the teachers of religious law, and the elders came up to him. [2]They demanded, "By what authority are you doing all these things? Who gave you the right?"

[3]"Let me ask you a question first," he replied. [4]"Did John's authority to baptize come from heaven, or was it merely human?"

[5]They talked it over among themselves. "If we say it was from heaven, he will ask why we didn't believe John. [6]But if we say it was merely human, the people will stone us because they are convinced John was a prophet." [7]So they finally replied that they didn't know.

[8]And Jesus responded, "Then I won't tell you by what authority I do these things."

Parable of the Evil Farmers
[9]Now Jesus turned to the people again and told them this story: "A man planted a vineyard, leased it to tenant farmers, and moved to another country to live for several years. [10]At the time of the grape harvest, he sent one of his servants to collect his share of the crop. But the farmers attacked the servant, beat him up, and sent him back empty-handed. [11]So the owner sent another servant, but they also insulted him, beat him up, and sent him away empty-handed. [12]A third man was sent, and they wounded him and chased him away.

[13]"'What will I do?' the owner asked himself. 'I know! I'll send my cherished son. Surely they will respect him.'

[14]"But when the tenant farmers saw his son, they said to each other, 'Here comes the heir to this estate. Let's kill him and get the estate for ourselves!' [15]So they dragged him out of the vineyard and murdered him.

19:46 Isa 56:7; Jer 7:11.

"What do you suppose the owner of the vineyard will do to them?" Jesus asked. [16]"I'll tell you—he will come and kill those farmers and lease the vineyard to others."

"How terrible that such a thing should ever happen," his listeners protested.

[17]Jesus looked at them and said, "Then what does this Scripture mean?

'The stone that the builders rejected
    has now become the cornerstone.'*

[18]Everyone who stumbles over that stone will be broken to pieces, and it will crush anyone it falls on."

[19]The teachers of religious law and the leading priests wanted to arrest Jesus immediately because they realized he was telling the story against them—they were the wicked farmers. But they were afraid of the people's reaction.

Taxes for Caesar

[20]Watching for their opportunity, the leaders sent spies pretending to be honest men. They tried to get Jesus to say something that could be reported to the Roman governor so he would arrest Jesus. [21]"Teacher," they said, "we know that you speak and teach what is right and are not influenced by what others think. You teach the way of God truthfully. [22]Now tell us—is it right for us to pay taxes to Caesar or not?"

[23]He saw through their trickery and said, [24]"Show me a Roman coin.* Whose picture and title are stamped on it?"

"Caesar's," they replied.

[25]"Well then," he said, "give to Caesar what belongs to Caesar, and give to God what belongs to God."

[26]So they failed to trap him by what he said in front of the people. Instead, they were amazed by his answer, and they became silent.

Discussion about Resurrection

[27]Then Jesus was approached by some Sadducees—religious leaders who say there is no resurrection from the dead. [28]They posed this question: "Teacher, Moses gave us a law that if a man dies, leaving a wife but no children, his brother should marry the widow and have a child who will carry on the brother's name.* [29]Well, suppose there were seven brothers. The oldest one married and then died without children. [30]So the second brother married the widow, but he also died. [31]Then the third brother married her. This continued with all seven of them, who died without children. [32]Finally, the woman also died. [33]So tell us, whose wife will she be in the resurrection? For all seven were married to her!"

[34]Jesus replied, "Marriage is for people here on earth. [35]But in the age to come, those worthy of being raised from the dead will neither marry nor be given in marriage. [36]And they will never die again. In this respect they will be like angels. They are children of God and children of the resurrection.

[37]"But now, as to whether the dead will be raised—even Moses proved this when

---

20:17 Ps 118:22.   20:24 Greek *a denarius.*   20:28 See Deut 25:5-6.

he wrote about the burning bush. Long after Abraham, Isaac, and Jacob had died, he referred to the Lord* as 'the God of Abraham, the God of Isaac, and the God of Jacob.'* ³⁸So he is the God of the living, not the dead, for they are all alive to him."

³⁹"Well said, Teacher!" remarked some of the teachers of religious law who were standing there. ⁴⁰And then no one dared to ask him any more questions.

Whose Son Is the Messiah?

⁴¹Then Jesus presented them with a question. "Why is it," he asked, "that the Messiah is said to be the son of David? ⁴²For David himself wrote in the book of Psalms:

'The LORD said to my Lord,
    Sit in the place of honor at my right hand
⁴³   until I humble your enemies,
        making them a footstool under your feet.'*

⁴⁴Since David called the Messiah 'Lord,' how can the Messiah be his son?"

⁴⁵Then, with the crowds listening, he turned to his disciples and said, ⁴⁶"Beware of these teachers of religious law! For they like to parade around in flowing robes and love to receive respectful greetings as they walk in the marketplaces. And how they love the seats of honor in the synagogues and the head table at banquets. ⁴⁷Yet they shamelessly cheat widows out of their property and then pretend to be pious by making long prayers in public. Because of this, they will be severely punished."

CHAPTER 21

The Widow's Offering

While Jesus was in the Temple, he watched the rich people dropping their gifts in the collection box. ²Then a poor widow came by and dropped in two small coins.*

³"I tell you the truth," Jesus said, "this poor widow has given more than all the rest of them. ⁴For they have given a tiny part of their surplus, but she, poor as she is, has given everything she has."

Jesus Foretells the Future

⁵Some of his disciples began talking about the majestic stonework of the Temple and the memorial decorations on the walls. But Jesus said, ⁶"The time is coming when all these things will be completely demolished. Not one stone will be left on top of another!"

⁷"Teacher," they asked, "when will all this happen? What sign will show us that these things are about to take place?"

⁸He replied, "Don't let anyone mislead you, for many will come in my name, claiming, 'I am the Messiah,'* and saying, 'The time has come!' But don't believe them. ⁹And when you hear of wars and insurrections, don't panic. Yes, these things

---

20:37a Greek *when he wrote about the bush. He referred to the Lord.* 20:37b Exod 3:6. 20:42-43 Ps 110:1.
21:2 Greek *two lepta* [the smallest of Jewish coins]. 21:8 Greek *claiming, 'I am.'*

must take place first, but the end won't follow immediately." ¹⁰Then he added, "Nation will go to war against nation, and kingdom against kingdom. ¹¹There will be great earthquakes, and there will be famines and plagues in many lands, and there will be terrifying things and great miraculous signs from heaven.

¹²"But before all this occurs, there will be a time of great persecution. You will be dragged into synagogues and prisons, and you will stand trial before kings and governors because you are my followers. ¹³But this will be your opportunity to tell them about me.* ¹⁴So don't worry in advance about how to answer the charges against you, ¹⁵for I will give you the right words and such wisdom that none of your opponents will be able to reply or refute you! ¹⁶Even those closest to you—your parents, brothers, relatives, and friends—will betray you. They will even kill some of you. ¹⁷And everyone will hate you because you are my followers.* ¹⁸But not a hair of your head will perish! ¹⁹By standing firm, you will win your souls.

²⁰"And when you see Jerusalem surrounded by armies, then you will know that the time of its destruction has arrived. ²¹Then those in Judea must flee to the hills. Those in Jerusalem must get out, and those out in the country should not return to the city. ²²For those will be days of God's vengeance, and the prophetic words of the Scriptures will be fulfilled. ²³How terrible it will be for pregnant women and for nursing mothers in those days. For there will be disaster in the land and great anger against this people. ²⁴They will be killed by the sword or sent away as captives to all the nations of the world. And Jerusalem will be trampled down by the Gentiles until the period of the Gentiles comes to an end.

²⁵"And there will be strange signs in the sun, moon, and stars. And here on earth the nations will be in turmoil, perplexed by the roaring seas and strange tides. ²⁶People will be terrified at what they see coming upon the earth, for the powers in the heavens will be shaken. ²⁷Then everyone will see the Son of Man* coming on a cloud with power and great glory.* ²⁸So when all these things begin to happen, stand and look up, for your salvation is near!"

²⁹Then he gave them this illustration: "Notice the fig tree, or any other tree. ³⁰When the leaves come out, you know without being told that summer is near. ³¹In the same way, when you see all these things taking place, you can know that the Kingdom of God is near. ³²I tell you the truth, this generation will not pass from the scene until all these things have taken place. ³³Heaven and earth will disappear, but my words will never disappear.

³⁴"Watch out! Don't let your hearts be dulled by carousing and drunkenness, and by the worries of this life. Don't let that day catch you unaware, ³⁵like a trap. For that day will come upon everyone living on the earth. ³⁶Keep alert at all times. And pray that you might be strong enough to escape these coming horrors and stand before the Son of Man."

³⁷Every day Jesus went to the Temple to teach, and each evening he returned to spend the night on the Mount of Olives. ³⁸The crowds gathered at the Temple early each morning to hear him.

21:13 Or *This will be your testimony against them.*   **21:17** Greek *on account of my name.*   **21:27a** "Son of Man" is a title Jesus used for himself.   **21:27b** See Dan 7:13.

CHAPTER 22

Judas Agrees to Betray Jesus

The Festival of Unleavened Bread, which is also called Passover, was approaching. [2]The leading priests and teachers of religious law were plotting how to kill Jesus, but they were afraid of the people's reaction.

[3]Then Satan entered into Judas Iscariot, who was one of the twelve disciples, [4]and he went to the leading priests and captains of the Temple guard to discuss the best way to betray Jesus to them. [5]They were delighted, and they promised to give him money. [6]So he agreed and began looking for an opportunity to betray Jesus so they could arrest him when the crowds weren't around.

The Last Supper

[7]Now the Festival of Unleavened Bread arrived, when the Passover lamb is sacrificed. [8]Jesus sent Peter and John ahead and said, "Go and prepare the Passover meal, so we can eat it together."

[9]"Where do you want us to prepare it?" they asked him.

[10]He replied, "As soon as you enter Jerusalem, a man carrying a pitcher of water will meet you. Follow him. At the house he enters, [11]say to the owner, 'The Teacher asks: Where is the guest room where I can eat the Passover meal with my disciples?' [12]He will take you upstairs to a large room that is already set up. That is where you should prepare our meal." [13]They went off to the city and found everything just as Jesus had said, and they prepared the Passover meal there.

[14]When the time came, Jesus and the apostles sat down together at the table.* [15]Jesus said, "I have been very eager to eat this Passover meal with you before my suffering begins. [16]For I tell you now that I won't eat this meal again until its meaning is fulfilled in the Kingdom of God."

[17]Then he took a cup of wine and gave thanks to God for it. Then he said, "Take this and share it among yourselves. [18]For I will not drink wine again until the Kingdom of God has come."

[19]He took some bread and gave thanks to God for it. Then he broke it in pieces and gave it to the disciples, saying, "This is my body, which is given for you. Do this to remember me."

[20]After supper he took another cup of wine and said, "This cup is the new covenant between God and his people—an agreement confirmed with my blood, which is poured out as a sacrifice for you.*

[21]"But here at this table, sitting among us as a friend, is the man who will betray me. [22]For it has been determined that the Son of Man* must die. But what sorrow awaits the one who betrays him." [23]The disciples began to ask each other which of them would ever do such a thing.

22:14 Or *reclined together.*   **22:19-20** Some manuscripts do not include 22:19b-20, *which is given for you . . . which is poured out as a sacrifice for you.*   **22:22** "Son of Man" is a title Jesus used for himself.

²⁴Then they began to argue among themselves about who would be the greatest among them. ²⁵Jesus told them, "In this world the kings and great men lord it over their people, yet they are called 'friends of the people.' ²⁶But among you it will be different. Those who are the greatest among you should take the lowest rank, and the leader should be like a servant. ²⁷Who is more important, the one who sits at the table or the one who serves? The one who sits at the table, of course. But not here! For I am among you as one who serves.

²⁸"You have stayed with me in my time of trial. ²⁹And just as my Father has granted me a Kingdom, I now grant you the right ³⁰to eat and drink at my table in my Kingdom. And you will sit on thrones, judging the twelve tribes of Israel.

Jesus Predicts Peter's Denial

³¹"Simon, Simon, Satan has asked to sift each of you like wheat. ³²But I have pleaded in prayer for you, Simon, that your faith should not fail. So when you have repented and turned to me again, strengthen your brothers."

³³Peter said, "Lord, I am ready to go to prison with you, and even to die with you."

³⁴But Jesus said, "Peter, let me tell you something. Before the rooster crows tomorrow morning, you will deny three times that you even know me."

³⁵Then Jesus asked them, "When I sent you out to preach the Good News and you did not have money, a traveler's bag, or an extra pair of sandals, did you need anything?"

"No," they replied.

³⁶"But now," he said, "take your money and a traveler's bag. And if you don't have a sword, sell your cloak and buy one! ³⁷For the time has come for this prophecy about me to be fulfilled: 'He was counted among the rebels.'* Yes, everything written about me by the prophets will come true."

³⁸"Look, Lord," they replied, "we have two swords among us."

"That's enough," he said.

Jesus Prays on the Mount of Olives

³⁹Then, accompanied by the disciples, Jesus left the upstairs room and went as usual to the Mount of Olives. ⁴⁰There he told them, "Pray that you will not give in to temptation."

⁴¹He walked away, about a stone's throw, and knelt down and prayed, ⁴²"Father, if you are willing, please take this cup of suffering away from me. Yet I want your will to be done, not mine." ⁴³Then an angel from heaven appeared and strengthened him. ⁴⁴He prayed more fervently, and he was in such agony of spirit that his sweat fell to the ground like great drops of blood.*

⁴⁵At last he stood up again and returned to the disciples, only to find them asleep, exhausted from grief. ⁴⁶"Why are you sleeping?" he asked them. "Get up and pray, so that you will not give in to temptation."

22:37 Isa 53:12.   **22:43-44** Verses 43 and 44 are not included in many ancient manuscripts.

Jesus Is Betrayed and Arrested

[47]But even as Jesus said this, a crowd approached, led by Judas, one of the twelve disciples. Judas walked over to Jesus to greet him with a kiss. [48]But Jesus said, "Judas, would you betray the Son of Man with a kiss?"

[49]When the other disciples saw what was about to happen, they exclaimed, "Lord, should we fight? We brought the swords!" [50]And one of them struck at the high priest's slave, slashing off his right ear.

[51]But Jesus said, "No more of this." And he touched the man's ear and healed him.

[52]Then Jesus spoke to the leading priests, the captains of the Temple guard, and the elders who had come for him. "Am I some dangerous revolutionary," he asked, "that you come with swords and clubs to arrest me? [53]Why didn't you arrest me in the Temple? I was there every day. But this is your moment, the time when the power of darkness reigns."

Peter Denies Jesus

[54]So they arrested him and led him to the high priest's home. And Peter followed at a distance. [55]The guards lit a fire in the middle of the courtyard and sat around it, and Peter joined them there. [56]A servant girl noticed him in the firelight and began staring at him. Finally she said, "This man was one of Jesus' followers!"

[57]But Peter denied it. "Woman," he said, "I don't even know him!"

[58]After a while someone else looked at him and said, "You must be one of them!"

"No, man, I'm not!" Peter retorted.

[59]About an hour later someone else insisted, "This must be one of them, because he is a Galilean, too."

[60]But Peter said, "Man, I don't know what you are talking about." And immediately, while he was still speaking, the rooster crowed. [61]At that moment the Lord turned and looked at Peter. Suddenly, the Lord's words flashed through Peter's mind: "Before the rooster crows tomorrow morning, you will deny three times that you even know me." [62]And Peter left the courtyard, weeping bitterly.

[63]The guards in charge of Jesus began mocking and beating him. [64]They blindfolded him and said, "Prophesy to us! Who hit you that time?" [65]And they hurled all sorts of terrible insults at him.

Jesus before the Council

[66]At daybreak all the elders of the people assembled, including the leading priests and the teachers of religious law. Jesus was led before this high council,* [67]and they said, "Tell us, are you the Messiah?"

But he replied, "If I tell you, you won't believe me. [68]And if I ask you a question, you won't answer. [69]But from now on the Son of Man will be seated in the place of power at God's right hand.*"

22:66 Greek *before their Sanhedrin.*   **22:69** See Ps 110:1.

208

⁷⁰They all shouted, "So, are you claiming to be the Son of God?" And he replied, "You say that I am."

⁷¹"Why do we need other witnesses?" they said. "We ourselves heard him say it."

CHAPTER 23

Jesus' Trial before Pilate

Then the entire council took Jesus to Pilate, the Roman governor. ²They began to state their case: "This man has been leading our people astray by telling them not to pay their taxes to the Roman government and by claiming he is the Messiah, a king."

³So Pilate asked him, "Are you the king of the Jews?"

Jesus replied, "You have said it."

⁴Pilate turned to the leading priests and to the crowd and said, "I find nothing wrong with this man!"

⁵Then they became insistent. "But he is causing riots by his teaching wherever he goes—all over Judea, from Galilee to Jerusalem!"

⁶"Oh, is he a Galilean?" Pilate asked. ⁷When they said that he was, Pilate sent him to Herod Antipas, because Galilee was under Herod's jurisdiction, and Herod happened to be in Jerusalem at the time.

⁸Herod was delighted at the opportunity to see Jesus, because he had heard about him and had been hoping for a long time to see him perform a miracle. ⁹He asked Jesus question after question, but Jesus refused to answer. ¹⁰Meanwhile, the leading priests and the teachers of religious law stood there shouting their accusations. ¹¹Then Herod and his soldiers began mocking and ridiculing Jesus. Finally, they put a royal robe on him and sent him back to Pilate. ¹²(Herod and Pilate, who had been enemies before, became friends that day.)

¹³Then Pilate called together the leading priests and other religious leaders, along with the people, ¹⁴and he announced his verdict. "You brought this man to me, accusing him of leading a revolt. I have examined him thoroughly on this point in your presence and find him innocent. ¹⁵Herod came to the same conclusion and sent him back to us. Nothing this man has done calls for the death penalty. ¹⁶So I will have him flogged, and then I will release him."*

¹⁸Then a mighty roar rose from the crowd, and with one voice they shouted, "Kill him, and release Barabbas to us!" ¹⁹(Barabbas was in prison for taking part in an insurrection in Jerusalem against the government, and for murder.) ²⁰Pilate argued with them, because he wanted to release Jesus. ²¹But they kept shouting, "Crucify him! Crucify him!"

²²For the third time he demanded, "Why? What crime has he committed? I have found no reason to sentence him to death. So I will have him flogged, and then I will release him."

²³But the mob shouted louder and louder, demanding that Jesus be crucified,

---

23:16 Some manuscripts add verse 17, *Now it was necessary for him to release one prisoner to them during the Passover celebration.* Compare Matt 27:15; Mark 15:6; John 18:39.

and their voices prevailed. ²⁴So Pilate sentenced Jesus to die as they demanded. ²⁵As they had requested, he released Barabbas, the man in prison for insurrection and murder. But he turned Jesus over to them to do as they wished.

The Crucifixion

²⁶As they led Jesus away, a man named Simon, who was from Cyrene,* happened to be coming in from the countryside. The soldiers seized him and put the cross on him and made him carry it behind Jesus. ²⁷A large crowd trailed behind, including many grief-stricken women. ²⁸But Jesus turned and said to them, "Daughters of Jerusalem, don't weep for me, but weep for yourselves and for your children. ²⁹For the days are coming when they will say, 'Fortunate indeed are the women who are childless, the wombs that have not borne a child and the breasts that have never nursed.' ³⁰People will beg the mountains, 'Fall on us,' and plead with the hills, 'Bury us.'* ³¹For if these things are done when the tree is green, what will happen when it is dry?*"

³²Two others, both criminals, were led out to be executed with him. ³³When they came to a place called The Skull,* they nailed him to the cross. And the criminals were also crucified—one on his right and one on his left.

³⁴Jesus said, "Father, forgive them, for they don't know what they are doing."* And the soldiers gambled for his clothes by throwing dice.*

³⁵The crowd watched and the leaders scoffed. "He saved others," they said, "let him save himself if he is really God's Messiah, the Chosen One." ³⁶The soldiers mocked him, too, by offering him a drink of sour wine. ³⁷They called out to him, "If you are the King of the Jews, save yourself!" ³⁸A sign was fastened above him with these words: "This is the King of the Jews."

³⁹One of the criminals hanging beside him scoffed, "So you're the Messiah, are you? Prove it by saving yourself—and us, too, while you're at it!"

⁴⁰But the other criminal protested, "Don't you fear God even when you have been sentenced to die? ⁴¹We deserve to die for our crimes, but this man hasn't done anything wrong." ⁴²Then he said, "Jesus, remember me when you come into your Kingdom."

⁴³And Jesus replied, "I assure you, today you will be with me in paradise."

The Death of Jesus

⁴⁴By this time it was about noon, and darkness fell across the whole land until three o'clock. ⁴⁵The light from the sun was gone. And suddenly, the curtain in the sanctuary of the Temple was torn down the middle. ⁴⁶Then Jesus shouted, "Father, I entrust my spirit into your hands!"* And with those words he breathed his last.

⁴⁷When the Roman officer* overseeing the execution saw what had happened, he worshiped God and said, "Surely this man was innocent.*" ⁴⁸And when all the crowd that came to see the crucifixion saw what had happened, they went home in deep sorrow.* ⁴⁹But Jesus' friends, including the women who had followed him from Galilee, stood at a distance watching.

23:26 *Cyrene* was a city in northern Africa.   **23:30** Hos 10:8.   **23:31** Or *If these things are done to me, the living tree, what will happen to you, the dry tree?*   **23:33** Sometimes rendered *Calvary,* which comes from the Latin word for "skull."   **23:34a** This sentence is not included in many ancient manuscripts.   **23:34b** Greek *by casting lots.* See Ps 22:18.   **23:46** Ps 31:5.   **23:47a** Greek *the centurion.*   **23:47b** Or *righteous.*   **23:48** Greek *went home beating their breasts.*

The Burial of Jesus

⁵⁰Now there was a good and righteous man named Joseph. He was a member of the Jewish high council, ⁵¹but he had not agreed with the decision and actions of the other religious leaders. He was from the town of Arimathea in Judea, and he was waiting for the Kingdom of God to come. ⁵²He went to Pilate and asked for Jesus' body. ⁵³Then he took the body down from the cross and wrapped it in a long sheet of linen cloth and laid it in a new tomb that had been carved out of rock. ⁵⁴This was done late on Friday afternoon, the day of preparation,* as the Sabbath was about to begin.

⁵⁵As his body was taken away, the women from Galilee followed and saw the tomb where his body was placed. ⁵⁶Then they went home and prepared spices and ointments to anoint his body. But by the time they were finished the Sabbath had begun, so they rested as required by the law.

CHAPTER 24

The Resurrection

But very early on Sunday morning* the women went to the tomb, taking the spices they had prepared. ²They found that the stone had been rolled away from the entrance. ³So they went in, but they didn't find the body of the Lord Jesus. ⁴As they stood there puzzled, two men suddenly appeared to them, clothed in dazzling robes.

⁵The women were terrified and bowed with their faces to the ground. Then the men asked, "Why are you looking among the dead for someone who is alive? ⁶He isn't here! He is risen from the dead! Remember what he told you back in Galilee, ⁷that the Son of Man* must be betrayed into the hands of sinful men and be crucified, and that he would rise again on the third day."

⁸Then they remembered that he had said this. ⁹So they rushed back from the tomb to tell his eleven disciples—and everyone else—what had happened. ¹⁰It was Mary Magdalene, Joanna, Mary the mother of James, and several other women who told the apostles what had happened. ¹¹But the story sounded like nonsense to the men, so they didn't believe it. ¹²However, Peter jumped up and ran to the tomb to look. Stooping, he peered in and saw the empty linen wrappings; then he went home again, wondering what had happened.

The Walk to Emmaus

¹³That same day two of Jesus' followers were walking to the village of Emmaus, seven miles* from Jerusalem. ¹⁴As they walked along they were talking about everything that had happened. ¹⁵As they talked and discussed these things, Jesus himself suddenly came and began walking with them. ¹⁶But God kept them from recognizing him.

23:54 Greek *It was the day of preparation.*   **24:1** Greek *But on the first day of the week, very early in the morning.*
24:7 "Son of Man" is a title Jesus used for himself.   **24:13** Greek *60 stadia* [11.1 kilometers].

[17]He asked them, "What are you discussing so intently as you walk along?"

They stopped short, sadness written across their faces. [18]Then one of them, Cleopas, replied, "You must be the only person in Jerusalem who hasn't heard about all the things that have happened there the last few days."

[19]"What things?" Jesus asked.

"The things that happened to Jesus, the man from Nazareth," they said. "He was a prophet who did powerful miracles, and he was a mighty teacher in the eyes of God and all the people. [20]But our leading priests and other religious leaders handed him over to be condemned to death, and they crucified him. [21]We had hoped he was the Messiah who had come to rescue Israel. This all happened three days ago.

[22]"Then some women from our group of his followers were at his tomb early this morning, and they came back with an amazing report. [23]They said his body was missing, and they had seen angels who told them Jesus is alive! [24]Some of our men ran out to see, and sure enough, his body was gone, just as the women had said."

[25]Then Jesus said to them, "You foolish people! You find it so hard to believe all that the prophets wrote in the Scriptures. [26]Wasn't it clearly predicted that the Messiah would have to suffer all these things before entering his glory?" [27]Then Jesus took them through the writings of Moses and all the prophets, explaining from all the Scriptures the things concerning himself.

[28]By this time they were nearing Emmaus and the end of their journey. Jesus acted as if he were going on, [29]but they begged him, "Stay the night with us, since it is getting late." So he went home with them. [30]As they sat down to eat,* he took the bread and blessed it. Then he broke it and gave it to them. [31]Suddenly, their eyes were opened, and they recognized him. And at that moment he disappeared!

[32]They said to each other, "Didn't our hearts burn within us as he talked with us on the road and explained the Scriptures to us?" [33]And within the hour they were on their way back to Jerusalem. There they found the eleven disciples and the others who had gathered with them, [34]who said, "The Lord has really risen! He appeared to Peter.*"

Jesus Appears to the Disciples

[35]Then the two from Emmaus told their story of how Jesus had appeared to them as they were walking along the road, and how they had recognized him as he was breaking the bread. [36]And just as they were telling about it, Jesus himself was suddenly standing there among them. "Peace be with you," he said. [37]But the whole group was startled and frightened, thinking they were seeing a ghost!

[38]"Why are you frightened?" he asked. "Why are your hearts filled with doubt? [39]Look at my hands. Look at my feet. You can see that it's really me. Touch me and make sure that I am not a ghost, because ghosts don't have bodies, as you see that I do." [40]As he spoke, he showed them his hands and his feet.

[41]Still they stood there in disbelief, filled with joy and wonder. Then he asked them, "Do you have anything here to eat?" [42]They gave him a piece of broiled fish, [43]and he ate it as they watched.

24:30 Or *As they reclined.*   **24:34** Greek *Simon.*

⁴⁴Then he said, "When I was with you before, I told you that everything written about me in the law of Moses and the prophets and in the Psalms must be fulfilled." ⁴⁵Then he opened their minds to understand the Scriptures. ⁴⁶And he said, "Yes, it was written long ago that the Messiah would suffer and die and rise from the dead on the third day. ⁴⁷It was also written that this message would be proclaimed in the authority of his name to all the nations,* beginning in Jerusalem: 'There is forgiveness of sins for all who repent.' ⁴⁸You are witnesses of all these things.

⁴⁹"And now I will send the Holy Spirit, just as my Father promised. But stay here in the city until the Holy Spirit comes and fills you with power from heaven."

The Ascension
⁵⁰Then Jesus led them to Bethany, and lifting his hands to heaven, he blessed them. ⁵¹While he was blessing them, he left them and was taken up to heaven. ⁵²So they worshiped him and then returned to Jerusalem filled with great joy. ⁵³And they spent all of their time in the Temple, praising God.

24:47 Or *all peoples.*

THE GOSPEL OF JOHN

Author

Though John's authorship is not explicitly stated anywhere in the Gospel, the text itself points to his authorship. The writer of this Gospel calls himself "the one whom Jesus loved"[20] and identifies himself at the end of the Gospel as a disciple who witnessed the events he wrote about, concluding with the personal "I" in the very last verse.[21] This disciple was one of the Twelve, and among them, he was one of those few who were very close to Jesus (for example, see 13:23-25, where this disciple is said to have been reclining on Jesus' bosom during the Last Supper).

From the synoptic Gospels we can conclude that three disciples were very close to Jesus: Peter, James, and John. Peter could not have been the author of this Gospel because he who named himself as "the disciple Jesus loved" communicated with Peter at the Last Supper,[22] raced Peter to the empty tomb on the morning of the Resurrection,[23] and walked with Jesus and Peter along the shore of the Sea of Galilee during another of Jesus' post-Resurrection appearances.[24]

Thus, someone other than Peter authored this Gospel. And that someone could not have been James, for he was martyred many years before this Gospel was written.[25] That someone must have been John, who shared an intimate relationship with Jesus. Most likely, it was also John who was the other disciple with Andrew (Peter's brother), the first two to follow Jesus,[26] and he was likely the one who was known to the high priest, gaining access for himself and Peter into the courtyard of the place where Jesus stood trial.[27] This one, "the disciple Jesus loved," stood by Jesus during his crucifixion[28] and walked with Jesus after his resurrection.[29] This is, then, the same disciple who wrote the Gospel that bears his name.[30]

Irenaeus (ca. A.D. 180) attributes the Gospel to John,[31] as does the Muratorian Canon and the Anti-Marcionite Prologue (late second century). Irenaeus, in that same statement, says he heard Polycarp talking about being tutored by John the apostle, who had seen the Lord. By the end of the second century (and from that point on), there was near-unanimous acceptance that the fourth Gospel was authored by John.

Date

The latest possible date for the writing of John's Gospel is between A.D. 110 and 120 because there is an early papyrus fragment of John (P52) dated to this period.[32] Another papyrus fragment of an unknown Gospel known as Egerton Papyrus 2, which was largely based on John's Gospel, is dated around A.D. 130–150. These copies give evidence of the existence of John's

Gospel in at least the beginning of the second century, if not earlier. The earliest possible date for John's Gospel is probably the late A.D. 60s. Most assign it to the 80s or early 90s because of John 21:23, which probably was penned while he was near the end of his life.

Manuscripts

There are more extant early manuscripts for the Gospel of John than for any other book of the New Testament. Manuscripts of the second and third centuries include the following:

P5 (John 1; 16; 20)
P22 (John 15–16)
P28 (John 6)
P39 (John 8)
P45 (John 4–5; 10–11)
P52 (John 18)[33]
P66 (all of the Gospel)
P75 (John 1–15)
P80 (John 3)
P90 (John 18–19)
P95 (John 5)
P107 (John 17)
P108 (John 17–18)
P109 (John 21)

Among these, P52 (also called P. Rylands 457) belongs to the early second century (ca. A.D. 110, the earliest extant manuscript of the New Testament); P66 belongs to the middle of the second century; and P75, to the end of the second century.[34] Of all these manuscripts, P75 is the most accurate copy of John. The manuscript, produced by a very careful scribe, was valued enough to be used by another careful scribe to produce the fourth-century manuscript known as Codex Vaticanus. According to textual critics, P75 and B provide the best textual witness to the original wording of John's Gospel. The corrected text of P66 (known as P66c) is also a good witness, as is P39 and P90.

Other manuscripts of the fourth and fifth centuries that provide good witness to the original text of John are Codex Sinaiticus (Aleph, from John 9–21), T, and W.

JOHN

CHAPTER 1

Prologue: Christ, the Eternal Word

¹ In the beginning the Word already existed.
    The Word was with God,
    and the Word was God.
² He existed in the beginning with God.
³ God created everything through him,
    and nothing was created except through him.
⁴ The Word gave life to everything that was created,*
    and his life brought light to everyone.
⁵ The light shines in the darkness,
    and the darkness can never extinguish it.*

⁶God sent a man, John the Baptist,* ⁷to tell about the light so that everyone might believe because of his testimony. ⁸John himself was not the light; he was simply a witness to tell about the light. ⁹The one who is the true light, who gives light to everyone, was coming into the world.

¹⁰He came into the very world he created, but the world didn't recognize him. ¹¹He came to his own people, and even they rejected him. ¹²But to all who believed him and accepted him, he gave the right to become children of God. ¹³They are reborn—not with a physical birth resulting from human passion or plan, but a birth that comes from God.

¹⁴So the Word became human* and made his home among us. He was full of unfailing love and faithfulness.* And we have seen his glory, the glory of the Father's one and only Son.

¹⁵John testified about him when he shouted to the crowds, "This is the one I was talking about when I said, 'Someone is coming after me who is far greater than I am, for he existed long before me.'"

¹⁶From his abundance we have all received one gracious blessing after another.* ¹⁷For the law was given through Moses, but God's unfailing love and faithfulness came through Jesus Christ. ¹⁸No one has ever seen God. But the unique One, who is himself God,* is near to the Father's heart. He has revealed God to us.

The Testimony of John the Baptist

¹⁹This was John's testimony when the Jewish leaders sent priests and Temple assistants* from Jerusalem to ask John, "Who are you?" ²⁰He came right out and said, "I am not the Messiah."

1:3-4 Or *and nothing that was created was created except through him. The Word gave life to everything.*   1:5 Or *and the darkness has not understood it.*   1:6 Greek *a man named John.*   1:14a Greek *became flesh.*   1:14b Or *grace and truth;* also in 1:17.   1:16 Or *received the grace of Christ rather than the grace of the law;* Greek reads *received grace upon grace.*   1:18 Some manuscripts read *But the one and only Son.*   1:19 Greek *and Levites.*

²¹"Well then, who are you?" they asked. "Are you Elijah?"

"No," he replied.

"Are you the Prophet we are expecting?"*

"No."

²²"Then who are you? We need an answer for those who sent us. What do you have to say about yourself?"

²³John replied in the words of the prophet Isaiah:

"I am a voice shouting in the wilderness,
    'Clear the way for the LORD's coming!'"*

²⁴Then the Pharisees who had been sent ²⁵asked him, "If you aren't the Messiah or Elijah or the Prophet, what right do you have to baptize?"

²⁶John told them, "I baptize with* water, but right here in the crowd is someone you do not recognize. ²⁷Though his ministry follows mine, I'm not even worthy to be his slave and untie the straps of his sandal."

²⁸This encounter took place in Bethany, an area east of the Jordan River, where John was baptizing.

Jesus, the Lamb of God

²⁹The next day John saw Jesus coming toward him and said, "Look! The Lamb of God who takes away the sin of the world! ³⁰He is the one I was talking about when I said, 'A man is coming after me who is far greater than I am, for he existed long before me.' ³¹I did not recognize him as the Messiah, but I have been baptizing with water so that he might be revealed to Israel."

³²Then John testified, "I saw the Holy Spirit descending like a dove from heaven and resting upon him. ³³I didn't know he was the one, but when God sent me to baptize with water, he told me, 'The one on whom you see the Spirit descend and rest is the one who will baptize with the Holy Spirit.' ³⁴I saw this happen to Jesus, so I testify that he is the Chosen One of God.*"

The First Disciples

³⁵The following day John was again standing with two of his disciples. ³⁶As Jesus walked by, John looked at him and declared, "Look! There is the Lamb of God!" ³⁷When John's two disciples heard this, they followed Jesus.

³⁸Jesus looked around and saw them following. "What do you want?" he asked them.

They replied, "Rabbi" (which means "Teacher"), "where are you staying?"

³⁹"Come and see," he said. It was about four o'clock in the afternoon when they went with him to the place where he was staying, and they remained with him the rest of the day.

⁴⁰Andrew, Simon Peter's brother, was one of these men who heard what John said and then followed Jesus. ⁴¹Andrew went to find his brother, Simon, and told him, "We have found the Messiah" (which means "Christ"*).

1:21 Greek *Are you the Prophet?* See Deut 18:15, 18; Mal 4:5-6.   **1:23** Isa 40:3.   **1:26** Or *in;* also in 1:31, 33.   **1:34** Some manuscripts read *the Son of God.*   **1:41** *Messiah* (a Hebrew term) and *Christ* (a Greek term) both mean "the anointed one."

⁴²Then Andrew brought Simon to meet Jesus. Looking intently at Simon, Jesus said, "Your name is Simon, son of John—but you will be called Cephas" (which means "Peter"*).

⁴³The next day Jesus decided to go to Galilee. He found Philip and said to him, "Come, follow me." ⁴⁴Philip was from Bethsaida, Andrew and Peter's hometown.

⁴⁵Philip went to look for Nathanael and told him, "We have found the very person Moses* and the prophets wrote about! His name is Jesus, the son of Joseph from Nazareth."

⁴⁶"Nazareth!" exclaimed Nathanael. "Can anything good come from Nazareth?"

"Come and see for yourself," Philip replied.

⁴⁷As they approached, Jesus said, "Now here is a genuine son of Israel—a man of complete integrity."

⁴⁸"How do you know about me?" Nathanael asked.

Jesus replied, "I could see you under the fig tree before Philip found you."

⁴⁹Then Nathanael exclaimed, "Rabbi, you are the Son of God—the King of Israel!"

⁵⁰Jesus asked him, "Do you believe this just because I told you I had seen you under the fig tree? You will see greater things than this." ⁵¹Then he said, "I tell you the truth, you will all see heaven open and the angels of God going up and down on the Son of Man, the one who is the stairway between heaven and earth.*"

CHAPTER 2

The Wedding at Cana

The next day* there was a wedding celebration in the village of Cana in Galilee. Jesus' mother was there, ²and Jesus and his disciples were also invited to the celebration. ³The wine supply ran out during the festivities, so Jesus' mother told him, "They have no more wine."

⁴"Dear woman, that's not our problem," Jesus replied. "My time has not yet come."

⁵But his mother told the servants, "Do whatever he tells you."

⁶Standing nearby were six stone water jars, used for Jewish ceremonial washing. Each could hold twenty to thirty gallons.* ⁷Jesus told the servants, "Fill the jars with water." When the jars had been filled, ⁸he said, "Now dip some out, and take it to the master of ceremonies." So the servants followed his instructions.

⁹When the master of ceremonies tasted the water that was now wine, not knowing where it had come from (though, of course, the servants knew), he called the bridegroom over. ¹⁰"A host always serves the best wine first," he said. "Then, when everyone has had a lot to drink, he brings out the less expensive wine. But you have kept the best until now!"

1:42 The names *Cephas* (from Aramaic) and *Peter* (from Greek) both mean "rock."   1:45 Greek *Moses in the law.*
1:51 Greek *going up and down on the Son of Man;* see Gen 28:10-17. "Son of Man" is a title Jesus used for himself.
2:1 Greek *On the third day;* see 1:35, 43.   2:6 Greek *2 or 3 measures* [75 to 113 liters].

¹¹This miraculous sign at Cana in Galilee was the first time Jesus revealed his glory. And his disciples believed in him.

¹²After the wedding he went to Capernaum for a few days with his mother, his brothers, and his disciples.

Jesus Clears the Temple

¹³It was nearly time for the Jewish Passover celebration, so Jesus went to Jerusalem. ¹⁴In the Temple area he saw merchants selling cattle, sheep, and doves for sacrifices; he also saw dealers at tables exchanging foreign money. ¹⁵Jesus made a whip from some ropes and chased them all out of the Temple. He drove out the sheep and cattle, scattered the money changers' coins over the floor, and turned over their tables. ¹⁶Then, going over to the people who sold doves, he told them, "Get these things out of here. Stop turning my Father's house into a marketplace!"

¹⁷Then his disciples remembered this prophecy from the Scriptures: "Passion for God's house will consume me."*

¹⁸But the Jewish leaders demanded, "What are you doing? If God gave you authority to do this, show us a miraculous sign to prove it."

¹⁹"All right," Jesus replied. "Destroy this temple, and in three days I will raise it up."

²⁰"What!" they exclaimed. "It has taken forty-six years to build this Temple, and you can rebuild it in three days?" ²¹But when Jesus said "this temple," he meant his own body. ²²After he was raised from the dead, his disciples remembered he had said this, and they believed both the Scriptures and what Jesus had said.

Jesus and Nicodemus

²³Because of the miraculous signs Jesus did in Jerusalem at the Passover celebration, many began to trust in him. ²⁴But Jesus didn't trust them, because he knew human nature. ²⁵No one needed to tell him what mankind is really like.

CHAPTER 3

There was a man named Nicodemus, a Jewish religious leader who was a Pharisee. ²After dark one evening, he came to speak with Jesus. "Rabbi," he said, "we all know that God has sent you to teach us. Your miraculous signs are evidence that God is with you."

³Jesus replied, "I tell you the truth, unless you are born again,* you cannot see the Kingdom of God."

⁴"What do you mean?" exclaimed Nicodemus. "How can an old man go back into his mother's womb and be born again?"

⁵Jesus replied, "I assure you, no one can enter the Kingdom of God without being born of water and the Spirit.* ⁶Humans can reproduce only human life, but

---

2:17 Or *"Concern for God's house will be my undoing."* Ps 69:9.   3:3 Or *born from above;* also in 3:7.   3:5 Or *and spirit.* The Greek word for *Spirit* can also be translated *wind;* see 3:8.

the Holy Spirit gives birth to spiritual life.* ⁷So don't be surprised when I say, 'You* must be born again.' ⁸The wind blows wherever it wants. Just as you can hear the wind but can't tell where it comes from or where it is going, so you can't explain how people are born of the Spirit."

⁹"How are these things possible?" Nicodemus asked.

¹⁰Jesus replied, "You are a respected Jewish teacher, and yet you don't understand these things? ¹¹I assure you, we tell you what we know and have seen, and yet you won't believe our testimony. ¹²But if you don't believe me when I tell you about earthly things, how can you possibly believe if I tell you about heavenly things? ¹³No one has ever gone to heaven and returned. But the Son of Man* has come down from heaven. ¹⁴And as Moses lifted up the bronze snake on a pole in the wilderness, so the Son of Man must be lifted up, ¹⁵so that everyone who believes in him will have eternal life.*

¹⁶"For God loved the world so much that he gave his one and only Son, so that everyone who believes in him will not perish but have eternal life. ¹⁷God sent his Son into the world not to judge the world, but to save the world through him.

¹⁸"There is no judgment against anyone who believes in him. But anyone who does not believe in him has already been judged for not believing in God's one and only Son. ¹⁹And the judgment is based on this fact: God's light came into the world, but people loved the darkness more than the light, for their actions were evil. ²⁰All who do evil hate the light and refuse to go near it for fear their sins will be exposed. ²¹But those who do what is right come to the light so others can see that they are doing what God wants.*"

John the Baptist Exalts Jesus

²²Then Jesus and his disciples left Jerusalem and went into the Judean countryside. Jesus spent some time with them there, baptizing people.

²³At this time John the Baptist was baptizing at Aenon, near Salim, because there was plenty of water there; and people kept coming to him for baptism. ²⁴(This was before John was thrown into prison.) ²⁵A debate broke out between John's disciples and a certain Jew* over ceremonial cleansing. ²⁶So John's disciples came to him and said, "Rabbi, the man you met on the other side of the Jordan River, the one you identified as the Messiah, is also baptizing people. And everybody is going to him instead of coming to us."

²⁷John replied, "No one can receive anything unless God gives it from heaven. ²⁸You yourselves know how plainly I told you, 'I am not the Messiah. I am only here to prepare the way for him.' ²⁹It is the bridegroom who marries the bride, and the best man is simply glad to stand with him and hear his vows. Therefore, I am filled with joy at his success. ³⁰He must become greater and greater, and I must become less and less.

³¹"He has come from above and is greater than anyone else. We are of the

---

3:6 Greek *what is born of the Spirit is spirit.*   **3:7** The Greek word for *you* is plural; also in 3:12.   **3:13** Some manuscripts add *who lives in heaven.* "Son of Man" is a title Jesus used for himself.   **3:15** Or *everyone who believes will have eternal life in him.*   **3:21** Or *can see God at work in what he is doing.*   **3:25** Some manuscripts read *some Jews.*

earth, and we speak of earthly things, but he has come from heaven and is greater than anyone else.* [32]He testifies about what he has seen and heard, but how few believe what he tells them! [33]Anyone who accepts his testimony can affirm that God is true. [34]For he is sent by God. He speaks God's words, for God gives him the Spirit without limit. [35]The Father loves his Son and has put everything into his hands. [36]And anyone who believes in God's Son has eternal life. Anyone who doesn't obey the Son will never experience eternal life but remains under God's angry judgment."

CHAPTER 4

Jesus and the Samaritan Woman

Jesus* knew the Pharisees had heard that he was baptizing and making more disciples than John [2](though Jesus himself didn't baptize them—his disciples did). [3]So he left Judea and returned to Galilee.

[4]He had to go through Samaria on the way. [5]Eventually he came to the Samaritan village of Sychar, near the field that Jacob gave to his son Joseph. [6]Jacob's well was there; and Jesus, tired from the long walk, sat wearily beside the well about noontime. [7]Soon a Samaritan woman came to draw water, and Jesus said to her, "Please give me a drink." [8]He was alone at the time because his disciples had gone into the village to buy some food.

[9]The woman was surprised, for Jews refuse to have anything to do with Samaritans.* She said to Jesus, "You are a Jew, and I am a Samaritan woman. Why are you asking me for a drink?"

[10]Jesus replied, "If you only knew the gift God has for you and who you are speaking to, you would ask me, and I would give you living water."

[11]"But sir, you don't have a rope or a bucket," she said, "and this well is very deep. Where would you get this living water? [12]And besides, do you think you're greater than our ancestor Jacob, who gave us this well? How can you offer better water than he and his sons and his animals enjoyed?"

[13]Jesus replied, "Anyone who drinks this water will soon become thirsty again. [14]But those who drink the water I give will never be thirsty again. It becomes a fresh, bubbling spring within them, giving them eternal life."

[15]"Please, sir," the woman said, "give me this water! Then I'll never be thirsty again, and I won't have to come here to get water."

[16]"Go and get your husband," Jesus told her.

[17]"I don't have a husband," the woman replied.

Jesus said, "You're right! You don't have a husband—[18]for you have had five husbands, and you aren't even married to the man you're living with now. You certainly spoke the truth!"

[19]"Sir," the woman said, "you must be a prophet. [20]So tell me, why is it that you

---

3:31 Some manuscripts do not include *and is greater than anyone else.*   **4:1** Some manuscripts read *The Lord.*
4:9 Some manuscripts do not include this sentence.

Jews insist that Jerusalem is the only place of worship, while we Samaritans claim it is here at Mount Gerizim,* where our ancestors worshiped?"

²¹Jesus replied, "Believe me, dear woman, the time is coming when it will no longer matter whether you worship the Father on this mountain or in Jerusalem. ²²You Samaritans know very little about the one you worship, while we Jews know all about him, for salvation comes through the Jews. ²³But the time is coming—indeed it's here now—when true worshipers will worship the Father in spirit and in truth. The Father is looking for those who will worship him that way. ²⁴For God is Spirit, so those who worship him must worship in spirit and in truth."

²⁵The woman said, "I know the Messiah is coming—the one who is called Christ. When he comes, he will explain everything to us."

²⁶Then Jesus told her, "I AM the Messiah!"*

²⁷Just then his disciples came back. They were shocked to find him talking to a woman, but none of them had the nerve to ask, "What do you want with her?" or "Why are you talking to her?" ²⁸The woman left her water jar beside the well and ran back to the village, telling everyone, ²⁹"Come and see a man who told me everything I ever did! Could he possibly be the Messiah?" ³⁰So the people came streaming from the village to see him.

³¹Meanwhile, the disciples were urging Jesus, "Rabbi, eat something."

³²But Jesus replied, "I have a kind of food you know nothing about."

³³"Did someone bring him food while we were gone?" the disciples asked each other.

³⁴Then Jesus explained: "My nourishment comes from doing the will of God, who sent me, and from finishing his work. ³⁵You know the saying, 'Four months between planting and harvest.' But I say, wake up and look around. The fields are already ripe* for harvest. ³⁶The harvesters are paid good wages, and the fruit they harvest is people brought to eternal life. What joy awaits both the planter and the harvester alike! ³⁷You know the saying, 'One plants and another harvests.' And it's true. ³⁸I sent you to harvest where you didn't plant; others had already done the work, and now you will get to gather the harvest."

Many Samaritans Believe

³⁹Many Samaritans from the village believed in Jesus because the woman had said, "He told me everything I ever did!" ⁴⁰When they came out to see him, they begged him to stay in their village. So he stayed for two days, ⁴¹long enough for many more to hear his message and believe. ⁴²Then they said to the woman, "Now we believe, not just because of what you told us, but because we have heard him ourselves. Now we know that he is indeed the Savior of the world."

Jesus Heals an Official's Son

⁴³At the end of the two days, Jesus went on to Galilee. ⁴⁴He himself had said that a prophet is not honored in his own hometown. ⁴⁵Yet the Galileans welcomed him,

---

4:20 Greek *on this mountain.*   **4:26** Or *"The 'I AM' is here";* or *"I am the* LORD*";* Greek reads *"I am, the one speaking to you."* See Exod 3:14.   **4:35** Greek *white.*

for they had been in Jerusalem at the Passover celebration and had seen everything he did there.

⁴⁶As he traveled through Galilee, he came to Cana, where he had turned the water into wine. There was a government official in nearby Capernaum whose son was very sick. ⁴⁷When he heard that Jesus had come from Judea to Galilee, he went and begged Jesus to come to Capernaum to heal his son, who was about to die.

⁴⁸Jesus asked, "Will you never believe in me unless you see miraculous signs and wonders?"

⁴⁹The official pleaded, "Lord, please come now before my little boy dies."

⁵⁰Then Jesus told him, "Go back home. Your son will live!" And the man believed what Jesus said and started home.

⁵¹While the man was on his way, some of his servants met him with the news that his son was alive and well. ⁵²He asked them when the boy had begun to get better, and they replied, "Yesterday afternoon at one o'clock his fever suddenly disappeared!" ⁵³Then the father realized that that was the very time Jesus had told him, "Your son will live." And he and his entire household believed in Jesus. ⁵⁴This was the second miraculous sign Jesus did in Galilee after coming from Judea.

CHAPTER 5

Jesus Heals a Lame Man

Afterward Jesus returned to Jerusalem for one of the Jewish holy days. ²Inside the city, near the Sheep Gate, was the pool of Bethesda,* with five covered porches. ³Crowds of sick people—blind, lame, or paralyzed—lay on the porches.* ⁵One of the men lying there had been sick for thirty-eight years. ⁶When Jesus saw him and knew he had been ill for a long time, he asked him, "Would you like to get well?"

⁷"I can't, sir," the sick man said, "for I have no one to put me into the pool when the water bubbles up. Someone else always gets there ahead of me."

⁸Jesus told him, "Stand up, pick up your mat, and walk!"

⁹Instantly, the man was healed! He rolled up his sleeping mat and began walking! But this miracle happened on the Sabbath, ¹⁰so the Jewish leaders objected. They said to the man who was cured, "You can't work on the Sabbath! The law doesn't allow you to carry that sleeping mat!"

¹¹But he replied, "The man who healed me told me, 'Pick up your mat and walk.'"

¹²"Who said such a thing as that?" they demanded.

¹³The man didn't know, for Jesus had disappeared into the crowd. ¹⁴But afterward Jesus found him in the Temple and told him, "Now you are well; so stop sinning, or something even worse may happen to you." ¹⁵Then the man went and told the Jewish leaders that it was Jesus who had healed him.

5:2 Other manuscripts read *Beth-zatha;* still others read *Bethsaida.*   5:3 Some manuscripts add an expanded conclusion to verse 3 and all of verse 4: *waiting for a certain movement of the water,* ⁴*for an angel of the Lord came from time to time and stirred up the water. And the first person to step in after the water was stirred was healed of whatever disease he had.*

Jesus Claims to Be the Son of God

[16]So the Jewish leaders began harassing* Jesus for breaking the Sabbath rules. [17]But Jesus replied, "My Father is always working, and so am I." [18]So the Jewish leaders tried all the harder to find a way to kill him. For he not only broke the Sabbath, he called God his Father, thereby making himself equal with God.

[19]So Jesus explained, "I tell you the truth, the Son can do nothing by himself. He does only what he sees the Father doing. Whatever the Father does, the Son also does. [20]For the Father loves the Son and shows him everything he is doing. In fact, the Father will show him how to do even greater works than healing this man. Then you will truly be astonished. [21]For just as the Father gives life to those he raises from the dead, so the Son gives life to anyone he wants. [22]In addition, the Father judges no one. Instead, he has given the Son absolute authority to judge, [23]so that everyone will honor the Son, just as they honor the Father. Anyone who does not honor the Son is certainly not honoring the Father who sent him.

[24]"I tell you the truth, those who listen to my message and believe in God who sent me have eternal life. They will never be condemned for their sins, but they have already passed from death into life.

[25]"And I assure you that the time is coming, indeed it's here now, when the dead will hear my voice—the voice of the Son of God. And those who listen will live. [26]The Father has life in himself, and he has granted that same life-giving power to his Son. [27]And he has given him authority to judge everyone because he is the Son of Man.* [28]Don't be so surprised! Indeed, the time is coming when all the dead in their graves will hear the voice of God's Son, [29]and they will rise again. Those who have done good will rise to experience eternal life, and those who have continued in evil will rise to experience judgment. [30]I can do nothing on my own. I judge as God tells me. Therefore, my judgment is just, because I carry out the will of the one who sent me, not my own will.

Witnesses to Jesus

[31]"If I were to testify on my own behalf, my testimony would not be valid. [32]But someone else is also testifying about me, and I assure you that everything he says about me is true. [33]In fact, you sent investigators to listen to John the Baptist, and his testimony about me was true. [34]Of course, I have no need of human witnesses, but I say these things so you might be saved. [35]John was like a burning and shining lamp, and you were excited for a while about his message. [36]But I have a greater witness than John—my teachings and my miracles. The Father gave me these works to accomplish, and they prove that he sent me. [37]And the Father who sent me has testified about me himself. You have never heard his voice or seen him face to face, [38]and you do not have his message in your hearts, because you do not believe me—the one he sent to you.

[39]"You search the Scriptures because you think they give you eternal life. But the Scriptures point to me! [40]Yet you refuse to come to me to receive this life.

5:16 Or *persecuting.*   **5:27** "Son of Man" is a title Jesus used for himself.

[41]"Your approval means nothing to me, [42]because I know you don't have God's love within you. [43]For I have come to you in my Father's name, and you have rejected me. Yet if others come in their own name, you gladly welcome them. [44]No wonder you can't believe! For you gladly honor each other, but you don't care about the honor that comes from the one who alone is God.*

[45]"Yet it isn't I who will accuse you before the Father. Moses will accuse you! Yes, Moses, in whom you put your hopes. [46]If you really believed Moses, you would believe me, because he wrote about me. [47]But since you don't believe what he wrote, how will you believe what I say?"

CHAPTER 6

Jesus Feeds Five Thousand

After this, Jesus crossed over to the far side of the Sea of Galilee, also known as the Sea of Tiberias. [2]A huge crowd kept following him wherever he went, because they saw his miraculous signs as he healed the sick. [3]Then Jesus climbed a hill and sat down with his disciples around him. [4](It was nearly time for the Jewish Passover celebration.) [5]Jesus soon saw a huge crowd of people coming to look for him. Turning to Philip, he asked, "Where can we buy bread to feed all these people?" [6]He was testing Philip, for he already knew what he was going to do.

[7]Philip replied, "Even if we worked for months, we wouldn't have enough money* to feed them!"

[8]Then Andrew, Simon Peter's brother, spoke up. [9]"There's a young boy here with five barley loaves and two fish. But what good is that with this huge crowd?"

[10]"Tell everyone to sit down," Jesus said. So they all sat down on the grassy slopes. (The men alone numbered about 5,000.) [11]Then Jesus took the loaves, gave thanks to God, and distributed them to the people. Afterward he did the same with the fish. And they all ate as much as they wanted. [12]After everyone was full, Jesus told his disciples, "Now gather the leftovers, so that nothing is wasted." [13]So they picked up the pieces and filled twelve baskets with scraps left by the people who had eaten from the five barley loaves.

[14]When the people saw him* do this miraculous sign, they exclaimed, "Surely, he is the Prophet we have been expecting!"* [15]When Jesus saw that they were ready to force him to be their king, he slipped away into the hills by himself.

Jesus Walks on Water

[16]That evening Jesus' disciples went down to the shore to wait for him. [17]But as darkness fell and Jesus still hadn't come back, they got into the boat and headed across the lake toward Capernaum. [18]Soon a gale swept down upon them, and the sea grew very rough. [19]They had rowed three or four miles* when suddenly they saw Jesus walking on the water toward the boat. They were terrified, [20]but

---

5:44 Some manuscripts read *from the only One.*   **6:7** Greek *Two hundred denarii would not be enough.* A denarius was equivalent to a laborer's full day's wage.   **6:14a** Some manuscripts read *Jesus.*   **6:14b** See Deut 18:15, 18; Mal 4:5-6.   **6:19** Greek *25 or 30 stadia* [4.6 or 5.5 kilometers].

he called out to them, "Don't be afraid. I am here!*" ²¹Then they were eager to let him in the boat, and immediately they arrived at their destination!

Jesus, the Bread of Life

²²The next day the crowd that had stayed on the far shore saw that the disciples had taken the only boat, and they realized Jesus had not gone with them. ²³Several boats from Tiberias landed near the place where the Lord had blessed the bread and the people had eaten. ²⁴So when the crowd saw that neither Jesus nor his disciples were there, they got into the boats and went across to Capernaum to look for him. ²⁵They found him on the other side of the lake and asked, "Rabbi, when did you get here?"

²⁶Jesus replied, "I tell you the truth, you want to be with me because I fed you, not because you understood the miraculous signs. ²⁷But don't be so concerned about perishable things like food. Spend your energy seeking the eternal life that the Son of Man* can give you. For God the Father has given me the seal of his approval."

²⁸They replied, "We want to perform God's works, too. What should we do?"

²⁹Jesus told them, "This is the only work God wants from you: Believe in the one he has sent."

³⁰They answered, "Show us a miraculous sign if you want us to believe in you. What can you do? ³¹After all, our ancestors ate manna while they journeyed through the wilderness! The Scriptures say, 'Moses gave them bread from heaven to eat.'*"

³²Jesus said, "I tell you the truth, Moses didn't give you bread from heaven. My Father did. And now he offers you the true bread from heaven. ³³The true bread of God is the one who comes down from heaven and gives life to the world."

³⁴"Sir," they said, "give us that bread every day."

³⁵Jesus replied, "I am the bread of life. Whoever comes to me will never be hungry again. Whoever believes in me will never be thirsty. ³⁶But you haven't believed in me even though you have seen me. ³⁷However, those the Father has given me will come to me, and I will never reject them. ³⁸For I have come down from heaven to do the will of God who sent me, not to do my own will. ³⁹And this is the will of God, that I should not lose even one of all those he has given me, but that I should raise them up at the last day. ⁴⁰For it is my Father's will that all who see his Son and believe in him should have eternal life. I will raise them up at the last day."

⁴¹Then the people* began to murmur in disagreement because he had said, "I am the bread that came down from heaven." ⁴²They said, "Isn't this Jesus, the son of Joseph? We know his father and mother. How can he say, 'I came down from heaven'?"

⁴³But Jesus replied, "Stop complaining about what I said. ⁴⁴For no one can come to me unless the Father who sent me draws them to me, and at the last day I will raise them up. ⁴⁵As it is written in the Scriptures,* 'They will all be taught by God.' Everyone who listens to the Father and learns from him comes to me. ⁴⁶(Not that anyone has ever seen the Father; only I, who was sent from God, have seen him.)

6:20 Or *The 'I AM' is here;* Greek reads *I am.* See Exod 3:14.   **6:27** "Son of Man" is a title Jesus used for himself.
6:31 Exod 16:4; Ps 78:24.   **6:41** Greek *Jewish people;* also in 6:52.   **6:45** Greek *in the prophets.* Isa 54:13.

[47]"I tell you the truth, anyone who believes has eternal life. [48]Yes, I am the bread of life! [49]Your ancestors ate manna in the wilderness, but they all died. [50]Anyone who eats the bread from heaven, however, will never die. [51]I am the living bread that came down from heaven. Anyone who eats this bread will live forever; and this bread, which I will offer so the world may live, is my flesh."

[52]Then the people began arguing with each other about what he meant. "How can this man give us his flesh to eat?" they asked.

[53]So Jesus said again, "I tell you the truth, unless you eat the flesh of the Son of Man and drink his blood, you cannot have eternal life within you. [54]But anyone who eats my flesh and drinks my blood has eternal life, and I will raise that person at the last day. [55]For my flesh is true food, and my blood is true drink. [56]Anyone who eats my flesh and drinks my blood remains in me, and I in him. [57]I live because of the living Father who sent me; in the same way, anyone who feeds on me will live because of me. [58]I am the true bread that came down from heaven. Anyone who eats this bread will not die as your ancestors did (even though they ate the manna) but will live forever."

[59]He said these things while he was teaching in the synagogue in Capernaum.

Many Disciples Desert Jesus

[60]Many of his disciples said, "This is very hard to understand. How can anyone accept it?"

[61]Jesus was aware that his disciples were complaining, so he said to them, "Does this offend you? [62]Then what will you think if you see the Son of Man ascend to heaven again? [63]The Spirit alone gives eternal life. Human effort accomplishes nothing. And the very words I have spoken to you are spirit and life. [64]But some of you do not believe me." (For Jesus knew from the beginning which ones didn't believe, and he knew who would betray him.) [65]Then he said, "That is why I said that people can't come to me unless the Father gives them to me."

[66]At this point many of his disciples turned away and deserted him. [67]Then Jesus turned to the Twelve and asked, "Are you also going to leave?"

[68]Simon Peter replied, "Lord, to whom would we go? You have the words that give eternal life. [69]We believe, and we know you are the Holy One of God.*"

[70]Then Jesus said, "I chose the twelve of you, but one is a devil." [71]He was speaking of Judas, son of Simon Iscariot, one of the Twelve, who would later betray him.

CHAPTER 7

Jesus and His Brothers

After this, Jesus traveled around Galilee. He wanted to stay out of Judea, where the Jewish leaders were plotting his death. [2]But soon it was time for the Jewish Festival of Shelters, [3]and Jesus' brothers said to him, "Leave here and go to Judea, where

---

6:69 Other manuscripts read *you are the Christ, the Holy One of God;* still others read *you are the Christ, the Son of God;* and still others read *you are the Christ, the Son of the living God.*

your followers can see your miracles! [4]You can't become famous if you hide like this! If you can do such wonderful things, show yourself to the world!" [5]For even his brothers didn't believe in him.

[6]Jesus replied, "Now is not the right time for me to go, but you can go anytime. [7]The world can't hate you, but it does hate me because I accuse it of doing evil. [8]You go on. I'm not going* to this festival, because my time has not yet come." [9]After saying these things, Jesus remained in Galilee.

Jesus Teaches Openly at the Temple

[10]But after his brothers left for the festival, Jesus also went, though secretly, staying out of public view. [11]The Jewish leaders tried to find him at the festival and kept asking if anyone had seen him. [12]There was a lot of grumbling about him among the crowds. Some argued, "He's a good man," but others said, "He's nothing but a fraud who deceives the people." [13]But no one had the courage to speak favorably about him in public, for they were afraid of getting in trouble with the Jewish leaders.

[14]Then, midway through the festival, Jesus went up to the Temple and began to teach. [15]The people* were surprised when they heard him. "How does he know so much when he hasn't been trained?" they asked.

[16]So Jesus told them, "My message is not my own; it comes from God who sent me. [17]Anyone who wants to do the will of God will know whether my teaching is from God or is merely my own. [18]Those who speak for themselves want glory only for themselves, but a person who seeks to honor the one who sent him speaks truth, not lies. [19]Moses gave you the law, but none of you obeys it! In fact, you are trying to kill me."

[20]The crowd replied, "You're demon possessed! Who's trying to kill you?"

[21]Jesus replied, "I did one miracle on the Sabbath, and you were amazed. [22]But you work on the Sabbath, too, when you obey Moses' law of circumcision. (Actually, this tradition of circumcision began with the patriarchs, long before the law of Moses.) [23]For if the correct time for circumcising your son falls on the Sabbath, you go ahead and do it so as not to break the law of Moses. So why should you be angry with me for healing a man on the Sabbath? [24]Look beneath the surface so you can judge correctly."

Is Jesus the Messiah?

[25]Some of the people who lived in Jerusalem started to ask each other, "Isn't this the man they are trying to kill? [26]But here he is, speaking in public, and they say nothing to him. Could our leaders possibly believe that he is the Messiah? [27]But how could he be? For we know where this man comes from. When the Messiah comes, he will simply appear; no one will know where he comes from."

[28]While Jesus was teaching in the Temple, he called out, "Yes, you know me, and you know where I come from. But I'm not here on my own. The one who sent me is true, and you don't know him. [29]But I know him because I come from him, and he sent me to you." [30]Then the leaders tried to arrest him; but no one laid a hand on him, because his time* had not yet come.

7:8 Some manuscripts read *not yet going.*   **7:15** Greek *Jewish people.*   **7:30** Greek *his hour.*

³¹Many among the crowds at the Temple believed in him. "After all," they said, "would you expect the Messiah to do more miraculous signs than this man has done?"

³²When the Pharisees heard that the crowds were whispering such things, they and the leading priests sent Temple guards to arrest Jesus. ³³But Jesus told them, "I will be with you only a little longer. Then I will return to the one who sent me. ³⁴You will search for me but not find me. And you cannot go where I am going."

³⁵The Jewish leaders were puzzled by this statement. "Where is he planning to go?" they asked. "Is he thinking of leaving the country and going to the Jews in other lands?* Maybe he will even teach the Greeks! ³⁶What does he mean when he says, 'You will search for me but not find me,' and 'You cannot go where I am going'?"

Jesus Promises Living Water

³⁷On the last day, the climax of the festival, Jesus stood and shouted to the crowds, "Anyone who is thirsty may come to me! ³⁸Anyone who believes in me may come and drink! For the Scriptures declare, 'Rivers of living water will flow from his heart.'"* ³⁹(When he said "living water," he was speaking of the Spirit, who would be given to everyone believing in him. But the Spirit had not yet been given,* because Jesus had not yet entered into his glory.)

Division and Unbelief

⁴⁰When the crowds heard him say this, some of them declared, "Surely this man is the Prophet we've been expecting."* ⁴¹Others said, "He is the Messiah." Still others said, "But he can't be! Will the Messiah come from Galilee? ⁴²For the Scriptures clearly state that the Messiah will be born of the royal line of David, in Bethlehem, the village where King David was born."* ⁴³So the crowd was divided about him. ⁴⁴Some even wanted him arrested, but no one laid a hand on him.

⁴⁵When the Temple guards returned without having arrested Jesus, the leading priests and Pharisees demanded, "Why didn't you bring him in?"

⁴⁶"We have never heard anyone speak like this!" the guards responded.

⁴⁷"Have you been led astray, too?" the Pharisees mocked. ⁴⁸"Is there a single one of us rulers or Pharisees who believes in him? ⁴⁹This foolish crowd follows him, but they are ignorant of the law. God's curse is on them!"

⁵⁰Then Nicodemus, the leader who had met with Jesus earlier, spoke up. ⁵¹"Is it legal to convict a man before he is given a hearing?" he asked.

⁵²They replied, "Are you from Galilee, too? Search the Scriptures and see for yourself—no prophet ever comes* from Galilee!"

_____

[*The most ancient Greek manuscripts do not include John 7:53–8:11.*]

⁵³Then the meeting broke up, and everybody went home.

7:35 Or *the Jews who live among the Greeks?*   **7:37-38** Or *"Let anyone who is thirsty come to me and drink.* ³⁸*For the Scriptures declare, 'Rivers of living water will flow from the heart of anyone who believes in me.'"*   **7:39** Some manuscripts read *But as yet there was no Spirit.* Still others read *But as yet there was no Holy Spirit.*   **7:40** See Deut 18:15, 18; Mal 4:5-6.   **7:42** See Mic 5:2.   **7:52** Some manuscripts read *the prophet does not come.*

CHAPTER 8

A Woman Caught in Adultery

Jesus returned to the Mount of Olives, [2]but early the next morning he was back again at the Temple. A crowd soon gathered, and he sat down and taught them. [3]As he was speaking, the teachers of religious law and the Pharisees brought a woman who had been caught in the act of adultery. They put her in front of the crowd.

[4]"Teacher," they said to Jesus, "this woman was caught in the act of adultery. [5]The law of Moses says to stone her. What do you say?"

[6]They were trying to trap him into saying something they could use against him, but Jesus stooped down and wrote in the dust with his finger. [7]They kept demanding an answer, so he stood up again and said, "All right, but let the one who has never sinned throw the first stone!" [8]Then he stooped down again and wrote in the dust.

[9]When the accusers heard this, they slipped away one by one, beginning with the oldest, until only Jesus was left in the middle of the crowd with the woman. [10]Then Jesus stood up again and said to the woman, "Where are your accusers? Didn't even one of them condemn you?"

[11]"No, Lord," she said.

And Jesus said, "Neither do I. Go and sin no more."

Jesus, the Light of the World

[12]Jesus spoke to the people once more and said, "I am the light of the world. If you follow me, you won't have to walk in darkness, because you will have the light that leads to life."

[13]The Pharisees replied, "You are making those claims about yourself! Such testimony is not valid."

[14]Jesus told them, "These claims are valid even though I make them about myself. For I know where I came from and where I am going, but you don't know this about me. [15]You judge me by human standards, but I do not judge anyone. [16]And if I did, my judgment would be correct in every respect because I am not alone. The Father* who sent me is with me. [17]Your own law says that if two people agree about something, their witness is accepted as fact.* [18]I am one witness, and my Father who sent me is the other."

[19]"Where is your father?" they asked.

Jesus answered, "Since you don't know who I am, you don't know who my Father is. If you knew me, you would also know my Father." [20]Jesus made these statements while he was teaching in the section of the Temple known as the Treasury. But he was not arrested, because his time* had not yet come.

The Unbelieving People Warned

[21]Later Jesus said to them again, "I am going away. You will search for me but will die in your sin. You cannot come where I am going."

8:16 Some manuscripts read *The One.*   **8:17** See Deut 19:15.   **8:20** Greek *his hour.*

²²The people* asked, "Is he planning to commit suicide? What does he mean, 'You cannot come where I am going'?"

²³Jesus continued, "You are from below; I am from above. You belong to this world; I do not. ²⁴That is why I said that you will die in your sins; for unless you believe that I AM who I claim to be,* you will die in your sins."

²⁵"Who are you?" they demanded.

Jesus replied, "The one I have always claimed to be.* ²⁶I have much to say about you and much to condemn, but I won't. For I say only what I have heard from the one who sent me, and he is completely truthful." ²⁷But they still didn't understand that he was talking about his Father.

²⁸So Jesus said, "When you have lifted up the Son of Man on the cross, then you will understand that I AM he.* I do nothing on my own but say only what the Father taught me. ²⁹And the one who sent me is with me—he has not deserted me. For I always do what pleases him." ³⁰Then many who heard him say these things believed in him.

Jesus and Abraham

³¹Jesus said to the people who believed in him, "You are truly my disciples if you remain faithful to my teachings. ³²And you will know the truth, and the truth will set you free."

³³"But we are descendants of Abraham," they said. "We have never been slaves to anyone. What do you mean, 'You will be set free'?"

³⁴Jesus replied, "I tell you the truth, everyone who sins is a slave of sin. ³⁵A slave is not a permanent member of the family, but a son is part of the family forever. ³⁶So if the Son sets you free, you are truly free. ³⁷Yes, I realize that you are descendants of Abraham. And yet some of you are trying to kill me because there's no room in your hearts for my message. ³⁸I am telling you what I saw when I was with my Father. But you are following the advice of your father."

³⁹"Our father is Abraham!" they declared.

"No," Jesus replied, "for if you were really the children of Abraham, you would follow his example.* ⁴⁰Instead, you are trying to kill me because I told you the truth, which I heard from God. Abraham never did such a thing. ⁴¹No, you are imitating your real father."

They replied, "We aren't illegitimate children! God himself is our true Father."

⁴²Jesus told them, "If God were your Father, you would love me, because I have come to you from God. I am not here on my own, but he sent me. ⁴³Why can't you understand what I am saying? It's because you can't even hear me! ⁴⁴For you are the children of your father the devil, and you love to do the evil things he does. He was a murderer from the beginning. He has always hated the truth, because there is no truth in him. When he lies, it is consistent with his character; for he is a liar and the father of lies. ⁴⁵So when I tell the truth, you just naturally don't believe

---

8:22 Greek *Jewish people;* also in 8:31, 48, 52, 57.   **8:24** Greek *unless you believe that I am.* See Exod 3:14.
8:25 Or *Why do I speak to you at all?*   **8:28** Greek *When you have lifted up the Son of Man, then you will know that I am.* "Son of Man" is a title Jesus used for himself.   **8:39** Some manuscripts read *if you are really the children of Abraham, follow his example.*

me! [46]Which of you can truthfully accuse me of sin? And since I am telling you the truth, why don't you believe me? [47]Anyone who belongs to God listens gladly to the words of God. But you don't listen because you don't belong to God."

[48]The people retorted, "You Samaritan devil! Didn't we say all along that you were possessed by a demon?"

[49]"No," Jesus said, "I have no demon in me. For I honor my Father—and you dishonor me. [50]And though I have no wish to glorify myself, God is going to glorify me. He is the true judge. [51]I tell you the truth, anyone who obeys my teaching will never die!"

[52]The people said, "Now we know you are possessed by a demon. Even Abraham and the prophets died, but you say, 'Anyone who obeys my teaching will never die!' [53]Are you greater than our father Abraham? He died, and so did the prophets. Who do you think you are?"

[54]Jesus answered, "If I want glory for myself, it doesn't count. But it is my Father who will glorify me. You say, 'He is our God,*' [55]but you don't even know him. I know him. If I said otherwise, I would be as great a liar as you! But I do know him and obey him. [56]Your father Abraham rejoiced as he looked forward to my coming. He saw it and was glad."

[57]The people said, "You aren't even fifty years old. How can you say you have seen Abraham?*"

[58]Jesus answered, "I tell you the truth, before Abraham was even born, I AM!*" [59]At that point they picked up stones to throw at him. But Jesus was hidden from them and left the Temple.

CHAPTER 9

Jesus Heals a Man Born Blind

As Jesus was walking along, he saw a man who had been blind from birth. [2]"Rabbi," his disciples asked him, "why was this man born blind? Was it because of his own sins or his parents' sins?"

[3]"It was not because of his sins or his parents' sins," Jesus answered. "This happened so the power of God could be seen in him. [4]We must quickly carry out the tasks assigned us by the one who sent us.* The night is coming, and then no one can work. [5]But while I am here in the world, I am the light of the world."

[6]Then he spit on the ground, made mud with the saliva, and spread the mud over the blind man's eyes. [7]He told him, "Go wash yourself in the pool of Siloam" (Siloam means "sent"). So the man went and washed and came back seeing!

[8]His neighbors and others who knew him as a blind beggar asked each other, "Isn't this the man who used to sit and beg?" [9]Some said he was, and others said, "No, he just looks like him!"

8:54 Some manuscripts read *your God.*   **8:57** Some manuscripts read *How can you say Abraham has seen you?*
8:58 Or *before Abraham was even born, I have always been alive;* Greek reads *before Abraham was, I am.* See Exod 3:14.
9:4 Other manuscripts read *I must quickly carry out the tasks assigned me by the one who sent me;* still others read *We must quickly carry out the tasks assigned us by the one who sent me.*

But the beggar kept saying, "Yes, I am the same one!"

[10]They asked, "Who healed you? What happened?"

[11]He told them, "The man they call Jesus made mud and spread it over my eyes and told me, 'Go to the pool of Siloam and wash yourself.' So I went and washed, and now I can see!"

[12]"Where is he now?" they asked.

"I don't know," he replied.

[13]Then they took the man who had been blind to the Pharisees, [14]because it was on the Sabbath that Jesus had made the mud and healed him. [15]The Pharisees asked the man all about it. So he told them, "He put the mud over my eyes, and when I washed it away, I could see!"

[16]Some of the Pharisees said, "This man Jesus is not from God, for he is working on the Sabbath." Others said, "But how could an ordinary sinner do such miraculous signs?" So there was a deep division of opinion among them.

[17]Then the Pharisees again questioned the man who had been blind and demanded, "What's your opinion about this man who healed you?"

The man replied, "I think he must be a prophet."

[18]The Jewish leaders still refused to believe the man had been blind and could now see, so they called in his parents. [19]They asked them, "Is this your son? Was he born blind? If so, how can he now see?"

[20]His parents replied, "We know this is our son and that he was born blind, [21]but we don't know how he can see or who healed him. Ask him. He is old enough to speak for himself." [22]His parents said this because they were afraid of the Jewish leaders, who had announced that anyone saying Jesus was the Messiah would be expelled from the synagogue. [23]That's why they said, "He is old enough. Ask him."

[24]So for the second time they called in the man who had been blind and told him, "God should get the glory for this,* because we know this man Jesus is a sinner."

[25]"I don't know whether he is a sinner," the man replied. "But I know this: I was blind, and now I can see!"

[26]"But what did he do?" they asked. "How did he heal you?"

[27]"Look!" the man exclaimed. "I told you once. Didn't you listen? Why do you want to hear it again? Do you want to become his disciples, too?"

[28]Then they cursed him and said, "You are his disciple, but we are disciples of Moses! [29]We know God spoke to Moses, but we don't even know where this man comes from."

[30]"Why, that's very strange!" the man replied. "He healed my eyes, and yet you don't know where he comes from? [31]We know that God doesn't listen to sinners, but he is ready to hear those who worship him and do his will. [32]Ever since the world began, no one has been able to open the eyes of someone born blind. [33]If this man were not from God, he couldn't have done it."

[34]"You were born a total sinner!" they answered. "Are you trying to teach us?" And they threw him out of the synagogue.

9:24 Or *Give glory to God, not to Jesus;* Greek reads *Give glory to God.*

Spiritual Blindness

³⁵When Jesus heard what had happened, he found the man and asked, "Do you believe in the Son of Man?*"

³⁶The man answered, "Who is he, sir? I want to believe in him."

³⁷"You have seen him," Jesus said, "and he is speaking to you!"

³⁸"Yes, Lord, I believe!" the man said. And he worshiped Jesus.

³⁹Then Jesus told him,* "I entered this world to render judgment—to give sight to the blind and to show those who think they see* that they are blind."

⁴⁰Some Pharisees who were standing nearby heard him and asked, "Are you saying we're blind?"

⁴¹"If you were blind, you wouldn't be guilty," Jesus replied. "But you remain guilty because you claim you can see.

CHAPTER 10

The Good Shepherd and His Sheep

"I tell you the truth, anyone who sneaks over the wall of a sheepfold, rather than going through the gate, must surely be a thief and a robber! ²But the one who enters through the gate is the shepherd of the sheep. ³The gatekeeper opens the gate for him, and the sheep recognize his voice and come to him. He calls his own sheep by name and leads them out. ⁴After he has gathered his own flock, he walks ahead of them, and they follow him because they know his voice. ⁵They won't follow a stranger; they will run from him because they don't know his voice."

⁶Those who heard Jesus use this illustration didn't understand what he meant, ⁷so he explained it to them: "I tell you the truth, I am the gate for the sheep. ⁸All who came before me* were thieves and robbers. But the true sheep did not listen to them. ⁹Yes, I am the gate. Those who come in through me will be saved.* They will come and go freely and will find good pastures. ¹⁰The thief's purpose is to steal and kill and destroy. My purpose is to give them a rich and satisfying life.

¹¹"I am the good shepherd. The good shepherd sacrifices his life for the sheep. ¹²A hired hand will run when he sees a wolf coming. He will abandon the sheep because they don't belong to him and he isn't their shepherd. And so the wolf attacks them and scatters the flock. ¹³The hired hand runs away because he's working only for the money and doesn't really care about the sheep.

¹⁴"I am the good shepherd; I know my own sheep, and they know me, ¹⁵just as my Father knows me and I know the Father. So I sacrifice my life for the sheep. ¹⁶I have other sheep, too, that are not in this sheepfold. I must bring them also. They will listen to my voice, and there will be one flock with one shepherd.

¹⁷"The Father loves me because I sacrifice my life so I may take it back again. ¹⁸No one can take my life from me. I sacrifice it voluntarily. For I have the author-

---

9:35 Some manuscripts read *the Son of God?* "Son of Man" is a title Jesus used for himself.   **9:38-39a** Some manuscripts do not include *"Yes, Lord, I believe!" the man said. And he worshiped Jesus. Then Jesus told him.* **9:39b** Greek *those who see.*   **10:8** Some manuscripts do not include *before me.*   **10:9** Or *will find safety.*

ity to lay it down when I want to and also to take it up again. For this is what my Father has commanded."

¹⁹When he said these things, the people* were again divided in their opinions about him. ²⁰Some said, "He's demon possessed and out of his mind. Why listen to a man like that?" ²¹Others said, "This doesn't sound like a man possessed by a demon! Can a demon open the eyes of the blind?"

Jesus Claims to Be the Son of God

²²It was now winter, and Jesus was in Jerusalem at the time of Hanukkah, the Festival of Dedication. ²³He was in the Temple, walking through the section known as Solomon's Colonnade. ²⁴The people surrounded him and asked, "How long are you going to keep us in suspense? If you are the Messiah, tell us plainly."

²⁵Jesus replied, "I have already told you, and you don't believe me. The proof is the work I do in my Father's name. ²⁶But you don't believe me because you are not my sheep. ²⁷My sheep listen to my voice; I know them, and they follow me. ²⁸I give them eternal life, and they will never perish. No one can snatch them away from me, ²⁹for my Father has given them to me, and he is more powerful than anyone else.* No one can snatch them from the Father's hand. ³⁰The Father and I are one."

³¹Once again the people picked up stones to kill him. ³²Jesus said, "At my Father's direction I have done many good works. For which one are you going to stone me?"

³³They replied, "We're stoning you not for any good work, but for blasphemy! You, a mere man, claim to be God."

³⁴Jesus replied, "It is written in your own Scriptures* that God said to certain leaders of the people, 'I say, you are gods!'* ³⁵And you know that the Scriptures cannot be altered. So if those people who received God's message were called 'gods,' ³⁶why do you call it blasphemy when I say, 'I am the Son of God'? After all, the Father set me apart and sent me into the world. ³⁷Don't believe me unless I carry out my Father's work. ³⁸But if I do his work, believe in the evidence of the miraculous works I have done, even if you don't believe me. Then you will know and understand that the Father is in me, and I am in the Father."

³⁹Once again they tried to arrest him, but he got away and left them. ⁴⁰He went beyond the Jordan River near the place where John was first baptizing and stayed there awhile. ⁴¹And many followed him. "John didn't perform miraculous signs," they remarked to one another, "but everything he said about this man has come true." ⁴²And many who were there believed in Jesus.

CHAPTER 11

The Raising of Lazarus

A man named Lazarus was sick. He lived in Bethany with his sisters, Mary and Martha. ²This is the Mary who later poured the expensive perfume on the Lord's

---

10:19 Greek *Jewish people;* also in 10:24, 31.   **10:29** Other manuscripts read *for what my Father has given me is more powerful than anything;* still others read *for regarding that which my Father has given me, he is greater than all.* **10:34a** Greek *your own law.*   **10:34b** Ps 82:6.

feet and wiped them with her hair.* Her brother, Lazarus, was sick. [3]So the two sisters sent a message to Jesus telling him, "Lord, your dear friend is very sick."

[4]But when Jesus heard about it he said, "Lazarus's sickness will not end in death. No, it happened for the glory of God so that the Son of God will receive glory from this." [5]So although Jesus loved Martha, Mary, and Lazarus, [6]he stayed where he was for the next two days. [7]Finally, he said to his disciples, "Let's go back to Judea."

[8]But his disciples objected. "Rabbi," they said, "only a few days ago the people* in Judea were trying to stone you. Are you going there again?"

[9]Jesus replied, "There are twelve hours of daylight every day. During the day people can walk safely. They can see because they have the light of this world. [10]But at night there is danger of stumbling because they have no light." [11]Then he said, "Our friend Lazarus has fallen asleep, but now I will go and wake him up."

[12]The disciples said, "Lord, if he is sleeping, he will soon get better!" [13]They thought Jesus meant Lazarus was simply sleeping, but Jesus meant Lazarus had died.

[14]So he told them plainly, "Lazarus is dead. [15]And for your sakes, I'm glad I wasn't there, for now you will really believe. Come, let's go see him."

[16]Thomas, nicknamed the Twin,* said to his fellow disciples, "Let's go, too— and die with Jesus."

[17]When Jesus arrived at Bethany, he was told that Lazarus had already been in his grave for four days. [18]Bethany was only a few miles* down the road from Jerusalem, [19]and many of the people had come to console Martha and Mary in their loss. [20]When Martha got word that Jesus was coming, she went to meet him. But Mary stayed in the house. [21]Martha said to Jesus, "Lord, if only you had been here, my brother would not have died. [22]But even now I know that God will give you whatever you ask."

[23]Jesus told her, "Your brother will rise again."

[24]"Yes," Martha said, "he will rise when everyone else rises, at the last day."

[25]Jesus told her, "I am the resurrection and the life.* Anyone who believes in me will live, even after dying. [26]Everyone who lives in me and believes in me will never ever die. Do you believe this, Martha?"

[27]"Yes, Lord," she told him. "I have always believed you are the Messiah, the Son of God, the one who has come into the world from God." [28]Then she returned to Mary. She called Mary aside from the mourners and told her, "The Teacher is here and wants to see you." [29]So Mary immediately went to him.

[30]Jesus had stayed outside the village, at the place where Martha met him. [31]When the people who were at the house consoling Mary saw her leave so hastily, they assumed she was going to Lazarus's grave to weep. So they followed her there. [32]When Mary arrived and saw Jesus, she fell at his feet and said, "Lord, if only you had been here, my brother would not have died."

11:2 This incident is recorded in chapter 12.   **11:8** Greek *Jewish people;* also in 11:19, 31, 33, 36, 45, 54.
11:16 Greek *Thomas, who was called Didymus.*   **11:18** Greek *was about 15 stadia* [about 2.8 kilometers].
11:25 Some manuscripts do not include *and the life.*

[33]When Jesus saw her weeping and saw the other people wailing with her, a deep anger welled up within him,* and he was deeply troubled. [34]"Where have you put him?" he asked them.

They told him, "Lord, come and see." [35]Then Jesus wept. [36]The people who were standing nearby said, "See how much he loved him!" [37]But some said, "This man healed a blind man. Couldn't he have kept Lazarus from dying?"

[38]Jesus was still angry as he arrived at the tomb, a cave with a stone rolled across its entrance. [39]"Roll the stone aside," Jesus told them.

But Martha, the dead man's sister, protested, "Lord, he has been dead for four days. The smell will be terrible."

[40]Jesus responded, "Didn't I tell you that you would see God's glory if you believe?" [41]So they rolled the stone aside. Then Jesus looked up to heaven and said, "Father, thank you for hearing me. [42]You always hear me, but I said it out loud for the sake of all these people standing here, so that they will believe you sent me." [43]Then Jesus shouted, "Lazarus, come out!" [44]And the dead man came out, his hands and feet bound in graveclothes, his face wrapped in a headcloth. Jesus told them, "Unwrap him and let him go!"

The Plot to Kill Jesus

[45]Many of the people who were with Mary believed in Jesus when they saw this happen. [46]But some went to the Pharisees and told them what Jesus had done. [47]Then the leading priests and Pharisees called the high council* together. "What are we going to do?" they asked each other. "This man certainly performs many miraculous signs. [48]If we allow him to go on like this, soon everyone will believe in him. Then the Roman army will come and destroy both our Temple* and our nation."

[49]Caiaphas, who was high priest at that time,* said, "You don't know what you're talking about! [50]You don't realize that it's better for you that one man should die for the people than for the whole nation to be destroyed."

[51]He did not say this on his own; as high priest at that time he was led to prophesy that Jesus would die for the entire nation. [52]And not only for that nation, but to bring together and unite all the children of God scattered around the world.

[53]So from that time on, the Jewish leaders began to plot Jesus' death. [54]As a result, Jesus stopped his public ministry among the people and left Jerusalem. He went to a place near the wilderness, to the village of Ephraim, and stayed there with his disciples.

[55]It was now almost time for the Jewish Passover celebration, and many people from all over the country arrived in Jerusalem several days early so they could go through the purification ceremony before Passover began. [56]They kept looking for Jesus, but as they stood around in the Temple, they said to each other, "What do you think? He won't come for Passover, will he?" [57]Meanwhile, the leading priests and Pharisees had publicly ordered that anyone seeing Jesus must report it immediately so they could arrest him.

11:33 Or *he was angry in his spirit.*   **11:47** Greek *the Sanhedrin.*   **11:48** Or *our position;* Greek reads *our place.*
11:49 Greek *that year;* also in 11:51.

CHAPTER 12

Jesus Anointed at Bethany

Six days before the Passover celebration began, Jesus arrived in Bethany, the home of Lazarus—the man he had raised from the dead. ²A dinner was prepared in Jesus' honor. Martha served, and Lazarus was among those who ate* with him. ³Then Mary took a twelve-ounce jar* of expensive perfume made from essence of nard, and she anointed Jesus' feet with it, wiping his feet with her hair. The house was filled with the fragrance.

⁴But Judas Iscariot, the disciple who would soon betray him, said, ⁵"That perfume was worth a year's wages.* It should have been sold and the money given to the poor." ⁶Not that he cared for the poor—he was a thief, and since he was in charge of the disciples' money, he often stole some for himself.

⁷Jesus replied, "Leave her alone. She did this in preparation for my burial. ⁸You will always have the poor among you, but you will not always have me."

⁹When all the people* heard of Jesus' arrival, they flocked to see him and also to see Lazarus, the man Jesus had raised from the dead. ¹⁰Then the leading priests decided to kill Lazarus, too, ¹¹for it was because of him that many of the people had deserted them* and believed in Jesus.

Jesus' Triumphant Entry

¹²The next day, the news that Jesus was on the way to Jerusalem swept through the city. A large crowd of Passover visitors ¹³took palm branches and went down the road to meet him. They shouted,

"Praise God!*
Blessings on the one who comes in the name of the LORD!
Hail to the King of Israel!"*

¹⁴Jesus found a young donkey and rode on it, fulfilling the prophecy that said:

¹⁵ "Don't be afraid, people of Jerusalem.*
Look, your King is coming,
    riding on a donkey's colt."*

¹⁶His disciples didn't understand at the time that this was a fulfillment of prophecy. But after Jesus entered into his glory, they remembered what had happened and realized that these things had been written about him.

¹⁷Many in the crowd had seen Jesus call Lazarus from the tomb, raising him from the dead, and they were telling others* about it. ¹⁸That was the reason so many went out to meet him—because they had heard about this miraculous sign.

12:2 Or *who reclined.*   **12:3** Greek *took 1 litra* [327 grams].   **12:5** Greek *worth 300 denarii.* A denarius was equivalent to a laborer's full day's wage.   **12:9** Greek *Jewish people;* also in 12:11.   **12:11** Or *had deserted their traditions;* Greek reads *had deserted.*   **12:13a** Greek *Hosanna,* an exclamation of praise adapted from a Hebrew expression that means "save now."   **12:13b** Ps 118:25-26; Zeph 3:15.   **12:15a** Greek *daughter of Zion.*
12:15b Zech 9:9.   **12:17** Greek *were testifying.*

¹⁹Then the Pharisees said to each other, "There's nothing we can do. Look, everyone* has gone after him!"

Jesus Predicts His Death

²⁰Some Greeks who had come to Jerusalem for the Passover celebration ²¹paid a visit to Philip, who was from Bethsaida in Galilee. They said, "Sir, we want to meet Jesus." ²²Philip told Andrew about it, and they went together to ask Jesus.

²³Jesus replied, "Now the time has come for the Son of Man* to enter into his glory. ²⁴I tell you the truth, unless a kernel of wheat is planted in the soil and dies, it remains alone. But its death will produce many new kernels—a plentiful harvest of new lives. ²⁵Those who love their life in this world will lose it. Those who care nothing for their life in this world will keep it for eternity. ²⁶Anyone who wants to be my disciple must follow me, because my servants must be where I am. And the Father will honor anyone who serves me.

²⁷"Now my soul is deeply troubled. Should I pray, 'Father, save me from this hour'? But this is the very reason I came! ²⁸Father, bring glory to your name."

Then a voice spoke from heaven, saying, "I have already brought glory to my name, and I will do so again." ²⁹When the crowd heard the voice, some thought it was thunder, while others declared an angel had spoken to him.

³⁰Then Jesus told them, "The voice was for your benefit, not mine. ³¹The time for judging this world has come, when Satan, the ruler of this world, will be cast out. ³²And when I am lifted up from the earth, I will draw everyone to myself." ³³He said this to indicate how he was going to die.

³⁴The crowd responded, "We understood from Scripture* that the Messiah would live forever. How can you say the Son of Man will die? Just who is this Son of Man, anyway?"

³⁵Jesus replied, "My light will shine for you just a little longer. Walk in the light while you can, so the darkness will not overtake you. Those who walk in the darkness cannot see where they are going. ³⁶Put your trust in the light while there is still time; then you will become children of the light."

After saying these things, Jesus went away and was hidden from them.

The Unbelief of the People

³⁷But despite all the miraculous signs Jesus had done, most of the people still did not believe in him. ³⁸This is exactly what Isaiah the prophet had predicted:

"LORD, who has believed our message?
    To whom has the LORD revealed his powerful arm?"*

³⁹But the people couldn't believe, for as Isaiah also said,

⁴⁰   "The Lord has blinded their eyes
        and hardened their hearts—

12:19 Greek *the world.*   **12:23** "Son of Man" is a title Jesus used for himself.   **12:34** Greek *from the law.*
12:38 Isa 53:1.

> so that their eyes cannot see,
>   and their hearts cannot understand,
> and they cannot turn to me
>   and have me heal them."*

⁴¹Isaiah was referring to Jesus when he said this, because he saw the future and spoke of the Messiah's glory. ⁴²Many people did believe in him, however, including some of the Jewish leaders. But they wouldn't admit it for fear that the Pharisees would expel them from the synagogue. ⁴³For they loved human praise more than the praise of God.

⁴⁴Jesus shouted to the crowds, "If you trust me, you are trusting not only me, but also God who sent me. ⁴⁵For when you see me, you are seeing the one who sent me. ⁴⁶I have come as a light to shine in this dark world, so that all who put their trust in me will no longer remain in the dark. ⁴⁷I will not judge those who hear me but don't obey me, for I have come to save the world and not to judge it. ⁴⁸But all who reject me and my message will be judged on the day of judgment by the truth I have spoken. ⁴⁹I don't speak on my own authority. The Father who sent me has commanded me what to say and how to say it. ⁵⁰And I know his commands lead to eternal life; so I say whatever the Father tells me to say."

CHAPTER 13

Jesus Washes His Disciples' Feet

Before the Passover celebration, Jesus knew that his hour had come to leave this world and return to his Father. He had loved his disciples during his ministry on earth, and now he loved them to the very end.* ²It was time for supper, and the devil had already prompted Judas,* son of Simon Iscariot, to betray Jesus. ³Jesus knew that the Father had given him authority over everything and that he had come from God and would return to God. ⁴So he got up from the table, took off his robe, wrapped a towel around his waist, ⁵and poured water into a basin. Then he began to wash the disciples' feet, drying them with the towel he had around him.

⁶When Jesus came to Simon Peter, Peter said to him, "Lord, are you going to wash my feet?"

⁷Jesus replied, "You don't understand now what I am doing, but someday you will."

⁸"No," Peter protested, "you will never ever wash my feet!"

Jesus replied, "Unless I wash you, you won't belong to me."

⁹Simon Peter exclaimed, "Then wash my hands and head as well, Lord, not just my feet!"

¹⁰Jesus replied, "A person who has bathed all over does not need to wash, except for the feet,* to be entirely clean. And you disciples are clean, but not all

---

12:40 Isa 6:10.   **13:1** Or *he showed them the full extent of his love.*   **13:2** Or *the devil had already intended for Judas.*
13:10 Some manuscripts do not include *except for the feet.*

of you." [11]For Jesus knew who would betray him. That is what he meant when he said, "Not all of you are clean."

[12]After washing their feet, he put on his robe again and sat down and asked, "Do you understand what I was doing? [13]You call me 'Teacher' and 'Lord,' and you are right, because that's what I am. [14]And since I, your Lord and Teacher, have washed your feet, you ought to wash each other's feet. [15]I have given you an example to follow. Do as I have done to you. [16]I tell you the truth, slaves are not greater than their master. Nor is the messenger more important than the one who sends the message. [17]Now that you know these things, God will bless you for doing them.

Jesus Predicts His Betrayal

[18]"I am not saying these things to all of you; I know the ones I have chosen. But this fulfills the Scripture that says, 'The one who eats my food has turned against me.'* [19]I tell you this beforehand, so that when it happens you will believe that I AM the Messiah.* [20]I tell you the truth, anyone who welcomes my messenger is welcoming me, and anyone who welcomes me is welcoming the Father who sent me."

[21]Now Jesus was deeply troubled,* and he exclaimed, "I tell you the truth, one of you will betray me!"

[22]The disciples looked at each other, wondering whom he could mean. [23]The disciple Jesus loved was sitting next to Jesus at the table.* [24]Simon Peter motioned to him to ask, "Who's he talking about?" [25]So that disciple leaned over to Jesus and asked, "Lord, who is it?"

[26]Jesus responded, "It is the one to whom I give the bread I dip in the bowl." And when he had dipped it, he gave it to Judas, son of Simon Iscariot. [27]When Judas had eaten the bread, Satan entered into him. Then Jesus told him, "Hurry and do what you're going to do." [28]None of the others at the table knew what Jesus meant. [29]Since Judas was their treasurer, some thought Jesus was telling him to go and pay for the food or to give some money to the poor. [30]So Judas left at once, going out into the night.

Jesus Predicts Peter's Denial

[31]As soon as Judas left the room, Jesus said, "The time has come for the Son of Man* to enter into his glory, and God will be glorified because of him. [32]And since God receives glory because of the Son,* he will soon give glory to the Son. [33]Dear children, I will be with you only a little longer. And as I told the Jewish leaders, you will search for me, but you can't come where I am going. [34]So now I am giving you a new commandment: Love each other. Just as I have loved you, you should love each other. [35]Your love for one another will prove to the world that you are my disciples."

[36]Simon Peter asked, "Lord, where are you going?"

And Jesus replied, "You can't go with me now, but you will follow me later."

13:18 Ps 41:9.   13:19 Or that the 'I AM' has come; or that I am the LORD; Greek reads that I am. See Exod 3:14.
13:21 Greek was troubled in his spirit.   13:23 Greek was reclining on Jesus' bosom. The "disciple Jesus loved" was probably John.   13:31 "Son of Man" is a title Jesus used for himself.   13:32 Some manuscripts do not include And since God receives glory because of the Son.

³⁷"But why can't I come now, Lord?" he asked. "I'm ready to die for you."

³⁸Jesus answered, "Die for me? I tell you the truth, Peter—before the rooster crows tomorrow morning, you will deny three times that you even know me.

CHAPTER 14

Jesus, the Way to the Father

"Don't let your hearts be troubled. Trust in God, and trust also in me. ²There is more than enough room in my Father's home.* If this were not so, would I have told you that I am going to prepare a place for you?* ³When everything is ready, I will come and get you, so that you will always be with me where I am. ⁴And you know the way to where I am going."

⁵"No, we don't know, Lord," Thomas said. "We have no idea where you are going, so how can we know the way?"

⁶Jesus told him, "I am the way, the truth, and the life. No one can come to the Father except through me. ⁷If you had really known me, you would know who my Father is.* From now on, you do know him and have seen him!"

⁸Philip said, "Lord, show us the Father, and we will be satisfied."

⁹Jesus replied, "Have I been with you all this time, Philip, and yet you still don't know who I am? Anyone who has seen me has seen the Father! So why are you asking me to show him to you? ¹⁰Don't you believe that I am in the Father and the Father is in me? The words I speak are not my own, but my Father who lives in me does his work through me. ¹¹Just believe that I am in the Father and the Father is in me. Or at least believe because of the work you have seen me do.

¹²"I tell you the truth, anyone who believes in me will do the same works I have done, and even greater works, because I am going to be with the Father. ¹³You can ask for anything in my name, and I will do it, so that the Son can bring glory to the Father. ¹⁴Yes, ask me for anything in my name, and I will do it!

Jesus Promises the Holy Spirit

¹⁵"If you love me, obey* my commandments. ¹⁶And I will ask the Father, and he will give you another Advocate,* who will never leave you. ¹⁷He is the Holy Spirit, who leads into all truth. The world cannot receive him, because it isn't looking for him and doesn't recognize him. But you know him, because he lives with you now and later will be in you.* ¹⁸No, I will not abandon you as orphans—I will come to you. ¹⁹Soon the world will no longer see me, but you will see me. Since I live, you also will live. ²⁰When I am raised to life again, you will know that I am in my Father, and you are in me, and I am in you. ²¹Those who accept my commandments and obey them are the ones who love me. And because they love me, my Father will love them. And I will love them and reveal myself to each of them."

14:2a Or *There are many rooms in my Father's house.*   **14:2b** Or *If this were not so, I would have told you that I am going to prepare a place for you.* Some manuscripts read *If this were not so, I would have told you. I am going to prepare a place for you.*   **14:7** Some manuscripts read *If you have really known me, you will know who my Father is.* **14:15** Other manuscripts read *you will obey;* still others read *you should obey.*   **14:16** Or *Comforter,* or *Encourager,* or *Counselor.* Greek reads *Paraclete;* also in 14:26.   **14:17** Some manuscripts read *and is in you.*

²²Judas (not Judas Iscariot, but the other disciple with that name) said to him, "Lord, why are you going to reveal yourself only to us and not to the world at large?"

²³Jesus replied, "All who love me will do what I say. My Father will love them, and we will come and make our home with each of them. ²⁴Anyone who doesn't love me will not obey me. And remember, my words are not my own. What I am telling you is from the Father who sent me. ²⁵I am telling you these things now while I am still with you. ²⁶But when the Father sends the Advocate as my representative—that is, the Holy Spirit—he will teach you everything and will remind you of everything I have told you.

²⁷"I am leaving you with a gift—peace of mind and heart. And the peace I give is a gift the world cannot give. So don't be troubled or afraid. ²⁸Remember what I told you: I am going away, but I will come back to you again. If you really loved me, you would be happy that I am going to the Father, who is greater than I am. ²⁹I have told you these things before they happen so that when they do happen, you will believe.

³⁰"I don't have much more time to talk to you, because the ruler of this world approaches. He has no power over me, ³¹but I will do what the Father requires of me, so that the world will know that I love the Father. Come, let's be going.

CHAPTER 15

Jesus, the True Vine

"I am the true grapevine, and my Father is the gardener. ²He cuts off every branch of mine that doesn't produce fruit, and he prunes the branches that do bear fruit so they will produce even more. ³You have already been pruned and purified by the message I have given you. ⁴Remain in me, and I will remain in you. For a branch cannot produce fruit if it is severed from the vine, and you cannot be fruitful unless you remain in me.

⁵"Yes, I am the vine; you are the branches. Those who remain in me, and I in them, will produce much fruit. For apart from me you can do nothing. ⁶Anyone who does not remain in me is thrown away like a useless branch and withers. Such branches are gathered into a pile to be burned. ⁷But if you remain in me and my words remain in you, you may ask for anything you want, and it will be granted! ⁸When you produce much fruit, you are my true disciples. This brings great glory to my Father.

⁹"I have loved you even as the Father has loved me. Remain in my love. ¹⁰When you obey my commandments, you remain in my love, just as I obey my Father's commandments and remain in his love. ¹¹I have told you these things so that you will be filled with my joy. Yes, your joy will overflow! ¹²This is my commandment: Love each other in the same way I have loved you. ¹³There is no greater love than to lay down one's life for one's friends. ¹⁴You are my friends if you do what I command. ¹⁵I no longer call you slaves, because a master doesn't confide in his slaves. Now you are my friends, since I have told you everything the Father told me. ¹⁶You didn't choose me. I chose you. I appointed you to go and produce lasting fruit, so

that the Father will give you whatever you ask for, using my name. [17]This is my command: Love each other.

The World's Hatred

[18]"If the world hates you, remember that it hated me first. [19]The world would love you as one of its own if you belonged to it, but you are no longer part of the world. I chose you to come out of the world, so it hates you. [20]Do you remember what I told you? 'A slave is not greater than the master.' Since they persecuted me, naturally they will persecute you. And if they had listened to me, they would listen to you. [21]They will do all this to you because of me, for they have rejected the one who sent me. [22]They would not be guilty if I had not come and spoken to them. But now they have no excuse for their sin. [23]Anyone who hates me also hates my Father. [24]If I hadn't done such miraculous signs among them that no one else could do, they would not be guilty. But as it is, they have seen everything I did, yet they still hate me and my Father. [25]This fulfills what is written in their Scriptures*: 'They hated me without cause.'

[26]"But I will send you the Advocate*—the Spirit of truth. He will come to you from the Father and will testify all about me. [27]And you must also testify about me because you have been with me from the beginning of my ministry.

CHAPTER 16

"I have told you these things so that you won't abandon your faith. [2]For you will be expelled from the synagogues, and the time is coming when those who kill you will think they are doing a holy service for God. [3]This is because they have never known the Father or me. [4]Yes, I'm telling you these things now, so that when they happen, you will remember my warning. I didn't tell you earlier because I was going to be with you for a while longer.

The Work of the Holy Spirit

[5]"But now I am going away to the one who sent me, and not one of you is asking where I am going. [6]Instead, you grieve because of what I've told you. [7]But in fact, it is best for you that I go away, because if I don't, the Advocate* won't come. If I do go away, then I will send him to you. [8]And when he comes, he will convict the world of its sin, and of God's righteousness, and of the coming judgment. [9]The world's sin is that it refuses to believe in me. [10]Righteousness is available because I go to the Father, and you will see me no more. [11]Judgment will come because the ruler of this world has already been judged.

[12]"There is so much more I want to tell you, but you can't bear it now. [13]When the Spirit of truth comes, he will guide you into all truth. He will not speak on his own but will tell you what he has heard. He will tell you about the future. [14]He will bring me glory by telling you whatever he receives from me. [15]All that belongs to the Father is mine; this is why I said, 'The Spirit will tell you whatever he receives from me.'

15:25 Greek *in their law.* Pss 35:19; 69:4.   15:26 Or *Comforter,* or *Encourager,* or *Counselor.* Greek reads *Paraclete.*
16:7 Or *Comforter,* or *Encourager,* or *Counselor.* Greek reads *Paraclete.*

Sadness Will Be Turned to Joy

[16]"In a little while you won't see me anymore. But a little while after that, you will see me again."

[17]Some of the disciples asked each other, "What does he mean when he says, 'In a little while you won't see me, but then you will see me,' and 'I am going to the Father'? [18]And what does he mean by 'a little while'? We don't understand."

[19]Jesus realized they wanted to ask him about it, so he said, "Are you asking yourselves what I meant? I said in a little while you won't see me, but a little while after that you will see me again. [20]I tell you the truth, you will weep and mourn over what is going to happen to me, but the world will rejoice. You will grieve, but your grief will suddenly turn to wonderful joy. [21]It will be like a woman suffering the pains of labor. When her child is born, her anguish gives way to joy because she has brought a new baby into the world. [22]So you have sorrow now, but I will see you again; then you will rejoice, and no one can rob you of that joy. [23]At that time you won't need to ask me for anything. I tell you the truth, you will ask the Father directly, and he will grant your request because you use my name. [24]You haven't done this before. Ask, using my name, and you will receive, and you will have abundant joy.

[25]"I have spoken of these matters in figures of speech, but soon I will stop speaking figuratively and will tell you plainly all about the Father. [26]Then you will ask in my name. I'm not saying I will ask the Father on your behalf, [27]for the Father himself loves you dearly because you love me and believe that I came from God.* [28]Yes, I came from the Father into the world, and now I will leave the world and return to the Father."

[29]Then his disciples said, "At last you are speaking plainly and not figuratively. [30]Now we understand that you know everything, and there's no need to question you. From this we believe that you came from God."

[31]Jesus asked, "Do you finally believe? [32]But the time is coming—indeed it's here now—when you will be scattered, each one going his own way, leaving me alone. Yet I am not alone because the Father is with me. [33]I have told you all this so that you may have peace in me. Here on earth you will have many trials and sorrows. But take heart, because I have overcome the world."

CHAPTER 17

The Prayer of Jesus

After saying all these things, Jesus looked up to heaven and said, "Father, the hour has come. Glorify your Son so he can give glory back to you. [2]For you have given him authority over everyone. He gives eternal life to each one you have given him. [3]And this is the way to have eternal life—to know you, the only true God, and Jesus Christ, the one you sent to earth. [4]I brought glory to you here on earth by completing the work you gave me to do. [5]Now, Father, bring me into the glory we shared before the world began.

16:27 Some manuscripts read *from the Father.*

⁶"I have revealed you* to the ones you gave me from this world. They were always yours. You gave them to me, and they have kept your word. ⁷Now they know that everything I have is a gift from you, ⁸for I have passed on to them the message you gave me. They accepted it and know that I came from you, and they believe you sent me.

⁹"My prayer is not for the world, but for those you have given me, because they belong to you. ¹⁰All who are mine belong to you, and you have given them to me, so they bring me glory. ¹¹Now I am departing from the world; they are staying in this world, but I am coming to you. Holy Father, you have given me your name;* now protect them by the power of your name so that they will be united just as we are. ¹²During my time here, I protected them by the power of the name you gave me.* I guarded them so that not one was lost, except the one headed for destruction, as the Scriptures foretold.

¹³"Now I am coming to you. I told them many things while I was with them in this world so they would be filled with my joy. ¹⁴I have given them your word. And the world hates them because they do not belong to the world, just as I do not belong to the world. ¹⁵I'm not asking you to take them out of the world, but to keep them safe from the evil one. ¹⁶They do not belong to this world any more than I do. ¹⁷Make them holy by your truth; teach them your word, which is truth. ¹⁸Just as you sent me into the world, I am sending them into the world. ¹⁹And I give myself as a holy sacrifice for them so they can be made holy by your truth.

²⁰"I am praying not only for these disciples but also for all who will ever believe in me through their message. ²¹I pray that they will all be one, just as you and I are one—as you are in me, Father, and I am in you. And may they be in us so that the world will believe you sent me.

²²"I have given them the glory you gave me, so they may be one as we are one. ²³I am in them and you are in me. May they experience such perfect unity that the world will know that you sent me and that you love them as much as you love me. ²⁴Father, I want these whom you have given me to be with me where I am. Then they can see all the glory you gave me because you loved me even before the world began!

²⁵"O righteous Father, the world doesn't know you, but I do; and these disciples now you sent me. ²⁶I have revealed you to them, and I will continue to do so. Then your love for me will be in them, and I will be in them."

CHAPTER 18

Jesus Is Betrayed and Arrested
After saying these things, Jesus crossed the Kidron Valley with his disciples and entered a grove of olive trees. ²Judas, the betrayer, knew this place, because Jesus had often gone there with his disciples. ³The leading priests and Pharisees had given Judas a contingent of Roman soldiers and Temple guards to accompany him. Now with blazing torches, lanterns, and weapons, they arrived at the olive grove.

17:6 Greek *have revealed your name;* also in 17:26.   **17:11** Some manuscripts read *you have given me these [disciples].*   **17:12** Some manuscripts read *I protected those you gave me, by the power of your name.*

4Jesus fully realized all that was going to happen to him, so he stepped forward to meet them. "Who are you looking for?" he asked.

5"Jesus the Nazarene,"* they replied.

"I AM he,"* Jesus said. (Judas, who betrayed him, was standing with them.) 6As Jesus said "I AM he," they all drew back and fell to the ground! 7Once more he asked them, "Who are you looking for?"

And again they replied, "Jesus the Nazarene."

8"I told you that I AM he," Jesus said. "And since I am the one you want, let these others go." 9He did this to fulfill his own statement: "I did not lose a single one of those you have given me."*

10Then Simon Peter drew a sword and slashed off the right ear of Malchus, the high priest's slave. 11But Jesus said to Peter, "Put your sword back into its sheath. Shall I not drink from the cup of suffering the Father has given me?"

Jesus at the High Priest's House

12So the soldiers, their commanding officer, and the Temple guards arrested Jesus and tied him up. 13First they took him to Annas, the father-in-law of Caiaphas, the high priest at that time.* 14Caiaphas was the one who had told the other Jewish leaders, "It's better that one man should die for the people."

Peter's First Denial

15Simon Peter followed Jesus, as did another of the disciples. That other disciple was acquainted with the high priest, so he was allowed to enter the high priest's courtyard with Jesus. 16Peter had to stay outside the gate. Then the disciple who knew the high priest spoke to the woman watching at the gate, and she let Peter in. 17The woman asked Peter, "You're not one of that man's disciples, are you?"

"No," he said, "I am not."

18Because it was cold, the household servants and the guards had made a charcoal fire. They stood around it, warming themselves, and Peter stood with them, warming himself.

The High Priest Questions Jesus

19Inside, the high priest began asking Jesus about his followers and what he had been teaching them. 20Jesus replied, "Everyone knows what I teach. I have preached regularly in the synagogues and the Temple, where the people* gather. I have not spoken in secret. 21Why are you asking me this question? Ask those who heard me. They know what I said."

22Then one of the Temple guards standing nearby slapped Jesus across the face. "Is that the way to answer the high priest?" he demanded.

23Jesus replied, "If I said anything wrong, you must prove it. But if I'm speaking the truth, why are you beating me?"

24Then Annas bound Jesus and sent him to Caiaphas, the high priest.

18:5a Or *Jesus of Nazareth;* also in 18:7.   **18:5b** Or *"The 'I AM' is here";* or *"I am the LORD";* Greek reads *I am;* also in 18:6, 8. See Exod 3:14.   **18:9** See John 6:39 and 17:12.   **18:13** Greek *that year.*   **18:20** Greek *Jewish people;* also in 18:38.

Peter's Second and Third Denials

[25]Meanwhile, as Simon Peter was standing by the fire warming himself, they asked him again, "You're not one of his disciples, are you?"

He denied it, saying, "No, I am not."

[26]But one of the household slaves of the high priest, a relative of the man whose ear Peter had cut off, asked, "Didn't I see you out there in the olive grove with Jesus?" [27]Again Peter denied it. And immediately a rooster crowed.

Jesus' Trial before Pilate

[28]Jesus' trial before Caiaphas ended in the early hours of the morning. Then he was taken to the headquarters of the Roman governor.* His accusers didn't go inside because it would defile them, and they wouldn't be allowed to celebrate the Passover. [29]So Pilate, the governor, went out to them and asked, "What is your charge against this man?"

[30]"We wouldn't have handed him over to you if he weren't a criminal!" they retorted.

[31]"Then take him away and judge him by your own law," Pilate told them.

"Only the Romans are permitted to execute someone," the Jewish leaders replied. [32](This fulfilled Jesus' prediction about the way he would die.*)

[33]Then Pilate went back into his headquarters and called for Jesus to be brought to him. "Are you the king of the Jews?" he asked him.

[34]Jesus replied, "Is this your own question, or did others tell you about me?"

[35]"Am I a Jew?" Pilate retorted. "Your own people and their leading priests brought you to me for trial. Why? What have you done?"

[36]Jesus answered, "My Kingdom is not an earthly kingdom. If it were, my followers would fight to keep me from being handed over to the Jewish leaders. But my Kingdom is not of this world."

[37]Pilate said, "So you are a king?"

Jesus responded, "You say I am a king. Actually, I was born and came into the world to testify to the truth. All who love the truth recognize that what I say is true."

[38]"What is truth?" Pilate asked. Then he went out again to the people and told them, "He is not guilty of any crime. [39]But you have a custom of asking me to release one prisoner each year at Passover. Would you like me to release this 'King of the Jews'?"

[40]But they shouted back, "No! Not this man. We want Barabbas!" (Barabbas was a revolutionary.)

CHAPTER 19

Jesus Sentenced to Death

Then Pilate had Jesus flogged with a lead-tipped whip. [2]The soldiers wove a crown of thorns and put it on his head, and they put a purple robe on him. [3]"Hail! King of the Jews!" they mocked, as they slapped him across the face.

18:28 Greek *to the Praetorium;* also in 18:33.   **18:32** See John 12:32-33.

⁴Pilate went outside again and said to the people, "I am going to bring him out to you now, but understand clearly that I find him not guilty." ⁵Then Jesus came out wearing the crown of thorns and the purple robe. And Pilate said, "Look, here is the man!"

⁶When they saw him, the leading priests and Temple guards began shouting, "Crucify him! Crucify him!"

"Take him yourselves and crucify him," Pilate said. "I find him not guilty."

⁷The Jewish leaders replied, "By our law he ought to die because he called himself the Son of God."

⁸When Pilate heard this, he was more frightened than ever. ⁹He took Jesus back into the headquarters* again and asked him, "Where are you from?" But Jesus gave no answer. ¹⁰"Why don't you talk to me?" Pilate demanded. "Don't you realize that I have the power to release you or crucify you?"

¹¹Then Jesus said, "You would have no power over me at all unless it were given to you from above. So the one who handed me over to you has the greater sin."

¹²Then Pilate tried to release him, but the Jewish leaders shouted, "If you release this man, you are no 'friend of Caesar.'* Anyone who declares himself a king is a rebel against Caesar."

¹³When they said this, Pilate brought Jesus out to them again. Then Pilate sat down on the judgment seat on the platform that is called the Stone Pavement (in Hebrew, *Gabbatha*). ¹⁴It was now about noon on the day of preparation for the Passover. And Pilate said to the people,* "Look, here is your king!"

¹⁵"Away with him," they yelled. "Away with him! Crucify him!"

"What? Crucify your king?" Pilate asked.

"We have no king but Caesar," the leading priests shouted back.

¹⁶Then Pilate turned Jesus over to them to be crucified.

The Crucifixion

So they took Jesus away. ¹⁷Carrying the cross by himself, he went to the place called Place of the Skull (in Hebrew, *Golgotha*). ¹⁸There they nailed him to the cross. Two others were crucified with him, one on either side, with Jesus between them. ¹⁹And Pilate posted a sign on the cross that read, "Jesus of Nazareth,* the King of the Jews." ²⁰The place where Jesus was crucified was near the city, and the sign was written in Hebrew, Latin, and Greek, so that many people could read it.

²¹Then the leading priests objected and said to Pilate, "Change it from 'The King of the Jews' to 'He said, I am King of the Jews.'"

²²Pilate replied, "No, what I have written, I have written."

²³When the soldiers had crucified Jesus, they divided his clothes among the four of them. They also took his robe, but it was seamless, woven in one piece from top to bottom. ²⁴So they said, "Rather than tearing it apart, let's throw dice* for it." This fulfilled the Scripture that says, "They divided my garments among themselves and threw dice for my clothing."* So that is what they did.

19:9 Greek *the Praetorium.*   19:12 "Friend of Caesar" is a technical term that refers to an ally of the emperor.
19:14 Greek *Jewish people;* also in 19:20.   19:19 Or *Jesus the Nazarene.*   19:24a Greek *cast lots.*   19:24b Ps 22:18.

²⁵Standing near the cross were Jesus' mother, and his mother's sister, Mary (the wife of Clopas), and Mary Magdalene. ²⁶When Jesus saw his mother standing there beside the disciple he loved, he said to her, "Dear woman, here is your son." ²⁷And he said to this disciple, "Here is your mother." And from then on this disciple took her into his home.

The Death of Jesus

²⁸Jesus knew that his mission was now finished, and to fulfill Scripture he said, "I am thirsty."* ²⁹A jar of sour wine was sitting there, so they soaked a sponge in it, put it on a hyssop branch, and held it up to his lips. ³⁰When Jesus had tasted it, he said, "It is finished!" Then he bowed his head and released his spirit.

³¹It was the day of preparation, and the Jewish leaders didn't want the bodies hanging there the next day, which was the Sabbath (and a very special Sabbath, because it was the Passover). So they asked Pilate to hasten their deaths by ordering that their legs be broken. Then their bodies could be taken down. ³²So the soldiers came and broke the legs of the two men crucified with Jesus. ³³But when they came to Jesus, they saw that he was already dead, so they didn't break his legs. ³⁴One of the soldiers, however, pierced his side with a spear, and immediately blood and water flowed out. ³⁵(This report is from an eyewitness giving an accurate account. He speaks the truth so that you also can believe.*) ³⁶These things happened in fulfillment of the Scriptures that say, "Not one of his bones will be broken,"* ³⁷and "They will look on the one they pierced."*

The Burial of Jesus

³⁸Afterward Joseph of Arimathea, who had been a secret disciple of Jesus (because he feared the Jewish leaders), asked Pilate for permission to take down Jesus' body. When Pilate gave permission, Joseph came and took the body away. ³⁹With him came Nicodemus, the man who had come to Jesus at night. He brought about seventy-five pounds* of perfumed ointment made from myrrh and aloes. ⁴⁰Following Jewish burial custom, they wrapped Jesus' body with the spices in long sheets of linen cloth. ⁴¹The place of crucifixion was near a garden, where there was a new tomb, never used before. ⁴²And so, because it was the day of preparation for the Jewish Passover* and since the tomb was close at hand, they laid Jesus there.

CHAPTER 20

The Resurrection

Early on Sunday morning,* while it was still dark, Mary Magdalene came to the tomb and found that the stone had been rolled away from the entrance. ²She ran and found Simon Peter and the other disciple, the one whom Jesus loved. She said,

---

19:28 See Pss 22:15; 69:21.   **19:35** Some manuscripts read *can continue to believe.*   **19:36** Exod 12:46; Num 9:12; Ps 34:20.   **19:37** Zech 12:10.   **19:39** Greek *100 litras* [32.7 kilograms].   **19:42** Greek *because of the Jewish day of preparation.*   **20:1** Greek *On the first day of the week.*

"They have taken the Lord's body out of the tomb, and we don't know where they have put him!"

³Peter and the other disciple started out for the tomb. ⁴They were both running, but the other disciple outran Peter and reached the tomb first. ⁵He stooped and looked in and saw the linen wrappings lying there, but he didn't go in. ⁶Then Simon Peter arrived and went inside. He also noticed the linen wrappings lying there, ⁷while the cloth that had covered Jesus' head was folded up and lying apart from the other wrappings. ⁸Then the disciple who had reached the tomb first also went in, and he saw and believed—⁹for until then they still hadn't understood the Scriptures that said Jesus must rise from the dead. ¹⁰Then they went home.

Jesus Appears to Mary Magdalene

¹¹Mary was standing outside the tomb crying, and as she wept, she stooped and looked in. ¹²She saw two white-robed angels, one sitting at the head and the other at the foot of the place where the body of Jesus had been lying. ¹³"Dear woman, why are you crying?" the angels asked her.

"Because they have taken away my Lord," she replied, "and I don't know where they have put him."

¹⁴She turned to leave and saw someone standing there. It was Jesus, but she didn't recognize him. ¹⁵"Dear woman, why are you crying?" Jesus asked her. "Who are you looking for?"

She thought he was the gardener. "Sir," she said, "if you have taken him away, tell me where you have put him, and I will go and get him."

¹⁶"Mary!" Jesus said.

She turned to him and cried out, "Rabboni!" (which is Hebrew for "Teacher").

¹⁷"Don't cling to me," Jesus said, "for I haven't yet ascended to the Father. But go find my brothers and tell them, 'I am ascending to my Father and your Father, to my God and your God.'"

¹⁸Mary Magdalene found the disciples and told them, "I have seen the Lord!" Then she gave them his message.

Jesus Appears to His Disciples

¹⁹That Sunday evening* the disciples were meeting behind locked doors because they were afraid of the Jewish leaders. Suddenly, Jesus was standing there among them! "Peace be with you," he said. ²⁰As he spoke, he showed them the wounds in his hands and his side. They were filled with joy when they saw the Lord! ²¹Again he said, "Peace be with you. As the Father has sent me, so I am sending you." ²²Then he breathed on them and said, "Receive the Holy Spirit. ²³If you forgive anyone's sins, they are forgiven. If you do not forgive them, they are not forgiven."

Jesus Appears to Thomas

²⁴One of the twelve disciples, Thomas (nicknamed the Twin),* was not with the others when Jesus came. ²⁵They told him, "We have seen the Lord!"

20:19 Greek *In the evening of that day, the first day of the week.*   **20:24** Greek *Thomas, who was called Didymus.*

But he replied, "I won't believe it unless I see the nail wounds in his hands, put my fingers into them, and place my hand into the wound in his side."

²⁶Eight days later the disciples were together again, and this time Thomas was with them. The doors were locked; but suddenly, as before, Jesus was standing among them. "Peace be with you," he said. ²⁷Then he said to Thomas, "Put your finger here, and look at my hands. Put your hand into the wound in my side. Don't be faithless any longer. Believe!"

²⁸"My Lord and my God!" Thomas exclaimed.

²⁹Then Jesus told him, "You believe because you have seen me. Blessed are those who believe without seeing me."

Purpose of the Book

³⁰The disciples saw Jesus do many other miraculous signs in addition to the ones recorded in this book. ³¹But these are written so that you may continue to believe* that Jesus is the Messiah, the Son of God, and that by believing in him you will have life by the power of his name.

CHAPTER 21

Epilogue: Jesus Appears to Seven Disciples

Later, Jesus appeared again to the disciples beside the Sea of Galilee.* This is how it happened. ²Several of the disciples were there—Simon Peter, Thomas (nicknamed the Twin),* Nathanael from Cana in Galilee, the sons of Zebedee, and two other disciples.

³Simon Peter said, "I'm going fishing."

"We'll come, too," they all said. So they went out in the boat, but they caught nothing all night.

⁴At dawn Jesus was standing on the beach, but the disciples couldn't see who he was. ⁵He called out, "Fellows,* have you caught any fish?"

"No," they replied.

⁶Then he said, "Throw out your net on the right-hand side of the boat, and you'll get some!" So they did, and they couldn't haul in the net because there were so many fish in it.

⁷Then the disciple Jesus loved said to Peter, "It's the Lord!" When Simon Peter heard that it was the Lord, he put on his tunic (for he had stripped for work), jumped into the water, and headed to shore. ⁸The others stayed with the boat and pulled the loaded net to the shore, for they were only about a hundred yards* from shore. ⁹When they got there, they found breakfast waiting for them—fish cooking over a charcoal fire, and some bread.

¹⁰"Bring some of the fish you've just caught," Jesus said. ¹¹So Simon Peter went aboard and dragged the net to the shore. There were 153 large fish, and yet the net hadn't torn.

20:31 Some manuscripts read *that you may believe.*   **21:1** Greek *Sea of Tiberias,* another name for the Sea of Galilee.
21:2 Greek *Thomas, who was called Didymus.*   **21:5** Greek *Children.*   **21:8** Greek *200 cubits* [90 meters].

¹²"Now come and have some breakfast!" Jesus said. None of the disciples dared to ask him, "Who are you?" They knew it was the Lord. ¹³Then Jesus served them the bread and the fish. ¹⁴This was the third time Jesus had appeared to his disciples since he had been raised from the dead.

¹⁵After breakfast Jesus asked Simon Peter, "Simon son of John, do you love me more than these?*"

"Yes, Lord," Peter replied, "you know I love you."

"Then feed my lambs," Jesus told him.

¹⁶Jesus repeated the question: "Simon son of John, do you love me?"

"Yes, Lord," Peter said, "you know I love you."

"Then take care of my sheep," Jesus said.

¹⁷A third time he asked him, "Simon son of John, do you love me?"

Peter was hurt that Jesus asked the question a third time. He said, "Lord, you know everything. You know that I love you."

Jesus said, "Then feed my sheep.

¹⁸"I tell you the truth, when you were young, you were able to do as you liked; you dressed yourself and went wherever you wanted to go. But when you are old, you will stretch out your hands, and others* will dress you and take you where you don't want to go." ¹⁹Jesus said this to let him know by what kind of death he would glorify God. Then Jesus told him, "Follow me."

²⁰Peter turned around and saw behind them the disciple Jesus loved—the one who had leaned over to Jesus during supper and asked, "Lord, who will betray you?" ²¹Peter asked Jesus, "What about him, Lord?"

²²Jesus replied, "If I want him to remain alive until I return, what is that to you? As for you, follow me." ²³So the rumor spread among the community of believers* that this disciple wouldn't die. But that isn't what Jesus said at all. He only said, "If I want him to remain alive until I return, what is that to you?"

²⁴This disciple is the one who testifies to these events and has recorded them here. And we know that his account of these things is accurate.

²⁵Jesus also did many other things. If they were all written down, I suppose the whole world could not contain the books that would be written.

21:15 Or *more than these others do?*   **21:18** Some manuscripts read *and another one.*   **21:23** Greek *the brothers.*

CHAPTER 6

The Many Other Gospels

This chapter pertains to all the Gospels that did not make it into the New Testament canon. Some of these Gospels may have been very orthodox and very well read, as in the case of the *Gospel of the Nazareans* and the *Gospel of Peter,* but they lacked apostolic authorship and therefore never made it into the canon. Others—specifically, many of those known as Gnostic Gospels—contradicted earlier apostolic teaching and were eventually classified as heretical. Some of the other Gospels were composed to cover the unrecorded years of Jesus' life, especially his early years. Because of the scarcity of information about such matters as the childhood, adolescence, and early manhood of Jesus, the Infancy Gospels undertook to supply the reader with what was meant to pass for historical fact.

Much of the material, however, was entirely within the realm of fantasy and would never have been accepted as fact by any intelligent reader of the Gospels. For example, in the *Infancy Gospel of Thomas,* the five-year-old Jesus is accused of breaking the Sabbath by making sparrows of clay beside a stream. When his father Joseph investigates the situation, Jesus claps his hands and the clay birds come to life and fly away chirping. This supposed display of immaturity, disobedience, and secrecy is in direct contrast to the life and message of the Jesus written about in all those manuscripts that have stood the test of the canon. And then there were Passion and Resurrection Gospels, which were written to embellish the canonical accounts of Christ's crucifixion and resurrection.

Most of the noncanonical books are pseudepigrapha—that is, they are books ascribed to a pseudonymous author. In other words, the main characteristic of these writings is the fictitious claim that the author of the book was a well-known biblical person (such as Peter, Thomas, Philip, Mary). By the nature of the contents of the pseudepigrapha, they were recognized only by certain groups.

Writings that failed to gain acceptance into the New Testament canon were described in the writings of some early Christian scholars by the term *apocrypha.* The Greek word means "hidden things," and when applied to books, it described those works that religious authorities wished to be concealed from the reading public. The reason was that such books were thought to contain mysterious or secret lore, meaningful only to the initiate and therefore unsuitable for the ordinary reader. But the word *apocrypha* was also applied in a less complimentary sense to works that deserved to be concealed. Such works contained harmful doctrines or false teachings calculated to unsettle or pervert rather than to edify those who read them. The suppression of undesirable writings was comparatively easy at a time when only a few copies of any book were in circulation at a given time.

There are four broad classes of noncanonical Gospels:

1. Noncanonical Orthodox Gospels

   These are Gospels that appear to be orthodox in content but did not get accepted into the New Testament canon. There is not enough extant text to make a definitive decision about the content of these Gospels. It could be that some other parts of these Gospels had unorthodox content and therefore were rejected by the early Christians. Or it could be that these Gospels got lost or soon went out of publication after the time of writing. After all, Luke did say that "many" had written a narrative about Jesus' life prior to his writing the third Gospel.[1] Some of these Gospels could have been among the "many": the *Gospel of Peter* and the *Gospel of the Nazareans,* as well as the papyrus fragments P. Oxyrhynchus 840, P. Oxyrhynchus 1224, and P. Egerton 2.

2. Gnostic Gospels

   These are Gospels written in the second century A.D. that promote heresy stressing philosophical knowledge (gnosis) of the cosmos and humanity. They are often in the form of dialogues between Jesus and his disciples, such as the Coptic *Gospel of Thomas,* the *Apocryphon of John,* the *Sophia of Jesus Christ,* and the *Dialogue of the Savior.* In this category are also those Gospels attributed to the Twelve as a group, such as the *Memoria of the Apostles.*

3. Infancy Gospels

   These purport to supply otherwise unknown information of a legendary nature about Christ's earliest years. These narratives were written to satisfy curiosity about Christ's birth and childhood. Much of their content was fantastical, as described in the example above of the five-year-old Jesus in the *Infancy Gospel of Thomas.*

4. Passion and Resurrection Gospels
   These were written to embellish the canonical accounts of Christ's crucifixion and resurrection. As supplements to Christian teaching, many of the apocryphal writings seemed to be proclaiming ideas that were actually outside the scope of New Testament doctrine. Attempts to fill in the hidden years of Christ's life had no foundation whatsoever in the traditions of the Gospels. Works dealing with the last state of unbelievers were embellished in a manner that went far beyond anything stated in the New Testament.

In some notable instances, as in the writings of various gnostic sects, the authors set out deliberately to propagate heretical teachings they had accepted under the authority of some apostolic figure. The *Gospel of Thomas* is an example of an attempt to spread curious sayings and dogmas by attributing them to Jesus so that they would receive wide circulation and acceptance.

A comparison of the general dates represented by these four categories with those of the canonical Gospels, as judged by discovered manuscripts and ancient testimony, helps us evaluate their merit. All four canonical Gospels are dated within the second half of the first century A.D.—Mark being written as early as A.D. 50–60. The manuscripts we have for them date to A.D. 100–150 for Matthew and John and to A.D. 175–250 for Mark and Luke. A couple of the noncanonical orthodox Gospels were written around A.D. 100–150.[2] Others in this category come from the third century.

Some Gnostic Gospels must have been written as early as A.D. 180 because Irenaeus wrote about them at that time. It is notable, however, that Marcion, who had gnostic leanings, did not include any Gnostic Gospels (or even revisions of Gnostic Gospels) in his canon list around A.D. 140. This would seem to indicate that Gnostic Gospels had not yet been composed or that they were still so new they could not be regarded as having the authority of eyewitness accounts. The earliest manuscripts for Gnostic Gospels are early third century, which is the date assigned to P. Oxyrhynchus 1, 654, and 655, each of which has portions of the *Gospel of Thomas*.

The earliest Infancy Gospels date to around A.D. 150 (*Protoevangelium of James*) and perhaps to around A.D. 180 (*Infancy Gospel of Thomas*). The manuscripts for these are as early as the third century. The other Infancy Gospels are later—as late as the fifth century. Of the Passion and Resurrection Gospels, the earliest seems to be the *Letter of Peter to Philip*, which dates to the late second or early third century.

From these findings, it is clear that the canonical Gospels are the earliest compositions. Taking A.D. 70 as a median date for their composition, we may observe that the earliest of the noncanonical orthodox Gospels followed right on the heels of the evangelists, while some eighty years passed before the appearance of the earliest Infancy Gospels, Gnostic Gospels, and Passion and Resurrection Gospels. With the passage of time, it is impossible that the apostles could have verified these later Gospels, and it is notable that pseudonyms were increasingly supplied in a bid for authority.

NONCANONICAL ORTHODOX GOSPELS

Egerton Gospel (P. Egerton 2 + P. Köln 608)

This Gospel was probably composed in the early part of the second century, while the copy that was discovered could be dated no later than A.D. 150.[3] The paleographic dating came about by a morphological comparison with the following manuscripts: P52 (dated early second century A.D.) with which it bears unmistakable likeness; P. Berolinensis 6854 (a document dated in the reign of Trajan, who died in A.D. 117); P. London 130 (a horoscope calculated from A.D. April 1, 81, and therefore not likely to be later than the early years of the second century); and P. Oxyrhynchus 656 (Genesis, mid-to-late second century). All these comparable manuscripts are dated within the period of late first century to second century, and most of them have solid documentary dating. As Harold Bell wrote, "This papyrus almost certainly falls within the period A.D. 120–170, and it is on the whole likely to date from the first rather than the second half of that period."[4] As such, this is a very early Gospel, which could be dated to the beginning of the second century, or perhaps even the end of the first. The translation that follows is primarily based on P. Egerton 2; P. Köln 608 supplies portions of sections one and two.

The orthodoxy of this Gospel is largely based on the fact that the passages are quite parallel to those found in the canonical Gospels. Section one parallels John 5:39-47; 10:31; section two parallels Matthew 8:1-4; section three parallels Matthew 22:16-17; 15:8-9. Section four has no clear-cut parallels in the canonical Gospels.

I. A Conversation between Jesus and Some Jewish Rulers

[Jesus said] to the teachers of the law, [judge] every evildoer [and] transgressor, but not me, [because you don't know] how he does what he does.

[And] turning to the rulers of the people, he said, "Search the scriptures, in which you think you have life. These are they [which testify] concerning me. Do not think I have come to accuse [you] to my Father. There is [one who] accuses you, even Moses, upon whom you have set your hope."

And they said, "We know that God spoke to Moses, but as for you—we don't know."

Jesus answered and said, "Now your failure to believe Moses' testimonies accuses. If you had believed Moses you would have believed me, for he wrote of me to your fathers."

And [they wanted] to stone him. And the rulers laid their hands on him that they might take him and [hand him over] to the crowd. And they could not take him because the hour of his betrayal had not yet come. But he himself, the Lord, escaping [their hands], departed from [them].

A small fragment of the P. Egerton 2 follows this text; it could read something like this:

[Jesus said, "I and my Father are] one. [Hereafter,] I remain no more [among you."]

They carried [stones to the place where] they might kill him. [But Jesus] says [to them] . . .

2. Jesus' Healing of a Leper

And behold, a leper came to him and said, "Teacher Jesus, while traveling with lepers and eating with them in the inn, I also myself got leprosy. If you will, therefore, I am made clean."

The Lord said to him, "I will. Be clean." Immediately the leprosy left him. And Jesus said to him, "Go show yourself to the priests and make an offering for your cleansing [as Moses] prescribed. [And] do not sin any more."

3. Jesus Being Questioned and Tested

They came to him and began to test him, saying, "Teacher Jesus, we know that you have come [from God] because the prophets testify about the things you are doing. [Tell] us, [therefore,] is it lawful to pay kings the things that pertain to their rule? Should we pay them or not?"

But Jesus, knowing their thoughts, was moved with indignation. He said [to them], "Why do you call me Teacher with your mouth when you don't hear what I say? Well did Isaiah prophesy of you, saying, 'This people [honors] me with their lips but their hearts are far from me. In vain [they] worship me.'"

4. A Miracle by the Jordan

Having shut something up in a place . . . has it been placed secretly beneath. [. . .] its weight unweighed [?]. [. . .] And they were perplexed at the strange question. Jesus walked and then stood still on the edge of the Jordan. And stretching forth his right hand, he filled it [with water] and sprinkled it on. [. . .] And then the water that was sprinkled before their eyes brought forth fruit [. . .] there was much joy.

Gospel of the Nazareans

This Gospel is unlike all the other noncanonical Gospels and like the canonical Gospels in that it apparently included a narrative of Jesus' baptism, public ministry, death, and resurrection. Written in Aramaic in the first half of the second century, it was popular among Jewish Christians living near and around Palestine, who were sometimes called Nazareans. The Gospel was not read by the Christian community at large because they did not read Aramaic and because the Jewish emphases were suspect. As such, some Christians thought it was nothing other than an Aramaic revision of Matthew's Gospel.

Eusebius and Jerome appear to have quoted from it as an authoritative account, sometimes calling it the *Gospel of the Hebrews*. The work exists only through quotations by church fathers.

Eusebius (*Theophania* 4.12)

> The reason for divisions in certain houses is what Christ himself taught, as we have discovered in a place in the Gospel read by the Jews in the Hebrew language, which says, "I will select for myself the best the Father in heaven has given me."

Jerome, commenting on Matthew 6:11

> In the Gospel [. . .] for "substantial bread" I found mahar, which signifies "tomorrow's."
>
> Therefore, the meaning would be, "give us today tomorrow's bread."

Jerome, commenting on Matthew 12:13

> In the Gospel that the Nazareans and Ebionites use, which recently translated from the Hebrew into the Greek, and which most people designate as the authentic text of Matthew, we read that the man with the withered [palsied] hand was a mason. He asked [Jesus] for help in these words: "I was a mason, working for my food with these hands. I beseech you, Jesus, restore my health so that I don't eat my food with shame."

Jerome, commenting on Matthew 23:35

> In the Gospel which the Nazareans use we find it written for "son of Barachias," "son of Johoiada."

Jerome, commenting on Matthew 27:16

> In the so-called *Gospel of the Hebrews*, Barabbas, who was condemned for sedition and murder has a name that is interpreted to mean "son of their teacher."

Jerome, commenting on Matthew 27:51

> In the Gospel frequently mentioned we read, "The great lintel of the Temple broke and fell into pieces."

259

Jerome, *Dialogi contra Pelagianos* 3.2

In the *Gospel of the Hebrews* which is written in the Syro-Chaldean language (though in Hebrew letters), which the Nazareans make use of even in this day, which is also called the *Gospel of the Apostles*, or as many think, the Gospel of Matthew, and which is in the library at Caesarea, the following story is written:

"Look, the mother of the Lord and his brothers said to him, 'John the Baptist baptizes for the forgiveness of sins, let us be baptized by him.'"

"But he [Jesus] said, 'What [sin] have I done that I should be baptized by him—unless I am speaking in ignorance?'"

In the same [Gospel] we read:

"If your brother has sinned against you by something he has said and has made amends, forgive him up to seven times a day."

Simon, his disciple, asked him, "Seven times?"

The Lord replied, "Truly I tell you, seventy times seven. For even the prophets sinned in their speech after they were anointed by the Holy Spirit."

The *Gospel of the Nazareans* is also referred to in the margins of several Greek manuscripts of Matthew's Gospel—especially 566 and 1424, as well as 4, 273, 566, 899. These notes refer to this as the Jewish Gospel. Some of the notes in Matthew are as follows:

4:5 The Jewish copy reads "in Jerus'alem" instead of "to the holy city" (MS 566).

5:22 The words "without cause" are not found in some copies, nor in the Jewish copy (MS 1424).

7:5 The Jewish copy reads here: "If you are in my bosom and do not do the will of my Father in heaven, I will cast you way from my bosom" (MS 1424).

11:12 The Jewish copy has "the kingdom of heaven is ravished" instead of "suffers violence" (MS 1424).

12:40 The Jewish copy does not have "three days and three nights" (MS 899).

16:2-3 This is omitted in the Jewish copy and many other manuscripts.

18:22 After the words "seventy times seven" the Jewish copy has "For in the prophets, after they were anointed with the Holy Spirit, there was found in them a matter of sin" (MSS 566, 899).

26:74 The Jewish copy reads, "and he denied and swore and cursed" (MSS 4, 273, 566, 899, 1424).

27:65 The Jewish copy reads, "and he delivered to them armed men, that they might sit opposite the cave and keep watch on it day and night" (MS 1424).

Gospel of Peter

In 1884 a Greek manuscript was found in Akhmim, Egypt, in the tomb of a Christian monk. This little codex contains a portion of the book of *Enoch,* a description of heaven and hell, and the present fragment known as the *Gospel of Peter.* This manuscript is P. Cairo 10759. Two other fragments are found in P. Oxyrhynchus 2949 and probably P. Oxyrhynchus 4009.

The last verse of the Akhmim Manuscript says, "I, Simon Peter, and Andrew my brother, took our nets and went to the sea." This would seem to indicate that Peter was the narrator of this Gospel and therefore the presumed author. But there is not one scholar who thinks Peter wrote it because the writing has all the markings of having been composed in the second century, many decades after Peter's death. As such, this Gospel is pseudepigraphal: Some unknown author falsely assumed the name of Peter in order to promote his own writing. The extant fragments present a narrative of Jesus' death and resurrection. This narrative draws from all four canonical Gospels, but adds its own unorthodox slant here and there by casting doubt on the reality of Jesus' sufferings and by consequence on the reality of Jesus' human body. In short, it may be Docetic—subscribing to a heresy that purported that Jesus only *appeared* to have a physical body but actually did not. This was the charge laid against this so-called *Gospel by Serapion of Antioch.* In addition to its unorthodoxy, this Gospel is anti-Jewish in that it makes "the Jews" categorically responsible for Jesus' death.

The fourth-century church historian Eusebius of Caesarea observed that the *Gospel of Peter* had not been accepted by any ancient authorities,[5] though he was probably not aware of its acceptance by Clement of Alexandria. Even though only fragments of the document have survived, they are important in that they reveal a transitional stage in the history of early Christian literature. During the first century, Christian literature, including all of the New Testament, was written for the consumption of other Christians. During the second century, Christian writers began to feel the need to defend their faith against the criticisms of their pagan and Jewish opponents. A new kind of Christian literature, the apology (from *apologia,* meaning "defense"), began to appear in the early second century with the writings of the earliest Christian apologists, Quadratus and Aristides. The *Gospel of Peter* represents a transition from the kind of apologetic writing found in the Acts of the

Apostles and the sermons contained in that book and the kind found in the writings of the early apologists.

Clement quoted randomly from the *Gospel of Peter*. By reading these quotes, we can gather some of the major emphases of the document. According to Clement, Peter called the Lord both "Law and Word" in the "Preaching."[6] Mankind must recognize that one God created the beginning of all things and has the power to bring all things to an end.[7] The pagans, whom the author of the *Gospel of Peter* opposed, believed the universe was uncreated and eternal. God, the author contended, is invisible, incomprehensible, inconceivable, everlasting, imperishable, uncreated, and self-sustaining.

The God of the *Gospel of Peter* must not be worshiped in the manner of the Greeks, for they had foolishly fashioned images of ordinary materials and worshiped them as gods. Further, they sacrificed to these idols animals that should be used for food. The Jews' worship should not be emulated either, according to this Gospel, for they revered angels, archangels, months, and the moon. But if any of the nation of Israel should repent, they would find forgiveness.[8]

In one place the *Gospel of Peter* narrates the Lord's sending of his disciples to preach the gospel throughout the world after the Resurrection,[9] though the precise connection between this narrative and the preceding apologetic statements is not clear. It may be that the document began with a special version of the great commission.[10] Elsewhere the document states that the Old Testament prophets speak of Christ, sometimes in parables and enigmas, yet at other times very clearly and directly.[11] The major events in the life of Christ—his coming, torture, crucifixion, death, resurrection, and ascension into heaven—were predicted in detail by the prophets.

The Akhmim Manuscript

[1]None of the Jews washed their hands, nor did Herod or even one of his judges. Because they did not want to wash, Pilate rose up. [2]Then King Herod commanded the Lord to be taken away by them, saying to them, "Do everything I commanded you to do to him." [3]Now Joseph, the friend of Pilate and of the Lord, was standing there. When he realized that they were about to crucify him, he came to Pilate and asked for the body of the Lord for burial. [4]Pilate sent a message to Herod, asking for the body.* [5]Herod said, "Brother Pilate, even if no one had asked for him, we would have buried him, because the Sabbath is about to dawn. For it is written in the Law, 'The sun should not set on one who has been murdered.'" [And he handed him over to the people] the day before the Festival of Unleavened Bread.

[6]Having taken the Lord, they pushed him as they ran, and said, "Let us take the Son of God away, since we have authority over him." [7]And they clothed him in purple and made him sit upon the seat of judgment, saying,

"King of Israel, give just judgment." [8]And one of them brought a crown of thorns and put it on the Lord's head. [9]And others standing there were spitting on his eyes; others slapped his cheeks; others were hitting him with a reed; and some flogged him, saying, "This is how we honor the Son of God!"

[10]And they brought two criminals and crucified the Lord between them. But he was silent, as one having no pain. [11]And on the cross which they set upright, they wrote, "This is the King of Israel." [12]Placing his clothes in front of him, they divided them and threw dice for them. [13]But one of the criminals reproached them, saying, "We have suffered for the crimes we have done, but as for this one who has become the Savior of people—what crime has he done?" [14]And they were furious with him; they ordered that his legs should not be broken so that he would die in torment.

[15]It was noon and darkness prevailed over all Judea. The people were troubled and disturbed that the sun would set while [Jesus] was still alive. [16]And one of them said, "Give him gall with vinegar to drink." And they mixed them and gave it to him to drink. [17]And they fulfilled all things such that this fulfillment brought down upon their heads all their sins. [18] And many were wandering around with lamps, thinking it was night. [Some of them] stumbled. [19]And the Lord cried out loud, saying, "My power, my power, you have forsaken me!" And when he said this, he was taken up. [20][In the same] hour the veil of the Temple of Jerusalem was split in two.

[21]And then they pulled the nails from the Lord's hands and placed him on the ground. And all the ground shook, so that everyone was really afraid. [22]As the sun began to shine, people realized it was three in the afternoon. [23]But the Jews rejoiced, and they gave his body to Joseph to bury it since he had seen all the good [Jesus] had done. [24]After taking the Lord, he washed him and wrapped him in linen and took him to his own burial vault, called Joseph's Garden.

[25]Then, when the Jews and the elders and the priests saw what kind of evil they had done to themselves, they began beating their breasts and saying, "Woe to us because of our sins! The judgment and the end of Jerusalem are near." [26]But I and my companions were experiencing very sad thoughts, and we went into hiding. We were being pursued as if we were criminals who wanted to burn the Temple. [27]Because of all this, we fasted and sat mourning and weeping night and day until the Sabbath came.

[28]The scribes and Pharisees and elders gathered with one another, having heard that all the people were murmuring and beating their breasts, saying, "Since these great signs happened during his death, you can see [how] righteous he is!" [29]The elders were afraid; they came to Pilate and entreated him: [30]"Give us soldiers so that we may guard his tomb for three days. This will keep his disciples from stealing him and the people from thinking he was raised from the dead. Otherwise, they will harm us." [31]Pilate gave them Petronius, the centurion, with soldiers to guard the tomb. The elders and the scribes came with them to the tomb. [32]Everyone who was there, including

the centurion and the soldiers, rolled a great stone over the entrance to the tomb. ³³After they plastered seven seals on it, they pitched tents and began their watch.

³⁴Early in the morning as the Sabbath dawned, a multitude from Jerusalem and the surrounding area came to see the tomb that had been sealed. ³⁵During the night on which the Lord's Day dawned, while the soldiers were keeping watch two by two, there was a great sound in heaven. ³⁶They saw the heavens open and two men descend from there. These men, who were brightly shining, approached the tomb. ³⁷The stone on the entrance to the tomb rolled away by itself, moving over to one side. Both young men entered the open tomb. ³⁸ When the soldiers saw this, they awakened the centurion and the elders who were also keeping watch. ³⁹And while they were telling them what they had seen, they saw three men come out of the tomb. Two of them were holding up the other, and a cross was following them. ⁴⁰The heads of the two reached up to the sky, but the head of the one they were leading reached above the sky. ⁴¹And they heard from the heavens, "Have you preached to those who are asleep?" ⁴²And an answer was heard from the cross: "Yes."

⁴³The men made a decision to go to Pilate and report these things to him. ⁴⁴While they were thinking about these things, heaven opened again and a man descended and entered the tomb. ⁴⁵Those who were with the centurion saw these things and hurried to Pilate during the night. They left the tomb they had been watching and reported everything they had seen. With deep agitation they said, "This one was really the Son of God." ⁴⁶Pilate replied, "I am innocent of the blood of the Son of God. It was you who thought of this."

⁴⁷Then they all came to him and urged him to command the centurion and the soldiers to say nothing about what they had seen. ⁴⁸For they said, "It is better for us to incur the greatest sin against God than for us to fall into the hands of the Jews, who will stone us." ⁴⁹Therefore, Pilate commanded the centurion and the soldiers to say nothing.

⁵⁰Mary Magdalene, a female disciple of the Lord, had been afraid to come to the tomb to do what women customarily do for their deceased loved ones. She had been afraid of what the Jews might do because they were so inflamed with anger. But on the Lord's Day early in the morning, ⁵¹ she brought some of her female friends to the tomb where he had been buried. ⁵²Even though they were afraid the Jews might see them, they said, "Even if we were not able to weep and lament on the day he was crucified, we should do so now at his tomb. ⁵³But who will roll away for us the stone that is set on the entrance to the tomb, so that we can enter, sit next to him, and do what we should do? ⁵⁴For it is a large stone, and we are afraid someone might see us. If we cannot move it, we can lay down the things we have brought before the entrance to the tomb. They will be a memorial for him. And we will weep and beat our breasts in sorrow until we return home."

[55]When they got there, they discovered that the tomb was open. As they stooped down and looked in, they saw a young man sitting in the middle of the tomb. This beautiful young man dressed in very bright clothing said to them, "Why have you come here? Whom are you seeking? Surely not the one who was crucified? He is risen and returned to where he came from. If you don't believe it, stoop down to look and you will see that he is not here." [57]Then the women fled because they were afraid.

[58]Now it was the last day of the Festival of Unleavened Bread, and many people were leaving the city to return to their own homes because the Festival had ended. [59]But we, the twelve disciples of the Lord, were weeping in sorrow. And each one returned to his own home, grieved for what had happened. But I, Simon Peter, and my brother Andrew, took our nets and went off to the sea. And accompanying us was Levi, the son of Alphaeus, whom the Lord [. . .].[†]

P. OXYRHYNCHUS 4009

The manuscript known as P. Oxyrhynchus 4009, though fragmented, most likely preserves a portion of the *Gospel of Peter*. This same portion was quoted by Clement as coming from an apocryphal Gospel.[12] A probable translation of the reconstructed text is as follows:

> [Jesus said,] "Be innocent as doves and wise as serpents. You will be as lambs in the midst of wolves."
> I [presumably Peter] said, "What if we are torn to pieces?"
> He [Jesus] says to me, "The wolves that tear the lamb no longer have power to do anything to it."
> I [Jesus] say to you all, "Do not fear the one killing you because after the killing he can't do anything to you."

An Unknown Gospel (?) (P. Oxyrhynchus 406)

This manuscript should probably be dated to the late second or early third century A.D.; the script strongly suggests a date slightly later than that of P4, which is dated around A.D. 175. Though it could be a fragment of a homily or a theological treatise, it may just as likely preserve a portion of an unknown Gospel. The verso of the manuscript has a quotation from Isaiah 6:9-10, an Old Testament text cited in each of the four canonical Gospels.[13] This citation in the canonical Gospels provides a reason for the rejection by certain people of Jesus' claims to be the Christ, the Son of God.

It can be ascertained that P. Oxyrhynchus 406 is not a portion of any known Gospel because the recto has the unique wording "the Son of God"

[†]P. Oxyrhynchus 2949 has nearly the same wording as verses 3 and 4. In both the Akhmim Manuscript and P. Oxyrhynchus 2949, Joseph's request to have the body of Jesus for burial is placed before the execution, contrary to the order of events in the canonical Gospels.

(*huios theou*) and "Christ crucified" (*Christos estaurōmenos*) in close proximity—a scenario not found in any other extant Gospel. The rest of the extant wording on the recto is difficult to decipher, even when examined in person, as I have done. However, it appears to suggest that the speaker, perhaps Jesus or a Gospel writer, was arguing that certain people, presumably the Jewish leadership in Jesus' day, did not recognize that Jesus was the Son of God and were thus responsible for crucifying the Christ. The reason they rejected Jesus is foretold in Isaiah 6:9-10, which could be one of several passages the speaker in this fragment cited—per the wording "I speak from another [passage]."

> [recto]
> I speak from another [passage] . . . because their [minds] . . . [did not
> recognize] the Son of God . . . [who is] Christ crucified . . .
> because the [heart] of [this] people is calloused
> and they hardly hear with their ears,
>
> [verso]
> and they have closed [their] eyes
> lest [they see] with their eyes
> [and] hear with [their] ears,
> [and] understand [with their hearts],
> and turn, and I would heal them.

Unknown Gospel (P. Oxyrhynchus 840)

This is one vellum leaf dated to the fourth century. It was probably a Gospel composed in the third century or later because Jesus is referred to as "the Savior," whereas in early Gospels he is typically referred to as "Lord." Furthermore, the term *Savior* is written as a nomen sacrum, a trend that was not current in the second and early third centuries.

The majority of the manuscript involves a conversation between Jesus and a chief priest, which takes place in the Temple at Jerusalem. The dramatic episode is preserved nearly complete. A translation is as follows:

> Jesus said to his disciples: "Beware lest you suffer the same things as they because the evildoers receive their reward not among the living only, but also await punishment and much torment." And he brought them into the very place of purification and was walking in the Temple.
>
> A certain Pharisee, a chief priest, whose name was Levi, met them and said to the Savior, "Who allowed you to walk in this place of purification and to see the holy vessels, when you have not washed and your disciples have not bathed their feet? But you were defiled when you walked into this temple, which is a pure place, wherein no other person walks unless he has washed himself and changed his clothes—he will not venture to see these holy vessels."

The Savior immediately stood still with his disciples and answered them, "Are you clean, then, as you are here in the Temple?"

He said, "I am clean because I washed in the pool of David. I descended by one staircase and then I ascended by another. And I put on white and clean clothes. Then I came and looked upon these holy vessels."

The Savior answered him, "Woe to you. You are blind. You do not see. You have washed in these running waters wherein dogs and swine have been thrown night and day and have cleansed the outside skin, which also the harlots and flute girls anoint and wipe and beautify for the lust of men. But within they are full of scorpions and all wickedness. But I and my disciples, whom you say have not bathed, have been dipped in the waters of eternal life."

Unknown Gospel (P. Oxyrhynchus 1224)

This manuscript, dated to the late third century or early fourth, is composed of several fragments. The content has some parallels with the wording in the synoptic Gospels, yet it is also quite distinct.[14] The original Gospel of which this is a copy could be as early as the second century. Four sayings can be discerned from the very fragmented text:

Jesus stood by in a vision and said, "Why are you cast down? For it is not you who [. . .] but he who gave [. . .]" [Someone asks Jesus] "[. . .] did you say?" He gave no answer.

"What then have you forbidden? What is the new doctrine they say you teach? Or what is the new baptism you preach?"

The scribes and Pharisees and priests, seeing him, were indignant because he reclined in the midst of sinners. And Jesus hearing them said, "They who are healthy do not need a physician."

"And pray for your enemies. For he who is not against you is with you. He who today is far off will tomorrow be near you. And in [. . .] of the adversary."

GNOSTIC GOSPELS

The Birth of Mary

This gnostic writing is known only through its detractors. "The Gnostics have a book which they call the Birth (or Descent) of Mary, in which are horrible and deadly things," said the fourth-century bishop Epiphanius,[15] in describing *The Birth of Mary,* a work that has not survived. *The Birth of Mary* claimed to reveal what Zechariah, father of John the Baptist, saw in the Temple—namely, the Jewish God in the form of an ass. That Jews and Christians worshiped an ass-god was commonly held by their critics in those days.[16] This evidently blasphemous work should not be confused with the *Gospel of the Nativity of Mary* (see page 335), a fanciful early account of Mary's birth, early life, and marriage to Joseph that shows no strong gnostic tendencies.

Book of John the Evangelist

This writing is preserved only in Latin and in its present form is dated no earlier than the twelfth century. This book was used most extensively by the Albigenses and was commonly regarded as stemming from the Bogomils before them. (See chapter three for descriptions of these groups.) It was written in the form of questions and answers purported to have come from the apostle John while he leaned upon the breast of Jesus at the Last Supper. This pattern of questions and answers is found in other early gnostic writings, especially the *Gospel of Bartholomew.*

The writing contains gnostic theology. It portrays a world created by Satan, not God, and portrays Christ as an angel sent to the earth rather than a human born of Mary—he "entered in by the ear and came forth by the ear" of Mary. It further indicates that John the Baptist was sent by Satan, that his disciples were not disciples of Christ, and that baptism and apparently also the Lord's Supper were valueless.

Dialogue of the Savior

This gnostic document was found in the ancient Nag Hammadi Library at the modern city of Nag Hammadi (Upper Egypt) in 1946. The *Dialogue* is a fictitious account of a conversation between Jesus and some of his disciples in which they discuss questions about the universe, humanity, the end times, and salvation. The manuscript is in very poor condition and does not allow for a coherent translation. Its authorship and origin are unknown, though it was possibly written in Egypt during the second or third century A.D.

Gospel of Bartholomew

This is one of many Gospels appearing after the second century under the name of some illustrious person. The early church was aware not only of the existence of these writings but also of their fictitious character. In the fourth century, the church historian Eusebius described such writings as heretical, spurious, absurd, and impious. Later a *Gospel of Bartholomew* was mentioned by name, along with several other Gnostic Gospels, in the prologue of Jerome's commentary on Matthew's Gospel. However, there is no evidence that Jerome had seen such a book or that it actually existed.

A work called *Questions of Bartholomew* does exist in Greek, Latin, and Slavonic texts—the Greek dating possibly from the fifth or sixth century. Its text has Bartholomew asking Jesus where he went after the Crucifixion, with Jesus replying that he went into Hades. Later, Bartholomew is pictured as asking Mary to tell how she conceived the Incomprehensible or bore him who cannot be carried. Mary warns him that if she began to tell him, fire would come forth from her mouth and consume the whole world, yet the apostle persists. As she tells the story of the angelic visitation and the Annunciation, fire comes from her mouth. The world is about to come to an end, but Jesus intervenes and places his hand over Mary's mouth.

Also, the apostles ask to see the bottomless pit and "the things which are in the heavens." Bartholomew is shown the adversary of men, Beliar, restrained by 660 angels and bound with fiery chains. When Bartholomew treads upon his neck, Beliar explains that he had first been called Satanael and later Satan, he describes the creation of the angels, and he tells how he fell and was able to deceive Eve. Finally, Bartholomew is said to have asked Jesus about the greatest sin. Jesus replies that to say anything evil against a faithful worshiper of God is to sin against the Holy Spirit.

Gospel of Basilides

This was apparently a polemic commentary on the Gospels by a second-century Gnostic. The writings of Basilides remain only as allusions and fragments in later works by several church fathers. Basilides taught in Alexandria sometime during the reign of the Roman emperor Hadrian (A.D. 117–138). His teacher, Glaucias, claimed to be a firsthand interpreter of the apostle Peter. Basilides asserted that his gnostic scheme emerged from Peter's views on the relationship between God and Christ. He described God paradoxically as a nonexistent "Being" who generated three "Sonships." Through successive ascents and enlightenments, the *Gospel of the Supreme God* (the *Gospel of Light*) eventually descended upon Jesus.

Origen stated that "Basilides dared to write a gospel according to Basilides." Clement of Alexandria and the writer of a fourth-century fragment, *Acta Archelai,* thought that Origen referred to an apocryphal Gospel, the teaching of which was deduced from Irenaeus's account. Today, more in line with Hippolytus's understanding of Basilides, this work is regarded as merely a commentary on the Gospels. Basilides was probably not responsible for the magical rites and libertinism of the Basilidians, a gnostic sect led by his son Isidore in Egypt.

Gospel of the Ebionites

This Gospel was quoted by one early Christian writer, Epiphanius (fourth century), in his book *Against Heresies.* Epiphanius preserves seven quotations based on all three Gospels, primarily based on Matthew. Ebionite theology is evident in the quotations. This group rejected the Virgin Birth and held to an adoptionistic view of Christology—that is, Jesus became the Christ at the time of his baptism. The citations also stress the vegetarian diets of John the Baptist and Jesus.

These are quotes from Epiphanius's *Against Heresies:*[17]

There was a man named Jesus, who was about thirty years old. After he chose us, he came to Capernaum and entered the house of Simon called Peter.

Opening his mouth, Jesus said, "As I walked by the sea of Tiberias, I chose John and James, the sons of Zebedee, and Simon, Andrew, Thaddaeus, Simon Zelotes, Judas Iscariot, as well as you, Matthew, when you were sitting at the customs booth. When I called you, you followed me. It is my will that you will be the twelve apostles as a testimony to Israel."

As John was baptizing, the Pharisees came to him and were baptized, as well as all Jerusalem. He wore a garment of camel's hair and a leather belt around his waist.

His food was wild honey, which tasted like manna, formed into cakes with oil.

The beginning of this Gospel reads as follows:

It came to pass in the days of Herod, King of Judea, that John came to the Jordan River and baptized with a baptism of repentance. He is said to be from the tribe of Aaron and the son of Zechariah, the priest, and of Elizabeth. All went out to [hear] him.

And after many other words it reads:

After the people had been baptized, Jesus also came and was baptized. As he came out of the water, the heavens opened, and he saw the Holy Spirit descending in the form of a dove and entering into him. And a voice was heard from heaven: "You are my dearly loved Son with whom I am very pleased." And again [the voice said]: "I have begotten you this day." Suddenly a bright light shone in that place—and John, seeing him, asked, "Who are you, Lord?" Then a voice from heaven was heard: "This is my dearly loved Son with whom I am very pleased." Hearing this, John fell at Jesus' feet and said, "Lord, please baptize me!" But he refused, saying, "No, we must carry out all that is supposed to be accomplished."

[In Epiphanius's view,] they [the Ebionites] also deny that he is a man, basing their position on the words [Jesus] said, "Look, your mothers and brothers are standing outside."

[He replied,] "Who is my mother and who are my brothers?" And he stretched forth his hand toward his disciples and said, "My brothers and my mother and sisters are those who do my Father's will."

[In Epiphanius's view,] they [the Ebionites] say that he [Jesus] is not begotten by God the Father, but was created like one of the archangels— though he is greater than them. They say he rules over the angels and all the beings created by God. As the Gospel used by them says, Jesus came and proclaimed, "I have come to abolish the sacrifices. If you do not stop your sacrifices, [God's] anger will continue to weigh upon you."

[In Epiphanius's view,] those who reject eating meat have fallen into serious error. They [the Ebionites] cite Jesus as saying, "I have no desire to eat the flesh of the Passover lamb with you." They change the true order of these words and distort them, which is clear to all when the words are read in context. They make the disciples ask Jesus: "Where do you want us to prepare the Passover meal for you?" To which he replied, "I have no desire to eat the flesh of the Passover lamb with you."

Gospel of the Egyptians

There are two noncanonical books of the same name. The first, a Greek manuscript from the second century A.D., is currently lost. It was mentioned by the early church writers Clement of Alexandria and Origen. It was used by Gentile Christians in Egypt but was apparently superseded by the canonical Gospels in orthodox circles. It contained gnostic "statements of Jesus" also found in the *Gospel of Thomas*.[18] This Gospel seems to have contained and propagated gnostic teachings, especially those advocated in Syria by Simon and Menander. According to these Gnostics, marriage, eating meat, and procreation were evil. Clement may have quoted from this writing to refute the beliefs of the Encratites, a gnostic group who practiced abstinence and self-restraint and who broadly agreed with the Syrian Gnostics on those matters. The Gnostics' depreciation of women is reflected in the quotations Clement used. The primary information we have is found in the quotes below:

> Clement of Alexandria (*Stromata* 3.9.63)
> But those who stand against God's creation for the sake of continence, which is a nice sounding word, quote also those words which were spoken to Salome, of which I made mention before. (These are contained, I believe, in the *Gospel according to the Egyptians*.) For they say that "the Savior himself said: 'I came to destroy the works of the female.'" By female he means lust: by works, birth and decay.

> (*Stromata* 3.13.92)
> When Salome inquired as to when the things she asked about would be known, the Lord said: "When you have trod underfoot the garment of shame [i.e., the flesh], and when the two become one and the male together with the female is neither male nor female." First of all, we

271

do not have this saying in any of the four Gospels that have been delivered to us, but in that which is according to the Egyptians.[19]

Hippolytus (*Refutation of All Heresies* 5.7)
[The Naassenes] say that the soul is very difficult to discover and perceive because it does not continue in the same manner or shape or in one emotion so that one can describe it or comprehend its essence. And they have these various changes of the soul set forth in a Gospel entitled "According to the Egyptians."

Epiphanius (*Heresies* 62.2) on the Sabellians, followers of the heretic Sabellius, promoter of modalism
They draw their entire error (falsehood) and the support for it from some apocryphal books, especially from what is called the Egyptian Gospel, to which some have given that name. For in it many similar things are attributed to the person of the Savior, said in a corner, claiming that he demonstrated for his disciples that the same person was Father, Son, and Holy Spirit.

The second *Gospel of the Egyptians* is a composition discovered in 1946 at Chenoboskeia (Egypt) in the Nag Hammadi collection of gnostic writing. The principal title of the work, described in the colophon as "Gospel of the Egyptians," was the "Sacred Book of the Great Invisible Spirit." It exists in two copies with variations: Nag Hammadi Codices III, 40–69; and Nag Hammadi Codices IV, 50–81. This work deals with emanations from "the primal spirit of the cosmos" and perhaps was a product of the Barbelo gnostic sect. It is very much distinct from the Gospel genre. Instead, it is a gnostic treatise on salvation history. The text below incorporates some elements of both texts, which are used to supply material missing in each other. Except for a section of about five pages, the page numbers in the text below follow Nag Hammadi Codices III. The page numbers from Nag Hammadi Codices IV are noted by the Roman numeral IV; the page numbers are approximate and are here inserted in brackets in the text.

[40] The holy book of the Egyptians regarding the great invisible Spirit, the Parent[†] whose name is unutterable, he who came forth from the peaks of perfection, the light of the light of the aeons of light, the light of the silence of forethought, and the Father of the silence, the light of the Word and the truth, the light of the incorruptions, [41] the infinite light, the radiance from the aeons of light of the unrevealable, unmarked, ageless, unspeakable Parent, the Aeon of the aeons, who is the self-generated, self-begotten, self-producing, wholly other—the genuine Aeon.

---

† Literally, "Father."

Three powers emanated from him: the Father, the Mother, and the Son. These came from the living silence, from the incorruptible Parent. They emanated from the silence of the unknown Parent.

And from that place, Domedon-Doxomedon came forth, the place of the aeons. And [. . .] the light of each one of their powers. Thus the Son was the fourth emanation, the Mother was the fifth, and the Father was the sixth. He was [. . .]; it is he who is unmarked among all the powers, the glories, and those things that are imperishable.

From that place the three powers emanated, the three octets that the Parent brings forth in silence by his forethought, [42] from his bosom—the Father, the Mother, and the Son.

The first octet, on account of which the thrice-male[†] child came forth, which is the thought, and the word, and the incorruption, and the eternal life, the will, the mind, and the foreknowledge, the androgynous Father.

The second octet-power, the Mother, the masculine female virgin, Barbelo, Epititioch[. . .]ai, Memeneaimen[. . .], [. . .]kaba, Adone, [. . .] who presides over the heaven [. . .] the inexplicable power, the ineffable Mother. She had emanated and then radiated from herself [. . .] and she delighted in the Parent of the silent silence.

The third octet-power, the Son of the silent silence, the crown of the silent silence, the glory of the Father, the virtue of the Mother, [43] the one from whose bosom the seven powers of the great light of the seven vowels[‡] go forth. And the word is their perfection.

These are the three powers, the three octets that the Parent brought forth from his bosom according to his forethought. He brought them forth at that place.

Domedon-Doxomedon came forth, the Aeon of the aeons, and the throne which is in him, and the powers which surround him, the glories and the incorruptions. The Parent of the great light who came forth from the silence, he is the great Doxomedon-aeon, in which the thrice-male child rests. And the throne of his glory was established in it, this one on which his unrevealable name is inscribed, on the tablet [. . .] one is the word, the Parent of the light of everything, he who came forth from the silence, while he rests in the silence, [44] he whose name is in an invisible symbol. A hidden, invisible mystery came forth: iiiiiiiiiiiiiiiiiiii, EEEEEEEEEEEEEEEEEEEEEEE, ooooooooooooooooooooooo, uuuuuuuuuuuuuuuuuuuuuu, eeeeeeeeeeeeeeeeeeeeeee, aaaaaaaaaaaaaaaaaaaaaa, OOOOOOOOOOOOOOOOOOOOOO.[§]

[†]I.e., superior, a genuine member of the incorruptible aeon or age.

[‡]Or, "seven voices."

[§]Each of the seven Greek vowels are repeated twenty-two times (the number of letters in the Hebrew alphabet). Their use here is much like that in ancient spells or incantations, though there are various theories as to their order and its significance.

And so the three powers praised the great, invisible, unnamable, virginal, uninvokable Spirit, and his masculine female virgin.[†] They asked for a power, and a silence from living silence came forth, namely glories and incorruptions in the aeons [. . .] aeons, [IV 55] myriads added on [. . .], the thrice-males, the thrice-male offspring, and the male races[‡] [. . .] filled the great Doxomedon-aeon with the power of the word of the whole fullness.

Then the thrice-male child of the great Christ, who had been anointed by the great invisible Spirit—he whose power is named "Ainon"—gave praise to the great invisible Spirit and his masculine female virgin Youel, and the silence of silent silence, and the greatness that [. . .] ineffable. [. . .] ineffable [. . .] unanswerable and inexplicable, the first one who has come forth, and unproclaimable, [. . .] which is wonderful [. . .] ineffable [. . .], [IV 56] he who has all the greatnesses of greatness of the silence there. The thrice-male child offered praise and asked for a power from the great, invisible, virgin Spirit.

Then there appeared at that place [. . .], who [. . .], who sees glories [. . .] treasures in a [. . .] invisible mysteries to [. . .] of the silence, who is the masculine female virgin Youel. Then Esephekh, the child of the child, appeared.

In this way he was completed, namely, the Father, the Mother, the Son, the five seals, the invincible power that is the great Christ of all the incorruptible ones. [*** one line missing ***] [IV 57] holy [. . .] the end, the incorruptible [. . .], and [. . .], they are powers and glories and incorruptions [. . .]. They came forth [*** 5 lines missing ***]

[. . .] This one praised the unrevealable, hidden mystery [. . .] the hidden [*** 4 lines missing ***]

[. . .] him in the [. . .], and the aeons [. . .] thrones, [. . .] and each [. . .] innumerable myriads of powers surround them, glories and incorruptions [. . .] and they [. . .] of [IV 58] the Father, and the Mother, and the Son, and the whole fullness, which I mentioned earlier, and the five seals, and the mystery of mysteries. They appeared [*** 3 lines missing ***]

[. . .] who rules over [. . .], and the aeons of [. . .] truly [. . .] and the [*** 4 lines missing ***]

[. . .] and the true and genuine eternal aeons.

Then forethought came out from silence together with the Spirit's living silence, and the Word of the Parent, and a light. She [. . .] the five seals which the Parent brought forth from his bosom, [IV 59] and she passed through all the aeons which I mentioned earlier. And she set up glorious thrones, and innumerable myriads of angels that surrounded them, powers and incorruptible glories, who sing and give glory, all giving praise with a single voice, together as one unceasing voice, [. . .] to the Father, and the Mother, and the Son [. . .], and all the fullnesses that I spoke of earlier, who is the great Christ,

---

[†] I.e., the Barbelo.

[‡] Nag Hammadi csodex IV 55 includes here "the glories of the Father, the glories of the great Christ, and the male offspring."

who is from silence, who is the incorruptible child Telmael Telmakhael Eli Eli Makhar Makhar Seth, the power which genuinely and truly lives, and Youel, the masculine female virgin who is with him, and Esephekh, holder of the glory, the child of the child, and his crowning glory, [. . .] of the five seals, the fullness that I mentioned earlier.

[IV 60] The great self-begotten living Word came forth in that place, the true god, the unborn physis, whose name I will tell, saying, [. . .] aia [. . .] thaOthOsth [. . .], who is the son of the great Christ,† who is the son of the ineffable silence, who came forth from the great invisible and incorruptible Spirit. The son of the silence and silence appeared [*** one line missing ***] not visible [. . .] man and his glorious treasures. Then he appeared in the manifest [. . .]. And he established the four aeons with a word.

He praised the great, invisible, virginal Spirit, the silence of the Parent, in a silence of the living silence of silence, the place where the man rests [*** two lines missing ***]. [III 49] Then there came forth from that place the intensely radiant cloud, the living power, the mother of the holy, incorruptible ones, the great power, the Mirothoe. And she bore him whose name I speak, saying, "[ien] ien ien Ea Ea Ea," three times.

Now this one, Adamas, is a light that shined forth from the light; he is the eye of the light. For he is the first human, he because of whom and for whom everything came to exist, and apart from whom nothing came into being. The unknowable, incomprehensible Parent came forth, descending in order to do away with the deficiency.

Then the great Word, the divine Self-Generated, and the incorruptible man Adamas mingled with each other. A Word of man came into existence, although the human had come into being through a word.

He praised the great, invisible, incomprehensible, virginal Spirit, and the masculine female virgin, and the thrice-male child, and [50] the masculine female virgin Youel, and Esephekh, holder of the glory, the child of the child and his crowning glory, and the great Doxomedon-aeon, and the thrones that exist in him, and the powers which surround him, the glories and the incorruptions, and their whole fullness which I mentioned earlier, and the ethereal earth that receives God, where the holy men of the great light are formed, the men of the Parent of the silent, living silence, the Parent and their whole fullness, as I mentioned earlier.

The great Word, the divine Self-Generated, and the incorruptible man Adamas offered praise, and requested a power and eternal strength for the Self-Generated, in order to perfect the four aeons, that through them [. . .] the glory and power of the invisible [51] Parent of the holy men of the great light that will come to the world might appear—it is the image of the night. The incorruptible human, Adamas, requested a son of his own for their sakes, in order that the son might become the father of the immovable,

---

†Here, the Word is understood as emanating from the eternal Christ.

incorruptible race, through which the silence and the voice should appear and the dead aeon raise itself, that it may dissolve.

And so there came forth from above the power of the great light, the Manifestation. She gave birth to the four great lights—Harmozel, Oroiael, Davithe, Eleleth—and to the great incorruptible Seth, the son of Adamas, the incorruptible human. In this way, the perfect septet that exists [52] in hidden mysteries became complete. When she receives the glory, she becomes eleven octets.

And the Parent approved, and the whole fullness of the lights was in agreement. Their consorts came forth for the completion of the octet of the divine Self-Generated: Favor for the first light Harmozel, Perception for the second light Oroiael, Understanding for the third light Davithe, and Sagacity for the fourth light Eleleth. This is the first octet of the divine Self-Generated.

And the Parent approved, and the whole fullness of the lights was in agreement. The attendants came forth: the first one, the mighty Gamaliel of the first great light Harmozel, and the mighty Gabriel of the second great light Oroiael, and the mighty Samlo of the great light Davithe, and the mighty Abrasax of the great light Eleleth. [53] And the consorts of the attendants came forth in accord with the Parent's desire and approval: Memory of the Great One for the first, Gamaliel; Love of the Great One for the second, Gabriel; Peace of the Great One for the third, Samblo; and Eternal Life of the Great One for the fourth, Abrasax. And so the emanation of the five octets was finished, a total of 40, as an inexplicable power.

Then the great Word, the Self-Generated, and the word of the fullness of the four lights gave praise to the great, invisible, uninvokable, virginal Spirit, and the masculine female virgin, and the great Doxomedon-aeon, and the thrones which are in them, and the powers which surround them, glories, authorities, and the powers, and the thrice-male child, and the masculine female virgin Youel, [54] and Esephekh, holder of the glory, the child of the child and his crowning glory, the whole fullness, and all the glories which are there, the infinite fullnesses and the unnamable aeons, in order that they might name the parent the fourth, with the incorruptible race, and that they may call the seed of the Parent the seed of the great Seth.

Then everything quaked, and trembling took hold of the incorruptible ones. Then the three male children came forth from above, down into the ones who are not born, and the self-begotten ones, and those who were begotten in what is begotten. The greatnesses came forth, all the greatnesses of the great Christ. He set up thrones in glory with [55] innumerable myriads in the four aeons, and around them innumerable myriads, powers and glories and incorruptions. And so it came to be.

And the incorruptible, spiritual church grew strong within the four lights of the great, living Self-Generated, the god of truth, praising, singing, and glorifying together with one voice, as with an unceasing mouth, the Father, and the Mother, and the Son, and their whole fullness, as I mentioned earlier [. . .] the five seals that possess the myriads, and they who rule over the aeons, and they who bear the glory of the leaders being given an order to show it to the worthy ones. Amen!

Then the great Seth, the son of the incorruptible human, Adamas, praised the great, invisible, uninvokable, unnamable, virginal Spirit, and the masculine female virgin, and the thrice-male child, and the masculine female virgin Youel, and Esephekh, holder of the glory and his crowning glory, the child of the child, and [56] the great Doxomedon-aeons, and the fullness that I mentioned earlier; and asked for his seed.

Then there emanated from that place the mighty power of the great light Plesithea—the mother of the angels, the mother of the lights, the glorious mother, the four-breasted virgin, bringing the fruit from Gomorrah as a spring, and of Sodom, which is the fruit of the spring of Gomorrah within her. She came forth through the great Seth.

Then the great Seth rejoiced over the grace given him by the incorruptible child. He took his seed from the four-breasted virgin, and he placed it with her among the four aeons, in the third great light, Davithe.

After 5,000 years, the great light Eleleth spoke: "Let someone reign over chaos and Hades." And a cloud appeared, called hylic Sophia [57] [. . .] She looked out on the parts of chaos, her face being like [. . .] in her way [. . .] blood. And the mighty angel Gamaliel said to the mighty Gabriel, the minister of the great light Oroiael, "Let an angel emerge to rule over chaos and Hades." Then the cloud, in agreement, came forth in the two units, each having light. [. . .] the throne that she had placed in the cloud above. Sakla, the great angel, saw Nebruel, the great demon who was with him. And together they became earthly spirits, begetting. They begot assisting angels. Sakla said to the great demon Nebruel, "Let there be 12 aeons in the [. . .] aeon, worlds [. . .]." [. . .] by the will of the Self-Generated, the great angel Sakla said, [58] "Let there be the [. . .] of the seven in number [. . .]." And he said to the great angels, "Each of you, go and reign over your world." So each one of these 12 angels went forth. The first angel is Athoth. He is the one called [. . .] by the great generations of men. The second is Harmas, who is the fiery eye. The third is Galila. The fourth is Yobel. The fifth is Adonaios, who is called Sabaoth. The sixth is Cain, who is called the sun by the great generations of men. The seventh is Abel; the eighth Akiressina; the ninth Yubel. The tenth is Harmupiael. The eleventh is Archir-Adonin. The twelfth is Belias. These are the ones who preside over Hades and the chaos.

And after the founding of the world, Sakla said to his angels, "Behold, I myself am a jealous god. And apart from me, nothing has come into being," for he trusted in his essence.

[59] But a voice from on high said, "The Man exists, and the Son of the Man." Because the image from above came down, which is like its voice in the superiority of the image.

The image gazed out, and through the gaze of the image above, the first creature was formed. Because of this, Metanoia[†] came into being. She received her completion and her power by the will of the Parent, and his approval, with which he approved of Seth's great, incorruptible, immovable race of the great and mighty men, in order that he may sow it in the aeons that were brought forth, so that through her, what is lacking may be supplied. For she emanated from above and descended to the world, the image of the night. After she came, she prayed for both the seed of the archon of this aeon, and the authorities who had emanated from him—that impure one of the demon-begetting god which will be destroyed—and the [60] seed of Adam and the great Seth, which is like the sun.

Then the great angel Hormos came to make, by means of the virgins of this aeon's corrupted sowing, in a Word-begotten, holy vessel, through the Holy Spirit, the seed of the great Seth.

Then the great Seth came and brought his seed. And it was sown in the aeons that had emanated, whose number is the quantity of Sodom. Some claim that the great Seth's pastureland in Sodom is Gomorrah. But others claim that the great Seth removed his plant from Gomorrah and planted it at the second place, which he called "Sodom."

This is the race that came forth through Edokla, who, through logic, gave birth to truth and righteousness, the source of the seed of eternal life, which is with those who will endure by means of the knowledge of their emanation. This is the great, incorruptible race that has emanated through three worlds into the world.

[61] And the flood came as a foreshadowing of the end of the aeon; because of this race, a conflagration will come upon the earth. And grace will come to the race by means of the prophets and the guardians who watch over the life of the race. Because of this race, famines and plagues will occur. Now, these things will happen on account of the great, incorruptible race. On account of this race, temptations will come by the deceit of false prophets.

The great Seth saw the devil's deeds and his many disguises and his plots—which will come upon Seth's incorruptible, immovable race—as well as the persecutions of his powers and his angels, and their error, that they acted recklessly.

Then the great Seth praised the great, uninvokable, virginal Spirit, and the masculine female virgin [62] Barbelo, and the thrice-male child Telmael Telmakhael Heli Heli Makhar Makhar Seth, the power which genuinely and truly lives, and the masculine female virgin Youel, and Esephekh, holder of the glory and his crowning glory, and the great Doxomedon-aeon, and the thrones which are in him, and the powers that surround them, and the whole fullness, as I mentioned earlier. And he requested guards for his seed.

And then from the great aeons, four hundred ethereal angels came forth,

---

[†] I.e., repentance.

along with the mighty Aerosiel and the mighty Selmekhel, to guard the great, incorruptible race, its fruit, and the great men of the great Seth, from the time and the moment of truth and righteousness, until the consummation of the aeon with its archons, whom the great judges have sentenced to death.

Then the great Seth was sent by the four lights, according to the desire of the Self-Generated and the whole fullness, and with [63] the favor and happy approval of the great invisible Spirit, and the five seals, and the whole fullness.

He endured the three existential events which I mentioned earlier: the flood, and the conflagration, and the judgment of the archons and the powers and the authorities, in order to save the race that went astray by the reconciliation of the world and baptism of the body, through a Word-begotten one whom the great Seth secretly prepared for himself through the virgin. He did this in order that the holy ones might be born of the holy Spirit by invisible, mysterious symbols, by reconciling the world with the world, by renouncing the world and the god of the thirteen aeons, and by the convocations of the holy ones and the indescribable ones, and by the incorruptible bosom, and by the great light pre-existing in forethought.

And by forethought, he set in place the holy baptism that exceeds the heaven through the incorruptible, Word-begotten one—he is [64] Jesus the living one, with whom the great Seth has clothed himself. And through him, he crucified[†] the powers of the thirteen aeons and set in place those who are delivered and caught away. He armed them with the armor of knowing this truth, an unconquerable power of incorruptibility.

There appeared to them the great minister Yesseus Mazareus Yessede-keus, the living water; the great governors, James the great and Theopemp-tos and Isauel; those who act as authorities over the spring of truth, Mikheus and Mikhar and Mnesinous; the one who acts as the authority over the baptism of the living, Sesengenpharanges the purifier; those who act as authorities over the gates of the waters, Mikheus and Mikhar; those who act as authorities over the mountain, Seldao and Elainos; the recipients of the great race, the great Seth's incorruptible, mighty men; the attendants of the four lights—the mighty Gamaliel, the mighty Gabriel, the mighty Samblo, and the mighty Abrasax; those who act [65] as authorities over the sun and its rising—Olses, Hypneus, and Heurumaious; those who act as authorities over the entrance into the rest of eternal life, the rulers Mixanther and Michanor; those who guard the souls of the chosen ones, Akramas and Strempsoukhos; the great power Heli Heli Makhar Makhar Seth; the great invisible, uninvokable, unnamable, virginal Spirit, and the silence; the first great light Harmozel—the place of the living Self-Generated, the God of the truth, and with him, the incorruptible human, Adamas; the second

---

†Literally, "nailed."

great light, Oroiael—the place of the great Seth, and Jesus, who has the life and who came and crucified that which is in the law; the third great light, Davithe—the place of the sons of the great Seth; the fourth great light, Eleleth—the place where the souls of the sons are resting; and also the fifth great light, Yoel, who exercises authority over the name of him to whom it will be granted to baptize with the holy baptism that surpasses the heaven, the incorruptible one.

But from now on, by the agency of [66] Poimael the incorruptible man on behalf of those who are worthy of petition and the repudiation of the five seals in the spring-baptism, those who, according to the instruction they receive, know their recipients and are known by them will certainly not taste death.

O Iesseus EO ou EO Oua!† Genuinely and truly, O Yesseus Mazareus Yes-sedekeus, O living water, O child of the child, O glorious name! O Genuine and true Aeon that exists, iiii EEEE eeee oooo uuuu OOOO aaaa. Genuinely and truly, Ei aaaa OOOO, O existing one who sees the aeons! Genuinely and truly, a ee EEE iiii ooooo uuuuuu OOOOOOOO, who is eternally eternal! Genuinely and truly, iEa aiO, in the heart, who exists, upsilon forever,‡ you are what you are, you are who you are!

Your great name is upon me, O self-begotten Perfect One, who is not outside me. I behold you, O you who may be seen by all, for who can com-prehend you by means of speech? Having come to know you, I have mixed myself with [67] that which is changeless; I have equipped myself with an armor of light; I have become light! For the Mother was there because of the lovely beauty of the gift. For this reason, I have stretched out my folded hands. I was fashioned in the circle of the bountiful light that is in my bosom, which fashions the many who are begotten by the irreproachable light. I shall accurately proclaim your glory, for I have comprehended you. Regard-ing you, O Jesus, eternal omega, eternal epsilon, O eternity of eternity, O God of silence! I honor you completely. You are my place of rest, O son, Es Es, the epsilon! You are one without outward form, existing among those without outward forms, raising a human by whom you will set me apart for your life, according to your incorruptible name. Thus the fragrance of life is within me. I mixed it with water as a pattern for the archons, so that I might live with you in the peace of the holy ones, you who genuinely and truly exist for eternity.

[68] This is the book that the great Seth wrote and set upon mountains so high that the sun cannot rise there, nor will it ever be able to. And since the days of the prophets and the apostles and the preachers [began], the name has never risen upon their hearts, nor will it ever be able to, and their ears have not heard it.

The great Seth wrote down the letters in this book in 130 years. He set it

---

†This and the following lines seem to have been a gnostic baptismal hymn.
‡ Or possibly "son forever."

in the mountain called Kharaxio, so that at the end of the times and the eras—according to the desire of the divine Self-Generated and the whole fullness and through the gift of untraceable, incomprehensible, fatherly love—it may emerge to reveal the great Savior's incorruptible, holy race, along with those who dwell with them in love, and the great, invisible, eternal Spirit, and his only-begotten Son, and the everlasting light, and [69] his great, incorruptible consort, and the incorruptible Sophia, and the Barbelo, and utter fullness in eternity. Amen.

The Gospel of the Egyptians.[†] The holy, secret book written by God. May Favor, Understanding, Perception, and Sagacity[‡] be with the one who has written it—Eugnostos the beloved, spiritually speaking (though according to the flesh, my name is Gogessos)—and to my fellow incorruptible lights. Jesus Christ, Son of God, Savior, Ichthus. The holy book of the great invisible Spirit is written by God. Amen.

The Holy Book of the Great Invisible Spirit. Amen.

Gospel of Eve

This is a gnostic and apocalyptic writing, known solely through a citation by Epiphanius, a late fourth-century bishop of Cyprus. Epiphanius quoted the *Gospel of Eve* in a biting refutation of gnostic and Origenistic teachings. Evidently a cult had formed around Eve, as if her name implied revelation simply because the serpent had spoken to her in the Garden of Eden. Epiphanius's quotation from the *Gospel of Eve* roughly translates as follows:

> I stood on a high mountain and saw a giant and a feeble man, and I heard a voice like thunder: "Come near me and listen." And he spoke to me saying, "I am you and you are me. Wherever you are, there I am. I am spread through all things, and any place you are able to retire into or take shelter in me; and, taking shelter in me, you take shelter in yourself."

Gospel According to the Hebrews

This Gospel, composed in the middle of the second century, is to be distinguished from the *Gospel of the Egyptians,* which was read by Gentile Christians in Egypt. Six fragments have been preserved in the writings of Clement of Alexandria, Origen, and Jerome. The sayings show no sign of being related to the canonical Gospels. The *Gospel According to the Hebrews* has an account of the risen Christ's appearance to his brother James. It appears that the Gospel embodies the gnostic emphasis on attaining salvation through release from the body and absorption in the Spirit. But there is too little extant text to be certain about this.

[†]These final two paragraphs are from the fragmentary copy of this work found in Nag Hammadi Codices III.

[‡]These virtues are also the names of the consorts given at 52.

Clement of Alexandria (*Stromata* 2.9.45)
>   It is also written in the *Gospel According to the Hebrews,* "He who marvels will reign, and who reigns will rest."

Origen (on John 2:12)
>   If anyone would trust the *Gospel According to the Hebrews,* where the Savior says, "My mother, the Holy Spirit, took me away by one of my hairs and carried me off to the great Mount Tabor," he will have difficulty explaining how the Holy Spirit can be the mother of the Christ.

Jerome (on Ephesians 5:4)
>   We read in the Hebrew Gospel where the Lord says to his disciples, "You can't be happy unless you show love to your brother."

Jerome (De viris illustribus 2)
>   The Gospel also titled as "According to the Hebrews," which I recently translated into Greek and Latin and which Origen often quotes, has this narrative after the resurrection:
>   Now the Lord, when he had given the cloth to the servant of the priest, went to James and appeared to him. James had previously taken an oath that he would not eat food (since the time he had partaken of the Lord's cup) until he saw him risen from the dead. A little later the Lord said, "Bring a table and bread." And then it says, "He took bread, blessed and broke it, and gave it to James the just, saying to him: 'My brother, eat your bread, for the Son of Man has risen from among those who sleep.'"

Jerome (on Ezekiel 18:7)
>   In the *Gospel of the Hebrews,* which the Nazareans customarily read, it is said that one of the greatest sins is when "one hurts the spirit of his brother."

Jerome (on Isaiah 11:2)
>   The Gospel, which is written in Hebrew and the Nazareans read, says, "The whole fountain of the Holy Spirit will descend on him." And the Lord is the Spirit, and where the Spirit of the Lord is, there is liberty. And in the Gospel just referred to I find this written: "And it came to pass, as the Lord came up out of the water, the whole fountain of the Holy Spirit descended upon him and rested upon him and said to him, 'My son, [as predicted] in all the prophets I expected you might come and that I might rest upon you. You are my rest, you are my firstborn Son, who reigns in eternity.'"

Gospel of Judas

This is one of the earlier gnostic writings, probably produced by the Cainite sect.[20] We know of it first through the writings of Irenaeus (ca. A.D. 180),[21] and it may have been written around A.D. 130–150. This work was considered lost for a long time but was found in a codex of Coptic writings in the 1970s in El Minya, Egypt. It was subsequently purchased by Frieda-Nussenberger Tchacos (who named the codex after her father). In recent years the *Gospel of Judas* in Codex Tchacos has been studied and published.[22] It gives an account of a special revelation of the nature of the universe that Jesus gave to Judas in the week before the Crucifixion.

After a brief summary of Jesus' ministry, the narrative opens with Jesus and his disciples in Judea during the week before his crucifixion. Jesus approaches the disciples as they say a prayer before a meal and reproaches them,[23] leading to a conflict that shows the disciples' ignorance but highlights Judas's unique understanding and ability to learn from Jesus. Following this, Jesus begins to teach Judas privately.

As Passover nears, further interaction between Jesus and the disciples reinforces the idea that all of them, except Judas, are on the wrong track in their worship of Israel's God. The narrative makes this point through parallel scenes; in the first, Jesus responds to a vision seen by the disciples. In the second, he responds at length to a vision seen by Judas. Jesus' response to Judas's vision contains a long cosmological discourse that is marked by an affinity to classical gnostic teachings and culminates in Jesus' revelation that Judas will "sacrifice the man that clothes [Jesus]."

Thus, the Gospel sets forth the "mystery of the betrayal" and explains how Judas through his treachery made the salvation of all humanity possible. This was accomplished by his preventing the destruction of the truth proclaimed by Christ or by his thwarting the designs of the evil powers, the Archons, who wished to prevent the crucifixion of Christ because they knew it would destroy their evil power. Because of its recent publication, we will give some extra space for the discussion of the *Gospel of Judas*.

A number of anachronisms show the *Gospel of Judas* to be a response to the Christian community, not a historical representation of Jesus' life; for example, the statement "That place is reserved for the holy. Neither the sun nor the moon will rule there, nor the day, but the holy will abide there always, in the eternal realm with the holy angels" (column 45, lines 18–24) shows the author's knowledge of Revelation 22:5 but places the words in Jesus' earthly ministry. Later we read "Jesus said to them, 'Why are you troubled? I tell you the truth, all the priests who stand before that altar invoke my name'" (column 39).[24] This statement seems to envision the setting of a church building, with priests and an altar—accoutrements not found in early house-churches or synagogues—but again, the words are spoken by Jesus in his earthly ministry.

Later we read, "Judas said to Jesus, 'Look, what will those who have been baptized in your name do?'" (column 55, lines 21–23). Since it is questionable whether baptism in the name of Jesus was practiced during Jesus' earthly ministry, this topic in the conversation between Jesus and Judas again reflects the conditions of the growing church after the first century rather than any historical teaching of Jesus.

In literary terms, then, the *Gospel of Judas* shows itself to be a gnostic, minority response to larger groups of Christians who rejected gnostic teachings.[25] It appears to have been designed to reinforce the superiority of gnostic ideas for this minority group by inviting them to stand in Judas's shoes. The implicit argument is that they are the only ones of Jesus' disciples who really understand his message and are destined for the higher realm. The other Christians invoking Christ's name at the altar (columns 38–39) are really serving Saklas (the evil Demiurge or Yaldabaoth) and are destined to vanish along with all that is merely material.

According to the *Gospel of Judas,* persecution or rejection by mainstream Christians is predictable (column 46) and is due to the gnostic minority's enlightened status in the midst of everyone else's blind service to Yaldabaoth. But the situation will one day be reversed, and followers of gnostic teaching should be reassured that their ability to attain the spiritual realm has not fallen under the power of the lesser gods—just as Judas, their "seed" was not under "the control of the rulers" (column 46). Understanding the implicit argument of the *Gospel of Judas* sheds light on its context, which is probably representative of the situation of the Christian gnostic sects in general: They were marginal groups whose teachings had been rejected from the beginning by most other Christians, but they remained convinced that the majority of Christians were unenlightened and were actually serving wicked subdeities while claiming the name of Christ.

In the following presentation of the text, some of the smaller *lacunae* (that is, gaps or missing spaces) have been omitted and reconstructions allowed in their place to facilitate easier reading. In addition, the column numbers are placed in brackets for general reference to different sections of the text. The text of the *Gospel of Judas* begins in column 33 of Codex Tchacos.

> The secret record of the revelation that Jesus told Judas Iscariot in a week's conversation, three days before he celebrated Passover
>
> When Jesus was manifest on the earth, he did miracles and great wonders for mankind's salvation. And because some walked in the way of righteousness while others walked in their sins, the twelve disciples were called.

He started to speak with them about the mysteries beyond the world and what would take place at the end. Often he did not appear to his disciples as himself, but he was found among them as a child.

Judas's Insight and the Other Disciples' Ignorance
On a day when Jesus was in Judea with his disciples, he found them seated in pious observance as a group. When he drew near to his disciples, [34] who were seated together and saying a prayer of thanksgiving over the bread, he laughed. The disciples said, "Teacher, why are you laughing at our prayer of thanksgiving? We have done what is right."

He answered them, "I am not laughing at you. You are not doing this because you desire to but because through this your God will be praised."

They said, "Teacher, you are [. . .] the son of our God."

And Jesus said, "How do you know me? I tell you the truth, no generation of the people that are among you will know me."

When the disciples heard this, they became angry and enraged and started blaspheming him in their hearts. Jesus, observing their lack of understanding, said to them, "Why has this disturbance made you angry? It is your God within you and [. . .] [35] have provoked your souls to anger. Let any of you men who has enough fortitude bring out the perfect man and stand in my presence."

They all said, "We are strong enough." But their spirits did not dare to stand, except for Judas Iscariot. He could stand in his presence, but he was not able to look him in the eyes, so he turned his face away.

Judas said to Jesus, "I know you and your origins. You have come from the eternal realm of Barbelo. And I am not worthy to speak the name of the one who sent you."

Recognizing that Judas was meditating on something exalted, Jesus said to him, "Step away from the others and I will speak to you of the mysteries of the Kingdom. To attain it is possible for you, but you will grieve much [36] because another will take your place, in order to restore the twelve disciples to completion with their God."

Judas asked him, "When will you speak to me about these things? When will the great day of light dawn for the generation?" But while he said this, Jesus left him.

After that, on the following morning, Jesus came again to his disciples. They said, "Teacher, where did you go and what did you do after you departed from us?"

Jesus said, "I went to another great and holy generation."

And his disciples said, "Lord, what is this great generation that is not presently in this realm, which is better than us and holier than us?"

Hearing this, Jesus laughed and said to them, "Why do you think in your hearts about the powerful and holy generation? [37] I tell you the truth, no one born of this age[†] will see that generation, and no company of angels of

---

[†]Or "aeon."

the stars will rule over that generation, and no mortal can associate with it because that generation does not originate from [. . .] which is [. . .]. Your generation of people is from the generation of humanity [. . .] forces, which [. . .] other forces [. . .] by which you have dominion."

Hearing this, his disciples were troubled in spirit. None could say a word.

Another day Jesus came to them, and they said, "Teacher, we have seen you in a vision, for we have had great dreams [. . .] night [. . .]."

He said, "Why have you [. . .] gone into hiding?" [38]

They said, "We have seen a large house with an altar in it, and twelve men (whom we would say are the priests) and a name. A large group of people waits at that altar for the priests [. . .] take the offerings. But we kept waiting."

Jesus said, "What are the priests like?"

They said, "[. . .] two weeks; some offer their own children as sacrifices, others their wives, in worship and humility with one another; some sleep with men; some are involved in murder; some commit myriad sins and lawless acts—and those who stand before that altar call on your name! [39] And in all their inadequate activities, the sacrifices are brought to an end† [. . .]."

After they spoke, they were silent, for they were troubled.

Jesus said to them, "Why are you troubled? I tell you the truth, all the priests who stand before that altar call on my name. Once more I tell you, my name has been inscribed on this [. . .] of the generations of the stars through the human generations. And in my name they have disgracefully planted trees without fruit."

Jesus said, "Those you saw by the altar receiving the offerings—they are you yourselves. That is the God you are serving, and the twelve men you have seen are you. The cattle you saw being brought for sacrifice are the numerous people you lead astray [40] before that altar. [. . .] will stand and use my name in this manner, and generations of the devoted will continue in loyalty to him. After him, another man will stand there who is one of the sexually immoral, and another will stand there who is one of the slayers of children, and another who is one of those who sleep with men, and those who abstain, and the rest of the defiled, lawless, and erring people, and those saying, 'We are like angels.' These are the stars that bring everything to its end, for it has been said to the human generations, 'Behold, God has accepted your sacrifice through the priest'—that is a false minister. But it is the Lord, the Lord of the universe, who gives the order: 'On the last day they will be put to shame.'" [41]

Jesus said, "Stop sacrificing [. . .] that you have [. . .] over the altar because they are over your stars and your angels and have already come to their end there. So let them be trapped in your presence, and let them depart

[*** about fifteen lines missing ***]

---

†Or "to completion."

[. . .] generations [. . .]. A baker is not able to feed all creation [42] under heaven. And [. . .] to them [. . .] and [. . .] to us and [. . .].

Jesus said to them, "Stop struggling with me. Each of you has his own star, and everybody

[*** about seventeen lines missing ***]

[43] in [. . .] who has come [. . .] for the tree [. . .] of this age† [. . .] for a season [. . .] but he has come to water God's paradise and the eternal generation, because he will not defile the course of that generation, but [. . .] for all eternity."

Judas said, "Rabbi, what kind of fruit is produced by this generation?"

Jesus said, "The souls of all human generations will die, but when these people have passed through the time set for the kingdom and the spirit leaves them, their bodies will die but their souls will remain alive and be taken up."

Judas said, "What will the other human generations do?"

Jesus said, "It is not possible [44] to harvest fruit from seed sown on the stones. This is also the way [. . .] the polluted generation [. . .] and corruptible Sophia [. . .] the hand that created mortals, so that their souls go up to the everlasting realms above. I tell you the truth, [. . .] angel [. . .] force will be able to see that [. . .] these to whom [. . .] holy generations [. . .]." After Jesus said this, he departed.

Judas Receives More Teaching in Private

Judas said, "Teacher, in the way that you listened to all of them, now listen to me, for I have seen an impressive vision."

Hearing this, Jesus laughed and said to him, "You thirteenth spirit, why do you try so hard? Nevertheless, speak, and I will indulge you."

Judas said to him, "In the vision I saw myself while the twelve disciples were stoning me and [45] persecuting me severely. And I also came to the place where [. . .] after you. I saw a house [. . .], and my eyes failed to take in its full size. Important people were all around it, and the house had a roof of greenery, and in the middle of the house was a crowd [*** two lines missing ***] [and I was] saying, 'Teacher, take me in along with these people.'"

Jesus answered and said, "Judas, your star has led you astray." He went on, "No mere mortal is worthy to enter the house you saw because it is reserved for the holy. Neither the sun nor the moon will rule there, nor the day, but the holy will abide there forever, in the everlasting realm with the holy angels. Look, I have made known to you the mysteries of the kingdom [46] and instructed you about the error of the stars; and [. . .] dispatch it [. . .] on the twelve aeons."

Judas said, "Teacher, could it be that my seed is under the control of the rulers?"

---

†Or "aeon."

Jesus answered, "Come, so that I [*** two lines missing ***], but when you see the kingdom and all its generation, you will grieve greatly."

Hearing this, Judas said to him, "What use is it that I have received it? For you have already set me apart for that generation."

Jesus answered, "You will become the thirteenth, and the other generations will curse you, and you will eventually rule over them. In the last days they will curse your ascent [47] to the holy generation."

Teachings on Cosmology

Jesus said, "Come, and I will teach you about secrets that no one has ever seen. For there exists a vast and noble realm, whose extent no angelic generation has seen, wherein there is a great invisible spirit,[†]

which no angelic eye has ever seen,[‡]

no thought of the heart has ever comprehended,

and which was never called by any name.

"And a radiant cloud appeared in that realm. It said, 'Let there be an angel, to be my attendant.' A mighty angel, the enlightened divine Self-Generated One, came out of a cloud. And because of him, four other angels emerged from another cloud and became attendants for the angelic Self-Generated One. The Self-Generated One said, [48] 'Let there be [. . .],' and it was [. . .]. And he made the first luminary to reign over him. He said, 'Let there be angels to serve him,' and so there were innumerable myriads. He said, 'Let there be an enlightened aeon,' and it was. He made the second luminary to reign over him, along with innumerable myriads of angels to offer service. That is how he created the rest of the enlightened aeons. He created them to rule over them, and he created innumerable myriads of angels to assist them.

"Adamas was in the first radiant cloud that no angel among all those called 'God' has ever seen. He [49] [. . .] that [. . .] the image [. . .] and in the likeness of this angel. He caused the imperishable generation of Seth to appear [. . .] the twelve [. . .] the twenty-four [. . .]. He made seventy-two luminaries appear in the imperishable generation, according to the will of the Spirit. The seventy-two luminaries then made 360 luminaries appear in the imperishable generation, according to the will of the Spirit, so that their number would be five for each.

"The twelve aeons of the twelve luminaries constitute their father, with six heavens for each aeon, so that there are seventy-two heavens for the seventy-two luminaries, and for each [50] of them five firmaments, totaling 360 firmaments [. . .]. They were given authority and an innumerable myriad of angels for glory and adoration, and virgin spirits as well, for the glory and adoration of all the aeons and the heavens and their firmaments.

"The multitude of those immortals is called the world[§] (that is, eternal

---

[†]Cf. the *Gospel of the Egyptians* [?].

[‡]Cf. 1 Cor. 2:9-10.

[§]Literally, "cosmos."

destruction) by the Father and the seventy-two luminaries who are with the Self-Generated One and his seventy-two aeons. There, the first man appeared with incorruptible powers. And the aeon that appeared with his generation, the aeon that the cloud of knowledge and the angel are in, is called [51] El. [. . .] Aeon [. . .] then [. . .] said, 'Let there be twelve angels to rule over chaos and the [underworld].' And behold, from the cloud came an angel whose face gleamed like a burning fire and whose appearance was contaminated by blood. He was called Nebro, which means 'rebel'; others call him Yaldabaoth. Another angel, Saklas, also appeared from the cloud. So Nebro created six angels—in addition to Saklas—as assistants. These then made twelve angels in the heavens, each one receiving a share of the heavens.

"The twelve rulers spoke to the twelve angels: 'Each of you should [52] [. . .] and they should [. . .] generation [*** one line missing ***] angels':

The first is Seth, who is called Christ.
The second is Harmathoth, who is [. . .].
The third is Galila.
The fourth is Yobel.
The fifth is Adonaios.
These are the five who ruled over the underworld, primarily over chaos.

"Saklas then said to his angels, 'Let us create a human after the resemblance and after the image.' Then they made Adam and Eve, his wife, who, in the cloud, is named Zoe. By these names all generations look for the man and speak of the woman. And Sakla did not [53] order [. . .] except [. . .] the generations [. . .] this [. . .]. And the ruler said to Adam, 'You shall have a long life, as will your children.'"

The End of the Human Spirit and the Other Generations
Judas said to Jesus, "How long is the time that humans will live?"

Jesus said, "Why do you wonder about how Adam and his generation have lived their span of life in that place where Adam has received his kingdom, with the length of life he received from his ruler?"

Judas said to Jesus, "Does the human spirit die?"

Jesus said, "This is why God ordered Michael to give people spirits as a loan: so that they would render service. But the Great One ordered Gabriel to grant spirits to the great generation with no ruler over it—that is, the spirit and the soul. Thus, the remaining souls [54] [*** one line missing ***].

"[. . .] light [*** nearly two lines missing ***] about [. . .] may [. . .] spirit that is within you dwell in this body among the angelic generations. But God imparted knowledge to Adam and those with him, so that the kings of chaos and the underworld could not presume to rule over them."

Judas said to Jesus, "What will those generations do, then?"

Jesus said, "I tell you the truth, for all of them the stars bring matters to their fulfillment. When Saklas finishes the span of time allotted to him, their first star will appear with the generations, and then they will complete that which they spoke of—then they will fornicate in my name and slaughter their children [55] and they will [. . .] and [*** about six and a half lines missing ***].

"[. . .] my name, and he will [. . .] your star over the thirteenth aeon."

And then Jesus laughed.

Judas asked, "Teacher, why are you laughing at us?"

Jesus answered, "I laugh not at you but at the error of the stars, for these six stars roam about with these five combatants, and they will all be annihilated along with their creations."

Those Baptized in Jesus' Name

Judas said to Jesus, "What will people who have been baptized in your name do?"

Jesus said, "I tell you the truth, this baptism [56] [. . .] my name [*** about four lines missing ***]."

Those Offering Sacrifice

"[*** about five lines missing ***] to me. I tell you the truth, Judas, those offering sacrifices to Saklas [. . .] God [*** three lines missing ***] all that is evil."

Judas's Personal Destiny

"But you will exceed them all, for you will sacrifice the man that clothes me.

Already your horn has been raised,

your anger has been ignited,

your star has shone brightly,

and your heart has [. . .]. [57]

"In truth [. . .] your final [. . .] be [*** about two and one half lines missing ***], grieve [*** about two lines missing ***]

"[. . .] the ruler, since he will be annihilated. And then the image of the great generation of Adam will be exalted, for that generation from the eternal realms existed before heaven and earth and the angels. Behold, you have heard everything. Lift up your eyes and see the cloud that has the light within it and stars surrounding it. The star that leads the way is your star."

Judas lifted up his eyes and saw the radiant cloud, and he entered it. The ones left standing on the ground heard a voice coming from the cloud, saying, [58] [. . .] great generation [. . .] image [. . .] [*** about five lines missing ***].

Judas Betrays Jesus

[. . .] Their high priests grumbled because he had gone into the guest room to pray. But some scribes were there keeping a careful watch so they could arrest him during the prayer, for they feared the people, since everyone considered him to be a prophet. They came to Judas and said to him, "Why are you here? You are Jesus' disciple." Judas gave them the desired reply, and he received some money and handed him over to them.

The Gospel of Judas

Gospel of Mary

This work is known only by two Greek fragments and one incomplete Coptic manuscript. The two Greek fragments, P. Rylands III 463 and P. Oxyrhynchus 3525 are of the third century. The partial Coptic manuscript is a translation of the Greek that dates to the fifth century (P. Berolinensis 8502) and was acquired by Carl Reinhardt in 1896 but not published until 1955 due to mitigating circumstances. The Coptic text contains pages 7–10, 15–19, which end with the subscription "Gospel according to Mary." The page numbers listed below are adjusted slightly for the sake of the English translation, noting the appropriate manuscripts. Where there is overlapping text of the Greek manuscripts and the Coptic, the following English translation depends on the Greek fragments as providing the primary text and the Coptic translation as providing the secondary text.

In the extant text, Jesus commissions his disciples and then departs. Mary of Magdala then serves as a sort of apostle to the apostles after Jesus leaves. She helps them overcome their fears about proclaiming the gospel, and she shares her special revelation from Jesus about the soul's escape from desire and its passage beyond various spiritual "powers" into salvation. The disciples at first doubt that "the Savior" (as Jesus is uniformly called throughout the manuscript) would have ever propounded such strange ideas, but Levi[26] persuades them that the Savior had rightly loved her more than other women and urges them to proclaim the gospel as they had been commanded. The words of Jesus, Mary, and Levi all show gnostic influence, marking them as ostensible protagonists in this gnostic work.

[Pages 1–6 are missing.]
[Pages 7–8, P. Berolinensis 8502]
The Savior said, "All natures, formations, and creatures exist in and with one another, and they will be resolved into their own roots. For the nature of matter is resolved into its own nature. Those who have ears to hear should listen."

Peter asked him, "Since you have explained everything to us, tell us also what the sin of this world is."

The Savior answered, "There is no sin. You create sin when you do things like adultery, which is called 'sin.' That is why the Good came to live among us—to restore the essence to its very root."

Then he continued, "That is why you [get sick] and die. Those who understand will understand this. Passion has no equal. It proceeds from something contrary to nature and creates disturbance in the entire body. That is why I said to you, 'Be of good courage.' But if you are discouraged, be encouraged in the presence of the different forms of nature. Those who have ears to hear should listen."

After the blessed One had said this, he greeted them all and said, "Peace be with you. Receive my peace into your being. Beware that no one lead you astray saying, 'Lo here' or 'lo there'! For the Son of Man is within you. Follow after him! Those who seek him will find him. Go then and preach the gospel of the Kingdom. Don't make any rules beyond what I appointed for you, and don't make laws lest you be constrained by them."

[Page 9, P. Oxyrhynchus 3525]

After he said this, he departed. [The disciples,] being grieved, wept greatly, saying, "How shall we go to the Gentiles and proclaim the gospel of the kingdom of the Son of Man? If they did not spare him, they will not spare us."

Then Mary stood up, greeted them all, and said to her brothers, "Do not weep and do not grieve nor be irresolute, for his grace will be entirely with you and will protect you. But rather, let us praise his greatness, for he has prepared us and made us into men."

When Mary said this, she turned their minds for the good, and they began to discuss the apothegms of the [Savior].

[Page 10]

Peter said to Mary, "Sister, we know the Savior loved you more than all other women. Tell us the Savior's words that you know and we don't because we didn't hear them."

Mary answered, "I will tell you what is hidden from you and I remember."

She began to speak to them these words, "I saw the Lord in a vision and I said to him, 'Lord, I saw you today in a vision.'

[P. Berolinensis 8502]

"He answered me, 'You are blessed because you did not falter when you saw me. For where the mind is, there is the treasure.'

"I said to him, 'Lord, does the person who sees the vision see it through the soul or through the spirit?'

"The Savior answered, 'The person does not see through the soul nor through the spirit, but the mind which is between the two sees the vision.'"

[Pages 11–14 are missing]

[Pages 15–16, P. Berolinensis 8502]

"[A certain power said], 'I did not see you descending but now I see you ascending. Why are you lying since you belong to me?'

"The soul answered, 'I saw you. You did not see me nor recognize me. I served you as a garment, and you did not know me.' When it had said this, it went away rejoicing greatly.

"Again it came to the third power, which is called arrogance. The power questioned the soul: 'Where are you going? You are bound up in evil. Since you are bound, do not judge!'

"And the soul asked, 'Why do you judge me when I have not judged? I was bound, though I have not bound. I was not recognized, but I have recognized that the All is being dissolved, both the earthly and the heavenly.'

"When the soul had overcome the third power, it went upward and saw the fourth power, which took seven forms. The first form is darkness, the second desire, the third ignorance, the fourth is the excitement of death, the fifth is the kingdom of the flesh, the sixth is the foolish wisdom of flesh, the seventh is the wrathful wisdom. These are the seven powers of wrath. They asked the soul, 'Where do you come from, slayer of men, or where are you going, conqueror of space?'

"The soul answered and said, 'What binds me has been slain, and what turns me about has been overcome, and my desire has been ended, and ignorance has died. In an aeon I was released from a world, and in a type from a type, and from the fetter of oblivion, which is transient.'

[Page 17, P. Rylands 463]

"From this time on, will I attain to the rest of the time, of the season, of the aeon, in silence."

After Mary said this, she became silent, because this was as far as the Savior had spoken.

Andrew said, "Brothers, what do you think about what she has told us? I do not believe the Savior said these things. For these teachings are different from his thinking on these matters."

[Peter said,] "When the Savior was questioned, did he really speak privately with a woman and not openly that we might all hear? Did he prefer her to us?"

[Page 18, P. Rylands 463]

Then Mary wept and said to Peter, "My brother Peter, what do you think? Do you think that I have thought this up myself in my heart, or that I am lying about the Savior?"

Levi said to Peter, "Peter, you have always been hot tempered. Now I see you contending against this woman as if she were an enemy. If the Savior made her worthy, who are you to reject her? Knowing her very well, he fully loved her. Let us be ashamed and put on the perfect man. Let us do what he commanded us: proclaim the gospel, not be angry, and not lay down laws. Because this is what the Savior said." After Levi had spoken, he departed and proclaimed the gospel.

[Page 19, P. Berolinensis 8502]

Gospel According to Mary

Gospel of Philip

This is known only by a single Coptic manuscript from Nag Hammadi that has been dated to A.D. 350 and that was very likely preceded by a Greek original. It is evidently a compilation of excerpts from other works, none of which have been discovered. As such, it is not properly a narrative, and the use of "Gospel" in the title must be taken as a reference to a "good news" proclamation. The date and place of its original compilation are unknown, but the text was clearly influenced by Valentinian teachings, probably from two or more branches of Valentinian thought. Although Philip is the only one of the apostles mentioned by name in the manuscript (*Gospel of Philip* 73), it is uncertain whether the title is intended to refer to the apostle Philip. The manuscript is too late to have come from Philip's hand, and Valentinian authors usually wrote using their own names.

The *Gospel of Philip* does contain seventeen sayings of Jesus, over half of which are included in the canonical Gospels, though these are generally interpreted differently here. The sayings of Jesus found here that do not occur in the four Gospels are rather obscure and seem to favor gnostic interpretation. In the presentation below, the page numbers of Nag Hammadi Codex II are given in brackets since there are various divisions of the sayings in use.

[51] A Hebrew makes another Hebrew, and they call this one "proselyte." But a proselyte does not make another proselyte. [. . .] are as they [. . .] and they make others [like themselves . . .] it suffices that they simply exist.

[52] The slave wants only to be free; he does not presume to obtain the estate of his master. But a son not only acts as a son but also claims the inheritance of the father. Those who inherit what is dead are themselves dead, and they inherit what is dead. Those who are heirs to what is living are alive, and they are heirs to what is living and what is dead. The dead are heirs to nothing. For how can he who is dead inherit? If he who is dead inherits what is living, he will not die, but he who is dead will live even more.

A Gentile does not die, for he has become alive that he may die. He who has believed in the truth has found life, and this one is in danger of dying, for he is alive. Since Christ came, the world has been created, the cities have been organized, and the dead carried out. When we were Hebrews, we were orphans and possessed our mother alone, but when we became Christians, we came to have both father and mother.

Whoever sows in winter reaps in summer. The winter is this world system, the summer is the other aeon [eternal realm]. Let us sow in this world system that we may reap in the summer. Because of this, we should not pray in the winter. Summer follows winter. But if anyone reaps in winter he will not actually reap but only uproot—this one will not provide a harvest. Not only will it [. . . (not)] come forth, but also on the Sabbath [. . .] is barren.

Christ came to ransom some, to rescue others, to redeem others. [53] He ransomed those who were strangers and brought them to himself. And he rescued those who came to him, whom he set as a pledge according to his desire. It was not only when he appeared that he laid down the soul, but he laid down the soul from the very day the world came into being. Then he came first in order to take it, since it had been given as a pledge. It fell into the hands of robbers and was taken captive, but he saved it. He redeemed the good people in the world and the bad.

Light and darkness, life and death, right and left are brothers to each other. They are inseparable. Because of this the good are not good, nor the evil evil; life is not life, nor death death. So each one will dissolve into its earliest origin. But the things that are exalted above the world are indissoluble, eternal.

Names given to the worldly are very deceptive, for they divert our hearts from what is established to that which is not established. Thus one who hears the word *God* does not perceive what is real, but conceives what is not reality. So also with *the Father* and *the Son* and *the Holy Spirit* and *life* and *light* and *resurrection* and *the Church* (or *assembly*) and all the rest—people do not perceive reality, they perceive what is not established, unless they have come to know what really is established. The names that one hears are in the world [. . .] deceive. [54] If they were in the eternal realm [the aeon], they would at no time be spoken in the world. Nor would they be set among worldly things; they have an end in the eternal realm.

Just one name is not uttered in the world, the name the Father gave to the Son; it is the name above all things, that is, the name of the Father. For the Son would not become Father unless he wore the name of the Father. Those who possess this name know it but do not speak it. But those who do not possess it do not think of it. But truth brought names into existence in the world for our sakes, for it cannot be spoken apart from these names. Truth is one single thing [. . .] is many things. For our sakes it teaches about this one thing in love through many things.

The archons [or, rulers] wanted to deceive mankind, since they saw that they had a kinship with what is truly good. They took the names of the good and gave them to those that are not good, so that through the names they might deceive mankind and bind them to what is not good. And afterward, what a favor they do for them! They take them from those that are not good and place them among those that are good. They themselves knew these things, for they wanted to take the free and make them their slaves permanently.

These are powers that [. . .] humans, not wanting them to be saved, in order that they may [. . .]. For if man is saved, there will not be any sacrifices [. . .], and animals will not be offered up unto the powers. [55] Indeed, the animals were the ones to whom they sacrificed. They were offered up alive, but when they offered them up, they died. As for humans, they were offered up dead to God and became alive.

Before Christ came, there was no bread in the world, just as Paradise, the place where Adam was, had many trees to nourish the animals but no wheat to sustain people, and people were nourished like the animals. But when Christ, the perfect human, came, he brought bread from heaven in order that people might be nourished with food for people.

The rulers thought that it was by their own power and will that they were doing what they did, but the Holy Spirit was secretly accomplishing everything through them as it wished. Truth, which existed since the beginning, is sown everywhere. And many see it being sown, but few are they who see it being reaped.

Some said, "Mary conceived by the Holy Spirit." They are mistaken. They do not know what they are saying. When did a woman ever conceive by another woman? Mary is the virgin whom the powers did not defile. She is a great anathema to the Hebrews, meaning the apostles and the apostolic men. This virgin whom no power defiled [. . .] the powers defiled themselves. And the Lord would not have said, "My Father who is in Heaven" (Matthew 16:17) unless he had had another father; he would have said simply "My father."

The Lord said to the disciples, "[. . .] from every house. [56] Bring into the house of the Father. But do not take from the house of the Father or carry [things] off."

"Jesus" is a hidden name; "Christ" is a revealed name. For this reason "Jesus" is not in any language; rather it is the name he is called: "Jesus." But as for "Christ," in Syriac it is "Messiah," in Greek it is "Christ," and probably all the others have it in their own language. "The Nazarene" is the revealed name of the hidden name. Christ has everything in himself, whether man, or angel, or mystery, and the Father.

Those who say that the Lord first died and [then] arose are in error, for he rose up first and [then] died. If one does not first attain the resurrection, he will not die. As God lives, he would [. . .].

No one will hide a large valuable object in something else of great value, but often one has put countless thousands inside something worth a penny. Compare the soul. It is a precious thing, and it came to be in a contemptible body.

Some are afraid lest they be resurrected naked. Because of this they wish to rise in the flesh, and they do not know that it is those who wear the flesh who are naked. Those who [. . .] to unclothe themselves who are not naked. "Flesh and blood will not inherit the kingdom of God."[†] What is this flesh which will not inherit it? [57] But what is this flesh that will inherit it? It is that which belongs to Jesus and his blood. Because of this he said, "He who will not eat my flesh and drink my blood has not life in him."[‡] What is it? His flesh is the word, and his blood is the Holy Spirit. He who has received these has food and has drink along with clothing.[§] (In addition) I find fault with those who say that the flesh will not rise. So then, both of them are at fault.

[†] Cf. 1 Cor. 15:50.
[‡] Cf. John 6:53.
[§] Possible allusion to 1 Tim. 6:8[?].

You say that the flesh will not rise. But tell me what element will rise, that we may honor you. You say it is the Spirit that is in the flesh, and also the light within the flesh. This, too, is a matter that is in the flesh, for whatever you shall say, you say nothing outside the flesh. It is necessary to rise in this flesh, since everything exists in it. In this world, those who put on clothes are better than the clothes. In the kingdom of heaven, the clothes are better than those who put them on.

It is by water and fire that the whole place is purified—the visible by the visible, the hidden by the hidden. Some things are hidden through the visible: There is water in water, there is fire in chrism.

Jesus tricked them all, for he did not appear as he was, but in a manner in which they would be able to see him. And he appeared to them all: He appeared to the great as great. He appeared to the small as small. He appeared to the angels as an angel, and to men as a man. [58] Because of this, his word was hidden from everyone; some indeed saw him and thought they were seeing themselves. But when he appeared to his disciples in glory on the mount, he was not small. He became great, or rather, he made the disciples great, that they might be able to see him in his greatness. He said on that day in the thanksgiving prayer, "O You who have joined the perfect light with the Holy Spirit, unite the angels with us also, as images."

Do not despise the lamb, for without it, it is not possible to see the door.[†] No one will be able to go in to the king while naked.

The heavenly man has many more sons than the earthly man. If the sons of Adam are many and yet die, how much more the sons of the perfect man, they who do not die but are always begotten?[‡] The father makes a son, and the son has not the power to make a son, for he who has recently been born has not the power to have children, but the son gets brothers for himself, not sons. All who are born in the world are born in a natural way, and the others are nourished from the place whence they have been born. Man receives nourishment from being promised to the heavenly place. [. . .] from the mouth. And had the word gone out from that place, he would be nourished from the mouth and would become perfect. [59] For it is by a kiss that the perfect conceive and give birth. For this reason we also kiss one another. We conceive by the grace that is in one another.

There were three women who always walked with the Lord: Mary his mother, his sister, and Magdalene, the one who was called his companion. For Mary is the name of his sister and his mother and his companion.

"The Father" and "the Son" are simple names; "the Holy Spirit" is a two-part name. For they are everywhere: They are above, they are below; they are in the concealed, they are in the revealed. The Holy Spirit is in the revealed: It is below. It is in the concealed: It is above.

[†]Some emend to "king."
[‡]Cf. Rom. 5:12-17.

The saints are served by evil powers, for they are blinded by the Holy Spirit into thinking that they are serving an [ordinary] person whenever they serve the saints. For this reason, a disciple asked the Lord one day for something of this world. He said to him, "Ask your mother, and she will give it to you from the things which are another's."

The apostles said to the disciples, "May our entire offering get salt." They referred to wisdom [sophia] as "salt." Without it, no offering is acceptable. But wisdom is barren, without children. For this reason, she is called "[. . .] of the salt." Wherever they can [. . .] in their own way, the Holy Spirit [. . .], [60] and many are her children.

What the father owns belongs also to his son. And the son, so long as he is little, is not entrusted with what is his. But when he has grown, his father will give him all that he possesses.

Those who have gone astray were begotten by the spirit and go astray also because of the spirit. Thus, from one and the same spirit, fire blazes and is quenched.

Echamoth is one thing and Echmoth is another. Echamoth is wisdom in a general sense, but Echmoth is the wisdom of death, which is the wisdom acquainted with death, which is called "the little wisdom."

There are domestic animals, like the bull and the donkey, and so forth. Others are undomesticated and live apart from where people live. People plough fields by means of the domestic animals, and both are thus nourished, the people and the animals, whether domesticated or not. Compare the perfect man: He ploughs by means of submissive powers, preparing for everything to come to pass. For it is because of this that the whole place remains established, whether the good or the evil, the right or the left. The Holy Spirit shepherds everyone and rules all the powers, the "domesticated" ones and the "undomesticated" ones, as well as those that are apart. For he [. . .] shuts them in, so that [. . .] wish, they might not escape.

He who was created was beautiful, but you would not find his sons noble creations. [61] If he were not created, but begotten, you would find that his descendants were noble. But instead, he was created and had children. What nobility is this? First, there was adultery, then murder: He [Cain] was begotten in adultery, for he was the son of the Serpent. So he became a murderer, just like his father, and he killed his brother. Indeed, every act of sexual intercourse that has occurred between beings that do not resemble each other is adultery.

God is a dyer. As the good dyes, which are called "true" dyes, dissolve into what is dyed in them, so it is with those whom God has dyed. Since his dyes are imperishable, those who are dyed become imperishable by means of his colors. Yet God submerses these in water.

It is not possible to see any of the things that actually exist unless one becomes them. This is not the way with people in the world: They see the sun without being the sun and see the sky and the earth, and so forth, without being them. This is quite in keeping with the truth. You, however, saw something of that place, and you have become those things. If you have seen the Spirit, you became the Spirit. You saw the Christ, you became the Christ. You saw the Father, you will become the Father. So in the world you see everything and do not see yourself, but in that place you see yourself; for you shall become what you see.[†]

Faith receives, love gives. No one can receive apart from faith. No one can give apart from love. [62] Therefore, in order to receive, we believe; and in order to love, we give, since if one gives without love, he has no profit from what he has given. He who has received something other than the Lord is still a Hebrew.

The apostles who were before us had these names for him: "Jesus, the Nazarene, Messiah"; that is, "Jesus, the Nazarene, the Christ." The final name is "Christ," the first is "Jesus," and that in the middle is "the Nazarene." *Messiah* has two meanings, both "the Christ" and "the measured." *Jesus* in Hebrew means "ransom." *Nazara* means "the truth," so *Nazarene* also means "the truth." *Christ,* then, [. . .] has been measured out: The *Nazarene* and *Jesus* have been measured out.

If a pearl is cast down into the mud, it is not despised, and if it is anointed with balsam oil, it does not become more precious. But it always has value to its owner. So also the sons of God have value in the eyes of their Father no matter where they are found.

If you say, "I am a Jew," no one will be shaken. If you say, "I am a Roman," no one will be upset. If you say, "I am a Greek," "a barbarian," "a slave," "a free man," no one will be troubled. If you say, "I am a Christian," the [. . .] will tremble. I wish that I could [. . .] like that—the person whose name [. . .] will not be able to endure hearing.

God is a cannibal. [63] Because of this, people are sacrificed to him. Before people were sacrificed, animals were sacrificed, because those to whom they were sacrificed were not gods.

Glass decanters and ceramic jugs are both made by means of fire. But if glass decanters break, they are remade, for they came into being through breath.[‡] If ceramic jugs break, however, they are destroyed because they were produced without breath.

A donkey that turns a millstone walked a hundred miles, and when it was loosed, it was still at the same place. There are also people who make many journeys but make no progress toward anywhere. When evening comes, they have seen neither city nor village, neither human artifact nor natural phenomenon, neither power nor angel. In vain have such wretches labored.

The Eucharist is Jesus. He is called *Pharisatha* in Syriac, which means "the one who is spread out," for Jesus came to crucify the world.

[†]Cf. 1 John 3:2.
[‡]Or "spirit."

The Lord entered the dye works of Levi. He took seventy-two different colors and threw them into the vat. He brought them out all white. And he said, "For this did the son of man come—to be a dyer."

As for the wisdom who is called the "barren wisdom," she is the mother of the angels. And the companion of the [Christ is] Mary Magdalene. [. . .] loved her more than all the disciples, and used to kiss her [more] often [on her mouth] than the rest of the disciples [. . .]. [64] They said to him, "Why do you love her more than all of us?" The Savior answered and said to them, "Why do I not love you like her? If a blind man and one who sees are both in the darkness, they are no different from one another. When the light comes, then he who sees will see the light, and he who is blind will remain in darkness."

The Lord said, "Blessed is that which was and came into being. For that which is, has been and shall be."

The supremacy of humanity is not obvious to the eye, but lies in what is hidden from view. Consequently, people have mastery over animals that are stronger than they are and larger in ways both external and internal. This enables them to survive. But if the animals are separated from people, they kill one another and bite one another. They ate one another because they did not find any food. But now they have found food because man tilled the soil.

If someone goes down into the water and comes up and says "I am a Christian" without having received anything, he has borrowed the name. But if he receives the Holy Spirit, he has the name as a gift. Someone who has received a gift will not have it taken away, but someone who borrows something must give it back. This is the way it happens to one who experiences a mystery.

Great is the mystery of marriage, for without it, the world would not exist. Now the structure of the world [. . .], and the structure of [. . .] marriage. Think of sexual intercourse [. . .] pollutes, for it possesses [. . .] power. Its image resides in pollution.

[65] Among the forms of evil spirits are male ones and female ones. The male ones have sexual intercourse with souls that inhabit a female form, and the female spirits mingle with those in a male form. No one is able to escape them if he or she does not receive a male power or a female power, namely a bridegroom or bride. One receives this from the imaged[†] bridal chamber. When the wanton female spirits see a male sitting alone, they leap down on him and fondle with him and defile him. So also the lecherous male spirits, when they see a pretty woman sitting alone, they seduce her and compel her, wishing to defile her. But if they see a man and his wife sitting side by side, the female ones cannot come to the man, nor can the male ones come to the woman. So also, if the image and the angel are joined with one another, no one can advance toward the man or the woman.

---

†Or "mirrored."

A person who comes out of the world can no longer be detained on the grounds that he was in the world. This person evidently is above the desire of the [. . .] and fear. He dominates [. . .] and is superior to envy. If [. . .] comes, they seize him and strangle him. And how can that person escape the great [. . .] powers? How can that person [. . .]? There are some who say, "We are faithful" in order that [. . .] the unclean spirits and the demons. For if they had the Holy Spirit, no unclean spirit would attach itself to them. Fear not the flesh nor love it. If you fear it, it will dominate you; if you love it, it will swallow and strangle you.

And so that person dwells either in this world or in the resurrection or in the middle place—God forbid that I be found there! In this world, there is good and evil, but the good things in the world are not good, and its evil things are not evil. But after this world, there are evils that are truly evil—it is called "the middle." It is death. While we are in this world, we must acquire the resurrection so that when we strip off the flesh, we may be at rest and not walk in the middle. For many go astray on the way. For it is good to leave the world before one has sinned.

There are some who neither want to nor have the power to. There are others who, if they want to, still do not profit, for they have not acted since [. . .] makes them sinners. And if they do not want to, justice will elude them in both cases: and it is always a matter of the desire, not the act.

In a vision, an apostolic man saw some people locked up in a house of fire and bound with fiery [. . .], lying [. . .] flaming [. . .], them in [. . .] faith [. . .]. And they said to them, "[. . .] them able to rescue [. . .]" but they did not desire it. They received [. . .] punishment, which is called "the [. . .] darkness, [67] because he [. . .]."

From water and fire the soul and the spirit came into being. From water and fire and light came a son of the bridal chamber. Fire is chrism, light is fire. I am not referring to earthly fire, but to the other fire whose appearance is white, which is bright and beautiful and gives beauty.

Truth did not come to the world naked; rather it came in types and images. The world will not accept truth in any other way. Rebirth exists as does an image of rebirth: Through the image one must be reborn. Which image? Resurrection. The image must rise again through the image. Through the image, both the bridal chamber and the image must enter into truth: This is the restoration. Not only must those who produce the name of Father and Son and Holy Spirit do so, but also those who have produced them for you. If one does not acquire them, the name will also be taken from him. But if one receives the chrism of [. . .] of the power of the cross, which the apostles called "the right and the left." For this person is no longer a Christian but a Christ.

The Lord did everything in a mystery: baptism, chrism, eucharist, redemption and bridal chamber. [. . .] he said, "I came to make the things below like

301

the things above, and the outer things like the inner, and to unite them in [. . .] here through types [. . .] and images."

Those who say, "There is a heavenly man and there is one higher still" are in error, for they call the revealed heavenly man "the one who is below," [68] and the one to whom the hidden (realm) belongs is that one who is above him. For it would be better for them to speak of the inner and outer and what is outside the outer. Thus the Lord called destruction the "the outer darkness"[+]; there is not another outside of it. He said, "My Father who is in secret," and said, "Go into your room and shut the door, and pray to your Father who is in secret,"[‡] that is, the one who is within them all. Now that which is within them all is the fullness. Beyond that, there is nothing further within. This is that which they call the "most high."

Before Christ, certain beings came from a place that they could no longer reenter, and they went to a place that they could no longer leave. Then Christ came and brought out those who went in and brought in those who went out.

When Eve was still with Adam, death did not exist. When she was separated from him, death came into existence. If he reenters and attains his former self, death will cease to exist.

"My God, my God, why, O Lord, have you forsaken me?"[§] It was from the cross that he spoke these words, for he had withdrawn from that place.

[. . .] who has been born through him who [. . .] from God.

The [. . .] from the dead. [. . .] to be, but now [. . .] perfect. [. . .] flesh, but this [. . .] is genuine flesh. [. . .] is not genuine, but [. . .] only possess an image of the genuine.

[69] A bridal chamber is not for animals, nor is it for slaves and defiled women, but it is for free men and virgins.

Through the Holy Spirit we are reborn, but we are born through Christ in two things. We are anointed through the Spirit. When we were born we were united. Nobody can see himself in water or in a mirror without light. Nor, again, can you see (yourself) by the light without a mirror or water. Thus it is fitting to baptize in two things: the light and the water. Now the light is the chrism.

There were three buildings for sacrifice in Jerusalem. The one facing west was called the holy. Another, facing south, was called the holy of the holy. The third, facing east, was called the holy of holies, and was the place where the high priest alone could enter. Baptism is the holy building, redemption is the holy of the holy, and the holy of holies is the bridal chamber. Baptism possesses resurrection and redemption; the redemption (occurs) in the bridal chamber. The bridal chamber is in that which is superior to [. . .] its [. . .] is

---

[+]Cf. Matt. 8:12; 22:13; 25:30.
[‡]Cf. Matt. 6:6.
[§]Cf. Mark 15:34.

like [. . .] those who pray [. . .] Jerusalem [. . .] Jerusalem, [. . .] Jerusalem, expecting [. . .] those called the holy of the holies [. . .] veil was rent, [. . .] bridal chamber except the image [. . .] above. [70] Because of this, its veil was rent from top to bottom because some from below had to ascend.

The powers do not see those who have put on the perfect light, and therefore cannot detain them. One will put on this light in a mystery, through the union.

If the woman had not separated from the man, she and the man would not die. His separation became the source of death. Christ came to repair the separation that had been there from the beginning and to reunite the two and to give life to those who died as a result of the separation, and join them together. Now, a woman is united to her husband in the bridal chamber, and those who have united in the bridal chamber will not be separated. Thus Eve separated from Adam because it was not in the bridal chamber that she united with him.

Adam's soul came into being by means of breath. His soul's partner is the spirit. His mother is the element that was given to him. His soul was taken from him and replaced by a spirit. When he was united [with the spirit], he spoke words superior to the powers. They envied him [. . .] spiritual partner [. . .] hidden [. . .] them alone [. . .] bridal chamber, so that [. . .].

Jesus appeared [. . .] Jordan—the fullness of the Kingdom of Heaven. The one who was born before everything was reborn. He who was once anointed was reanointed. He who was redeemed, redeemed others in turn.

[71] A person must indeed utter a mystery! The father of everything[†] united with the virgin who came down, and a fire illuminated him. He revealed the great bridal chamber when his body came into being that day. He left the bridal chamber as that which is born of the bridegroom and the bride. So Jesus established the repose of everything in it through these; thus, it is fitting also for each disciple to enter into his rest.

Adam came into being from two virgins: the Spirit and the virgin earth. Christ was born of a virgin in order to rectify the Fall that occurred in the beginning.

There are two trees growing in Paradise   one that bears animals and one that bears people. Adam ate from the tree that produces animals; he became an animal and begot animals. For this reason the children of Adam worship animals. The tree [. . .] fruit is [. . .] became numerous. [. . .] ate the [. . .] fruit of the [. . .] bears people, [. . .] people. [. . .] God created people. [. . .] people create God. [72] So also in the world—people make gods and worship their creation. It would be more appropriate for the gods to worship people!

What a man accomplishes comes from his abilities. Thus, we may call one's accomplishments "abilities." Children are a kind of accomplishment. They originate in a moment of rest. Thus his abilities are active in what he

---

†Or "parent of the entirety" (Layton, *Gnostic Scriptures,* 344).

accomplishes, but rest is clearly evident in the children. This applies also to the image: The man made after the image is accomplishing things with his abilities but producing his children while at rest.

In this world, servants serve free people. In the Kingdom of Heaven, the free will serve the servants: The bridegroom's attendants will serve the wedding guests. The bridegroom's attendants share one name: rest. Altogether, they need no other form, because they are in contemplation, [. . .]. They are [. . .] in [. . .].

[. . .] descend into the water. [. . .] will redeem it, [. . .] those who have [. . .] in his name. For he said, "In this way we shall fulfill all righteousness."[+]

[73] People who say they will die first and then rise are in error. If they do not receive the resurrection while they are alive, when they die they will receive nothing. So also it is said of baptism, "Baptism is a great thing," for if people receive it, they will live.

Philip the apostle said, "Joseph the carpenter planted a garden because he needed wood for his trade. It is he who made the cross from the trees that he had planted, and his own child hung from what he had planted. His child was Jesus, and what was planted was the cross. But in the midst of the garden stands the Tree of Life, and from the olive tree we get chrism,[‡] and from the chrism comes resurrection."

This world consumes corpses: all things eaten in it also die. The place of truth consumes life; therefore, nobody nourished by it will die. Jesus came and brought food from this place. He gave [life] to whoever desired it, that they might not die.

God [. . .] garden. People [. . .] garden. [. . .] there are [. . .] with God. [. . .] The things that are in [. . .] wish. In this garden they will say to me, "[. . . eat] this, or not, just as you desire." [74] The place where I will eat all things where the Tree of Knowledge is. The previous tree killed Adam, but here the Tree of Knowledge makes people alive. The law was the tree. It has power to give the knowledge of good and evil. It neither removed evil from him, nor did it put him in the right. It made death for those who ate of it, since when it said, "Eat this, do not eat that,"[§] it became the beginning of death.

Chrism[++] is better than baptism because it is from the word "chrism" that we have been called "Christians" and not because of the word "baptism." And it is from the term "chrism" that Christ has his name, for the Father anointed the Son—and the Son anointed the apostles, and the apostles anointed us. The person who has been anointed has it all: he possesses the resurrection, the light, the cross, the Holy Spirit. The Father gave that person these things in the bridal chamber; he merely accepted [them]. The

---

[+]Cf. Matt. 3:15.
[‡]I.e., consecrated oil.
[§]Cf. Col. 2:21.
[++]I.e., consecrated oil.

Father was in the Son, and the Son was in the Father. This is the Kingdom of Heaven.

The Lord said it well: "Some have gone into the Kingdom of Heaven laughing, and they have come out [. . .] for [. . .] a Christian, [. . .]. And [. . . went] down into the water, he came [. . .] all [. . .] because it [. . .] a trifle, but [. . .] full of contempt for this [. . .] the Kingdom of Heaven [. . .]. If he shows contempt [. . .], and despises it as a trifle, [. . .] forth laughing." So also are the bread and the cup and the oil, even though there are others greater than these.

[75] The world came about via transgression.[†] For he who created it wanted to make it incorruptible and immortal. He fell and did not attain his desire. For the world never was incorruptible, nor, for that matter, was that one who made the world. For there is no thing that is incorruptible, but sons are. Nothing will be able to receive incorruptibility if it does not first become a son. What has no ability to receive is even less able to give.

The cup of prayer contains wine and water, since it is in place as the representation of the blood for which thanks is given. And it is full of the Holy Spirit and belongs to the entirely perfect man. When we drink this, we receive in ourselves the perfect man. The living water is a body and it is necessary that we "wear" the living man. Therefore, when one is about to go down into the water, he takes his clothes off so that he may put on the living man.

A horse produces a horse, a human begets a human, and a divinity brings forth a divinity. So also with the bridegroom and the bride: They come from the [. . .]. Jew [. . .] existed. And [. . .] from the Jews [. . .] Christians [. . .] this [. . .] is called "The chosen people of [. . .]," and the "True Man" and "Son of Man" and "the seed of the Son of Man." [76] This true race is renowned in the world [. . .]; here dwell the bridegroom's attendants.

Whereas in this world males and females are united—a case of strength complemented by weakness—in the eternal realm,[‡] the union is different. Although we refer to these things by the same names, there are other names that are superior to every other name and that are stronger than the strong. For where there is power, there are those who are superior to force. These are not different things; both of them are this one thing. This is incomprehensible to the heart of flesh.

Shouldn't all those who possess everything know themselves fully? Some, if they do not know themselves, will not make use of what they possess. But those who have come to know themselves will fully enjoy what they possess.

They cannot restrain the perfect man, nor indeed can they see him—for if they could see him, they would detain him. There is no way for a person to obtain this quality except by putting on the perfect light and also becoming

---

[†] Or "through a mistake."
[‡] Literally "aeon."

perfect light. Whoever has put it on will enter [. . .]. This is the perfect [. . .] that we [. . .] become [. . .] before we have come [. . .]. Whoever receives everything [. . .] hither [. . .] can [. . .] there, but will [. . .] in the Middle Place as imperfect. [77] Jesus alone knows the end of such a person.

The holy person is completely holy, even his very body. For if he has taken the bread, he will make it holy; and the cup or anything else that he gets, he will also sanctify. Then how will he not sanctify the body also?

When he completed the water of baptism, Jesus poured death out. Thus when we do go down into the water, we do not go down into death†—that we are not poured out into the wind‡ of the world. When that blows, it brings the winter, but when the Holy Spirit blows, summer comes.

The person who has knowledge of the truth is a free person, and the free person does not sin, for "He who sins is a slave to sin."§ Truth is the mother, knowledge the father. The world calls those who are not given to sin "free." Knowledge of the truth elevates†† such people—that is, it makes them "free." The elevation is in regard to the whole world. But "Love builds up."‡‡ In fact, the person who is really free, through knowledge, is also a slave because of love for those who have not yet attained the freedom of knowledge. Knowledge makes them capable of becoming free. Love never [. . .] anything [. . . belongs] to it [. . .] belongs to it. It does not say, "That is mine" or [. . .] but "All these are yours." Spiritual love is wine and perfume. Those who anoint themselves with it all enjoy it. While those who are anointed are nearby, those nearby also enjoy the fragrance. [78] If the ones anointed with ointment leave, then those who merely stood nearby and were not anointed still remain in their own odor. The Samaritan gave only wine and oil to the wounded man. This is nothing other than the ointment. It healed the wounds, for "love covers a multitude of sins."§§

The children a woman bears will resemble the man who loves her. If it is her husband, then they will resemble her husband. If she is with an adulterer, then they will resemble the adulterer. Often, if a woman sleeps with her husband as a matter of course but her heart is set on the adulterer with whom she usually has intercourse, the child she bears resembles the adulterer. Now then, you who live with the Son of God, do not love the world, but rather love the Lord in order that those you produce will not resemble the world but the Lord.

Human beings breed with human beings. Horses breed with horses, and donkeys with donkeys. Members of a species usually have associated with those of the same species. So spirit mingles with spirit, and thought consorts

---

†Cf. Rom. 6:3-4.
‡Or "spirit."
§Cf. John 8:34.
††Literally, "puffs up"; possibly with good or bad connotation.
‡‡Cf. 1 Cor. 8:1.
§§Cf. 1 Pet. 4:8.

with thought, and light has intercourse with light. If you become a human, humans will love you. If you become a spirit, the spirit will be joined to you. If you become thought, thought will mingle with you. If you become light, light will have intercourse with you. If you become part of the things above, the things above will rest on you. If you become a horse, donkey, bull, dog, sheep, or other animal that is outside or below, then neither human being nor spirit nor thought nor light will be able to love you. Neither the things above nor those that belong within will be able to rest in you; you will have no part in them.

A person who is a slave against his will is able to become free. But a person who has become free by his master's kindness and has again sold himself into slavery is no longer able to become free.

Earthly farming requires four essential elements; a good harvest is gathered into the barn only as a result of water, soil, air, and light. God's farming likewise has four elements: faith, hope, love, and knowledge. Faith is the soil in which we take root. Hope is the water by which we are nourished. Love is the air by which we grow. And knowledge is the light by which we ripen. Grace exists [. . .] on earth [. . .] it is above heaven [. . .].

Blessed is the one who has not [. . .] to a soul. [80] That is Jesus Christ; he came to the whole place and did not burden anyone. For this reason, blessed is the one who is like this, because he is a perfect man. For logic and reason[†] tell us that this is difficult to accomplish. How shall we be able to succeed at such a great thing? How can one give everyone comfort? Above all, it is not proper to cause anyone grief—whether important or ordinary, unbeliever or believer—and then give comfort only to those who take rest in their luxurious goods. Some find it advantageous to give comfort to those who are well to do. A person who does good deeds will not give comfort to such people, for he does not do whatever he likes most. Neither does such a person cause them distress, however, since he does not burden them. Of course, the one who is well to do sometimes causes people distress. But the person doing good does not; rather, it is others' own evil which is responsible for their grief. A person who possesses the qualities [of the perfect man] bestows joy upon the good. Some people are terribly distressed by all this.

There was an estate owner who had everything one could imagine: children, slaves, cattle, dogs, pigs, wheat, barley, chaff, fodder, [. . .] meat, and acorns. Now he was a smart man, and he knew what the food of each one should be. He served the children bread [. . .] and gave the slaves [. . .] and grain. And he threw barley and chaff and fodder to the cattle. He fed bones to the dogs, and to the pigs he gave acorns and slop. [81] Compare God's disciples: If they are smart, they understand what discipleship is all about. They are not deceived by outward forms but look at the condition of everyone's soul and speak with him accordingly. There are many animals in the world

---

†Or "the word."

that have a human form. When a disciple recognizes them, he gives acorns to the pigs, barley and chaff and fodder to the cattle, and bones to the dogs. He will give only the elementary lessons to the slaves, but to the children he will give the full instruction.

The Son of Man exists and the son of the Son of Man exists. The Lord is the Son of Man, and the son of the Son of Man is the one who creates by the Son of Man. The Son of Man received from God the capacity to create: He possesses in order to beget. One who has received the ability to create is a creature, and one who has received the ability to beget is begotten. One who creates cannot beget, but one who begets can create. One may say that creators beget, but the "offspring" is really a creature. Because of [. . .] of birth, they are not his offspring but [. . .]. One that creates works openly and is visible. One that begets, begets in secret and is hidden, since [. . .] image. So, a creator creates openly. But one who begets, begets offspring in secret.

No one can know when a husband and wife have intercourse with one another but they alone. [82] For the marriage of this world is a mystery for those who have married. If there is a hidden quality to this defiled marriage, how much more is the undefiled marriage a genuine mystery! It is not fleshly, but pure. It belongs not to lust, but to compassion, not to darkness or night, but to daytime and light. If the intimacy of the marriage is open to the public, it becomes prostitution, and the bride plays the harlot not only if she is impregnated by another man, but even if she leaves her bedroom and is seen. She should appear only to her father and mother, to the friend of the bridegroom, and to the bridegroom's attendants. They are permitted to enter the bridal chamber every day. But let the others desire just to hear her voice and to enjoy the smell of her perfume from afar—let them eat the scraps that fall from the table, like the dogs. Bridegrooms and brides belong to the bridal chamber. No one is able to see a bridegroom or a bride unless he becomes one.

When Abraham [. . .] to see what he was going to see, he circumcised the flesh of his foreskin, teaching us that it is proper to do away with the flesh.

Most things in this world remain alive while their inner parts are hidden. If their [innards] are exposed, they die, as is seen in people physically. As long as the intestines of the person are hidden, the person lives; [83] when their intestines are exposed and leave the body, people die. Similarly, a tree sprouts and grows while its root is hidden. If its root is exposed, the tree dries up. So it is with everything that is born in this world, not only the visible, but the hidden. For as long as the root of evil is hidden, it remains powerful, but once it is recognized, it disappears. When it is discovered, it ceases to be. That is why the Scripture says, "The axe is already set at the root of the trees."[+] It will not cut [only the trunk]—that would sprout again—but the axe will strike deep, extracting the root. Jesus extracted the

---

[+]Matt. 3:10.

roots of this whole place, while others only did so in part. Likewise, we ourselves should dig down to the root of evil that is within and uproot it from our heart. It will be removed if it is recognized, but if we are ignorant of it, it becomes rooted in us and bears its fruit in our heart. It controls us and we become its slaves. It makes us captives, so that we do what we do not want; and what we do want, we do not do.[†] It remains strong because we have not recognized it—and it is active while it exists.

Lack of knowledge is the mother of all evil. Lack of knowledge will cause death, for those who came from the lack of knowledge were not and never will be. [. . .] will become perfect when the entire truth is manifest.[‡] [84] For truth is like the lack of knowledge in that it rests in itself while it is hidden. When truth is revealed and is recognized, however, it is praised since it overpowers error and the lack of knowledge. It gives freedom. The Scripture[§] said, "If you know the truth, the truth will make you free."[††] Lack of knowledge is enslavement. Knowledge is freedom. If we know the truth, we will find its fruit within us. If we are joined to it, it will receive our fullness.

Currently, we have the visible things of creation. We say that they are strong and highly regarded, and what is obscure is weak and despised. Contrast the hidden parts of truth: While they are hidden, they are not weak and despised but strong and highly regarded. Now, the mysteries of truth are revealed as symbols and images. The bridal chamber remains hidden; it is the holy of holies. Before, the veil hid how God controlled creation, but when the veil is torn and the things inside are seen, the house will be left desolate—destroyed. And the entire deity will flee from here, but it will not go into the holies of holies, being unable to mix with the unmixed light and the flawless fullness. It will stay under the wings of the cross and under its arms. This ark will be their salvation when the floodwaters rage over them. [85] If others belong to the order of the priesthood, they will be able to go inside the veil along with the high priest. Therefore, the veil was not torn at the top only, since that would have opened only what is above; nor was it torn at the bottom only, since that would have revealed only what is below. Instead, it was torn from top to bottom: What is above was opened to what is below so that we might go in to the secret of the truth. That is truly what is highly regarded and strong! And by means of lowly symbols and weak forms we shall enter in. They are certainly lowly compared with the perfect glory. That glory outstrips glory. That power overwhelms power. So the perfect things have opened to us, along with the hidden parts of truth. The holies of holies was uncovered, and we were invited to enter the bridal chamber.

[†] Rom. 7:14-15.
[‡] Cf. 1 Cor. 13:10.
[§] Or "word."
[††] John 8:32.

As long as the seed of the Holy Spirit is hidden, evil has not been removed from their midst, though evil is ineffectual. They are slaves to evil, but the perfect light will shine forth upon everyone when the seed is revealed. Those who are in the light will receive the anointing.[†] Then the slaves will be freed and the captives ransomed. "Every plant that my father who is in heaven has not planted will be uprooted."[‡] The ones who are divided will unite [. . .] and will become full.

Everyone entering the bridal chamber will kindle the light, for [. . .] like the marriages that are [. . .] be night. That fire [. . .] night, is extinguished. [86] But the mysteries of that marriage are performed in the day and light. Neither that day nor its light ever sets.[§] If anyone becomes an attendant of the bridegroom, that person will receive the light. If anyone does not receive it here, that person will not be able to receive it in the other place. Whoever receives that light will not be seen and cannot be detained. Nothing will be able to trouble a person like this, even while they dwell in the world. Moreover, when that person leaves the world, they have already obtained the truth via the images. To this one, the world has already become the aeon,[††] for the aeon is his fullness and is revealed to him alone. It is not hidden in the darkness or the night, but in a perfect day and a holy light.

The Gospel According to Philip

Gospel of Thomas

In 1898 on the first day of their dig in Oxyrhynchus, Grenfell and Hunt discovered Greek portions of an unknown Gospel, which they entitled "Logia of Jesus." The extant manuscripts[27] provide sayings purported to have come from Jesus. Later, in 1946, a manuscript was discovered as part of the Nag Hammadi collection, a Coptic translation of an earlier Greek original. This was identified as the *Gospel of Thomas,* and it was determined by scholars that the logia were portions of the *Gospel of Thomas.* The manuscript has no narrative but is a collection of 114 "sayings of Jesus," which shed a great deal of light on the influence of Gnosticism on Egyptian Christianity. They claim to be the hidden sayings of Jesus as transmitted by Thomas. The Greek fragments of the *Gospel of Thomas* date to around A.D. 200, with the Coptic text still later, of course. The text was probably first written or compiled around the middle or late second century A.D.[28]

In the following translation, sayings 1–6, 26–32, 36–39, and 77 are from

---

[†] Or, "chrism."
[‡] Cf. Matt. 15:13.
[§] Cf. Rev. 21:23-25.
[††] I.e., the eternal.

the Greek and are all marked with an asterisk (*). The other sayings come from the Coptic version.

* These are the [hidden] sayings the living Jesus spoke and Judas who is also Thomas [recorded].

*¹And he said, "[whoever understands the] interpretations of these sayings will not taste [death].

*²"Let the one seeking not stop [seeking until] he finds. And when he finds, [he will marvel, and] marveling he will reign, and reigning he will rest."

*³Jesus said, "[If] those pulling you [say to you, 'Look,] the kingdom is in the sky,' the birds of the sky [will go before you. Or if they say] that it is beneath the ground, the fish [will go in,] preceding you. And the kingdom [of God] is within you [and outside you. Whoever] knows [himself] will find this [and when] you know yourselves [you will know] you are children of the living Father. [But if] you will [not] know yourselves, [you are] in [poverty] and you are the poverty."

*⁴[Jesus said,] "A person [old in] days will not hesitate to ask a child [seven] days old about his place in [life and] he will live. For many of the first will be [last and] many of the last will be first, and they [will become one.]"

*⁵Jesus said, "Know [what is in] front of your face, and [what has been hidden] from you will be revealed [to you. For there] is [nothing] hidden that will not be made clear and nothing buried that will not [be raised]."

*⁶[His disciples] asked him, "How should we fast and [how] should we [pray], and how [should we do charitable deeds] and what [food laws] should we observe?"

Jesus said, "[Do not tell lies,] and [do not do what] you hate because [everything] is evident before the truth. [For there is nothing] hidden [that will not be made clear]."

⁷Jesus said, "Blessings on the lion which becomes a human when eaten by a human. And cursings on the human whom the lion eats, and the lion becomes human."

⁸And he said, "The man is like a wise fisherman who cast his net into the sea and brought up from the sea a net full of small fish. Among them the wise fisherman found a good large fish. He threw out all the small fish and easily selected the large fish. Anyone with ears to hear should listen."

⁹Jesus said, "As the sower went out, he took a handful of seeds and scattered them. The seeds that fell on the road were taken by the birds. Those that fell on the rocks did not root in the soil and did not produce grain. Those that fell among thorns were choked by them, and they were eaten by worms. Those that fell on good soil produced good fruit: some measured at sixty and others at one hundred and twenty."

¹⁰Jesus said, "I have thrown fire on the world; and look, I am watching over it until it blazes."

¹¹Jesus said, "This heaven and the one above it will disappear. The dead are not alive, and the living will not die."

¹²The disciples asked Jesus, "We know that you will leave us. Who will be our leader?"

Jesus said to them, "Wherever you are, you should go to James the righteous, for whose sake heaven and earth came into being."

¹³Jesus said to his disciples, "Compare me to someone. Tell me whom I am like."

Simon Peter said to him, "You are like a righteous angel."

Matthew said to him, "You are like a wise philosopher."

Thomas said to him, "Master, my mouth is completely unable to say whom you are like."

Jesus said [to Thomas], "I am your Master. You have become drunk from the living spring I have dispensed to you."

And he took him away and told him three things. When Thomas returned to his companions, they asked him, "What did Jesus tell you?"

Thomas answered, "If I even tell you one of the things he told me, you will pick up stones and throw them at me. But a fire will come out of the stones and burn you up."

¹⁴Jesus said to them, "If you fast, you will give in to sin. If you pray, you will be condemned. If you do charitable deeds, you will hurt your spirits. When you travel to any region and they receive you, eat what they set before you. Heal the sick among them. For it is not that which goes into your mouth that defiles you, but that which comes out of your mouth defiles you."

¹⁵Jesus said, "When you see a person who was not born of a woman, fall on your face before him and worship him because he is your father."

¹⁶Jesus said, "People think I have come to give peace to the world. They do not know that I have come to cause dissension because I will cast fire, sword, and war on the earth. In a home of five, three will be against two, and two against three. A father will be against his son, and a son against his father. Each will stand alone."

¹⁷Jesus said, "I will give you what no eye has seen, no ear has heard, no hand has touched, and no human mind has ever conceived."

¹⁸The disciples said to Jesus, "Tell us how we will come to our end."

Jesus said, "Have you discovered the beginning, so that you are now looking for the end? For where the beginning is, there the end will be. Blessings on the one who lives in the beginning—he will know what the end is and not experience death."

¹⁹Jesus said, "Blessings on the one who came into being before he came into being. If you become my disciples and listen to my words, these stones will serve you. There are five trees for you in Paradise; remaining unchanged summer and winter, their leaves do not fall."

²⁰The disciples said to Jesus, "Tell us what the kingdom of heaven is like."

He said to them, "It is like a mustard seed, which is the smallest of all seeds, but when it falls into fallow soil it produces a large plant which provides shelter for birds of the sky."

²¹Mary said to Jesus, "Whom are your disciples like?"

He said, "They are like children who settled down in a field that did not belong to them. When the owners of the field come to them, they will say, 'Let us have our field back.' They will undress in their presence and give their field back to them.

"I say, if a home owner knows when a thief is coming, he will begin his watch before he comes and won't let him dig into his house, which is his domain, and steal away his possessions. You should be on guard against the world. Arm yourselves with mighty strength lest the thieves find a way to come to you and lest the difficulty you expect be realized.

"Let there be a man among you with understanding. When the grain ripened, he came quickly with his sickle in his hand and reaped it. Anyone with ears to hear should listen."

²²When Jesus saw some babies being suckled, he said to his disciples, "These infants being suckled are like those who enter the kingdom."

They asked him, "Should we enter the kingdom as children?"

Jesus said to them, "When you make the two one, and when you make the inside like the outside and the outside like the inside, and the above like below, and when you make the male and female one and the same, so that the male is not male and the female is not female, and when you make eyes in place of an eye, and a hand in place of a hand, and a foot in place of a foot, and an image in place of an image, then you will enter."

²³Jesus said, "I will choose you, one out of a thousand, and two out of ten thousand, and they will stand as a single unit."

²⁴His disciples said to him, "Reveal to us the place where you are because it is necessary for us to seek it."

He said to them, "Anyone with ears to hear should listen. There is light within a man of light, and he enlightens the whole world. If he does not shine, he is darkness."

²⁵Jesus said, "Love your brother like your own soul, guard him like the pupil of your eye."

*²⁶[Jesus said, "When you take the beam out of your own eye], then you will see clearly to take out the speck in your brother's eye."

*²⁷Jesus said, "If you do not fast from the world, you will not find the Kingdom of God. And if you do not keep the Sabbath as a Sabbath, you will not see the Father."

*²⁸Jesus said, "I stood in the midst of the world, and I appeared to them in the flesh. I found everyone drunk and none of them thirsty. My soul worries about the children of humanity because they are blind in their hearts."

*³⁰Jesus said, "Where there are three, they are [without] God. And when there is only one, I say, I am with him. Raise the stone and there you will find me, split the wood and I am there."†

---

†Compare saying 77.

*[31]Jesus said, "A prophet is not accepted in his own homeland. A physician does not perform healings for those who know him."

*[32]Jesus said, "A city that has been built and fortified on the summit of a high mountain can neither fall nor be hidden."

[33]Jesus said, "Preach from the rooftop of your houses what you will hear in your ears. For no one lights a lamp and puts it under a bushel, nor does he put it in a hidden place; rather, he puts it on a lampstand so that everyone who enters and leaves will see its light."

[34]Jesus said, "If a blind man leads a blind man, they will both fall into a ditch."

[35]Jesus said, "It is not possible to enter the home of a strong man and take it by force unless he ties his hands; then he can loot his house."

*[36][Jesus said, "Do not worry] from early to late, from morning until evening. Neither worry about your food, what you will eat, [nor] for [your] clothes, what you will wear. [You are] much greater than the lilies which neither card nor spin. When you have no clothing, what do you wear? Who can add to your time of life? He [it is who] will give you your clothing."

*[37]His disciples asked him, "When will you be revealed to us? And when will we see you?"

He said, "When you undress and are not ashamed."

*[38]Jesus said, "You have often wanted to hear these words I am telling you, and there is no one else you can hear them from. There will be days when you look for me but can't find me."

*[39][Jesus said, "The Pharisees and scribes] took the [keys] of knowledge. They hid them. They did not go in, [nor did] they [allow those] trying [to do so. You,] however, be wise as [snakes] and innocent as doves."

[40]Jesus said, "A grapevine has been planted outside of the Father, but since it is unhealthy, it will be pulled up by its roots and destroyed."

[41]Jesus said, "Whoever has something in his hand will receive more, and whoever has nothing will be deprived of even the little he has."

[42]Jesus said, "Become those who pass by."

[43]His disciples asked him, "Who are you that you should say such things to us?"

[He answered,] "You do not realize who I am by what I say to you because you have become like the Jews. They either love the tree and hate its fruit, or love the fruit and hate the tree."

[44]Jesus said, "Whoever blasphemes the Father will be forgiven, and whoever blasphemes the Son will be forgiven, but whoever blasphemes the Holy Spirit will not be forgiven on earth or in heaven."

[45]Jesus said, "Grapes are not harvested from thorns, nor are figs gathered from thistles because they do not produce fruit. A good man brings out good from his storehouse; an evil man brings out evil from his bad storehouse, which is in his heart—that is, he says evil things. Out of the storehouse of his heart he brings out evil words."

46Jesus said, "Among those born from women, from Adam until John the Baptist, there is no superior to John the Baptist—that person's face should not be lowered before him. Yet I have said that whoever becomes a child will know the Kingdom and will be superior to John."

47Jesus said, "As it is impossible for a man to mount two horses or to stretch two bows, so it is impossible for a servant to serve two masters. Otherwise, he will honor the one and despise the other. No one drinks old wine and soon desires to drink new wine. New wine is not put into old wineskins lest they burst, nor is old wine put into old wineskins lest it ruin it. An old unshrunken patch is not sewn onto a new garment because it would cause it to tear."

48Jesus said, "If two people in one home can make peace with one another, they can say to this mountain, 'Move' and it will move away."

49Jesus said, "Blessed are the [solitary] and the elect because you will discover the kingdom, which you have come from and will return to."

50Jesus said, "If they ask you, 'Where did you come from?' answer them, 'We came from the light, the place where the light came into being of its own volition, established itself, and became manifest through their image.' If they ask you, 'Is it you?' answer them, 'We are the children of light, and we are the chosen of the living Father.' If they ask you, 'What is the sign of your father in you?' answer them, 'It is movement and rest.'"

51His disciples asked him, "When will the dead find rest, and when will the new world come?"

He answered them, "What you are looking for has already come and you did not realize it."

52His disciples said to him, "Twenty-four prophets spoke in Israel, and all of them spoke in you."

He said to them, "You have excluded the one living in your presence and have spoken only of the dead."

53His disciples asked him, "Is circumcision beneficial?"

He said to them, "If it were beneficial, they would have already been circumcised when their father and mother conceived them. Rather, the true and profitable circumcision is in spirit."

54Jesus said, "Blessings on the poor, for the Kingdom of heaven belongs to you."

55Jesus said, "Whoever doesn't hate his father and his mother cannot be my disciple. And whoever doesn't hate his brothers and sisters and take up his cross in following my way will not be worthy of me."

56Jesus said, "Whoever has understood the world has discovered a corpse, and whoever has discovered a corpse is superior to the world."

57Jesus said, "The Father's kingdom is like a man who sowed good seed."

58Jesus said, "Blessings on the one who has suffered and discovered life."

59Jesus said, "Give your attention to the living one while you are alive, lest you die. Yet when you seek to see him, you cannot do so."

⁶⁰[Seeing] a Samaritan was carrying a lamb on his way to Judea, he said to his disciples, "That man is taking his lamb."

They said to him, "So he may kill it and eat it."

He said to them, "While it is alive, he will not eat it, but only when he has killed it and it has become a corpse."

They said to him, "He couldn't do otherwise."

He said to them, "You, too, should look within yourselves for a place of solace, lest you become a corpse and be eaten."

⁶¹Jesus said, "Two will rest on a bed; the one will die and the other will live."

Salome asked, "Who are you, man, that you have come to my couch and eaten from my table?"

Jesus said to her, "I am he who exists from the undivided. I was given some of the things of my Father."

[Someone said,] "I am your disciple."

Therefore I say, "If he is destroyed, he will be filled with light, but if he is divided, he will be filled with darkness."

⁶²Jesus said, "To those [who are chosen to know my] mysteries, I speak my mysteries. Do not let your left hand know what your right hand is doing."

⁶³Jesus said, "There was a rich man who had gained a lot of money. He said to himself, 'I will put my money to use so that I may sow, reap, plant, and fill my storehouse with crops. Then I will lack nothing.' Though these were his intentions, he died that same night. Anyone with ears to hear should listen."

⁶⁴Jesus said, "When a certain man had received some visitors, he prepared for them a dinner. He sent his servant to invite guests.

"The servant went to the first one and said, 'My master invites you to a dinner.'

"He replied, 'I have some merchants coming to me this evening who owe me some money. I must go and take care of some orders. I ask to be excused from the dinner.'

"The servant went to another and said, 'My master invites you to a dinner.'

"He replied, 'I have just bought a house and am required to be there for the day. I will not have any extra time.'

"The servant went to another and said, 'My master invites you to a dinner.'

"He replied, 'My friend is getting married, and I am about to prepare the banquet. So I won't be able to come. I ask to be excused from the dinner.'

"The servant went to another and said, 'My master invites you to a dinner.'

"He replied, 'I have just purchased a farm, and I am on my way to collect the rent. I won't be able to come.'

"The servant returned and said to his master, 'Those whom you invited to the dinner have asked to be excused.'

"The master said to his servants, 'Go into the streets outside and bring back anyone you meet so that they may dine.'

"Businessmen and merchants will not enter the places of my Father."

65 He said, "There was a good man who owned a vineyard. He leased it to tenant farmers so that they would work there and he would collect the produce. When he sent his servant to the tenants to collect the produce, they grabbed his servant and beat him, nearly killing him. The servant went back and told his master what happened. The master said, 'Perhaps they did not recognize him.' So he sent another servant, and tenant farmers beat him up also. Then the owner sent his son, saying, 'Perhaps they will respect my son.' But because the tenant farmers knew that the son was to be the heir, they grabbed him and killed him. Anyone with ears to hear should listen."

66 Jesus said, "Show me the stone the builders rejected. That one is the cornerstone."

67 Jesus said, "If one who knows the all still feels lacking, then he is completely lacking."

68 Jesus said, "Blessings on you when you are hated and persecuted. Wherever you have been persecuted, that place will be no more."

69 Jesus said, "Blessings on those who have been persecuted by those among you.

"It is they who have really come to know the Father.

"Blessings on those who are hungry, for the cravings of the stomach will be satisfied."

70 Jesus said, "That which you have will save you if you bring it out from your being. That which you do not have within you will kill you if you do not have it within your being."

71 Jesus said, "[I will tear down] this house, and no one will be able to build it."

72 [Someone said] to him, "Tell my brothers to divide my father's possessions with me."

He replied, "O man, who has made me an arbiter?"

Then he turned to his disciples and asked, "I am not an arbiter, am I?"

73 Jesus said, "The harvest is plentiful but the laborers are few. Ask the Lord to send out workers to the harvest."

74 A man said, "O Lord, there are many standing around the drinking trough, but there is nothing in the cistern."

75 Jesus said, "Many are standing at the door, but it is the loner who will enter the bridal chamber."

76 Jesus said, "The Father's kingdom is like a merchant who discovered a pearl among his consignment of merchandise. The shrewd merchant sold the merchandise and bought the pearl for himself. Likewise, you should seek his unfailing and enduring treasure which no moth can devour or worm destroy."

⁷⁷Jesus said, "I am the light above them all. And I am the all. From me the all came forth, and the all reaches to me.

*"Split the wood and I am there. Lift the stone and there you will find me."†

⁷⁸Jesus said, "Why have you come into the wilderness? To see a reed shaken by the wind? Or to see a man clothed in fine garments [as those worn by your] kings and great men? Those who wear the fine garments are not able to see the truth."

⁷⁹A woman from the crowd said to him, "Blessings on the womb which bore you and the breast which nourished you."

He replied, "Blessings on those who have heard the word of the Father and have really kept it. For there will be days when you will say, 'Blessed is the womb which has not conceived and the breasts which have not given milk.'"

⁸⁰Jesus said, "He who has recognized the world has discovered the body, but he who has discovered the body is superior to the world."

⁸¹Jesus said, "Let him who has become rich be king, and let him who has power relinquish it."

⁸²Jesus said, "He who is near me is near the fire, and he who is far from me is far from the kingdom."

⁸³Jesus said, "The images are manifest to man, but the light in them remains concealed in the image of the Father's light. Though he will be manifested, his image will be concealed by his light."

⁸⁴Jesus said, "When you see your likeness, you rejoice. But when you see your images that came into being before you did—images that neither die nor become manifest—how much more will you have to endure!"

⁸⁵Jesus said, "Adam came into being from great power and wealth, but he is not as worthy as you. For had he been worthy, [he would] not [have experienced] death."

⁸⁶Jesus said, "[The foxes have their holes] and the birds have their nests, but the Son of Man has nowhere to lay his head and rest."

⁸⁷Jesus said, "The body that relies on a body is miserable, and the soul that relies on these two is miserable."

⁸⁸Jesus said, "The angels and the prophets will come to you and give you those things you have. And you, too, should give them the things you have—then say to yourselves, 'When will they come and take what is theirs?'"

⁸⁹Jesus said, "Why do you wash the outside of a cup? Don't you know that the one who made the inside is the same one who made the outside?"

⁹⁰Jesus said, "Come to me, for my yoke is easy and my lordship is mild, and you will find rest."

⁹¹They said to him, "Tell us who you are so we can believe in you."

He replied, "You can read the face of the sky and of the earth, but you

---

†This saying is part of saying 30 in P. Oxyrhynchus 1; see page 313.

haven't recognized the one in front of you, and you do not know how to read this moment."

⁹²Jesus said, "Seek and you will find. What you asked me in former times and I did not answer is now what I want to tell you, but you do not ask."

⁹³[Jesus said,] "Do not give what is sacred to dogs lest they throw it on the manure pile. Do not throw pearls to swine, lest they [. . .]."

⁹⁴Jesus [said], "He who seeks will find, and [he who knocks] will enter."

⁹⁵[Jesus said], "Don't lend money with interest; rather, give it someone who will not give it back."

⁹⁶Jesus said, "The Father's kingdom is like a [certain] woman who placed a little leaven into some dough and made it into large loaves. Anyone with ears to hear should listen."

⁹⁷Jesus said, "The [Father's] kingdom is like a certain woman who was carrying a jar full of flour. While she was walking on the road, at some distance from her home, the jar handle broke and the flour poured out behind her onto the road. She did not realize there had been an accident. When she got home and set the jar down, she discovered that it was empty."

⁹⁸Jesus said, "The Father's kingdom is like a certain man who wanted to kill a powerful man. While this man was in his own home, he drew out the sword and thrust it into the wall to find out if his hand could take it through the wall. Then he killed the powerful man."

⁹⁹The disciples said to him, "Your brothers and your mother are standing outside."

He replied, "Those here who do my Father's will are my brothers and my mother. They will enter my Father's kingdom."

¹⁰⁰Showing Jesus a gold coin, they said to him, "Caesar's men demand taxes from us."

He replied, "Give Caesar what belongs to Caesar, give God what belongs to God, and give me what is mine."

¹⁰¹[Jesus said,] "Whoever does not hate his [father] and mother, as I do, cannot become my [disciple]. And whoever does [not] love his [father and] his mother, as I do, cannot become my [disciple]. For my mother [. . .] but [my] true [mother] gave me life."

¹⁰²Jesus said, "Woe to the Pharisees because they are like a dog sleeping in a stable of oxen. Neither does he eat nor does he [let] the oxen eat."

¹⁰³Jesus said, "Blessings on the man who knows where the robbers will enter. He can get up, prepare his domain, and arm himself before they invade."

¹⁰⁴They said to Jesus, "Come, let us pray and fast today."

Jesus replied, "What sin have I done or how have I been defeated? But when the bridegroom leaves the bridal chamber, then they can fast and pray."

¹⁰⁵Jesus said, "He who knows the father and the mother will be called a harlot's son."

¹⁰⁶Jesus said, "When you make the two one, you will become the sons of man. And when you say, 'Move, mountain,' it will move."

[107]Jesus said, "The Kingdom is like a shepherd who had a hundred sheep. One of the sheep, which was the biggest, wandered off. He left the ninety-nine and searched for that one until he found it. After he had exerted so much effort, he said to the sheep, 'I care more for you than the ninety-nine.'"

[108]Jesus said, "He who drinks from my mouth will become like me, and I will become him. And the hidden things will be revealed to him."

[109]Jesus said, "The Kingdom is like a man who didn't know he had a treasure [hidden] in his field. After he died, he left it to his son, who also didn't know about it. After the son inherited the field, he sold it. Then the person who bought it [found] the treasure while he was plowing. He started lending out money with interest to whomever he wanted."

[110]Jesus said, "Whoever finds the world and becomes rich should renounce the world."

[111]Jesus said, "The heavens and the earth will be rolled up in your presence. And the person who lives from the Living One will not see death."

Doesn't Jesus say, "Whoever discovers himself is superior to the world"?

[112]Jesus said, "Miserable is the flesh that relies on the soul; miserable is the soul that depends on the flesh."

[113]His disciples asked him, "When will the kingdom come?"

[Jesus said,] "It will not come by waiting for it. It will not be a matter of saying 'Here it is' or 'There it is.' Rather, the Father's kingdom is spread out over the earth, and people do not see it."

[114]Simon Peter said to them, "Mary should leave us because women are not worthy of life."

Jesus said, "I myself will lead her so as to make her male, so that she may become a living spirit resembling you males. Every woman who makes herself male will enter the Kingdom of heaven."

The Gospel According to Thomas

Gospel of Truth

This manuscript is part of the Nag Hammadi collection; it is a Coptic translation of an earlier Greek original. Part of Codex I (titled the Jung Codex because it now is owned by the Jung Institute in Vienna), it is unique among the thirteen works because it is in Sub-Achmimic Coptic, while the rest of the works are in the more usual Sahidic Coptic. Codex I contains five works, two of which are the *Gospel of Thomas* and the *Gospel of Truth*.

The *Gospel of Truth* has no heading, but rather draws its title from the first line of the text. It has no author; it contains no addressee. In fact, it is not a Gospel at all but rather a treatise expressive of Valentinian Gnosticism at its earliest stage. Because the Gnosticism expressed in the *Gospel of Truth* is lacking all later-Valentinian mythological development and because it is stated simply and in almost orthodox Christian thought forms, the majority of modern scholars credit it to Valentinus himself, though no final proof of this has been discovered. If Valentinus did not write this document himself, then it had to be someone in the immediate circle of his initial disciples.

Valentinus was born in Egypt around A.D. 100 to 110. He received a thorough education at Alexandria, became a Christian, and taught first in Egypt before moving to Rome around A.D. 136, where he stayed until A.D. 154 or 155. Tertullian, in his work refuting heresy (*Prescription against Heretics*), states that Valentinus was a brilliant and eloquent man who had hopes of becoming a bishop in Rome at one time. But Tertullian seems to imply that Valentinus was expelled from the church in Rome, not once but twice. Valentinus attracted able followers, who later expanded his teachings almost beyond recognition. By the time he left Rome sometime after A.D. 154 or 155, he had made a final break with orthodoxy and was teaching a form of gnostic heresy, the product of which was the *Gospel of Truth*. There is a surviving statement that Valentinus taught subsequently in Cyprus and then he vanished into the mists of history.

Irenaeus said the *Gospel of Truth* is no Gospel, for it is unlike the four Gospels.[29] Irenaeus was certainly correct. The work is not a narrative, nor does it contain any story about Jesus, any place-name of any type, any date, or any mention of any person other than Jesus, who himself is mentioned only five times.

More than sixty times this brief work refers to the notions of "knowledge" or "needing to know." This knowledge is born from within as the soul returns to itself, finding there what Deity deposited in it—or perhaps better, finding there the residue of Deity still entrapped within it. Whoever has this gnosis has simply taken what is his—or hers—and can know where he comes from and where he is bound. Christ's role was to present the "living book." The term *book* is understood not as the gospel proclamation of the life and teachings of Jesus, but rather as the primordial gospel or truth that existed before Creation. It was human error and ignorance that rebelled against the Savior and nailed him to the tree.

Implied in this, though not explicitly stated, is the gnostic understanding that it was also divine error and ignorance out of which matter emerged or was created. Salvation for living beings entrapped in this matter comes with return to unalloyed Deity. The path of this return is gnosis (knowledge). The pleroma, the fullness of the Deity, went out into the depths of matter in search of the elect among beings by way of Jesus and the Cross.

While these traits of Gnosticism are clear, this Gospel is much closer to orthodoxy than most of the gnostic Chenoboskion writings, because it mentions only one Son of God, not several aeons or emanations; it does not split Jesus into a human Jesus and a Divine Christ; and most strikingly, Sophia, the usual central character in the gnostic cosmic drama, does not appear at all. It is for these reasons among others that the *Gospel of Truth* is placed very close to Valentinus's break with orthodoxy.

The *Gospel of Truth* has some degree of importance in New Testament studies despite its heretical content because it repeatedly assumes the full New Testament canon. There are fewer than eighty-three places where the *Gospel of Truth* echoes New Testament canonical books, in spite of the fact that it does not directly cite a single saying of Jesus. It relies heavily on the book of Revelation and the Epistle to the Hebrews and shows an affinity to the apostle John's literature as well. The page numbers for this text[30] are included in brackets; the text pagination begins with page 16.

> The gospel of truth is joy to those who have received from the Father of truth the gift of knowing him by the power of the Word, who has come from the Fullness that is the thought and the mind of the Father; he is the one who is called "the Savior" because that is the name of the work which he was to do to redeem those who had [17] not known the Father. The term "gospel" refers to the manifestation of hope, the discovery made by those who seek him.
>
> Because the All searched for the one from whom they had come forth—for the All had been inside of him, that illimitable, inconceivable one, who is superior to all thought—lack of acquaintance with the Father caused terror and fear. And the terror became like a dense fog in which no one could see. Therefore, error grew powerful. But she worked on her hylic substance[†] vainly, because she did not know the truth. She took on a fashioned form—a fiction—while preparing, by power, an attractive substitute for truth. This, however, was not humiliating to the illimitable and inconceivable one. For this terror and forgetfulness, and the figure of falsehood were as nothing, whereas the established truth is unchanging, unperturbed, and entirely lovely.
>
> For this reason, do not take error too seriously—she has no basis or source. She was in a fog regarding the Father, engaged in making items and forgetfulness and fears in order to use them to beguile those in the Middle and to take them captive. The forgetfulness of error is not readily seen, it did not [. . .] [18] beside the Father. Forgetfulness did not exist with the Father, and further, it was not because of him.[‡] What exists in him is knowledge, which was revealed so that forgetfulness might be done away with and the Father made known. Because forgetfulness came about because the Father was unknown, it will cease to exist from the moment the Father is known.
>
> This is the gospel of the one they seek, which he has revealed to the perfect through the mercies of the Father. By this hidden mystery, Jesus Christ enlightened those who were in darkness because of their forgetfulness. He enlightened them and gave them a way: the truth that he taught them.[§] Because of this, error was angry with him and persecuted him. She

---

[†] I.e., the material universe.
[‡] Some render this "although it did exist because of him."
[§] Cf. John 14:6.

was distressed by him, being made powerless. He was nailed to a tree and became the fruit of the knowledge of the Father. It did not, however, destroy those who ate of it.[†] It rather made those who ate of it joyful because they discovered him.

And as for him, he found them in himself, and they found him in themselves—the illimitable, inconceivable one, that perfect Father who made the All, in whom the All is, and whom the All lacks. Because he retained their perfection in himself and had not given it to the All, the Father was not jealous. For what jealousy is there between him and his members? For, even if [19] this age had [been perfect] it would not have been able to [be as perfect as] the Father, because he kept their perfection in himself, giving it to them as a way to return to him and as a perfected knowledge. He is the one who created the All and in whom the All existed and whom the All lacked. As one who is unknown to some, he desires that they know him and love him. For what was it that the All lacked, if not the knowledge of the Father?

He became a guide, quiet and at rest. He came as a teacher to the middle of a school and spoke the Word. Those who considered themselves wise came to test him. But he showed them to be empty-headed people. Because they really were not wise men, they hated him. After all these, the little children came—those who possess the knowledge of the Father.[‡] When they became strong they learned the outward manifestations of the Father and they came to know him and be known by him; they were glorified and they gave glory. The living book of the Living was made manifest in their hearts, the very book which was written in the thought and in the mind of the Father [20] and, from before the foundation of the All, was in that incomprehensible part of him.[§]

And no one was able to take this book, for it was reserved for him who would take it and be slain.[††] Until the book appeared, nothing could be manifested among those who believed in salvation. Therefore, the compassionate and faithful Jesus endured his sufferings until he took that book, knowing that his death would mean life for many. As in the case of a sealed will, in which the fortune of the deceased master of the house is hidden, so also was the case with the All, which had been hidden as long as the Father of the All, in whom every way has its source, was invisible. Therefore, Jesus appeared, putting on that book, was nailed to a cross, and affixed the edict of the Father to the cross.[‡‡]

What an excellent lesson! Lowering himself unto death, though clothed

---

[†]Cf. Gen. 2:17.
[‡]1 John 2:13.
[§]Cf. John 1:1; Rev. 13:8.
[††]Cf. Rev. 5:3.
[‡‡]Cf. Col. 2:14.

in eternal life, he took off these perishable rags and clothed himself in incorruptibility, which no one can take from him. Having entered the empty territory of fear, he brought forth those who were stripped naked by forgetfulness, because he is both knowledge and perfection, reading aloud the things that are in the heart of the Father. [21] He became the wisdom of all who would receive instruction. But those who would learn—the living whose names are written in the book of the living—learn about themselves, receiving instructions from the Father, returning to him again.

Because the perfection of the All remains in the Father, the All must ascend to him. Then, when each gains knowledge, each obtains what is his and takes it as his own. For the one who is ignorant is lacking, and that lack is great because he lacks what would make him perfect. Because the perfection of the All exists in the Father, the All must ascend to him and each one must get the things that are his. He assigned these things in advance, preparing them to be given to those who would come forth from him.

Those whose names he foreknew were called last;[+] the Father has pronounced the names of those who have knowledge. Those whose names have not been spoken remain ignorant. How could a person hear if his name had not been read aloud? For the one who remains ignorant until the end is a creature belonging to forgetfulness and destined to perish with it. If this is not the case, then why don't these wretches have [22] names? Why are their names not heard? So, if a person has knowledge, he is from above. If he is called, he hears, replies, and turns toward the one who called him. He ascends to him and he knows what he is called. Because he has knowledge, he does the will of the one who called him, desiring to please him, and he finds rest. He receives a certain name. He who has such knowledge knows where he came from and where he is going.[+] He knows it as one who, having been intoxicated, abandoned his drunkenness and came to himself, and has now restored what is his own.

He has restored many who erred, going ahead of them to their ways (from which they had departed upon accepting error) because of the depth of the one that surrounds every place, while nothing can surround him. It was a marvel that they were in the Father without the knowledge of him and that they were able go forth because they could not grasp or perceive the one whom they were in. For if his will had not proceeded from him [. . .]. For he revealed it to give a knowledge that would correspond with all its emanations; specifically, it is the knowledge of the living book, which in the end, he revealed to the [23] aeons as his letters. He demonstrated for them that these are not simply vowels and consonants that a person might read and find devoid of meaning—just the opposite! They are letters that

---

[+]Cf. Rom. 8:29.
[+]Cf. John 3:8.

transfer the truth; they know and speak only of their subject. Each letter is like a complete book written as a unified whole; it is a perfect truth because the Father wrote them for the aeons, that through his letters they might come to know the Father.

Its wisdom meditates on the Word; its teaching tells of him.
Knowledge of him has been revealed; its honor crowns him.
Its joy corresponds to his person; its glory exalts him.
It has revealed his image; it has obtained his rest.
Its love put a bodily form around him; its faithfulness embraced him.

In this way the Word of the Father proceeds to the All, being the produce [24] of his heart and the declaration of his will. It supports the All and chooses it. It also takes the outward shape of the All and purifies it, bringing it back to the Father and to the Mother, Jesus of unsurpassable kindness. And the Father uncovers his bosom, which is indeed the Holy Spirit, revealing his secret—his son! Thus, through the Father's compassion, the aeons may come to know him and cease their exhausting search for the Father, resting in him and knowing that he is rest. After he had filled what was deficient, he did away with outward shapes. The outward shape of what is deficient is the world, that which it served. For wherever jealousy and quarreling are, there is a deficiency; but wherever unity is, there is perfection. Because the reason for the deficiency was that they had no knowledge of the Father, from the moment they know the Father, deficiency will cease to exist. Just as a person's ignorance dissolves when he gains knowledge, and just as darkness disappears when light shines, [25] so also imperfection is eliminated by perfection. To be sure, from that moment forward, an outward shape no longer appears; it rather dissolves in a fusion with unity. Although their works lie scattered now, unity will eventually perfect the spaces. Through unity each one will understand itself, and through knowledge it will rid itself of diversity in order to attain unity, consuming matter within itself like fire—as darkness is consumed by light and death by life.

Since these things have indeed happened to each one of us, it is, of course, fitting for us to meditate upon the All and let the house be holy and silent, favoring unity. Like people who are moving from one place to another, if they have some useless old dishes around, they typically dispose of them. And the owners are not upset to lose them but rather look forward, thinking happily of replacing the defective dishes with others that are completely perfect. For this is the ruling that has come [26] down from on high and judged everyone like a two-edged sword slicing this way and that, for the Word has appeared; it is in the heart of those who pronounce it.[†] It is not only a sound, though; it has become a body. A great disturbance has happened among the dishes: Some became empty, some were filled partway,

---

†Cf. John 1:14; Heb. 4:12.

some were completely filled, some were spilled, some were cleaned, and others were broken. All the spaces were jumbled and disturbed for they had no bearing or stability. Error was disturbed and didn't know what to do. She was afflicted; she grieved, she was greatly agitated because she lacked knowledge. When knowledge appeared, which meant the destruction of error and all her emanations, she became empty, since there never was anything within her. When truth appeared, all its emanations recognized it and they greeted the Father truly and powerfully, such that they were set in accord with the Father. For each one loves truth because truth is the Father's mouth. His tongue is the Holy Spirit, which unites any person [27] who clings to the truth to the Father's mouth. From this tongue such a person will receive the Holy Spirit, which is the Father's manifestation and his revelation to his aeons. He revealed his inner person and explained it. For who exists if not the Father himself?

All the spaces proceeded from him, and they knew that they originated with him as children from within a mature human. They knew that they had not yet received an outward shape or a name. Every one of them is produced by the father, with an outward shape, when they are moved toward the knowledge of him. Until then, even though they are in fact in him, they do not perceive him. But the Father is perfect and knows every space that is within him. If he desires to cause anyone to appear, and to give him an outward shape and a name, he does so, and the person comes into existence. Those who do not yet exist have no knowledge of the one who created them. That is not to say that they are nothing because they do not yet exist; they are [28] in him who will cause them to exist when he desires, like an event which is destined to occur. Before anything has appeared, he knows what he will produce. The fruit that has yet to appear, however, does not perceive anything, nor is it anything properly speaking. So each space that is itself in the Father comes from the existent one, who has established himself from the nonexistent. [. . .] what does not exist at all, will never exist. What then should it think? "I am similar to the shadows and phantoms of the night." And when morning arrives, this one understands that the fear it had experienced was nothing.

Thus they had no knowledge of the Father; he is the one [29] they could not perceive. Since there was fear and chaos and insecurity and doubt and division, there were many illusions which were conceived by him, the foregoing, as well as vain ignorance—as if they were fast asleep and found they were subject to nightmares: either they dream they must flee somewhere, but they lack strength to get anywhere, having chased or fled from the unknown. Or they are in a fight, or they themselves are beaten. Or they are falling from the heights, or flying through the air, but without wings. Still other times, they feel as if certain people are trying to murder them, although there is no one chasing them, or that they have just murdered someone next to them and are covered in their blood. Until the time when these people who are experiencing all these confusions awake, they perceive nothing because their dreams are nothing. In the same way, those who cast off the lack of knowledge as though it were sleep do not consider it to be anything; they do not consider its [30] elements as real things, but they renounce them like a dream in the night and they regard the knowledge of the Father to be the sunrise. Each person who gains knowledge acts in this manner: as though he was asleep when he lacked knowledge and awoke when he gained understanding—and he who awakes and gains his senses is happy. Indeed, blessed is he who has opened blind eyes.

And the Spirit came quickly to that person when he awoke, taking the hand of that one lying prone on the ground, and steadying him on his feet, for he had not yet arisen. He provided them the means of knowing the knowledge of the Father and the revelation of his son. For when they saw him and listened to him, he permitted them to taste and smell of himself and to touch the beloved son.

He appeared, telling them about the Father, the infinite one. And doing his will, he inspired them with what is in the mind. Many received the light and turned [31] toward him. But materially oriented men were foreign to him and could not discern his appearance or recognize him. For he came in the likeness of a human body and nothing obstructed his way because it was incorruptible and unstoppable. Furthermore, in saying new things and speaking about what is in the Father's heart, he proclaimed the flawless word. Light spoke through his mouth, and his voice brought forth life. He gave them thought and understanding and mercy and salvation and the Spirit of strength derived from the Father's infinite nature and kindness. He caused punishments and beatings to cease—for these were what caused many who needed mercy to stray from him in error and in chains—he mightily destroyed them and mocked them with knowledge. He became a way for those who went astray[†] and knowledge to those who lacked knowledge, a discovery for those who were searching, and strength for those who trembled, purity for those who were defiled.

He is the shepherd who left behind the ninety-nine [32] sheep that had not strayed and went in search of that one that was lost. He rejoiced when he had found it because ninety-nine is a number gestured by the left hand, but when he finds the one, the whole number[‡] is immediately signaled by the right hand. In this way, what is lacking the one, that is, the whole right hand, draws in that which it is missing, takes it from the left hand and transfers it to the right. In this way, then, the number becomes one hundred. This number signifies the Father: he labored even on the Sabbath for the sheep

---

[†]Cf. John 14:6.

[‡]I.e., one hundred. The Roman system of hand-gestures to indicate numbers counted from one to ninety-nine on the left hand and started at one hundred on the right hand (Layton, 260).

327

that he found stuck in a ditch. He worked to rescue the life of that sheep, bringing it out of the ditch.

So, understand fully what that Sabbath is, you who possess full understanding. It is not a day for salvation to be idle, so that you may merely talk about that heavenly day that has no night and about the sun that does not set because it is perfect.[†] Rather, say in your hearts that you are this perfect day and that that unfailing light dwells in you. Speak the truth to those who seek it and impart knowledge to those who, in their error, have committed sin. [33]

Steady the feet of those who stumble and lay hands on the sick. Feed the hungry and comfort those who are troubled. Wake up those who desire to arise, and arise from your own slumber. For you are this understanding which encourages. If the strong follow this course, they will be even stronger. Turn your attention to yourselves. Do not be concerned with others, namely, those whom you have cast out from among yourselves and dismissed. Do not return to eat what you have expelled. Do not be moth-eaten. Do not be worm-eaten, for you have already shaken them off. Do not be a place of the devil, for you have already destroyed him. Do not strengthen the things that impede you—those that fall—as if it were a beneficial undertaking. For the lawless one is nothing. He hurts himself rather than the law. For he acts as he does because he is a lawless person. But this one, because he is a righteous person, does his works among others. Do the Father's will, then, because you are from him.

For the Father is sweet, and his will is good. He knows the things that are yours, so that you may rest yourselves in them. For by the fruits one knows the things that are yours, that they are the Father's children, [34] and one knows his fragrance, that you originate from the grace of his countenance. For this reason, the Father loved his fragrance; and it manifests itself in every place; and when it is mixed with matter, he gives his fragrance to the light; and into his rest he causes it to ascend in every outward shape and in every sound. For there are no nostrils which smell the fragrance, but it is the Spirit that possesses the sense of smell and it draws it for itself to itself and sinks into the Father's fragrance. He is, indeed, the place for it, and he takes it to the place from which it has come, in the original, cold fragrance. And it is an outward form that possesses a soul, being like a cold liquid that has permeated some loose soil; and which those who see it think, "It is simply dirt." Afterward, it becomes soft again. If a breath is taken, it is usually hot. The cold aromas, then, are from the division. For this reason, God came and destroyed the division and brought love's warm fullness, so that the cold may not return, and that instead, the unity of perfect thought would be effectual.

This is the message of the good news about the discovery of the Fullness for those who strive for [35] the salvation that comes from above. When their

---

[†] Cf. Rev. 21:25.

hope, for which they strive, is also striving, then at that time the Fullness is about to come to them—they whose likeness is the light in which there is no shadow.[†] That which is lacking in matter, however, is not the result of the infinite nature of the Father, who came to bring time to the lack. And yet no one is able to say that the incorruptible One will come in this way. But the Father's depth is ever-increasing, and the thought of error is not with him. It is a matter of falling down and being willingly set upright upon discovery by the one who has come to restore him.

For this restoration is called "repentance." For this reason, incorruption has breathed. It ran after the one who sinned in order that he might find rest. For forgiveness is the light that remains within the lack; it is the word of the Fullness. For the physician hurries to the place where there is sickness, because he desires to. The sick man is in a lacking condition, but he does not hide himself because the physician possesses that which he lacks. Thus, what is lacking is filled by the Fullness, which has no lack, which has [36] given of itself in order to fill the one who is lacking, so that the person may have grace. While he is lacking, he has no grace. Because of this, a decrease occurred in the place where there was no grace, the place where the one who was small and lacking was taken hold of.

He revealed himself as a Fullness—the finding of the light of truth, which has shined toward him—because he is unchangeable. For this reason, they who have been troubled speak about Christ in their midst so that they may be restored and he may anoint them with the ointment. The ointment is the mercy of the Father, who will take pity on them. But those whom he has anointed are those who are perfected. For full vessels are customarily sealed,[‡] but when the seal is gone, the vessel becomes empty, and the cause of its lack is the absence of its seal. When the seal is gone, a breeze will evaporate the contents by its power. But the vessel that does not lack its seal is not emptied in any way. And what is lacking is filled again by the perfect Father.

He is good and he knows his plants because he is the one who has planted them in his Paradise; his Paradise is his place of rest; it [37] is the completion of the Father's thought, and these ones are the words of his reflection. Each one of his words is the work of his will alone, in the revelation of his Word. Since they were in the depth of his mind, the Word, who was the first to come forth, caused them to appear, along with an intellect that speaks the unique word by means of a silent grace. It was called "thought," because they were in it before becoming manifest. It happened, then, that at the moment he willed it, it was the first to come forth, and it is in the will that the Father is at rest. Nothing happens apart from what

---

[†]Cf. 1 John 1:5.

[‡]There is a word play here between "seal" and "anoint" and "ointment"; it is the same root word in Coptic.

pleases him, nor does anything occur outside the Father's will. But his will is incomprehensible. His will is his mark, but it is not possible for anyone to know it or to concentrate on it in order to possess it. But that which he desires takes place at the moment he wills it—even if the sight does not please them. It is God's will. For the Father knows the beginning and the end of them all. For when their end arrives, he will question them to their faces. The end, you see, is the recognition of the one who is hidden, that is, the Father, [38] from whom the beginning came forth and to whom all who have come from him will return. For they appeared for the glory and the joy of his name.

And the name of the Father is the Son. He is the one who, in the beginning, gave a name to him who proceeded from him—he is forever the same—and he begat him for a son.[+] He gave him the name that belonged to him[‡]—he, the Father, who possesses everything that exists around him. He has the name and he has the son. It is possible to see the son, but the name is invisible, for it alone is the mystery of the invisible, which is about to come into ears that are entirely filled with it, because of him. Further, as regards the Father, his name is not pronounced, but it is revealed through a son. Therefore, the name is great.

Who, then, can speak his name, the great name, except the only one to whom the name belongs and the sons of the name, in whom the Father's name rests, and who themselves are at rest in his name? As the Father has no beginning, it is he alone who engendered him for himself in the beginning to be a name. This was before he had created the aeons, that the name of the Father should be over their heads as a lord—that is, the [39] real name, which is secure by his authority and by his perfect power. For the name is not drawn from dictionaries or derived from common naming practices, but is invisible.

He alone gave him a name, because he alone saw him and because he alone was able to give himself a name. For he who does not exist has no name. For what name does one give that which does not exist? But the one who exists, exists along with his name. And the Father alone knows it, and to him only did he give a name. The Son is his name. That being the case, he did not keep it secretly hidden, but the son came into existence. He himself gave a name to him. The name, then, is that of the Father, so that the name of the Father is the Son. For otherwise, how would compassion find its name, if not from the Father?

But someone will probably say to his companion, "Who gives a name to a person who existed before he himself did?" as if children were not named [40] by those who give them birth? And it is quite fitting that we should consider this point: What is the name? It is the real name. It is, indeed, the

---

[+]Cf. Heb. 1:5.
[‡]Cf. John 17:11.

name that came from the Father, for it is he who owns the name. For you see, he did not borrow the name as a loan, as is the case for others because of the outward shape in which each is created. Rather, his is the genuine name. There is no one else to whom it has been given. But it remained unspoken, unuttered, until the moment when he who is perfect had spoken of him [the son]; and it was the latter alone who was able to express his name and to see it. When it pleased him, then, that his son should be his spoken name and when he who emerged from the depth gave this name to him, he spoke of his secrets because he knew that the Father was absolute goodness. Precisely because of this, he sent this one in order that he might speak concerning the place from which he came and his place of rest, [41] and that he might glorify the Fullness, the greatness of his name, and the kindness of his Father.

Every person will speak of the place from which he has emerged, and he will quickly move to return to the region where he received his essential being—the place he departed from but will return to in order to taste, be nourished, and grow.

And his own place of rest is his Fullness. All the emanations from the Father, therefore, are Fullnesses, and all his emanations have their roots in the one who caused them all to grow from himself. He appointed their destinies. Thus they appeared individually so that they might be in their own thought, for the place they extend their thought to is their root, which lifts them up above all the heights to the Father. They reach his head, which is rest for them, and they remain there near to it so that they receive embraces in his presence, but these [42] do not appear as though this were the case. They do not exceed themselves, and they do not fall short of the Father's glory,[†] nor do they think of him as small, or bitter, or angry, but as absolutely good, unperturbed, sweet, knowing all the spaces before they existed and having no need for instruction.

Such are they who possess from above something of this immeasurable greatness, as they strain toward that unique and perfect one who exists there for them. And they do not descend into Hades. They have neither envy nor moaning, nor is death in them. But they rest in him who rests, and as regards truth, they are not fatigued or encumbered—rather, they are the truth. And the Father is in them, and they are in the Father, since they are perfect, inseparable from him who is truly good. They lack nothing at all and receive rest, being refreshed by the Spirit. And they listen to their root; they are busy with things that can lead a person to his root and not do damage to his soul.

Such is the place of the blessed; this is their place. As for the rest, then, let them know in their place, that it is not appropriate for me [43] to say anything further, for I have been in the place of rest. And it is there I shall

---

[†]Cf. Rom. 3:23.

remain so that I may devote myself perpetually to the Father of the All and to the true brothers, those upon whom the Father's love is lavished, and among whom nothing of him is lacking. It is they who dwell openly in that true and eternal life and who speak of the perfect light that is filled with the Father's seed, and which is in his heart and in the Fullness. In this his Spirit rejoices and glorifies the one it was in, because the Father is good. And his children are perfect and worthy of his name, because he is the Father. It is children of this kind that the Father loves.

The Gospel of Truth

Gospel of the Twelve Apostles

This is one of a large number of heretical "Gospels" circulating in the earliest centuries of the Christian church along with the Gospels of Matthew, Mark, Luke, and John. The *Gospel of the Twelve Apostles* was first mentioned by name in comments by Origen on Luke 1:1. Some scholars think it may have been the same as the *Gospel of the Ebionites,* quoted in a few early Christian writings. Nothing is known directly of the *Gospel of the Twelve Apostles.* Origen's comment is that those (of whom Luke speaks in his prologue) who "took in hand" or "attempted" to write Gospels came to the task rashly, without the needful gifts of grace—unlike Matthew, Mark, John, and Luke himself. According to Origen, such were those who composed the Gospel entitled "of the Twelve." He gives no more specific indications of the content than this.

INFANCY GOSPELS

Arabic Gospel of the Infancy

This is one of several Infancy Gospels. This writing from around the fifth century A.D. contains an account of the birth of Jesus, including the visits of the shepherds and the magi, the flight to Egypt, and miracles performed by Jesus as a boy. Other details are given of the early period of Jesus' life, about which the four Gospels say nothing. An interesting facet of many of the miracle stories is the role of Mary, the mother of Jesus, in contrast to the record of the miracles in the four Gospels. The *Arabic Gospel* may have been written in Syriac and translated into Arabic. Some of its stories are also found in the Koran and other Islamic writings. Study of this apocryphal Gospel reveals a sharp contrast with the canonical accounts, but also indicates how much this and similar writings contributed to the growing veneration of the Virgin Mary.

Armenian Gospel of the Infancy

This is a legendary account of the infancy and boyhood of Jesus Christ, one of many apocryphal Gospels intended to supplement the four Gospels by providing more details about Jesus' early life. It was probably translated into Armenian from a Syriac original. Nestorian missionaries reportedly brought an infancy gospel into Armenia around A.D. 590, but evidently not the *Armenian Gospel* in its present form.

Sources for the *Armenian Gospel* include two books containing legendary material about Christ's infancy: the *Protoevangelium of James* and the *Infancy Gospel of Thomas*.

The *Armenian Gospel* amplifies the material of these two texts considerably, making many novel additions to the life of Jesus. For example, Joseph searches for a midwife and meets Eve, who has come to witness the fulfillment of the promised Redeemer-Seed.[31] Later the magi bring the testament Adam gave to Seth. Jesus, accused of causing a child's death, is cleared when the child is raised from the dead.

History of Joseph the Carpenter

This document glorifies Jesus' father and promotes a cult of Joseph. Words in chapter 18 of the book support a fourth-century A.D. date for it. There Jesus tells his mother, "You, too, must look for the same end of life as other mortals." By the fifth century the doctrine of the "Assumption of the Virgin Mary" was widely held.

The document, derived from the *Protoevangelium of James,* was contaminated by both Gnosticism and other religious beliefs of Egypt, the country in which it was written. It is extant in Coptic and Arabic, and also in a fourth-century translation of the Coptic text. The *History of Joseph the Carpenter* claims to give an account of Joseph's life and his model death at the age of 111. In this story, allegedly told by Jesus to his disciples on the Mount of Olives, Joseph, a carpenter,[32] is a widower well advanced in years when he marries Mary, who is only twelve. Also, he had six children from an earlier marriage. Joseph is buried according to the rites of the Egyptian Osiris cult after Jesus pronounces a eulogy.

History of Joseph the Carpenter in Arabic

This is a fourth-century A.D. account of the life and death of Joseph—with information supposedly supplied by Jesus. According to this account, Joseph the carpenter becomes a widower after fathering four sons and two daughters (chapter 2). He is entrusted with the care of Mary in his ninetieth year (chapter 14). Thus, according to this account, the brothers and sisters of Jesus are Joseph's children from a previous marriage. Joseph is said to have died at the age of 111 years. The document, which exists in both Arabic and Coptic versions, contains the statement that Mary "must look for the same end of life as other mortals" (chapter 18). Hence, it has been dated as earlier than the fifth century, when the idea of the "assumption of Mary into heaven" was being promoted.

Infancy Gospel of Thomas

The *Infancy Gospel of Thomas* is composed of a series of childhood miracles of Jesus and is preserved for us in four versions—two in Greek (one quite a bit longer than the other), one in Latin and one in Syriac. This is a non-canonical and heretical Gospel of gnostic origin that probably dates from the second or third century A.D. It is one of a large number of similar writings that flourished among early religious sects such as the Marcosians[33] and the Manichaeans.[34] In fact, Cyril of Jerusalem, who died in A.D. 386, says the *Infancy Gospel of Thomas* was written by "one of those wicked disciples of Mani," the founder of Manichaeism. Along with the *Protoevangelium of James,* it is one of the oldest and most widely known of the more than fifty apocryphal Gospels that circulated among the churches during the period of their early growth and expansion.

This Gospel was apparently known as early as Hippolytus (A.D. 155–235), who quotes it as saying "He who seeks me will find me in children from seven years old; for there will I, who am hidden in the fourteenth aeon, be found." Hippolytus claimed that it was used by the Naasenes, a gnostic sect that worshiped the serpent, in support of their doctrine of the nature of the inward man. The quotation above is not found in the extant versions, but this is understandable because there is evidence from the *Stichometry of Nicephorus* (possibly fourth century) that an earlier version was over twice the length of the surviving one. The *Infancy Gospel of Thomas* was known both to Origen (ca. A.D. 185–254) and Eusebius (ca. A.D. 260–340). Eusebius classed it with the heretical writings and said it should be "rejected as altogether absurd and impious."[35]

The stories that make up the *Infancy Gospel of Thomas* emphasized the miraculous power and supernatural wisdom of the boy Jesus. Some scholars think the stories were originally fabricated by orthodox Christians in opposition to the gnostic heresy that the "supernatural Christ" first came upon Jesus at the time of his baptism. It is much more likely, however, that they owe their origin to people's curiosity about what Jesus must have been like as a boy. Some of the tales may have come from pagan sources.

Apart from three or four miracles recorded here that could be considered beneficial, the supernatural feats said to be performed by the boy Jesus were destructive. For example, when a certain child spoiled some pools made by Jesus, Jesus cursed him, and the boy completely withered. Another boy, who provoked Jesus by running into him, "immediately . . . fell down and died." A teacher who struck Jesus on the head fell to the ground, cursed. The

French writer Renan referred to the Jesus of the *Infancy Gospel of Thomas* as "a vicious little guttersnipe."

Throughout the Gospel, Jesus is presented as infinitely wise—yet cruel. He ridicules his teacher Zacchaeus, saying, "You hypocrite, first, if you know it, teach the Alpha, and then we will believe you concerning the Beta." After Zacchaeus berates himself for being so inferior to the one he intended to take as a disciple, Jesus laughs and announces, "I am come from above that I may curse them." The text continues, "And no man after that dared to provoke him, lest he should curse him, and he should be maimed."

Other miracles include making twelve live sparrows out of clay, smiting his accusers with blindness, raising a child from the dead, healing a foot cut in two by an ax, carrying water in a cloth garment, reaping an enormous harvest from one kernel of wheat, stretching a piece of wood to its proper length, and healing his brother James, who had been bitten by a viper while gathering firewood.

It comes as no surprise that the orthodox church has always rejected the apocryphal *Infancy Gospel of Thomas* from its canon of sacred Scripture. It is, however, quoted in other later Gospels of the same sort. For example, in the *Gospel of Pseudo-Matthew,* chapter 18 through the end is based on the *Infancy Gospel of Thomas.* Along with other apocryphal materials, it has exercised a significant influence on Christian art and literature, especially from the tenth century A.D. on. For example, the account of Jesus making birds from clay shows up in the Koran.[36]

Protoevangelium of James

This Infancy Gospel, also known as the *Gospel of the Nativity of Mary,*[37] is the earliest expansion on the canonical accounts of Jesus' childhood. This work, along with the *Infancy Gospel of Thomas,* exerted influence on the text of many other apocryphal infancy narratives. Over one hundred Greek manuscripts contain all or part of this work, some as early as the third century. The internal evidence shows that the author was not a Jew, and most scholars date the original composition to around A.D. 150.

The material in the text shows strong influence from both the Septuagint and the canonical Gospel accounts. The narrative focuses primarily on the life of Mary, including her own birth to a previously barren woman (though not to a virgin), and emphasizing Mary's perpetual virginity—even after the birth of Jesus. Notably, the book says that Joseph was a widower following a previous marriage—the source of Jesus' siblings—and that Jesus was born in a "cave" in the presence of Joseph's adult sons.

The book is named for James because it claims to be written by James, the half-brother of Jesus. Its composition likely predates A.D. 150 since Justin Martyr, an early Christian writer, named it in his *Dialogues* (165). It was rediscovered for the West by Guillame Postel,[†] who translated it from Greek into Latin.[38] Before it was lost, two major Latin revisions of it were produced: *Pseudo-Matthew* and the *Gospel of the Nativity of Mary*, compiled around the sixth and ninth centuries A.D., respectively. These revisions amplified the *Book of the Nativity of Mary* with more fanciful legends and were the basis for the *Golden Legend of Jacobus de Voragine* (A.D. 1230–1298), which in turn became instrumental in fostering the veneration of Mary.

According to the *Gospel of the Nativity of Mary*, Mary was born to rich, barren parents (Joachim and Anna) through angelic response to their prayers. They dedicated Mary to the Lord. At six months of age, Mary walked seven steps, so Anna made her bedroom a sanctuary, allowing nothing unclean to enter, and vowed that Mary would walk again only in the Temple. At age three, Mary was placed in the Temple and received food from an angel. On Mary's twelfth birthday, the high priest asked God what to do and was told to marry her to a widower. Elderly Joseph was chosen when a dove sprang from his staff. Months later, Mary gave birth to Jesus in Bethlehem's cave through a light so bright that no one could see. The light gradually withdrew, and the Child appeared at Mary's breast. The narrative ends with King Herod's slaughter of the children in Bethlehem and with Mary's saving Jesus by wrapping him in swaddling clothes and laying him in a manger.

PASSION AND RESURRECTION GOSPELS
Apocryphon of James
This account of a dialogue between Jesus, Peter, and James has little narrative structure and actually is a letter, though included by some among the Gnostic Gospels. It speaks of each of the twelve disciples writing down his own book of the teachings of Jesus, apparently shortly after his resurrection and before his ascension. As the disciples do so, Jesus appears, asks Peter and James to come with him, and tells the others to continue their writing. Jesus gives a special revelation to Peter and James and then ascends to the Father. This manuscript was discovered at Nag Hammadi and is one of the tractates of the Jung Codex. The manuscript is in Coptic and dates to the fourth century; the original is thought by some to have been as early as the first half of the second century, but its frequent use of "the Savior"

[†] Sixteenth-century French linguist.

as a title for Jesus seems more characteristic of the third century and later. A few selections follow.

Bartholomew's Book of the Resurrection of Christ

This apocryphal work exists only in Coptic and probably dates from the fifth or sixth century A.D. The most complete text is in the British Museum in London. Several other fragments exist, probably from an earlier version.

Like many similar writings of doubtful authenticity, it claims to supplement the accounts of Jesus found in the biblical Gospels. The book was supposedly addressed by Bartholomew to his son, Thaddaeus, who was warned not to let this book "come into the hand of any man who is an unbeliever and a heretic." The book can hardly be regarded as a narrative; its aim is obviously the glorification of Bartholomew, who sees things that are hidden from others. The text contains many breaks, contradictions abound, and a disregard of history is evident. Two different persons bury the body of Jesus: Joseph and Philogenes, father of a boy healed by Jesus. Mary the mother of Jesus is confused with Mary Magdalene.

In the account of the Last Supper, the author goes far beyond biblical statements about the bread and wine: "His Body was on the Table about which they were assembled; and they divided it. They saw the blood of Jesus pouring out as living blood down into the cup." Imaginative details also embellish the account of the Resurrection. Christ, for example, brings Adam back with him from Hades, and the story of doubting Thomas has been greatly amplified.

Book of the Cock

This is a non-gnostic apocryphal story that was probably written in the middle of the fifth century A.D. It was preserved by the church of Ethiopia, where it is still read on the Thursday before Easter, though it is not considered canonical.[39] According to the *Book of the Cock*, on the night of the Last Supper, Akrosina, wife of Simon the Pharisee (not the apostle), presents Jesus with a nicely prepared rooster for dinner. After Judas leaves the room, Jesus touches the rooster and it comes to life. He instructs it to follow Judas and to report his dealings. The rooster returns and tells about the forthcoming betrayal, mentioning Paul of Tarsus as one of those involved. The disciples weep. Jesus sends the rooster into the sky for a thousand years.[40]

A similar story exists in a Sahidic Coptic fragment. In the Coptic version, the resurrection of the rooster is a symbol of the resurrection of Christ.

Letter of Peter to Philip

This letter is part of the gnostic material discovered in 1946 at Nag Hammadi. It probably dates to the late second or early third century A.D. The letter takes its name from a segment at the beginning of the tractate in which Peter claims to have sent the material to Philip. The letter is written in a dialogue form common in gnostic literature. The body of the writing consists of a series of questions the apostles ask the risen Lord and the answers he gives. The questions provide a basis for the exposition of gnostic philosophy about the structure of the world revealed by the "Divine Light." That light is the Christ, who is the heavenly Redeemer.

Pistis Sophia

This Gospel is a fourth-century A.D. Coptic manuscript[41] that represents one of the chief gnostic works extant today. Consisting of four chapters, this work derives its name from its heroine, Sophia, though only the first half of the work refers to her. This section explains that Jesus, during the first eleven years after his resurrection, returns to teach his disciples the highest mystery of all: the Treasury of the Light. He then returns to the Mount of Olives, where he is caught up through the aeons. On his journey, he comes to the thirteenth aeon, where he finds Sophia. She is in sorrow because she has caught a glimpse of the Treasury of the Light but is deceived by Authades (the Self-Willed), who flashes a false brightness before her, causing her to fall into the hands of the powers of matter. She maintains her hope and faith, however, and after twelve prayers, she is delivered from Authades and chaos by Jesus, who reinstates her at the lower limit of the thirteenth aeon.

The work is in dialogue form, with Jesus answering questions asked by his disciples. The theme is thoroughly gnostic in its view of salvation, which comes by knowing a hidden, illuminating doctrine.

aeon

Within gnostic cosmology, an emanation or divinity proceeding from the transcendent Spirit of spirits; also, an indefinite time period of great length.

Aphroditopolis

See map (Appendix C).

apocrypha

A group of Old Testament books, hidden (*apocrypha* means "hidden") from public view. Many of these books were included in the Septuagint and Vulgate (and thus in Orthodox and Roman Catholic editions), but excluded from the Masoretic Text (and thus from Jewish and Protestant editions).

apostolic age

The time period when the apostles of Jesus spread his teachings and planted churches (A.D. 30–100).

apostolicity

The criterion for a manuscript's inclusion in the canon of Scripture concerned with whether or not a particular early-church document was considered to have been written by an apostle.

Aramaic

A Semitic language known since the tenth century B.C., first used as the speech of the Aramaeans and later used extensively in southwest Asia for commercial and governmental purposes. It was adopted by the Jews during their captivity in Babylon (sixth century B.C.) and used up until the time of Jesus.

autograph

The original manuscript of an ancient document; the copy penned by the author or scribe who first wrote the document.

Bodmer

Martin Bodmer, a Swiss bibliophile, purchased large collections of ancient writings from Egypt, including many significant biblical manuscripts. The Bodmer Institute is located in Cologne-Geneva, Switzerland.

canon

The collection of works understood to be authoritative ("the *canon* of Scripture"); a rule or guideline for a particular discipline ("the *canons* of *textual criticism*").

canon, closed

An exclusive list of authoritative works; a canon that is not open for additions or deletions.

Chenoboskeia; Chenoboskion
Village across the Nile from Nag Hammadi; both locations were discovery sites of the Nag Hammadi Codices. Manuscripts discovered here are also referred to as the Chenoboskion manuscripts. See map (Appendix C).

Chester Beatty
Chester Beatty, an Irish bibliophile, purchased large collections of ancient writings from Egypt, including many significant biblical manuscripts. The Chester Beatty Library is located in Dublin, Ireland.

church fathers
Prominent leaders in the early church, from the second to the fifth centuries A.D. (from Ignatius to Augustine).

codex (pl. codices)
A manuscript arranged in the form of a book, with separate sheets of *vellum* or *papyrus* bound in a stack at one edge.

collation
The process of comparing and listing the *variant readings* in a particular manuscript or set of manuscripts.

conflation
The scribal technique of resolving a discrepancy between two or more variant readings by including all of them.

Coptic
The final stage of the Egyptian language, which followed Demotic and was written in a specially adapted version of the Greek alphabet.

corpus
A collection of writings.

critical edition
An edition of an ancient text that is based on a *collation* of *variant readings* and that includes editorial decisions about which readings are most likely original.

Dishna
See map (Appendix C).

Dead Sea Scrolls
A collection of very early (100 B.C.—A.D. 100) Old Testament and other Jewish manuscripts found in the late 1940s and early 1950s near the Dead Sea.

deuterocanonical books
These are the books of Judith, Tobit, Baruch, 1–2 Maccabees, Wisdom of Solomon, Ben Sirach, and the Additions to Daniel and Esther, all of which were affirmed by the Roman Catholic church at the Council of Trent, but are not regarded as Scripture by Judaism or the Protestant church. (See also *apocrypha*.)

340

Diaspora, the
Jews living outside Palestine.

diaspora
The "scattering" of Jewish people from Palestine (beginning in A.D. 70) throughout the Near East and Europe.

extant manuscripts/extant witnesses
Manuscript copies that survived the ruins of time and are currently available for study and collation.

folio
A leaf (sheet of paper, parchment, or papyrus) in a *codex*.

four Gospels, the
The four Gospels that are included in the canon of Scripture as authoritative: Matthew, Mark, Luke, and John.

Gnosticism
The belief system of a group that separated itself from the early Christian church in the second century A.D. (and thereafter) by claiming to possess secret knowledge not available to other believers. Gnostics rejected the physical world and its Creator as evil and claimed that Jesus Christ was the divine Spirit sent to deliver people from bondage to the physical realm.

Gospel, a
A written record, published in book form, of the life and sayings of Jesus Christ.

gospel, the
The message of Jesus Christ and his Kingdom.

Hebrew
The Semitic language of the ancient Hebrews (Jews).

inspiration
The process by which God enabled the writers of Scripture to record his words and thoughts.

internal evidence
Evidence for a given reading, or interpretation, based on how that reading and other variants most likely occurred.

lacunae (s. lacuna)
Missing portions of a manuscript.

lector
The person responsible for reading the Scriptures aloud in a synagogue or church.

logia
The sayings of Jesus passed on by oral tradition until they were included in the Gospels.

Majority Text
The majority of extant manuscripts, representing the Byzantine *text type.*

majuscules
Capital letters used in manuscript copying.

manuscript
A copy of an ancient text in the language in which it was written.

Marcion of Sinope
A gnosticizing teacher who created an edited list of authoritative books that accorded with his theology. He was excluded from church fellowship in A.D. 144.

Masoretic Text
The Hebrew text produced by a school of European Jewish scribes (called the Masoretes) who helped preserve the Old Testament text between A.D. 500 and 1000 and who standardized vowel pointings for the consonantal Hebrew text.

minuscule manuscript
A manuscript written in lowercase cursive script.

Muratorian Canon
The earliest known list of authoritative Christian manuscripts, named for Ludovico Muratori, the man who discovered the list on a fragment of paper (the Muratorian Fragment) around A.D. 1740. The list includes all those books in the current New Testament except the following: Hebrews, James, 1 Peter, 2 Peter, 2 John, and 3 John.

Nag Hammadi
See map (Appendix C).

Nag Hammadi Manuscripts
The group of about forty gnostic manuscripts found in the mid-1940s at Nag Hammadi, Upper Egypt.

nomina sacra
Special contractions (or abbreviations) used in early Christian manuscripts for the divine names—Lord, God, Jesus, Christ, and the Spirit.

orthodoxy
Teaching that accords with established doctrine.

Oxyrhynchus
See map (Appendix C).

palimpsest
An animal-skin manuscript on which the original writing was later scraped off and replaced with a newer text; very often the older manuscript is much more valuable and can be recovered as an important textual witness.

papyrus
A manuscript writing surface prepared from strips of papyrus reed pounded to make a flat surface.

parchment
A manuscript writing surface prepared from animal skins that have had the hair removed and have been rubbed smooth.

Pastoral Epistles
Three Epistles of Paul (1–2 Timothy, Titus) written to help Timothy and Titus pastor the churches under their care.

Pentateuch
The first five books of the Old Testament ("five scrolls"), consisting of the law of Moses; also called the *Torah*.

Peshitta
The *Syriac* version of the Old and New Testaments that became the common scriptural text for the Syriac church.

proto-Masoretic Text manuscript
An Old Testament manuscript that predates the Masoretic manuscripts but appears to have been used in composing those later manuscripts.

pseudepigrapha
A collective term for writings falsely ascribed to prominent people in Judaism (such as the *Psalms of Solomon*) or Christianity (such as the *Gospel of Peter*).

Quelle (abbreviated, Q.)
The German word *Quelle* means "source"; it is used in biblical criticism to ascertain the source of a Gospel writer's words.

recto
The side of a leaf of manuscript that is read first; in papyrus manuscripts it is almost always the smoother side of the leaf.

Samaritan Pentateuch
The Samaritan text for the five books of Moses, which shows a different text type from the *Masoretic Text*.

scholia
Notes written by a scribe in the margin of a manuscript.

scribes
Scholars whose vocation was to make new copies of earlier manuscripts.

scriptorium (pl. scriptoria)
A room or building (usually attached to a library) set apart for scribes to do their work of copying.

Semitic languages
A family of languages that includes Hebrew, Aramaic, and Arabic.

Septuagint (LXX)
A translation of the Old Testament into Greek, made in the third and second centuries B.C. and widely used in the early church (and still in use in eastern Orthodox churches).

Shepherd of Hermas, the
A devotional book containing Visions, Mandates, and Parables (or "Similitudes," longer than the first two sections put together). Written mid–second century A.D. and very popular among Christians in the second and third centuries.

singular reading
A textual *variant* that occurs in only a single manuscript witness.

source criticism
The field of biblical studies that deals with determining the source (whether oral or written) of the words in the Gospels.

stichoi/stichometrical notes
Notations at the end of a manuscript, recording how many lines were copied (as a means of measuring how much the scribe should be paid).

stylus
A hard-pointed writing instrument.

Sub-Achmimic Coptic
A dialect of Coptic spoken in Egypt south of Asyut.

syncretism
A combination of different forms of religious beliefs and practices.

synoptic
A term that means "presenting the same common view." Matthew, Mark, and Luke are called synoptic Gospels because they present many of the same teachings of Jesus, as well as his places and times of travel.

Syriac
A literary language based on an eastern Aramaic dialect used by several Eastern Christian churches.

Targums, the
Aramaic paraphrases of the Old Testament.

textual criticism
The study of manuscripts and their copies (see *textual transmission*) to determine which reading among the *variants* is most likely the original wording of the *autograph*.

textual transmission
The process of manually transmitting a written text from copy to copy during the time period prior to the printing press.

Textus Receptus
The "received text"; a sixteenth-century edition of the Greek New Testament that formed the basis of the King James Version.

transposition
A scribal error in which two letters or words were accidentally reversed.

uncials
Uppercase letters used in writing a manuscript copy.

Uncial manuscript
A manuscript written on *vellum* or *parchment,* as opposed to *papyrus,* usually displaying *uncials.*

variant readings
All the different readings for a given section of text present in different manuscripts.

vellum
Animal skin (calf, sheep, or goat) specially prepared for use as a writing surface.

versions
Translations of ancient texts into other languages.

verso
The side of a leaf of manuscript that is read second; in papyrus manuscripts it is almost always the rougher side of the leaf.

Dates and Locations of Significant Gospel Manuscripts

This appendix provides manuscript information for all those texts that have been included in this volume. On the chart below, each place of discovery is in Egypt, and the language of each manuscript is Greek (here, sometimes abbreviated *Gr.*) unless otherwise noted. In a few cases, as we have indicated on the chart, a text is known only through the citations of various church fathers.

MANUSCRIPT	DATE	PLACE DISCOVERED	HOUSING LOCATION
CANONICAL GOSPELS			
All four canonical Gospels discovered in one codex			
P45 (Beatty Papyrus I)	3rd c.	Aphroditopolis	Dublin, Chester Beatty Museum
Aleph (Codex Sinaiticus)	4th c.	St. Catherine's Monastery	London, British Museum
A (Codex Alexandrinus)	5th c.	Fayum	London, British Museum
B (Codex Vaticanus)	4th c.	Egypt	Rome, Vatican Library
W (the Freer Gospels)	ca. 400	Gizeh	Washington D.C., Freer Gallery
Matthew			
P1 (P. Oxyrhynchus 2)	early 3rd c.	Oxyrhynchus	University of Pennsylvania
P64+P67	late 2nd c.	Coptos	P64 (Gr. 18) in Oxford, Magdalene College; P67 (inv. no. 1) in Barcelona, Fundacion San Lucas Evangelista
P77 (P. Oxyrhynchus 2683)	2nd c.	Oxyrhynchus	Oxford, Ashmolean Museum
P104 (P. Oxyrhynchus 4404)	early 2nd c.	Oxyrhynchus	Oxford, Ashmolean Museum
Mark			
P45 (Beatty Papyrus I)	3rd c.	Aphroditopolis	Dublin, Chester Beatty Museum
Luke			
P4+P64+P67 (three papyri of one codex) (Gr. 1120)	late 2nd c.	Coptos	Paris, Bibliotheque Nationale
P75 (P. Bodmer XIV)	late 2nd c.	Dishna Plain	Geneva, Bodmer Institute
John			
P5 (P. Oxyrhynchus 208, 1781)	3rd c.	Oxyrhynchus	London, British Library
P22 (P. Oxyrhynchus 1228)	3rd c.	Oxyrhynchus	Glasgow, University Library
P52 (Gr. P. 457)	110–125	Fayum	Manchester, John Rylands Library
P66 (P. Bodmer II)	late 2nd c.	Dishna Plain	Geneva, Bodmer Institute
P75 (P. Bodmer XV)	ca. 200	Dishna Plain	Geneva, Bodmer Institute
P90 (P. Oxyrhynchus 3523)	late 2nd c.	Oxyrhynchus	Oxford, Ashmolean Museum
NONCANONICAL ORTHODOX GOSPELS			
Egerton Gospel			
P. Egerton 2	ca. 150	Fayum	London, British Museum (Egerton Col.)
P. Köln 608	ca. 150	Fayum	Cologne, Institut fur Alterumskunde
Gospel of the Nazareans			
No manuscript; known only through citations of church fathers			

MANUSCRIPT	DATE	PLACE DISCOVERED	HOUSING LOCATION
Gospel of Peter			
P. Cairo 10759	8th c.	Ahkmim	Cairo, Museo Egizio del Cairo
P. Oxyrhynchus 2949	ca. 200	Oxyrhynchus	Oxford, Ashmolean Museum
P. Oxyrhynchus 4009	2nd c.	Oxyrhynchus	Oxford, Ashmolean Museum
Unknown Gospel			
P. Oxyrhynchus 406	ca. 200	Oxyrhynchus	Chicago, McCormick Theological Seminary
Unknown Gospel			
P. Oxyrhynchus 840	4th c.	Oxyrhynchus	Oxford, Bodleian Library
Unknown Gospel			
P. Oxyrhynchus 1224	4th c.	Oxyrhynchus	Oxford, Bodleian Library
GNOSTIC GOSPELS			
The Birth of Mary			
No manuscript; known only through citations of church fathers			
Book of John the Evangelist			
12th c. Latin manuscript; origin unknown			
Dialogue of the Savior			
Nag Hammadi codex III	4th c., Coptic	Chenoboskeia	Cairo, Coptic Museum
Gospel of Bartholomew			
No manuscript; known only through citations of church fathers			
Gospel of Basilides			
No manuscript; known only through citations of church fathers			
Gospel of the Ebionites			
No manuscript; known only through citations of church fathers			
Gospel of the Egyptians*			
Nag Hammadi codices III, IV	3rd c., Coptic	Chenoboskeia	Cairo, Coptic Museum
* Second work of the same name: no manuscript; known only through citations of church fathers			
Gospel of Eve			
No manuscript; known only through citations of church fathers			
Gospel According to the Hebrews			
No manuscript; known only through citations of church fathers			
Gospel of Judas Iscariot			
Codex Tchacos	ca. 300, Coptic	El Minya/Basel, Switzerland, Maecanas Foundation for Ancient Art	
Gospel of Mary			
P. Rylands 463	3rd c.	Oxyrhynchus	Manchester, John Rylands Library
P. Oxyrhynchus 3525	3rd c.	Oxyrhynchus	Oxford, Ashmolean Museum
P. Berolinensis 8502	5th c., Coptic	unknown	Berlin, Museum des Oberhessischen Geschichtsvereins
Gospel of Philip			
Nag Hammadi codex II	ca. 350, Coptic	Chenoboskeia	Cairo, Coptic Museum
Gospel of Thomas			
P. Oxyrhynchus 1	3rd c.	Oxyrhynchus	Oxford, Bodleian Library
P. Oxyrhynchus 654	3rd c.	Oxyrhynchus	London, British Museum
P. Oxyrhynchus 655	3rd c.	Oxyrhynchus	Cambridge, Harvard University
Nag Hammadi codex I (the Jung codex)	3rd c., Coptic	Chenoboskeia	Vienna, Jung Institute
Gospel of Truth			
Nag Hammadi codex I (the Jung codex)	3rd c., Coptic	Chenoboskeia	Vienna, Jung Institute
Gospel of the Twelve Apostles			
No manuscript; known only through citations of church fathers			

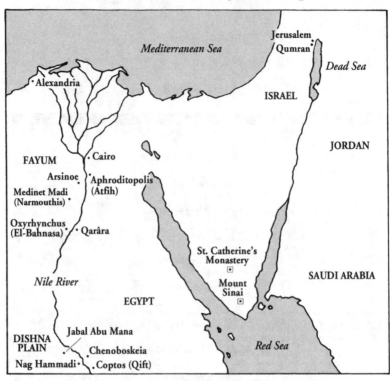

Modern names in parentheses.

DISCOVERY SITES	MANUSCRIPTS
Aphroditopolis (Atfih):	P45, P46, P47
Arsinoe:	P12
Coptos (Qift):	P4, P64/67
Dishna Plain—Jabal Abu Mana:	P66, P75
Fayum:	P37, P38, P52?, P53
Medinet Madi (Narmouthis):	P92
Nag Hammadi/Chenoboskeia:	Nag Hammadi Codices
Oxyrhynchus (El-Bahnasa):	P1, P5, P9, P10, P13, P15, P16, P17, P18, P20, P21, P22, P23, P24, P27, P28, P29, P30, P32?, P35, P39, P48, P51, P52?, P69, P70, P71, P77, P78, P82?, P85, P90, P100–116
Qarâra:	P40
Qumran:	Dead Sea Scrolls
St. Catherine's Monastery:	Codex Sinaiticus

NOTES

PREFACE
1. Published by the United Bible Societies.

INTRODUCTION
1. Michael Baigent, *The Jesus Papers: Exposing the Greatest Cover-Up in History* (New York: HarperOne, 2007), 241.

CHAPTER 1 WHAT IS A GOSPEL?
1. Irenaeus, *Against Heresies* 3.1.2.
2. For details concerning the publication and distribution of the Gospels, see Comfort, *Encountering the Manuscripts* (Nashville, TN: B&H Publishing Group, 2005), 15–54.
3. See Justin Martyr, *Dialogue with Trypho* 10.2, 100.1; Irenaeus, *Against Heresies* 3.1.1; Clement of Alexandria, *Stromata* 1.21.
4. See Luke 1:1.
5. Greek *chreiai*.
6. See Eusebius, *Ecclesiastical History* 3.39.15.
7. Greek *apomnemoneumata*.
8. Acts 1:1-2, NIV.
9. John 20:30-31, NIV.
10. A comparative study by Burridge also indicates that the closest ancient genre to the Gospels is ancient biography—in terms of literary and semantic evidence. See Richard A. Burridge, *What Are the Gospels? A Comparison with Greco-Roman Biography* (Cambridge: Cambridge University Press, 1992).
11. Harry Y. Gamble, *Books and Readers in the Early Church: A History of Early Christian Texts* (New Haven: Yale University Press, 1995), 101.
12. See John 14:26.
13. See Acts 1:21-22.
14. See Luke 10:1.
15. See Acts 1:15.
16. See Acts 2:42.
17. From *katechethes logon*, or "oral recitation."
18. See Eusebius, *Ecclesiastical History* 3.39.16.
19. See Eusebius, *Ecclesiastical History* 3.39.15.
20. John 1:14, NRSV.
21. See 1 John 1:1-2.
22. See Mark 3:5.
23. See Mark 8:12.
24. See John 11:33-38.
25. See John 12:27; 13:21.
26. Mark 5:41.
27. Mark 7:34.
28. Mark 14:36.
29. Mark 15:34.
30. See Mark 1–3; 5.
31. See John 1:39.
32. See John 2:6.

33. See John 5:2.
34. See John 21:9-11.
35. See Luke 1:1-3, NIV.
36. See John 1:14; 19:35; 21:24.
37. See Luke 1:1-4.
38. See Luke 24:48; 1 John 1:1-4.
39. See T. C. Skeat, "Irenaeus and the Four-Gospel Canon," *Novum Testamentum* 34 (1992):194–199; Skeat, "The Earliest Gospel Codex?" *New Testament Studies* 43 (1997); and Graham Stanton, "The Fourfold Gospel," *New Testament Studies* 43 (1997): 317–346.
40. T. C. Skeat, "The Oldest Manuscript of the Four Gospels?" *New Testament Studies* 43 (1997).
41. See 2 Peter 3:15-16.
42. Irenaeus *Against Heresies* 3.3.

CHAPTER 2 EXPLORING THE RELIGIOUS CONTEXT

1. Opinion is divided as to whether the Achamenid Dynasty of the Persians really did become Zoroastrian—none of their inscriptions mention Zoroaster, and many of their practices were at odds with his teaching. Further, while we grant here that Zoroaster preached monotheism, it remains difficult to prove this from the earliest writings. For more on these questions, see Edwin Yamauchi, *Persia and the Bible* (Grand Rapids: Baker, 1996), 419ff.
2. See Ezra 7:10; Nehemiah 8:1-8; *2 Baruch* 85:3.
3. Dio Chrysostom, *Discourse* 32.9.
4. See Acts 17:18.
5. The classical authors Plutarch and Apuleius are examples of thinkers from this school.
6. Everett Ferguson, *Backgrounds of Early Christianity* (Grand Rapids: Eerdmans, 1993), 364.
7. The Seleucids were the dynasty of one of Alexander's generals; they ruled from Persia to eastern Asia Minor and fought the Ptolemies (from another of Alexander's generals) early on to gain control of Judea.
8. 1 Maccabees 1:44-50, 62-63, RSV.
9. 1 Maccabees 2:15, 19-28, RSV.
10. See Philo of Alexandria, *Migration of Abraham* 89–90.
11. Some have identified the Qumran sect with the Essene sect mentioned in various passages of Josephus and Philo. While this falls short of being completely substantiated, the similarities are quite compelling. For further discussion of the relationship between the two groups, see T. S. Beall, *Josephus' Description of the Essenes Illustrated by the Dead Sea Scrolls* (Cambridge: Cambridge University Press, 1988). Another sect of Judaism, called the Theraputae, is described by Philo (quoted by Eusebius in *Preparation for the Gospel* 8.11) as a celibate Jewish communal group dedicated to worship, contemplation, and asceticism, but none of their literature remains. They may have had some connection to the Essenes.

CHAPTER 3 WHAT IS GNOSTICISM?

1. *Secret Book According to John* 18:2-5, as translated in Bentley Layton, *The Gnostic Scriptures* (New York: Doubleday, 1987), 42.

2. *Gospel of Truth*, 17:11ff.

3. *Gospel of Judas*, column 34, lines 3–10.

4. An interesting bit of trivia is that *Samael,* a gnostic name for the creator of matter (found, e.g., in *Triple Protennoia* 39:28 and *Hypostasis of the Archons* 87:3), made its way down through the centuries to be used along with the name *Lillith* by the French occultist Stanislas de Guaita in the earliest printed drawing of a baphomet, the image of a goat's head in a five-pointed star (*La Clef de la Magie Noire* [1897], 387).

5. This description follows Valentinian and Ptolemaic Gnosticism. *Triple Protennoia* 35:13 gives a classical gnostic reference to the hylic, but little detail.

6. Cf. Irenaeus, *Against Heresies* 1.6.1-2.

7. Interestingly, this concept is reminiscent of one that appeared later in the church: Las Casas, missionary to the Americas, apparently held that while the Europeans had souls and the Africans did not, the Native Americans had half a soul, and hence some spiritual potential.

8. Bob Larson, *Larson's Book of World Religions and Alternative Spirituality* (Carol Stream, IL: Tyndale), 224.

9. *Gospel of Thomas,* saying #114.

10. *Zöstrianos*, 131:5-8.

11. *Dialogue of the Savior*, 144.15–22 [Nag Hammadi Codices III, 5].

12. The name *Mandaean* is a word from a dialect of Aramaic that simply means "gnostic."

13. Even the bold folks at www.enemies.com appear unlikely to consider any such pilgrimage.

14. Elwell, Walter A., *Evangelical Dictionary of Theology* (Baker, 1995), 682.

15. Sam Harris, for example, is an atheist author who suggests that spirituality can remain, even apart from faith (*The End of Faith: Religion, Terror, and the Future of Reason* [New York: W. W. Norton, 2005]).

16. This is not to say that there is no element of subjectivity in orthodox Christian spirituality but simply that the objective aspects dominate the subjective. Similarly, most Spiritualists recognize some objective realities, but very little is integral to their spirituality.

17. See Irenaeus, *Against Heresies* 1.6.1.

18. See Irenaeus, *Against Heresies* 1.11.1.

19. See *Gospel of Truth* 18:11-31.

20. See Ignatius, *To the Trallians* 9.

21. Some examples of Jewish gnostic works, not included in this book because they are not Gospels, are the *Apocalypse of Adam*, the *Paraphrase of Shem*, "Poimandres," and the *Three Steles of Seth*. Orthodox Judaism also rejected Gnosticism, on much the same grounds as orthodox Christianity did.

22. See John 20:17, 27; cf. John 5:28-29.

23. See John 1:14, 34; 9:35-38; 14:6-9.

24. See John 3:16; 4:39-42; 5:24; 6:47; 8:51; 12:44-50.

25. Gnostic philosophy, though not necessarily considered or attributed as such, often turns up in contemporary thought.

26. See b. *Sanhedrin* 91a; *Leviticus Rabbah* 4:5.

27. Genesis 1:31.

28. See Galatians 1:6-9 in regard to alterations to the Christian gospel message.

29. This is also sometimes called the *Reality of the Rulers*.

30. See Nag Hammadi Codices II, 86:27–87:4; see also *Apocryphon of John* 28:6-29.

31. *Hypostasis of the Archons*, 95:5-10.

32. Ibid., 88:32–89:2.

33. Ibid., 89:3-10.

34. Ibid., 90:6-11.

35. Ibid., 91:34–92:3; 96:19.

36. See Timothy of Constantinople, *On the Reception of Heretics*.

37. See *Migration of Abraham*, 89–92.

38. See y. *Haggigah*, 77a; Sirach, 3:21–24. Jewish opposition to Gnosticism is discussed more fully in B. A. Pearson, *Gnosticism, Judaism, and Egyptian Christianity* (Minneapolis: Fortress, 1990). In particular, Pearson reviews the ideas of Moritz Friedländer (pp. 12ff).

39. See Lucian, *Passing of Peregrinus* 5.13 and Celsus, *True Doctrine*.

40. See Nag Hammadi Codices I, 16:36.

41. See Nag Hammadi Codices I, 18:7.

42. See *Gospel of Philip*, 66:21.

43. Nag Hammadi Codices II, 27:20.

44. *Hypostasis of the Archons*, 96:19-25.

45. In the gnostic view, the real God would have been the one true transcendent spirit, the Spirit of spirits, who was too pure a spirit to be associated with matter. The creator God, from the gnostic perspective, was the God of Genesis, who created matter—a weaker and misguided or even evil being.

46. *Gospel of Truth*, 16:36.

47. *Gospel of Thomas*, saying #70 (Nag Hammadi Codices II, 45:29).

48. *Gospel of Thomas*, saying #3 (Nag Hammadi Codices II, 32:25-27).

49. *Gospel of Judas*, columns 47–50.

50. See Matthew 4:17; Mark 1:15; Luke 4:15-21; 24:46-48.

51. See Matthew 5:17-20.

52. See Matthew 19:28-29.

53. See Matthew 7:21-23.

54. See Matthew 5–7.

55. N.T. Wright gives a nice discussion of this vis-à-vis Gnosticism in *Judas and the Gospel of Jesus* (Grand Rapids: Baker, 2006), 85.

56. Everett Ferguson, *Backgrounds of Early Christianity*, 2nd ed. (Grand Rapids: Eerdmans, 1993).

57. See Leviticus 19:3, 9, 13, 17, 32, 35.

58. Leviticus 20:8.

59. See Wright, *Judas and the Gospel of Jesus*.

60. One wonders whether some gnostic groups would have likewise guarded against the entry of orthodox Christians into their midst. Pearson (*Gnosticism, Judaism, and Egyptian Christianity*, 183) notes that Christians were called animals (*psuchikoi*) by some Gnostics and points out anti-Christian polemics by Gnostics such as that in the *Second Treatise of the Great Seth* (Nag Hammadi Codices VII, 2).

61. See Augustine, *Confessions* 1.11.
62. See Irenaeus, *Against Heresies* 1.26.1.
63. See Acts 15.
64. See Acts 15:22.
65. See 2 Peter 3:16.
66. See 1 Corinthians 15.
67. Ignatius, *To the Trallians* 9.
68. Clement of Alexandria, *Stromata* 5.3.3.
69. See Acts 2, 8, 10, and 16.
70. Revelation 7:9.
71. Irenaeus, *Against Heresies* 5.1.63.
72. These guiding factors are evident in Origen's rejection of reincarnation: "[. . .] lest I fall into the doctrine of transmigration [i.e., reincarnation], which is foreign to the Church of God, and not handed down by the apostles, nor anywhere set forth in the scriptures" (Origen's *Commentary on the Gospel of Matthew* 13:1:46-53).
73. See Acts 9.
74. See Galatians 1:6-9.
75. Space does not permit us to discuss the views of various unorthodox, nongnostic sects such as the Montanists, the Ebionites, the Encratites, or others.
76. John 10:1.
77. See John 14:26; Acts 1:21-22.
78. See Eusebius, *Ecclesiastical History* 3.25.
79. See Matthew 5:17; Luke 24:27, 44-47.
80. See 1 Corinthians 15:3.
81. See 1Timothy 5:18; 2 Peter 3:15-16.
82. See, for example, *1–2 Clement*.
83. Incidentally, the authors of the book *Reinventing Jesus* point out that even Marcion's choice of books to alter attests to the early authority perceived in what would later be recognized as canonical books (J. Ed Komoszewski, M. James Sawyer, and D. B. Wallace, *Reinventing Jesus* [Grand Rapids: Kregel, 2006], 125). He is not mentioned as having considered any of the gnostic literature for his canon; such books were either not written or were so recent that they were not regarded as authoritative.
84. The noncanonical books that *were* most frequently discussed in regard to the canon, but ultimately rejected, were the *Shepherd of Hermas*, *Barnabas*, the *Didache*, the *Apocalypse of Peter*, and *1–2 Clement*.
85. That is, a work written under an assumed name, usually the name of a famed or respected person, such as one of the apostles.
86. Eusebius, *Ecclesiastical History* 5.8; cf. Irenaeus, *Against Heresies* 2.27.2; 3.3.3; 3.11.8; 3.12.15; 3.14.1–15.1; 3.17.4; 3.21.3-4.

CHAPTER 4 DISCOVERING THE EVIDENCE

1. Manuscripts found in rubbish heaps are not "rubbish" per se, or defective copies. When a manuscript became old and worn, it was customary to replace it with a fresh copy and then discard the old one. The Egyptians are known to have disposed of such copies, not by burning them but by putting them into rubbish heaps.

2. As numbered by Kurt Aland.
3. Philip Comfort has studied many of these manuscripts in person and all the rest of them through photographs (those dated prior to A.D. 300). For an updated transcription of these papyri, see Philip Comfort and David P. Barrett, *The Text of the Earliest New Testament Greek Manuscripts* (Carol Stream, IL: Tyndale, 2001).
4. Jewish copies of the Old Testament were done on scrolls and so lack nomina sacra.
5. Philip Comfort, *Encountering the Manuscripts: An Introduction to New Testament Paleography and Textual Criticism* (Nashville: Broadman & Holman, 2005), 131–139.
6. Gnosticism is important to the study of the psychology of religious experience.
7. Members of a revolutionary Jewish political party.
8. G. W. Nebe, "7Q4—Möglichkeit und Grenze einer Identifikation," *Revue de Qumran* 13 (1988): 629–633.
9. Jose O'Callaghan, "Papiros neotestamentarios en la cueva 7 de Qumran?" *Biblica* 53 (1972): 91–93 [translated into English by W. L. Holladay in *Journal of Biblical Literature* 91 supplement (1972): 1–14.]; *Los Papiros Griegos de la Cueva 7 de Qumran* (Madrid: Editorial Catolica, 1974).
10. Orsolina Montevecchi, *Aegyptus* 74 (1994), 206–207.
11. Herbert Hunger, "7Q5: Markus 6.52–53—oder Die Meinung des Paprologen," in B. Mayer, ed., *Christen und Christliches in Qumran?* (Regensburg, 1992), 33–56.
12. See Sergio Daris's review of Thiede's *Die alteste Evangelien-Handschrift?* in *Biblica* 68 (1987), 431–433.
13. Victoria Spottorno, "Una nueva posible identificacion de 7Q5" in *Sefarad* 52:541–543.
14. *Dead Sea Scrolls Study Edition,* eds. Florentino Garcia-Martinez and Eibert J. C. Tigchelaar, vol. 2 (Grand Rapids: Eerdmans, 2000), 1164—so also for 7Q3, 6-7, 9-10, 15-18.
15. Philip Comfort has dated P66 to the middle of the second century and P75 to the end of the second century on the basis of very extensive research. See Comfort, *Encountering the Manuscripts,* 143–150.
16. Much more can be and has been said about this subject. See Bruce Metzger, *The Text of the New Testament: Its Transmission, Corruption, and Restoration, 3rd ed.* (New York: Oxford University Press USA, 1992); or my own book *Encountering the Manuscripts: An Introduction to New Testament Paleography and Textual Criticism* (Nashville: Broadman & Holman, 2005).

CHAPTER 5 THE FOUR CANONICAL GOSPELS

1. See Eusebius, *Ecclesiastical History* 3.39.15.
2. See Aland's *Text of the New Testament,* 96–101, 105, 128.
3. See Eusebius, *Ecclesiastical History* 3.39.
4. Ibid., 6.14.
5. Ibid., 6.25.4.
6. See Irenaeus, *Against Heresies* 3.1.1.
7. Eusebius, *Ecclesiastical History* 3.39.16.

8. I have examined P104, P64, P77, P103, and P1 in person and in photographs. For an updated transcription of these manuscripts, see Philip Comfort and David P. Barrett, *The Text of the Earliest New Testament Greek Manuscripts* (Carol Stream, IL: Tyndale, 2001). The early dates for each of these manuscripts are defended in my book, *Encountering the Manuscripts*, 127–149. I believe P104 could be the earliest extant New Testament manuscript, even earlier than P52 (ibid., 139–152 on P52, 160–163 on P104).

9. Eusebius, *Ecclesiastical History* 3.39.16.

10. See Irenaeus, *Against Heresies* 3.1.1.

11. As reported in Eusebius, *Ecclesiastical History* 6.14.6.

12. Ibid.

13. See Acts 12:12, 25; 13:13; 15:37-39; Colossians 4:10; 1 Peter 5:13; and Philemon 1:24.

14. See Irenaeus, *Against Heresies* 3.1.1.

15. As cited in Eusebius, *Ecclesiastical History* 2.15.2.

16. See Acts 16:10-18; 20:5-15; 21:1-18; 27:1–28:16.

17. See Colossians 4:14; 2 Timothy 4:11; Philemon 1:24.

18. Luke 1:1.

19. P4 is most likely a part of the same codex as P64+67. See *Encountering the Manuscripts*, 127–130.

20. John 20:2; see also 13:23; 19:26; 21:7, 20.

21. John 21:24-25.

22. John 13:23-25.

23. See John 20:2-4.

24. See John 21:20-23.

25. See Acts 12:2.

26. See John 1:35-40.

27. See John 18:15-16.

28. John 19:25-26.

29. See John 21:20.

30. See John 21:24-25.

31. See Irenaeus, *Against Heresies* 3.1.1.

32. See P. Rylands 457.

33. For a discussion on the dating of P52, see *Encountering the Manuscripts*, 139–143.

34. I have dated P66 to the middle of the second century, and P75 to the end of the second century on the basis of extensive research. See *Encountering the Manuscripts*, 143–150.

CHAPTER 6 THE MANY OTHER GOSPELS

1. See Luke 1:1.

2. See P. Egerton 2.

3. See Colin H. Roberts and T. C. Skeat, *The Birth of the Codex* (London: Oxford University Press, 1983), 41.

4. H. I. Bell and T. C. Skeat, *Fragments of an Unknown Gospel and Other Early Christian Papyri* (London: Oxford University Press, 1935), 1–2.

5. See Eusebius, *Ecclesiastical History* 3.3.1-4.

6. Clement, *Stromata* 1.29.182; 2.15.68.

7. See Clement, *Stromata* 6.5.39-41.
8. See Clement, *Stromata* 6.5.43.
9. See Clement, *Stromata* 6.6.48.
10. See Matthew 28:18-20.
11. See Clement, *Stromata* 6.15.128.
12. See *2 Clement* 5:2-4.
13. Matthew 13:14; Mark 4:12; Luke 8:10; John 12:40.
14. For saying 3 see Matthew 9:12, Mark 2:17, and Luke 5:31; for saying 4 see Matthew 5:44, Mark 9:40, and Luke 6:27, 35.
15. Epiphanius, *Against Heresies* 26.12.1.
16. This was possibly prompted by the coincidence that *iao* or *yahu* in old Coptic meant "donkey," and the similar word *Yahweh* was taken as equivalent to this in Egypt; see Bentley Layton, *The Gnostic Scriptures* (New York: Doubleday, 1987), 212.
17. Epiphanius, *Against Heresies* 30:1-3, 14, 16, 22.
18. See *Gospel of Thomas,* sayings #22 and 37.
19. A similar statement, though without reference to the *Gospel of the Egyptians,* seems to be alluded to in excerpts from *Theodotus* 67; *2 Clement* 12.2; cf. *Gospel of Thomas,* saying #114.
20. Like Jesus in the *Gospel of Judas*, the Cainite sect considered the God of Israel to be an opponent and a lesser spiritual being. They therefore considered Cain a hero for killing Abel, who was aligned with the God of Israel. It should also be noted that the *Gospel of Judas* has some parallels with the Sethian gnostics.
21. See Irenaeus, *Against Heresies* 1.1.35.
22. Bart D. Ehrman, Rudolphe Kasser, Marvin Meyer, and Gregor Wurst, the *Gospel of Judas* (Washington, D.C.: National Geographic, 2006).
23. His reproach is evident in his laughter, a laughter parallel to what is seen in another gnostic work, *The Second Treatise of the Great Seth,* Nag Hammadi Codices, 56.6-19.
24. The setting cannot be taken to be the Jewish Temple because Jesus speaks of the priests there invoking *his name,* something the Jews in his time period would never have done.
25. N.T. Wright appears to arrive at a similar conclusion when he writes "[The *Gospel of Judas*] explicitly and scornfully rejects the emerging church and its practices." In *Judas and the Gospel of Jesus* (Grand Rapids: Baker, 2006), 74.
26. See Luke 5:27.
27. P. Oxyrhynchus 1, 654, 655.
28. Nicholas Perrin, *Thomas and Tatian: The Relationship between the Gospel of Thomas and Tatian's Diatesseron,* Academia Biblica (Leiden: Brill, 2002).
29. Irenaeus, *Against Heresies* 3.2.9.
30. From Nag Hammadi Codex I.
31. See Genesis 3:15.
32. See Matthew 13:55.
33. A second-century group that built an elaborate sacramental system around numbers.
34. A group who espoused a third-century dualistic heresy based on the primeval conflict between light and darkness.
35. Eusebius, *Ecclesiastical History* 3.25.

36. Sura 3:49.
37. Titled *The Birth of Mary: Revelation of James* in the Bodmer Papyrus V text.
38. Postel, *Protoevangelium Jacobi* 1552.
39. R. W. Cowley, "The Biblical Canon of the Ethiopian Orthodox Church Today" *Ostkirchliche Studien* 23 (1974), 318–323.
40. For further reading on this see Pierluigi Piovanelli, "Exploring the Ethiopic Book of the Cock, An Apocryphal Passion Gospel from Late Antiquity," *Harvard Theological Review* 96 (2003): 427–454.
41. Codex Askewanus.